NIGEL CAWTHORNE is the author of *The World's Greatest Serial Killers*, and *Killers: The Most Barbaric Murderers of Our Times*, as well as numerous other books. His writing has appeared in over a hundred and fifty newspapers, magazines and partworks – from the *Sun* to the *Financial Times*, and from *Flatbush Life* to *The New York Trib*. He lives in London.

Also available

THE MAMMOTH BOOK OF
Killers at Large

Nigel Cawthorne

ROBINSON
London

Constable & Robinson Ltd
3 The Lanchesters
162 Fulham Palace Road
London W6 9ER
www.constablerobinson.com

First published in the UK by Robinson,
an imprint of Constable & Robinson Ltd, 2007

A copy of the British Library Cataloguing in
Publication Data is available from the British Library.

ISBN: 978-1-84529-631-5

Printed and bound in the EU

1 3 5 7 9 10 8 6 4 2

Contents

Introduction

There are serial killers everywhere. They inhabit our nightmares. Some have long careers. It took detectives 15 years to track down Gary Leon Ridgway, the Green River Killer who was responsible for the murder of at least 49 women in Washington State. Having passed a polygraph test in 1984, he was arrested in 2001 after DNA evidence linked him to his victims. He plea-bargained his way out of a death sentence and was sentenced to 49 life terms with no possibility of parole.

Dennis Rader – the BTK "Bind Torture Kill" Strangler – murdered ten in Kansas between 1974 and 1991. He was only caught in 2005 after he began taunting the authorities in a series of letters to the *Wichita Eagle*. Eventually he was persuaded to send in his writings on floppy disk. Forensic examination of the disk revealed it had previously been used by the Christ Lutheran Church, along with the name Dennis. A quick Internet search revealed that Rader was president of the church council. He showed no remorse and was given ten consecutive life terms, requiring that the 61-year-old Rader serves at least 175 years before being eligible for parole. He is held in solitary confinement.

Fred and Rosemary West went on a killing spree that lasted 37 years. He was charged with 11 murders, though boasted he had killed many more before he hanged himself in his cell in 1995. Rosemary West was found guilty of ten murders and sentenced to life with a recommendation from the judge that she never be released.

Dr Harold Shipman killed more than 250 over his 30-year career, though the true number will never be known. After being convicted on 15 sample charges – and sentenced to 15 life terms – he committed suicide in jail without confessing or explaining his crimes. Prolific American serial killer Henry Lee Lucas claimed to have killed over 3,000 people in a career that might have lasted for 32 years. A more likely number is 350 – among the victims was his own mother, whom he killed in 1960. Released in 1975, he went on the rampage with fellow serial killer Otis Toole until they were arrested in 1983. Toole died from cirrhosis of the liver in prison in Florida while serving six life sentences. George W. Bush agreed to the commutation of Lucas's death sentence – the only time he did so while Governor of Texas – and Lucas died of heart failure in jail in March 2001.

While these killers were eventually caught, there are plenty who have not been caught. The FBI estimate that there are between 35 to 50 serial killers at large in the United States. Other estimates put the number of killers closer to 500. In either case officials expect these numbers to continue their dramatic rise. As long ago as 1984 the FBI Behavioral Unit study of serial murder said that serial killing had reached "an almost epidemic proportion". It is believed that presently there are up to 6,000 people a year dying in the hands of a serial killer in the US alone.

Until recently serial killing has been thought of as a North American activity, though the British have struggled to produce some notably colourful cases. But now serial killing seems to be on the rise across the globe. Serial killing has become part of the national landscape in South Africa and the former Soviet Union. Even historically peaceful places such as Costa Rica and Belize now have their own serial killer.

Although it was once thought of as the province of predominantly brooding white loners, black men now join in, along with family men and those generally regarded as the life and soul of the party. Myra Hindley, Rosemary West and Aileen Wuornos have shown that even women are joining in.

But the *Mammoth Book of Killers at Large* concentrates on those killers who have not yet been caught. Many are current killers who might, at this very moment, be out stalking their victims. Others are less active, while some criminologists believe that serial killers only stop because they are dead or in jail. But Dennis Rader was dormant for 14 years before his boastfulness got the better of him. During that time he was a family man, a pillar of the community and an elected official. Other killers, once an area gets too hot for them, simply move on.

In some cases, the killer has been cleared by a court and is thus at large to kill again. In others, a man who is plainly not guilty has been railroaded by the system, while the real perpetrator goes free. And sometimes a culprit has been jailed for a series of killings, then blamed for others he has not been convicted of, or even charged with, that may well be the work of another. It is always tempting for a police department to clear its books by attributing numerous unsolved crimes to a fall guy who has already been convicted of something else.

I have also included some historic cases for completeness. True, Jack the Ripper can no longer be alive. But he was never caught or even convincingly identified. He is of enduring interest. New theories about him emerge regularly and he intersects interestingly with other, more up-to-date, cases.

Part I

American Psychos

Perhaps because murder is the stock in trade of the Hollywood thrillers, America seems to have cornered the market in cold-hearted killing. The United States has a history of violence that goes back to the foundation of the colonies there. Before Australia became Britain's penal colony, British felons could expect to be transported to North America to work on the plantations there.

Among them were numerous murderers who had escaped the hangman by taking "benefit of clergy". If a criminal could claim to the authorities that he was a clergyman, he would be handed over to be tried by the ecclesiastical courts which could not impose the death sentence. In the 16th, 17th and 18th centuries, to demonstrate that you were a clergyman, all you had to do was show that you were literate. And to do that, all you had to do was read aloud the 51st Psalm. This became known as the "neck verse" and illiterate ne'er-do-wells simply memorized it.

Other murderers turned up in the New World voluntarily. If you had killed in the old country, the easiest way to escape justice was to jump on a ship heading westwards. The law was hardly likely to find you if you put the North Atlantic between you and the courts. In America you could change your name and begin a new life – even kill again if you were so inclined. There were plenty of opportunities to make a career in homicide in the Indian wars and the lawless streets of the Wild West. And by the time gangsters began massacring each other during the Prohibition era, murder had become an American institution.

Because of the transient nature of American society, it is easy for a killer to up sticks and move on once one city or state gets too hot for them. And the victims are often transients too. If a person killed has no family or friends, the authorities are under little pressure to find out who murdered them. In the cases presented here, in a chilling number of instances, the victim could not be identified. No missing person report had been filed on anyone answering their description – so, presumably, no one missed them. If the police cannot identify the victim and cannot find out anything about them from those who knew them, finding the culprit is an all but impossible task and the killers are left at large.

As in so many other things, America leads the world in modern murder. Usually Jack the Ripper is thought to be the first serial killer – that is, the story of his killings came out as a serial, episode after episode, in the newspapers. But it is not true. Three years before Jack began killing ladies of the night in Whitechapel, an unidentified person began murdering a series of African-American servant girls in Austin, Texas – finishing his spree with two white society ladies, before he disappeared forever. As he was never caught, he is, like Jack the Ripper, technically still at large. Indeed he may even be the same man. One suspect in the Austin, Texas servant-girl murders jumped on a ship shortly afterwards, only to turn up in Whitechapel three years later where he was named in the Ripper investigation.

In America, it seems, you can get away with murder. For the killer at large, America is the land of opportunity. For those who enjoy killing, there are always plenty more potential victims out there. This is the dark side of the American dream. Indeed, thanks to cheap paperbacks, penny-dreadfuls and Hollywood, a nation heaving with uncaught killers has become the American nightmare.

Ann Arbor Hospital Homicides

Over six weeks during July and August 1975, 27 patients at the Michigan Veterans' Administration Hospital in Ann Arbor, Michigan, suffered respiratory failure that left them unable to breathe without mechanical assistance. Records showed that cardiopulmonary arrests rocketed to four times their usual rate. Some patients were struck by this life-threatening condition more than once. Eleven died. An analysis of the hospital's records found no changes in the type of patient in the hospital that could account for this dramatic upsurge. So many breathing failures could not be accidental, and patients and staff quickly figured that a medical serial killer was on the loose.

There were obvious clues; no tell-tale needle punctures or other marks on the patients' bodies. But a pharmacological investigation revealed that at least 18 of the victims – including nine of those who died – had been given Pavulon, the trade name of the drug pancuronium bromide. This is a synthetic version of curare, the lethal plant alkaloid used by South American Indians to tip poison arrows and darts. Anaesthesiologists sometimes administer Pavulon as a muscle relaxant during abdominal surgery. However hospital records showed that none of the victims had been prescribed the drug.

The FBI were called in and agents discovered that most of the breathing failures had occurred in the intensive-care unit during the afternoon shift. All of the victims were fed intravenously, but the drug could not have been added to the drip. In solution, Pavulon would have been too dilute to work. The FBI concluded that, to administer a lethal dose, the IV solution would have had to have been disconnected and the drug pumped directly down the feeding tubes.

Checking the work rosters, detectives found that two nurses from the Philippines, 29-year-old Filipina Narciso and 31-year-old Leonora Perez, were on duty in the intensive-care unit during the afternoon shifts when the trouble occurred. Subpoenaed to appear before a grand jury, the women denied responsibility for the deaths.

However, one of them was implicated by a survivor. During the investigation, New York psychiatrist Dr Herbert Spiegel hypnotized the survivors while FBI agents questioned them. Under hypnosis, 61-year-old retired auto worker Richard Neely, who was being treated for cancer of the bladder, remembered experiencing unexpected breathing difficulties and calling out to an

Asian nurse. But, instead of tending to him, she was frightened by his cry and fled. Later, he picked out one of the Filipino suspects from photographs of the hospital's nurses.

Although Federal authorities could come up with no motive for the crimes and psychological tests showed their behaviour patterns to be "normal", the two nurses were indicted. Fearing that Neely and other witnesses did not have long to live, the authorities moved the case speedily to trial. In a hearing that lasted three months, the prosecution introduced 89 witnesses and took testimony from 17 acknowledged experts. The medical testimony left little doubt that many of the patients had received a muscle relaxant without prescription. However, the testimony of the lay witnesses that sought to prove that the two nurses were always present when respiration failures occurred was seen as both "inconsistent" and "confusing". A proper epidemiological study was not introduced, and the prosecution was prohibited from introducing evidence concerning any respiratory arrests not in the original indictment. After 13 days of deliberation, the jury reached a verdict. On 13 July 1977, they found the nurses guilty of five counts of murder, ten counts of poisoning and conspiracy to commit murder. But the case went to appeal in February 1978 and the convictions were overturned.

In the closing argument at the trial, the prosecutor had asked: "What are the odds, ladies and gentlemen, what is the chance, what is the probability that these defendants have engaged in these activities and that all these factors that are incriminating could exist and the defendants would still nevertheless be innocent?" This argument, the appeal court held, was a "most egregious error" as it invited the jury "to engage in a speculative combination of the charges", while the court instructed them that "each charge, and the evidence pertaining to it must be considered separately. You may not consider evidence introduced as to one count in arriving at a verdict on any other count."

This meant that the prosecution could not use the unusually high incidence of cardiopulmonary arrest to suggest that criminal misconduct was taking place and that the incidence of it on their shifts did not mean that the two nurses were responsible.

Although the prosecution was give permission for a retrial, they dropped the case. No new suspects have been named, so the killers are still at large.

Atlanta's Child Killers

Atlanta, Georgia lived through a reign of terror from 1979 to 1981 when 29 African-American youths were killed. In 1982, Wayne Williams, himself black, was sentenced to life imprisonment for two of the slayings. After his conviction, the authorities blamed him for the other 22 deaths – though he was never charged for them – and the cases were closed. The other cases were reassigned to individual homicide investigations and remain unsolved to this day. However, there are now serious doubts that Wayne Williams had anything to do with the murders.

Heading those who believe in Williams' innocence is Louis Graham, the police chief of DeKalb County, which covers eastern Atlanta where some of the killings took place. In 2005, he took the extraordinary step of reopening five of the "Atlanta Child Murder" cases – those of ten-year-old Aaron Wyche, whose body was found on 24 June 1980; 11-year-old Patrick Baltazar, found 13 February 1981; 13-year-old Curtis Walker, found 6 March 1981; 15-year-old Joseph Bell, found 19 April 1981; and 17-year-old William Barrett, found 12 May 1981.

Chief Graham hopes his cold-case squad can either confirm or dismiss his gut feeling that Williams is innocent. Although Graham's renewed interest in the Williams case was sparked in December 2004, shortly after he became DeKalb County's new police chief, he has long held the view that Williams was not guilty. During the original murder spree, he was an assistant police chief in neighbouring Fulton County where most of the murders took place. He also worked on the task force that investigated the killings of the 29 victims – mostly male, in the age range of eight to 27.

Graham's wife taught at the Frederick Douglass High School, which Williams attended, and he met him as a young man. The veteran cop's assessment was that Williams, the only child of two Atlanta schoolteachers, was a spoiled, brash kid, but saw no harm in him and certainly could not see him as a serial killer.

"To me, he's just not the kind that would do something like this," said Graham.

When the serial killing task force narrowed its focus on the diminutive, bespectacled Williams, Graham began to have deep misgivings. How could such a puny wimp overpower so many people – some of whom were bigger than him, he wondered. And how come Williams had never been seen?

"He wasn't that smart," said Graham.

A college dropout, Williams still lived at home with his parents who doted on him. He had few other friends.

DeKalb County Sheriff Sidney Dorsey, who was the first Atlanta detective to search the Williams' home, concurred, claiming that most people who knew about the case believed that Williams was not guilty. But the pressure to make an arrest was enormous. State Representative Tyrone Brooks remembered George Bush Snr, then Vice President, coming to Atlanta and telling the local authorities that if they could not catch someone, the Feds would happily take over. Pressure was also applied by Georgia's Governor George Busbee.

Representative Brooks also believes that Williams is innocent. He knew Williams as a youth and sometimes helped to get leading lights of the civil rights movement to appear on the radio show that Williams broadcast from a station in his garage as a teenager. It was funded by his parents.

After dropping out of Georgia State University, Williams worked for a popular local radio station run by Benjamin Hooks, a leading light of the NAACP, and did odd jobs. He also dabbled in electronics and sold news footage to local TV stations. Using a scanner to listen in on police channels, he would often arrive at the scene with his video camera before the police themselves got there.

"I think he was too close to the scene too often with his camera," says Brooks. "He was a convenient scapegoat."

Despite the money he was making, Williams really fancied

himself as a music promoter and was determined to discover the next Jackson Five. Unfortunately, he was a fantasist with a tin ear and spent a fortune of his parents' money recording demos with local boys of limited talent.

The investigation of the case began on 28 July 1979. That afternoon, a woman searching for empty cans and bottles along a roadside in Atlanta stumbled on a pair of corpses dumped in the undergrowth. One victim was Alfred Evans, aged 13, who was last seen alive three days before when he left home to see a karate movie in downtown Atlanta. His death was ascribed by the coroner to asphyxiation, probably due to strangulation. The other was his friend Edward Smith, aged 14. He had been shot with a .22-caliber weapon and had gone missing the previous week after spending the evening at a skating rink with his girlfriend. Both dead boys were black. A story circulated that the two friends had fallen out with a third boy over drugs and the police investigation went little further.

On 4 September 1979, 14-year-old Milton Harvey was out riding his bicycle around the neighbourhood when he disappeared. The bike was found a week later. But Milton's badly decomposed remains were not found until mid-November outside the city limits, miles from both his home and where the bike was found. A post mortem could not determine how he had died and, as there were no signs of violence, his death was not initially considered a homicide.

Nine-year-old Yusef Bell's mother Camille sent him to the store on 21 October to buy tobacco for a neighbour. Witnesses saw him get into a blue car, thought to be that of Camille's former husband. Camille made an emotional appeal to the abductor to return her child. But on 8 November Yusef's body was found stuffed in a hole in the concrete floor of an abandoned elementary school. The coroner determined that he had been strangled manually by a powerful assailant. Yusef had been barefoot when he disappeared. Curiously, when he was found, the soles of his feet had been washed clean.

The death of Yusef Bell, by all accounts a gifted boy, seized the attention of the black community. City officials and civil rights leaders turned out for his funeral. Atlanta's newly elected African-American mayor Maynard Jackson promised an exhaustive investigation of Yusef's death. At that time, the four deaths were not considered connected – except by the fact that victims were all African-American youths and the murders had occurred in poor black neighbourhoods. However, Camille Bell and her supporters began to insist that the murders were racially motivated and that the Ku Klux Klan were behind them.

The spate of killings then took a grim new turn with the first female victim. Twelve-year-old Angel Lenair had gone missing on 4 March 1980. Six days later, she was found tied to a tree with her hands bound behind her. She had been sexually abused, strangled with an electrical cord, and a pair of panties, not her own, had been forced down her throat.

On 11 March, the day after Angel's body was found, ten-year-old Jeffrey Mathis was sent to the store to buy cigarettes for his mother – and disappeared. Again, a witness saw Jeffrey getting into a blue car, possibly a Buick. The driver was a white man. The witness said that he saw the man again some time later. This time the driver pulled a gun on him before speeding off. Jeffrey Mathis's two brothers said that they had seen a blue Buick parked in the drive of a house Jeffrey visited. Schoolmates said that two black men in a blue car had tried to lure them away from school. They had noted the car's licence plate number, but the police did little with the lead. The matter was handed over to the missing persons bureau, who assumed Jeffrey Mathis was a runaway. Eleven months later his badly decomposed body was discovered. With little more than a skeleton to go on, it was impossible to determine the cause of death.

Fourteen-year-old Eric Middlebrooks left home at 10.30 on the evening of 18 May after receiving a phone call from an unknown caller. His body was found early the following day a few blocks away. The cause of death – head wounds inflicted by a blunt instrument. Police believed that he had been a witness to a robbery.

With the police getting nowhere, Camille Bell, Willie Mae Mathis and Angel Lenair's mother Venus Taylor, along with the Reverend Earl Carroll formed the lobby group the Committee to Stop Children's Murders – STOP – to put pressure on the white establishment. Despite their best efforts the murder rate soared that summer. On 9 June, 12-year-old Christopher Richardson disappeared on his way to the local swimming pool. On 22 June, Latonya Wilson was snatched from her home, the night before her seventh birthday. Her body was found on 18 October, but was so badly decomposed that the cause of death could not be determined.

On 23 June, Aaron Wyche, aged ten, went missing. The next day, his body was found under a bridge where the highway passed over a railway track in DeKalb County. His neck was broken. His death was initially dismissed as an accident. It was assumed he had fallen off the bridge, even though the parapet was as high as the ten-year-old. Aaron was known to be afraid of heights and would not have climbed over the parapet unless he was fleeing from someone. Later he was added to the list of the victims of what STOP were now convinced was a serial killer.

On 6 July, nine-year-old Anthony Carter was playing hide and seek near his home when he vanished. His body was found the next day behind a warehouse less than a mile from his home. The cause of death was multiple stab wounds. Earl Terrill disappeared after being ejected from the South Bend Park swimming pool for misbehaviour on the afternoon of 30 July. Earl's aunt got a call from a man she took to be a white southerner saying that he had got Earl. He was in Alabama and it would cost her $200 to get him back. The man said he would call back that Friday. He didn't. Earl's badly decomposed body was found on 9 January 1981, but again the skeletal remains rendered no clue to the cause of death. A convicted paedophile named John David Wilcoxen, who had been found in possession of thousands of pornographic photographs of children, lived across the road from the South Bend Park swimming pool. Witnesses claimed that Earl Terrill had visited Wilcoxen's house on several occasions. The police dismissed the connection on the grounds that the pictures in Wilcoxen's possession were of white boys.

Mayor Jackson now appealed to the FBI on the grounds that

Latonya Wilson and Earl Terrill – then both still missing – may have been kidnapped and transported over a state line, making the crime a Federal offence.

On 20 August, the body of 12-year-old Clifford Jones, who was visiting his aunt in Atlanta, was found in a dumpster. He had been strangled with a ligature and was wearing shorts and underwear that did not belong to him. Three boys said that they had seen a black boy disappear into the back room of a Laundromat with the manager, a white male who was later jailed in 1981 for attempted rape and sodomy. One of the boys said he seen the manager "strangle and beat" the boy. The time they had seen the manager and boy together coincided with the time of death established by medical experts. Another witness said that he had seen the manager, whom he knew, drop a large object wrapped in plastic in the dumpster the night before Clifford's body was discovered. The manager admitted that he knew Clifford and failed two polygraph tests. However, he was not charged on the grounds that the boy who had said he had seen Clifford strangled was "retarded" and Jones' name was added to the growing list of the victims of the unidentified serial killer.

Eleven-year-old Darren Glass was also added to that list after he vanished near his home on 14 September 1980. Shortly afterwards his foster mother received an emergency call from someone the operator said claimed to be Darren. But when she was put through the line was dead. The police initially dismissed the case as Darren had run away several times before. But when he failed to turn up he joined the list, primarily because authorities did not know what else to do with his case. He was never found. On 9 October, Charles Stephens went missing. His body was found the following day. He had been asphyxiated.

That year, the citizens of Atlanta were particularly afraid that the killer would strike again at Halloween when children were out trick-or-treating. Police patrols were stepped up, to no avail. On 2 November, the body of nine-year-old Aaron Jackson, a friend of earlier victim Aaron Wyche, was found under a bridge over the South River, near where Wyche's body had been found. Like Charles Stephens he had been a victim of smothering.

Fifteen-year-old Patrick Rogers disappeared on 10 November. Like Darren Glass, he was thought to have run away several times before and it took some time before he was added to the list. His body was found face down in the Chattahoochee River on 21 December. His head had been crushed by heavy blows. "Pat Man" Rogers had known Aaron Jackson and had a crush on his sister. In fact, Rogers had connections to 17 other murder victims, some of which had not made the list. A week before he went missing, he had told his mother that he felt that the killer was closing in. A mother's friend told the police that Rogers had been looking for her son to tell him that he had found someone to manage their singing career. His name, she said, was Wayne Williams. It was the first time that Williams' name had come up in connection with the case.

On 2 January 1981 Lubie Geter, aged 14, disappeared. His body was found in a wood by a man walking his dog on 5 February. He was dressed only in his underwear and his decomposed corpse showed signs that he had been strangled manually. He was also connected to the paedophile John David Wilcoxen, who had been dismissed as a suspect in the Earl Terrill case, and another unnamed child molester – a white man whose apartment he had been seen in several times.

Lubie Geter's friend, 15-year-old Terry Pue, disappeared on 22 January after being seen in a hamburger joint on Memorial Drive. An anonymous caller – thought to be white – told the police where they could find his body. Pue's body was recovered the next day. He had been strangled with a rope or piece of cord. This time, the investigators used a new technique which allowed them to lift fingerprints from the boy's corpse. But the fingerprints they found did not match anyone on file. The caller had also indicated that the body of another victim might be found in the same place. Years later, other human remains were found nearby. These were thought to be those of Darren Glass.

On 6 February, 12-year-old Patrick Baltazar vanished shortly after calling the police and telling them that he thought the killer was coming after him. The Atlanta police task force did not respond. After he went missing, one of his teachers received a phonecall from a boy who said nothing, just cried. She said she thought it was Patrick. His body was found the following week by a man clearing up an office park. It showed signs of strangulation inflicted by rope. His corpse led FBI agents to the decomposed remains of Jeffrey Mathis that were found nearby. By this time, Atlanta's murder spree had become known across America and Jeffery Mathis's funeral made the national news.

Curtis Walker, aged 13, snuck off on the afternoon of 19 February to earn money by carrying elderly folks' bags at a local K-mart and never came home. He was strangled and his body was found later that day in Atlanta's South River. His uncle, Stanley Murray, who lived with Curtis and his mother Catherine Leach on the Bown Homes housing project in Atlanta, was also murdered, though his slaying did not make the list.

On 2 March, 16-year-old Joseph "Jo-Jo" Bell went missing. Two days later, a fellow employee of Cap'n Peg's seafood restaurant told the manager that Jo-Jo had called him and told him that he was "almost dead". After that, Jo-Jo's mother received a call from a woman who said she had Jo-Jo. She called back and spoke with Mrs Bell's other two children. Mrs Bell called the murder task force that had been set up by the Atlanta police. When they did not respond, she called the FBI. By then it was too late. On 19 April, Jo-Jo's body was found in the South River. Like many of the other victims, he had been asphyxiated.

Joseph Bell could be connected to a number of other victims. He had been to summer camp with Cynthia Montgomery, a murdered girl whose name did not make the list. However she had her own connections with a number of people on it. Jo-Jo's mother had been in prison for the murder of her husband. While incarcerated, she had befriended another inmate, who was the sister of Alfred Evans.

Jo-Jo was also a friend of 13-year-old Timothy Hill, who disappeared ten days later. Together they often visited the house of 63-year-old homosexual Thomas Terrell on Gray Street, which was known as Uncle Tom's. Terrell's next-door neighbour had seen Timothy Hill the day before he disappeared. Hill was a troubled youth with violent tendencies. A friend told the police that Terrell paid the under-age Hill for his sexual favours. Terrell admitted having sex with Hill. The last witness to see Hill alive said that Timothy had spent the night before he vanished at Terrell's house after missing his bus home. He also said he saw Timothy from his window, talking to a teenage girl. Timothy Hill also had connections with Alfred Evans, Anthony Carter, Jeffrey Mathis and Patrick Baltazar.

On 30 March 1981, Timothy's body was found in the Chattahoochee River. The cause of death was recorded as drowning, though it seems likely he was asphyxiated. Strangely, Terrell was never a suspect in the murders of Jo-Jo Bell or Timothy Hill.

By April 1981, the Atlanta "child murders" had become an embarrassment for the authorities. People took things into their own hands. Prayer vigils were held. Children were given safety instructions. Neighbourhood searches were made for missing children and curfews organized. Even the noted psychic Dorothy Allison was called in. Then FBI spokesmen announced that a number of the murders had been "substantially solved" – the victims had been killed by their own parents. This outraged Atlanta's African-American community. The civil rights struggles of the 1960s and 1970s were still fresh in their minds and the white supremacist group Ku Klux Klan was still active in the South.

Leader of the Congress of Racial Equality Roy Innis then blamed the murders on a Satanic cult involved with pornography and drugs, and he revealed the existence of an alleged ritual site, resplendent with large inverted crosses. He also produced a female witness who passed two polygraph tests, but the police took the investigation no further.

With the police and FBI investigations getting nowhere, the residents of the Techwood Homes housing project took matters into their own hands and began "bat patrols" – residents would patrol the streets armed with baseball bats. Some of the actions the communities had already undertaken may have had an effect. Detectives had already noted that the killer's area of activity seemed to have moved out from the centre of the city to more outlying areas and his victims were getting older. The same day

Hill's body was found, the Atlanta task force added 20-year-old Larry Rogers to their list. Although he was considerably older than the other victims, like many of them, he had been asphyxiated. He was mentally retarded and his body was found, not in a river, but in an abandoned apartment.

Although Larry Rogers was no relation of Patrick Rogers, he had a connection to Wayne Williams. Larry's young brother had been involved in a fight and suffered a head injury. Williams overheard reports of the incident on police channels. He beat the police to the scene and took the injured man to hospital. Later he picked up the boys' mother and took her to an apartment where the younger Rogers was holed up. This apartment, Mrs Rogers testified, was near the one where Larry's body was later found.

Then on 8 April 1981 – and the very day the bat patrols started – the body of 21-year-old Eddie "Bubba" Duncan was found. No cause of death could be established, but asphyxia was suspected and as Duncan was physically and mentally handicapped he was added to the list. Previously murder victims over 21 – and thus adults – were not included. But Eddie Duncan, it was discovered, had ties to Patrick Rogers.

On 1 April, another adult victim of asphyxiation, 23-year-old Michael McIntosh, an ex-convict, was pulled from the Chattahoochee River and ended up on the list. He had last been seen on 25 March, but a shopkeeper who said he saw McIntosh being beaten up by two black men. Again he had connection with other victims. He lived across the road from Cap'n Peg's seafood restaurant where Jo-Jo Bell had worked and had been seen at Tom Terrell's house along with Bell and Timothy Hill. It was thought that he was a homosexual himself.

It was plain that who made the official list was arbitrary. Critics pointed to the murder of 22-year-old Faye Yearby in January 1981. Like Angel Lenair, she had been found tied to a tree with her hands behind her back. She had also been stabbed to death, as had four of the acknowledged victims. However, the police refused to put her on the list on the grounds that she was female – though there were two girls on the list – and that she was too old – though McIntosh was a year older. Combing the police records, former assistant Atlanta police chief Chet Dettlinger came up with 63 murder victims that essentially met the same criteria as those of the list but were omitted – 25 of them occurred after the arrest of Williams that supposedly ended the killing spree. Some critics maintain that the list itself hampered the investigation as it led detectives to assume that everyone on it was been killed by the same hand when the various *modus operandi* employed suggested that more that one killer was at large.

Dettlinger also noted that, just as the victims were getting older and the murders were moving out of the centre of the city, they were also moving eastwards. However, the bodies were always found on the same 12 streets – if you extended them eastwards out of the central area. Even those dumped in the Chattahoochee and South Rivers were found in the vicinity of bridges carrying those same streets out to the eastern suburbs. Dettlinger first offered his help to the police, then to the families when the accuracy of his predictions of where the killer would strike next led him to become a suspect. After he was cleared, the FBI took him on as a consultant.

Meanwhile the death toll went on climbing. In April 1981, another ex-convict, 28-year-old John Porter, was found dead. He had been in and out of mental hospital and, shortly before he had disappeared, his grandmother had thrown him out of her house for fondling a two-year-old boy in her care. His body was found on a sidewalk in an empty lot. He had been stabbed six times. Porter did not make the list. However, at Williams' trial he was linked to the other murders by now disputed forensic evidence involving microscopic fibres and hairs.

Twenty-one-year-old ex-convict Jimmy Payne was reported missing on 22 April. His sister said that he had left the apartment they shared with their mother the day before to sell some old coins to a coin shop. His girlfriend said that he had walked her to the bus stop the day he went missing and she became concerned when he did not pick her up when she returned as they had planned. Payne was known to suffer from bouts of depression which had been particularly severe when he served time in jail for burglary.

Once he had tried to hang himself with his bed sheets, but had been cut down before he succeeded. Six days after he disappeared, his body was recovered from the Chattahoochee River. It appeared that he had been in the water for almost all that time. The cause of death could not be determined but it seemed probable that he had been suffocated and he was added to the list.

Seventeen-year-old juvenile delinquent William "Billy Star" Barrett went missing on 12 May. He was on his way to pay a bill for his mother. Found later that day not far from his home, he was another victim of asphyxiation, but he had also been stabbed after he had been strangled. At first he was not added to the list as the police had reports that he might have been the victim of a hit man. But then it transpired that he had been seen with paedophile John David Wilcoxen and had connections to the unnamed child molester in the Lubie Geter case. That man was seen at Barrett's funeral.

As several of the victims' bodies had been found in local rivers, the police began staking out the city's waterways. Officer Freddie Jacobs was stationed at the south end of James Jackson Parkway Bridge over the Chattahoochee River. Before dawn on 22 May, he saw the headlights of a slow-moving car approaching. It was a 1970 Chevrolet station wagon. Then Officer Bob Campbell, who was stationed on the river bank under the north end of the bridge, heard a splash in the water, saw ripples in the water and radioed Jacobs, who kept the car under surveillance.

At the far side of the bridge, veteran Officer Carl Holden was stationed outside a liquor store, watching for anything suspicious. He saw the station wagon standing on the bridge. It then moved off, turned in front of the liquor store, then re-crossed the bridge. He followed. A mile the other side, the car was stopped by FBI Agent Greg Gilliland.

The driver was 23-year-old Wayne Bertram Williams. He said that he had crossed the river to visit a woman named Cheryl Johnson whom he planned to audition, with the aim of promoting her as a singer. But the address he gave did not exist. The phone number was also bogus and there was no Cheryl Johnson in the phone book. The police searched Williams' car and spent two hours grilling him. Meanwhile the police dragged the river, but nothing was found. Nevertheless, the next day, Williams was interviewed again. He had been in trouble with the law once before. In 1976, he had been arrested for impersonating a police officer and illegally equipping his vehicle with red flashing lights, but he was not charged.

Released after the second interview, Williams and his father apparently undertook a major clean-up of the family house. Boxes were carted off in the station wagon and photographic prints and negatives were burnt.

Then, two days later, the naked body of 27-year-old convicted felon Nathaniel Cater was pulled out of the river downstream of James Jackson Parkway Bridge. He was the last victim to make it onto the list. An alcoholic, he supported himself by selling drugs, working as a homosexual prostitute and selling his blood to blood banks. He also lived in the same apartment block as Latonya Wilson and had connections to the Laundromat man- ager in the Clifford Jones case.

Although the cause of death could not be established, he had most certainly stopped breathing, so it was recorded as "probable asphyxia". At first, medical examiners thought he had not been in the water long, but they were prevailed on to extend the limits of error in their estimate of the time of death to include the dawn of 22 May, when Officer Campbell heard his splash. Authorities now concluded they had their man.

Not only could Cheryl Johnson not be found, none of the rest of Wayne Williams' alibi checked out. The FBI gave him three separate polygraph tests, all of which he failed. And Williams was his own worst enemy. Rather than keeping his own counsel, Williams held a huge press conference outside his house, during which he handed out a long and self-serving résumé that was littered with exaggeration and falsehood.

The FBI lab then claimed they could match fibres and dog hair from Williams' home and car to those found on the victims' clothing. However, perhaps niggled by the intervention of the FBI, Fulton Country District Attorney Lewis Slaton refused to proceed on forensic evidence alone. Although witnesses had come forward saying that they had seen Williams with a number of the victims, they had kept this information to themselves as Wayne Williams had not emerged as a suspect before. Others even claimed they had seen scratches on Williams' arms, implying that his alleged victims had fought back.

On 21 June, Wayne Williams was arrested and charged with the murder of Nathaniel Cater, despite testimony from four witnesses who had reported seeing Cater alive on 22 and 23 May, long after Officer Campbell had heard his splash. This information was not shared with the defence. On 17 July, Williams was indicted for killing Nathaniel Cater and Jimmy Payne. Although they were both adults, the newspapers headlined the indictment of Atlanta's infamous "child killer". In the case of Payne it had not even been clearly established that his death was a homicide. The death certificate said that the cause of death was "undetermined" and was only later changed to "homicide". The medical examiner had said that he had merely "checked the wrong box" – though there were no tick boxes on the certificate and the words "undetermined" or "homicide" had to be written in.

At Williams' trial, which began in December 1981, the prosecution described the defendant as an aggressive homosexual and a bigot, so disgusted with himself and the black race that he aimed to annihilate future generations of African-Americans by killing black children before they could reproduce. A 15-year-old testified that Williams had paid him $2 to fondle his penis. Another witness told the court that he had seen Nathaniel Cater and Williams holding hands on the evening of 21 May a few hours before "the splash". To counter this, a woman testified for the defence saying she had had "normal sex" with Williams. Others testified that Williams disliked homosexuals and his behaviour towards the boys whose singing careers he attempted to encourage was exemplary.

Prosecution turned the spotlight on the credibility and character of Wayne Williams, particularly when it came to his account of what had happened on the James Jackson Parkway Bridge. Williams was shown to be a liar and a fantasist. He had claimed to have flown jet fighters at Dobbins Air Force base, which was clearly ridiculous because of his defective eyesight. He also boasted that he could "knock out black street kids in a few minutes by putting his hands on their necks" and that, if enough evidence was gathered against him in the Atlanta child-killing case, he would confess. Despite his reputation for braggadocio, this was taken at face value.

The judge also allowed the prosecution to introduce testimony on ten other victims on the "child murder" list in an attempt to demonstrate a pattern in the killings. This was a problem for the defence. Although they knew that the prosecution would seek to introduce other cases, they did not know which ones they would choose and, consequently, did not know which to prepare for the defence. One of the cases admitted was that of Terry Pue, though no mention was made of the fingerprints thought to have been lifted from his corpse.

The other nine "pattern" cases were Alfred Evans, Eric Middlebrooks, Charles Stephens, Lubie Geter, Joseph Bell, Patrick Baltazar, William Barrett, Larry Rogers and John Porter. The pattern was that they were all black males, whom the defendant claimed not to know. They came from broken homes and poor families that did not own a car. They were street hustlers with no apparent motive for going missing. There was no evidence of forced abduction. All had died from asphyxiation by strangling. They had been transported, either before or after death, from where they had disappeared to where their bodies were dumped, which, the prosecution maintained, was usually near an expressway ramp or a major highway. Some of their clothing was missing and similar fibres were present in each case.

But on closer examination there was no pattern here at all. In only six of the ten cases was there evidence of strangulation. Not all these victims were found near expressway ramps or major highways. Indeed the pattern did not extend to the two murders that Williams was charged with. Nevertheless, the judge, a former prosecutor himself who had worked alongside District Attorney Lewis Slaton, accepted the DA's contention and prosecution witnesses testified that Williams had been seen with various victims. Their testimony was countered by the police sketch artist called in to draw up likenesses of the suspects on the instructions of the various witnesses. She said that none of the suspects that she had drawn up looked anything like Williams.

The most damning evidence came from forensic scientists who testified that fibres from a brand of carpet in the Williams home had been found on some of the bodies. Furthermore, they said that the victims Cater, Jones, Middlebrooks, Stephens, Terrill and Wyche all carried fibres from the trunk of the Williams family's 1979 Ford. Stephens' clothes were also said to have been covered in fibres from the 1970 Chevrolet station wagon subsequently owned by Wayne's parents. Twenty-eight matches were made with 19 items from Williams' home and cars.

Again the defence was at a disadvantage. They did not have to resources to match the FBI laboratories in West Virginia and could not afford expert witnesses to match those put up by the state. It has since been established that the fibre evidence is flawed. The prosecution claimed that the trilobal fibres concerned were rare when, in fact, they were commonly found in carpets through the region. Indeed, they were so common, it would have been difficult for victims not to have come in contact with them. Even more tellingly, no hairs or fibres from the victims or the clothes were found in the Williamses' home or cars.

What's more, Williams had no access to the Ford at the time Terrill, Stephens and Jones were killed. It had been taken into the shop for repairs at 9 am on 30 July 1980, nearly five hours before Terrill disappeared. It was only returned on 7 August long after Terrill was dead. The car refused to start the next morning and was taken back to the garage the next morning. The new estimate was so high that Wayne's father balked and they never got the car back. The family had no car when Clifford Jones was abducted on 20 August 1980 and Charles Stephens was murdered on 9 October. It was only on 21 October, 12 days after Stephens' death, that Wayne's parents bought the Chevrolet.

Blood-typing was used to link the deaths of John Porter and William Barrett to droplets found in the Williamses' car. However, there was controversy over how old the blood stains in the car were and they could easily have deposited there before Porter and Barrett had been murdered.

A hydrologist testified that, judging by where Cater's body had been found, it was highly unlikely that he had been thrown off the James Jackson Parkway Bridge. The defence also contended that there was no evidence that either Cater or Payne had even been murdered. Cater was a known drug addict and alcoholic, while Payne was a depressive who had previously tried to kill himself. Both of them had been found in the river. They might have committed suicide by jumping in, or they could simply have slipped in and drowned.

Williams took the stand in an attempt to demonstrate that, as a small man, he could not have hauled the body of the considerably larger and heavier Cater out of the back of the station wagon and flung him over the shoulder-height parapet – certainly not in the short time that the police maintain that he was on the bridge. However, this proved to be a mistake. Taking the stand gave the prosecution the chance to cross-examine him. Prosecutor Jack Mallard managed to rattle Williams, making him angry, and goaded him into insulting the FBI agents in the case. This did not impress the jury.

On 27 February 1982 Wayne Williams was convicted on two counts of murder and sentenced to two terms of life imprisonment. Two days later, the Atlanta "child murder" task force was disbanded and the other cases consigned to the files. However, Williams had only been convicted of killing two adults. None of the child murders has ever been solved.

In November 1985, new attorneys unearthed declassified documents from the Georgia Bureau of Investigation. In the early 1980s, they had an informant inside the Ku Klux Klan who told them that Klansmen aimed to provoke a race war by "killing the children" in Atlanta. A Klansman named Charles T. Sanders boasted of killing Lubie Geter, after the 14-year-old had run into Sanders' car with his go-cart. Sanders allegedly told a friend: "I'm gonna kill him. I'm gonna choke the black bastard to death." In early 1981, the spy in question warned the FBI that "after twenty black child killings, the Klan were going to start killing black women". It was noted that there was a cluster of unsolved murders of numerous black women in Atlanta in 1980–82, almost all of whom had been strangled. However, repeated attempts to secure a new trial in the Wayne Williams case have failed.

Nevertheless Police Chief Louis Graham has not given up. In 2000, he visited Williams in prison. At the end of the visit, he told Williams to look him in the eye and say he was innocent.

"To God almighty, I swear . . . I didn't do it," Williams replied – and Graham believes him.

Chet Dettlinger, who had been on the case since 1980, concurred. He told CNN: "I agree with Louis that Wayne Williams did not kill anybody."

Three of the cases that fall within Graham's jurisdiction and he has now reopened are among the ten "pattern cases" introduced in Williams' trial. Williams' new defence attorney Michael Lee Jackson, who is fighting the case in the Federal court, pointed out: "Wayne wasn't defending himself against two murder charges. He really had to defend himself against 12. But the state only had to prove two of them."

Jackson is confident that if Graham's cold-case squad can show that any of the "pattern-case" victims was killed by someone else, he can win Williams a new trial.

Despite the doubts about Williams' guilt, there are no protesters out on the streets demanding his release. *Los Angeles Times* journalist Jeff Prugh who co-wrote the book *The List* about the Williams case, says this is because the civil rights establishment that had taken over from the old white power structure around the time of the killings found it "politically expedient . . . to sit on their hands rather than to attack the black power structure that they helped put into office".

The Reverend Joseph Lowery, who co-founded the Southern Christian Leadership Conference with Dr Martin Luther King Jnr, blames Atlanta's current black police commissioner and a black mayor for allowing Williams to suffer such injustice. Lowery himself did not believe Williams responsible for the child killings – indeed, he handed over to the FBI a letter from a reputed

Ku Klux Klan member implicating the Klan in the murders. However, Lowery does feel that Williams was guilty of the two adult murders he was convicted of.

"I think the community settled into the position that if Wayne did not do it," he says, "at least those who were doing it had stopped."

Graham is worried that much of the physical evidence from the original cases no longer exists. Jackson says he would not be surprised to learn it had been destroyed, as were hours of surveillance tapes of Klan members. However, a judge has ordered that transcripts of the tapes, which still exist, should be handed over to the defence. But a review of the material says that the police dropped their investigation into Klan involvement in the murders after seven weeks. Although Klansman Charles T. Sanders voiced support for the killings, he denied involvement. He and two of his brothers passed lie-detector tests. However Williams has another ace up his sleeve. He says that he can prove that the witness who said he saw Williams and Nathaniel Cater holding hands on the night of the murder was, in fact, in jail at the time.

In a rare interview in 2005, Williams, then 46, told WVEE-FM that he was imprisoned with at least four relatives of his alleged victims, and that even they believe in his innocence.

"The Wayne Williams you see sitting right here today is just as much a victim of what happened as anybody else that was involved in this tragedy," he said from Hancock State Prison. "None of us have really had closure in this thing – not the families, not Wayne and not the people of Atlanta."

Williams claims that, as a black man, he was railroaded in order to prevent the race war the Klan sought to ignite. However, Janie Glenn, mother of victim Billy Barrett, is not convinced Williams is a victim. Twenty-four years before, on the day after Mother's Day, her 17-year-old son had cooked her breakfast, then he took the bus to go and pay a family friend for some guttering work he had done on the house.

"Be careful," she had said as he left.

Later that day, his body was found dumped on a road a few

miles from home – some witnesses say by a uniformed man in a squad car. He had been stabbed and smothered. Glenn says that Williams knew her son and had cruelly encouraged the smallish boy with a painful stutter into believing he could make it as a singer. A relative also told her that Williams had attended her son's funeral.

"I'm not going to say that his hands killed him, but I believe that he knows something," she says. "If Wayne knows who killed my son and the rest of the kids, then he needs to open his big mouth and let somebody else pay for what they did."

Catherine Leach, mother of 13-year-old victim Curtis Walker, shares Graham's belief in Williams' innocence but, to her, this is not about Williams.

"I don't know if he's innocent or not on those other crimes," she says. "All I want is justice for mine."

For her, the issue is her son, the boy who said he was going to Hollywood one day and make his momma rich. And she believes that her boy's killer is, almost certainly, still at large – along with the murderer of the other Atlanta child victims.

Atlanta's Prostitute Killers

In Atlanta, Georgia, more than ten African-American prostitutes have been murdered by a serial killer who likes to display their bodies in theatrical positions at the crime scene. Law enforcement personnel believe that this "lust killer" has been at large in Atlanta for the last 15 years.

Convicted killer Jeremy Bryan Jones confessed to killing eight women in metropolitan Atlanta, including five prostitutes. He talked of picking them up on streets lined with strip joints, murdering them and dumping their bodies in wooded areas and, in one case, dropping the body off a bridge in a river. Although he passed a polygraph test, he has since retracted his confession. His court-appointed lawyer, Habib Yazdi, said that he would confess to anything if he was allowed to talk to his mother and girlfriend.

Jones is certainly guilty of other killings. On 26 October 2005, Jones was convicted of burglary, sexual assault, rape, kidnapping and the homicide of 45-year-old Lisa Nichols. During the trial he blamed Nichols' neighbour for her death, but he had earlier confessed to killing Lisa and burning her body while high on crystal meth.

On 18 September 2004, Lisa Nichols, the divorced mother of two daughters from Mobile County, Alabama, had been found in her bathroom. She had been raped, shot in the head three times and her body set on fire. However, while the body and the room were scorched, the fire did not destroy the house as intended – and with it vital forensic evidence.

Neighbours recalled seeing a vehicle parked outside Nichols' home and one recalled part of the licence plate number. This lead to a itinerant labourer known locally as "Oklahoma". His employer gave the police his birth date and social security number. This identified him as John Paul Chapman, an alias used by Jeremy Bryan Jones.

Four days later, Chapman called Detective Paul Burch of the Mobile Country Police Department who was investigating the Nichols murder. The call was traced and Chapman was arrested, still on the phone, in a house not far from where Lisa Nichols lived.

Chapman was already known to the police as a small-time drug user. However, fingerprints had failed to link him to Jeremy Bryan Jones of Miami, Oklahoma, who had been in trouble with police since, at the age of 16, he had been charged with the assault of a boy and his mother. He was also suspected of murdering 20-year-old Jennifer Judd, the wife of a former schoolmate and next-door neighbour Justin Judd. She had been stabbed to death in the kitchen of her own home. Her body was discovered by her husband. They had been married just ten days. Justin Judd had regularly reported Jones to the police after hearing women's screams issuing from Jones' house.

Jones was charged with rape on 5 November 1995, and again on 10 January 1996. On the second occasion he was found in possession of methamphetamine – crystal meth. Out on bail the next day, he pointed a loaded gun at a woman's vulva and threatened to pull the trigger.

He pleaded guilty to three charges of sexual assault on 3 March 1997 and was sentenced to five years' probation. Two rape victims were afraid to testify. He defied court orders requiring him to provide DNA samples and was kicked off his sexual-offender counselling sessions. Then on 19 October 2000 his probation was revoked and a warrant was issued for his arrest, citing probable cause. Rather than go to jail, Jones skipped the state.

In Joplin, Missouri, he met the mother of convicted criminal John Paul Chapman who was serving time in Missouri State Penitentiary. She took pity on him and gave him her son's birth date and social security number. Equipped with a new identity, Jones headed for Atlanta.

As Chapman, he was picked up three times for minor offences in Georgia, but each time his fingerprints were run through, the FBI database in West Virginia failed to identify him as Jeremy Bryan Jones. Each time he was released, leaving him free to kill. He has been charged with three more murders during that period and remains a suspect in a fourth.

The first was that of 38-year-old Tina Mayberry in 2002. She was attending a Halloween fancy-dress party dressed as Betty Boop in Gipson's restaurant in Douglasville, Georgia, just outside Atlanta. Stepping outside for a breath of fresh of air, she staggered back into the party moments later, bleeding profusely from stab wounds. She died that night in an Atlanta hospital. She had not been robbed and there was no evidence of sexual assault. The murder appeared to be motiveless.

On 12 March 2003, 16-year-old Amanda Greenwell disappeared from a trailer park in Douglas County where Chapman also lived. She went to make a call from a local payphone and never returned home. In April, her badly decomposed body was found in a wooded area nearby. She had been stabbed and her neck had been broken "with great force", according to the post mortem report. But again, there were no clues, no suspect and no apparent motive.

Jones has been charged with the murder of Katherine Collins, who was found stabbed to death in the Garden District of New Orleans on 14 February 2004. Police say Katherine worked as a prostitute in the city.

He is also a suspect in the murder of Patrice Endres, who had gone missing from her beauty parlour Tambers' Trim-'n'-Tan in Chunchula, Alabama on 15 April 2004. Before leaving home that morning, she had left a billet-doux on her second husband's car saying: "The best is yet to come."

Although Endres' early life had been scarred by drugs, she had turned her life around. She had gone to hairdressing school and had opened her own salon. She married Rob Endres and had a 16-year-old son from a previous relationship whom she doted on. The family planned to move to Flagler, Florida, where they intended to buy a bed-and-breakfast.

At work that morning, Patrice was seen smiling and joking with the clientele, but when a client turned up for her 12 o'clock appointment, she found the salon empty. The front door was unlocked and her keys were on the table. Patrice's car was outside, though it was parked at an odd angle. Although the till was empty, her purse was on her desk and her lunch was in the microwave. The police were convinced she had run away. Family and friends protested that she had never been happier, but the offer of a $17,000 reward, a poster campaign and extensive search only elicited a witness who said they had seen a white utility van, that could have been Jones', outside the salon, but no further leads.

After he was arrested, the police say that Jones confessed to killing her and dumping her body in Sweetwater Creek in Forsyth County, Georgia. But after an exhaustive search of the creek, police still have no body and no physical evidence to base a charge on.

Jones is also suspected in the murder of a young prostitute whose decomposed torso was found near Wright City, Missouri on 28 June 2004. Passers-by told investigators that they saw a white utility van at the rest stop off Interstate 70, near where the torso was found.

While in custody, Chapman made a number of phonecalls from

the jail's pay phone to a number in Miami, Oklahoma. This belonged to Jeanne Beard, Jeremy Bryan Jones's mother. At last the police tied Chapman to the earlier outstanding warrants.

Awaiting trial, Jones confessed to numerous other murders including eight women in Atlanta. He even produced sketch maps of the places he had dumped bodies in Georgia, Oklahoma, Kansas and Alabama dating back to 1992. He confessed to murdering 19-year-old Justin Hutchings by "lethal injection" in Pitcher, Oklahoma. And police in Delaware County, Oklahoma, believe Jones was responsible for the murder of 38-year-old Daniel Oakley and 41-year-old Doris Harris in 1996. He is thought to have shot them, then set the trailer they lived in on fire to hide his crime.

However, before his trial, he recanted all his confessions. He has now been convicted in the Lisa Nichols' case and has been sentenced to death by lethal injection. Before that he faces trial in Georgia for the killing of Amanda Greenwell of Douglas County. No doubt other trials will follow.

The problem is that the Atlanta prostitute killings do not seem to fit into the random MO of his other slayings. Even if his jail-house confessions were not pure bravura, he did not admit all the current roster of prostitute killings in Atlanta, which means that, in all likelihood, there is at least one other killer at large in Atlanta.

Atlanta's Ripper

In 1911, Atlanta, Georgia, got its own Jack the Ripper. The horrific murders began on 20 May 1911. That night and on the following six Saturdays, the killer subdued his victims by throttling them before cutting their throats. The victims were all attractive black women. None had been raped, but their sexual organs had been mutilated in a way reminiscent of the fiend of Whitechapel.

However, things went wrong for the killer on the night of 1 July, when a young woman was stabbed while out looking for her mother, who had just become the culprit's seventh victim. The daughter survived and told the police that her assailant had been a well-dressed black man.

The killer then became more wary. He slowed his rate of killing, but did not stop. Over the next ten months, he would claim six more victims. After that he disappeared.

Atlanta's Son of Sam

Then in 1977, Atlanta got its own "Son of Sam" – the killer who was blithely killing youngsters at random in New York at the time. The Atlanta shootings began on 16 January 1977, when the "Lovers' Lane Killer" shot 26-year-old LaBrian Lovett and 20-year-old Veronica Hill.

The police were alerted when they were called to the scene of a car accident. A vehicle had veered across an intersection, coming to a halt when it collided with a traffic sign. Inside, a naked man lay slumped behind the steering wheel, his face and body streaked with blood. He had been shot four times – in the head, stomach, left arm and right leg. On the back seat was a naked woman covered by a coat. She had been shot twice – in the abdomen and the left leg. Both died of their wounds in the hospital, but detectives determined they were shot while making love in nearby Adams Park. Somehow Lovett had survived long enough to drive from the scene.

The killer struck again this time on 12 February. At 2.45 a.m., he approached a teenage couple who were necking in their car in West Manor Park, three miles north-west of Adams Park. He fired six shots into the car before trying to open the doors. Finding them locked, he fled on foot, leaving both victims seriously injured with chest wounds. They survived to describe the attacker as a large black man. Ballistics tests showed that the same .38-caliber pistol had been used in the murder of LaBrian Lovett and Veronica Hill. As with the Son of Sam killings, there was a bewildering lack of motive. The gunman seemed to have no interest in robbing or raping his victims, who appeared to be unknown to him.

The third attack occurred on 12 March when 20-year-old Diane Collins was canoodling with her fiancé in Adams Park. They had announced their engagement just a few days before. That evening they had been to the movies before stopping for a little intimacy in the park. Intent on what they were doing, neither noticed the lethal stalker as he approached their car and unloaded his .38 through the passenger window. Diane died instantly, but her fiancé, though wounded badly in the head, survived. With blood nearly blinding him, he managed to drive home and then telephone an ambulance.

With only the vaguest of descriptions, the police had little to go on. However, they did notice that there had been 27 days between the first two attacks and 28 between the second and third. The gunman seemed to be working on a four-week cycle.

The following month, they staked out the local parks, but the phantom gunman did not appear. He did not strike again. On 10 August 1977, David Berkowitz was arrested for the Son of Sam killings. He had been terrorizing New York for two years. Two years after the Atlanta Lovers' Lane killings the police admitted that they had no suspects and no leads in the case. Like the Atlanta Ripper of 1911, he remained at large.

Austin's Servant Girl Annihilator

Over three years before headlines presented Jack the Ripper as the "world's first serial killer", another mad slayer was stalking the streets of Austin, Texas. Known as the "Texas Servant Girl Annihilator", like his counterpart in London, he was never caught or identified with any certainty. It is plain that he was overshadowed in the historical record because most of his victims were poor and black.

The first killing took place on New Year's Eve 1884, when the remains of 25-year-old servant girl Mollie Smith were found outside the two-storey home of her employer William Hall in West Pecan Street. She cooked and kept house for the Halls, and lived in a room in the back with her common-law husband Walter

Spencer, who had also been attacked. He awoke in agony with a deep gash across his face to find Mollie had gone. The bedroom was covered with blood and there were bloody handprints on the threshold. He went for help and aroused Mr Hall, who followed the trail of blood and found Mollie lying in the snow by the outhouse. The wounds to her face and head indicated that she had been killed with an axe. Her nightdress was torn to shreds and, from the way she had been left, it was clear that she had been raped. The local marshal Grooms Lee brought in bloodhounds to track the killer, but the trail soon went cold. Later a bloody axe was found inside, which the killer had apparently brought with him.

William Sydney Porter, better known as the short-story writer O. Henry, was living in Austin at the time and coined the sobriquet "Servant Girl Annihilator" for his friends working at the *Austin Daily Statesman* – now the *Austin American-Statesman*. Porter, who was later jailed for bank fraud, was depicted as the perpetrator in the book *A Twist at the End* by Stephen Saylor, a fictionalized account of the murders, but it is clear that he had nothing to do with the killings.

Marshal Lee had a more obvious suspect, William "Lem" Brooks, whom Mollie had previously been involved with. The rape and murder had been motivated by jealousy, Lee reasoned. Brooks was arrested, but he protested his innocence and produced an alibi that would have made it hard, though not impossible, for him to have committed the murder. Nevertheless, a coroner's jury comprising six white male citizens, sitting on New Year's Day, concluded that Brooks had both the means and motive – and had, consequently, done it. He was later freed for lack of solid evidence.

On 6 May 1885, another African-American servant girl, Eliza Shelley, was murdered in the same blood-thirsty fashion. The newspapers immediately connected her murder with the slaughter of Mollie Smith. The *Statesman*'s headline ran: "The Foul Fiends Keep Up Their Wicked Work."

Lem Brooks had no connection to 30-year-old Shelley and was not a suspect. In those pre-Ripper times, this was a new kind of crime. A predatory killer was on the loose – a maniac who attacked at random without any discernible motive.

Eliza Shelley had been attacked on the property of Dr L. B. Johnson, a former state congressman who lived at the corner of Cypress and Jacinto Streets near the railroad track with his wife and niece. Hired as a cook the previous month, Shelley lived in a cabin behind the house with her three children. On the night of the attack, Mrs Johnson had heard screams emanating from Eliza's cabin, and sent her niece to find out what was happening. Seeing something was terribly wrong, she summoned Dr Johnson, who went to investigate.

He found Eliza Shelley lying on the floor, dead. She had sustained numerous grievous head wounds. One gash that appeared to have been made by an axe nearly cleaved her head in two and there were puncture wounds made by a sharp, pointed instrument. This time the killer had taken the murder weapons with him.

The pillows were covered in blood, indicating that she had been asleep in bed when she was attacked. Then she had been dragged to the floor and her nightdress pulled up. Her naked midriff was raised on a pile of blankets and her genitals exposed, so it was thought that she had been raped by her attacker.

Her eight-year-old son said that a man had come into the cabin in the middle of the night. The boy had woken up, but the man pushed him into a corner and told him to be quiet. He had placed a blanket over him and the child had passed out, possibly as the result of chloroform that had recently been stolen from a dentist's home in Austin. The boy had no recollection of what had happened to his mother. His younger brothers, who slept in the same bed as their mother, knew nothing.

Marshal Lee's bloodhounds failed once again. A set of shoeless footprints led to the cabin. At the time, Eliza's husband was in prison and it was not thought she had any other boyfriends, so it seemed clear that the shoeless person was to blame. Marshal Lee quickly arrested a 19-year-old, slightly backward black youth who walked around barefoot. But when the tracks were compared against his, it was clear that he had not made them.

Another African-American male who had once lived with Eliza was arrested. He had no alibi and had recently quarrelled with her. But he, too, was released when there was a third murder just over two weeks later.

On 23 May, another black servant girl was attacked in the middle of the night in her cabin, across the road from a beer garden. Her name was Irene Cross. This time the attacker had used a knife. But the attack was just as ferocious. Her arm had been practically severed from her body and the perpetrator had stabbed her so viciously in the head that she appeared to have been scalped. This time there was no suspect at all and no arrest was made.

The newspapers blamed the influx of migrant workers. Austin was then a city of just 23,000 people. But Texas was just recovering from the Civil War and the Reconstruction era and the attacker could have been any one of the thousands of strangers who had come to town, attracted by the prospect of work. There were even gangs of convicts employed in public building works. The newspapers were also unanimous that a black man was to blame – again, perhaps, a hangover from the Civil War.

A fourth attack took place on 29 August at the home of livery-stable owner Valentine Weed on Cedar and San Jacinto Streets, a block south of where Eliza Shelley had been raped and murdered. Weed's servant Rebecca Ramey had been attacked while she slept and left unconscious while her 12-year-old daughter Mary was dragged outside into an alley and brutally raped. Then she was stabbed through both ears with an iron rod and died sometime later. Rebecca survived but could remember little of the attack.

This time, the bloodhounds set off after a black man who was walking nearby. He was arrested, but released the next day. Even though news of the killings filled the papers, the white middle classes felt they had nothing to fear. However, their servants insisted on keeping the windows closed in the sweltering heat of summer. Soon the papers were gunning for Lee, who was now widely perceived as incompetent.

On 26 September, Lucinda Boddy, a cook in a house near the

newly founded University of Texas, went up to the nearby home of her friend Gracie Vance to tend her during an illness. Gracie lived in a servant's cabin behind the house of her employer, the attorney Major W. D. Dunham, with her boyfriend, Orange Washington. There was possibly a fourth person present, another servant girl named Patsie Gibson.

That evening Washington and Gracie had a row. The argument was so furious that the major overheard it and had reported it to the police. But by midnight, everything was quiet and everyone was asleep. At around 2 a.m., someone climbed in through the cabin window. Gracie woke and screamed. Orange jumped up, but a blow from an axe felled him, crushing his skull. Lucinda was also hit on the head, fracturing her skull. It seems she was raped and she blacked out. Patsie, too, had been badly beaten, possibly with a sandbag.

The attacker then dragged Gracie Vance out of the cabin and into some bushes near the stable, where she was also raped. It seems she put up a terrific fight before the killer finished her off by beating her skull with a brick.

During the attack Lucinda came round and lit an oil lamp to have a look around. She saw Orange lying unconscious on the floor and another man was in the room.

"Don't look at me," he said and, cursing, told her to put the light out. Instead, she threw it at him and ran. Her screams alerted the major, who came out of the house with a gun.

"We're all dead!" Lucinda screamed at him before she passed out again. He noticed the blood on her clothes and crept gingerly into the cabin. There he found Washington lying in a pool of blood on the floor. Beside him was an axe. Knowing of the other attacks on black servants in the area, the major called his neighbours for help.

Soon after he found Gracie's body. Her head had been turned to pulp and a bloody brick lay by her corpse. In her hand was a gold watch that did not belong to her, its chain wrapped around her arm. According to one source, a strange horse was found, saddled, in the stable. But neither the watch nor the horse led the authorities to the culprit.

Vigilante committees were set up and there were calls for all undesirables to be run out of town. The circumstances of the last attack indicated it was possible that more than one assailant was at work. Marshal Lee promptly arrested two black men, Dock Woods and Oliver Townsend. It seems that Lucinda Boddy implicated Woods, who was known to harass Gracie. When he was arrested, he was in possession of a blood-soaked shirt. Another witness claimed to have overheard Wood's friend Townsend, a petty thief, threaten to kill Gracie.

Lee also invited professional detectives from the Noble Detective Agency in Houston to assist him in the investigation. They immediately extracted a confession from a man named Alec Mack, who admitted killing Mary Ramey. But Mack said that they had threatened to lynch him unless he confessed. Bruises were found on his body from a beating. Lee said that Mack had sustained them resisting arrest. But confidence in Lee and his Houston detectives was so low that Mack, Woods and Townsend all had to be released. Lee then turned to an even more unlikely suspect. He arrested Walter Spence, who had been injured in the attack on Mollie Smith. After a three-day trial, Spence was acquitted.

It was clear that Lee's idea of going after suspects that might have had a motive in a single case was not working. Instead, state prosecutor E. T. Moore speculated that all the murders had been committed by a single culprit who hated women. No one had heard of such a thing before and he was mocked. Nevertheless, Lee was sacked from the case and a new marshal, a former Texas Ranger named James Lucy, was brought in.

Up until this point all the victims had been black. But that was to change on Christmas Eve 1885. After attending a concert at the State Institution for the Blind, Moses Hancock had been dozing in a chair at his home on San Jacinto Boulevard. When he woke he found his wife Susan missing. She had been dragged from her bed. He found her lying dead in the back yard, her head cleaved open with an axe, and a sharp, thin implement was sticking out of her brain. Blood was pouring from her ears and soaking into her hair. Amazingly she was not dead, though she never regained consciousness. It was also plain that she had been raped. But unlike the other victims Mrs Hancock was white.

Like his predecessor, Marshal Lucy brought in the blood-hounds. Again they drew a blank, but the killer had not finished for the night. Within an hour, society beauty Eula "Luly" Phillips was dead. One of the loveliest women in Austin, she had dark curly hair, pale skin, doe eyes and an exquisite figure that turned men's heads in the street. She lived with her husband and infant son in her father-in-law's house in one of the richest neighbour-hoods of Austin. But although she was married to the son of a prominent citizen, it seems that she also entertained other dis-tinguished lovers.

As before, she had been attacked at home in bed. Her husband Jimmy, who lay beside her, had also been assaulted. He was left unconscious with a huge gash on the back of his head. Their son, though, who was also present, was uninjured. The bloody axe was left in the middle of the bedroom floor. A trail of blood led from the bedroom, down the stairs, out of the house and into a nearby alley. There Eula Phillips had been raped and her head smashed in. Her naked body had been left spread-eagled with her arms pinned under timber. The only clue was a bloody shoeprint left on the porch. It was large and made by a man.

Now that leading – white – citizens were being struck down the newspapers went into overdrive. Some suggested that, as the killer could come and go without being seen, he had supernatural powers. Marshal Lucy brought in more detectives from out of town. Citizens kept loaded guns to hand. Five hundred attended a public meeting. Fresh rewards were raised and bars were closed at 12 o'clock. But the murders suddenly stopped.

With no fresh leads there was nowhere for the investigation to go. Consequently, both Moses Hancock and Jimmy Phillips were suspected of killing their wives – even though Phillips had been badly injured in the attack. The suggestion was that they had both raped their wives, then killed them with an axe to make it look like as the Servant Girl Annihilator had done, though that they had both chosen to do the deed at the same hour on the same night seemed something of a coincidence. Nevertheless they were both arrested. A letter found in a trunk at Hancock's house indicated that his wife had intended to leave him over his drinking. The DA maintained that Moses Hancock had found the letter, got drunk and attacked his wife, but the jury were not convinced that Hancock had even seen, or knew of, the letter. He was acquitted.

A more substantial case was brought against Jimmy Phillips, a known alcoholic. His two-year marriage had been troubled. The prosecution caused a sensation by suggesting that his wife had been prostituting herself at a "house of assignation". Indeed, she had even gone there on Christmas Eve. Witnesses were called to testify about her comings and goings and their suspicions that she had been seeing another man behind her husband's back. A number of local politicians were implicated. Phillips was known to have thrown things at his wife and threatened her with a knife. Indeed it was Eula who had brought the axe to the bedroom to protect herself from him. This had given him the opportunity for a copycat killing, murdering his wife for personal reasons and blaming it on the serial killer that was stalking the streets. He had attacked her with the axe then carried her body outside. A bloodhound called in to track the killer had returned to the Phillips' bedroom and the bloody footprint on the porch, the DA said, was his.

In court, Phillips had to ink his foot, so that the prints could be compared. When this ink print turned out to be much smaller than the print on the porch, the prosecution insisted that carrying the dead weight of his wife would have made Jimmy's foot spread, leaving a larger print. So Phillips picked up his own defence attorney. Still the footprints did not match.

Nevertheless, Phillips was convicted of second-degree murder and was sentenced to seven years. However, the Texas Court of Appeals overturned the conviction before the end of the year. No one was ever caught for the Servant Girl Annihilator killings and soon the Austin newpapers had the opportunity to compare their own killings with those in London's Whitechapel.

One of the largely overlooked suspects in the Ripper murders was a Malay cook named Maurice who sometimes worked on

ships. In October 1888, *The Times* of London said that he had
threatened to kill Whitechapel prostitutes, but had then disappeared. The *Austin Daily Statesman* discovered that he had been
employed at the Pearl House, a small hotel in Austin, in 1885,
leaving in January 1886, just after the last murder. Most of the
victims lived near the Pearl House. Jack the Ripper and the
Servant Girl Annihilator could have been one and the same
man. It is an intriguing theory but now, with the passage of
time, impossible to prove.

For over a hundred years, the Servant Girl Annihilator was
overshadowed by the famous Jack. But now he has come into his
own and Austin offers a tour of his murder sites.

The Baton Rouge Serial Killer

Nearly 120 years after the Texas Servant Girl Annihilator, another serial killer set to work in Louisiana. The first known victim
was Gina Wilson Green, a 41-year-old nurse and office manager
for Home Infusion Network. A divorcee, she lived alone in a
block on Stanford Avenue in Baton Rouge, near Louisiana State
University. Her body was found in her apartment on 23 September 2001. She had been sexually assaulted.

The cause of death was strangulation. According to the autopsy
report she died at about nine o'clock in the morning. Her purse
was missing, along with her Nokia cell phone. This was later
found in an alleyway on the other side of town.

Seven months later, there was a similar killing. At around
two in the afternoon on 31 May 2002, the body of 22-year-old
Charlotte Murray Pace, a graduate student at Louisiana State,
was found by her roommate at a townhouse on Sharlo Avenue
in Baton Rouge. Death was due to stab wounds, but she, too,
had been sexually assaulted. She had put up a fierce fight and it
was likely that her killer had been wounded. Another strange
coincidence linked the two killings. Charlotte Pace had moved
into the townhouse on Sharlo Avenue only two days before.
Previously she had lived just three doors away from Gina

Green, although there was no evidence that they ever knew each other.

Again items were missing. The killer had taken the keys to Charlotte's BMW along with a brown and tan Louis Vuitton wallet that contained her driver's licence. A silver ring had been stolen and, again, her cell phone was missing. However, her assailant left behind a clue in the form of a footprint. It been made by a man's Rawlings brand trainer, size 10 or 11. It was easy to identify because it had a unique pattern on the sole. Unfortunately it was a brand found widely in discount stores.

Then, on 12 July 2002, Pam Kinamore went missing. She was an antiques dealer who ran her own business, Comforts and Joys, in Denham Springs, a few miles east of Baton Rouge. It was a Friday evening and she shut up shop as usual before driving home to 8338 Briarwood Place in Baton Rouge itself.

Her husband arrived home later to find his wife's car in the driveway, but she was nowhere to be found. He was immediately concerned. She did not usually head off without telling him where she was going. Time passed and still she did not show up. Eventually he phoned the police and reported her missing.

As she had only been gone for a matter or hours and there was no sign of forced entry at the house, the police showed little interest. Maybe she had made plans for the evening and had forgotten to inform her husband, or there had been an emergency concerning a family member and she had been called away. Days passed. She did not return. Nothing was heard from her. All reasonable explanations had been checked out and discarded. The family grew gradually more convinced that she had been the victim of foul play. Posters were distributed offering a reward of $75,000 for information concerning her whereabouts or her safe return. After that, all they could do was pray that she would be found alive. Then came the hammer blow.

On 16 July 2002, a team of surveyors working in a boggy area of woodland under the Whisky Bay Bridge in Iberville Parish between Baton Rouge and Lafayette saw something at the water's edge. It was the naked body of a dead woman, later identified as Pam Kinamore.

At the post mortem conducted at the Orleans Parish Coroner's office, it was discovered that she had been sexually assaulted. The cause of death was a knife wound to the neck. Again something was missing. The killer had taken a silver toe ring from Kinamore's body. The police quickly tied her killing to those of Gina Green and Charlotte Pace – and another case.

Two days after Pam Kinamore had gone missing, a 28-year-old Mississippi woman was raped by a man who had forced her into a white pick-up on Interstate 10 that runs westwards from Baton Rouge to Layafette. After the assault, he had let her go and she gave the police a good enough description of her attacker for them to put together a composite.

Then, a week after Kinamore's body had been found, a woman came forward claiming that she had seen a woman answering Kinamore's description slumped in the passenger seat of a white pick-up truck the night she had gone missing. She appeared to be sleeping or, perhaps, dead. The truck had been speeding westwards down I–10 at around three o'clock in the morning. It had turned off at the Whisky Bay exit, the ramp nearest to where Pam Kinamore's body was found. The driver was a white male who, the witness said, had a slight build. This was surely the same man as the mystery rapist.

The police now put together a detailed description of the vehicle. They said they were looking for a white General Motors – or possibly a Chevrolet – pick-up truck, thought to be a 1996–97 single cab model. The licence plate was thought to contain JT341, though it was not known which state had issued it. The witness also said she had seen the shape of a fish on the rear off-side of the pickup.

In August 2002, a multi-agency murder task force was formed, comprising 40 officers from Baton Rouge Police Department, West Baton Rouge Parish Sheriff's Office, Lafayette Parish Sheriff's Office, Iberville Parish Sheriff's Office, the Louisiana State Police and the FBI. They believed that drawing on the resources of all their agencies would help catch the killer more quickly.

DNA evidence linked the murders of Gina Green and Charlotte Pace. Later the Louisiana State Crime Lab managed to show that

Kinamore had been killed by the same man. Now certain that they had a serial killer on the loose, the police began combing through unsolved homicides over the last ten years.

In mid-August another witness came forward. A woman told WDSU News Channel 6 that, when she was packing her groceries in the Winn Dixie food store, a strange man approached her. He said that he worked in construction and that his name was Joe. He then followed her out into the parking lot, carrying a jug of water. Ungallantly, he drew attention to her large size and said that he could lift her up. Even so he asked her to go out with him that night and appeared disappointed when she refused. But he was persistent and said he wanted to give her a gift. He went over to a large white truck that matched the description the police were now circulating. From the back of the truck, he took a tree vine which he gave to her. After he drove off, she called the police.

On 21 November 2002, 23-year-old Trineisha Dene Colomb disappeared. At around half-past-one in the afternoon her black 1994 Mazda MX3 was found on Robbie Road in the small town of Grand Coteau, 50 miles west of Baton Rouge and some 12 miles north of Layafette. The keys were still in the ignition, but Colomb was nowhere to be seen. Her naked body was found by a rabbit-hunter in a wood 30 miles away, three days later. Colomb was a US Marine and fought back before she had been bludgeoned to death. DNA evidence soon linked Colomb's killer with the Green, Pace and Kinamore murders.

There were other similarities with the earlier murders. Another footprint was found, again of a man's athletic shoe in size 10 or 11. CNN identified it as the latest model of a $40 Adidas-style basketball shoe on sale widely in the area. And some of the victim's possessions were missing, including a ring with the word "Love" inscribed on it. But there were some unique features. This was the first time the killer had struck outside Baton Rouge itself and Colomb was thought to be the Baton Rouge serial killer's first known black victim.

On the day Colomb went missing, a white pick-up truck was seen in the same wooded area where her body was found. The driver was described as around 35 years old and white, and investigators released a new composite showing "a person of interest".

The task force actively solicited help from the public. In November 2002, DNA samples were collected from 600 volunteers. Mouth swabs were taken from another 100 potential suspects the following month.

The police took the unusual step of issuing a detailed profile of the man they sought. He was, they thought, aged between 25 and 35. He earned less than the average income and his work did not bring him into contact with other people. It was probably an occupation that required physical strength, such as construction. He had shown himself strong enough to fend off a US Marine and carry the dead body of Pam Kinamore over a boggy terrain.

The killer was insecure around women, particularly women who displayed any sort of sophistication. Most women would have thought him awkward, but dismissed him as harmless. However, in some he might have developed an obsessive interest – to the point where they would have cause to become afraid. There was evidence he had stalked his victims before attacking them. And though the killer was sometimes impulsive, the murders seem to have been planned.

The profilers hoped that the killer would give himself away. They believed that he would be preoccupied with news of the killers and was likely to display anxiety, irritation and even intense anger at the coverage. He might even openly criticize any progress made in the investigation and blame the murdered women for their own deaths.

With the growing publicity surrounding the Baton Rouge serial killer, enrolment in self-defence classes soared, along with sales of guns and pepper spray. Attendance at Louisiana State also climbed with students turning up to class rather than staying at home where they feared being abducted and murdered.

The task force investigators began using roadside electronic billboards to keep the public up to date with the investigation. First two, then six in 2003, covering the Baton Rouge and Lafayette areas. However, after 18 months they seemed no closer to catching the killer. The task force then drew flak from Dr

Robert Keppel, the noted criminologist who had been involved in the investigation of the Green River killer and Ted Bundy. He identified four major mistakes made by the task force.

He criticized their use of the media. Releasing details of the killer's shoe prints might induce him to destroy the identifying footwear, making it more difficult to prove the case against him if and when he was caught. And revealing the DNA links between the victims might also hinder the investigation, Keppel said, as the killer would take more care about leaving behind genetic evidence in future crimes. Keppel was no fan of psychological profiling, which he believed only overloaded the investigation with extraneous information. Detectives should not be looking for the type of unusual character suggested by the profile, but rather the type of man who blends in and is easily overlooked. The task force should comb its files as they probably contained the killer's name already. Keppel maintained that investigators usually came across the name of the killer in the first 30 days of an investigation, which was overlooked as a deluge of fresh information flooded in.

In March 2003, the Baton Rouge serial killer struck again. The next victim was Carrie Lynn Yoder, a 26-year-old post-graduate student at Louisiana State. She lived alone at 4250 Dodson Avenue not far from Charlotte Pace and Gina Green. On 3 March, she told Lee Stanton, her boyfriend of three years standing, that she was going to the Winn Dixie grocery store on Burbank Drive. They arranged to talk again later that night or the following day. When she did not call he began to worry. On 4 March, he drove by her house and noted that the lights were on and her car was outside, but he left it at that. The next day, as he still had not heard from her, he went back to the house. The back door was open and he went in. Her keys, purse and cell phone were on the counter. Everything else seemed to be in order, except for a wall-mounted key rack near the front door. It was hanging by one screw as if it had been dislodged in an altercation. Stanton called the police.

Searching the house, they found a well-stocked fridge and cupboards, indicating that Carrie Yoder had returned from the store before she went missing. Questionnaires were handed out at the Winn Dixie. Meanwhile helicopters searched the area.

Ten days after Carrie Yoder went missing, an angler found her body in the Atchafalaya River near the Whisky Bay Bridge – not far from where Pam Kinamore's body had been dumped eight months before. She had been badly beaten and she had put up a fierce fight before she had been strangled. DNA evidence showed that she was the fifth victim of the Baton Rouge serial killer.

On 17 March 2003, the family and friends of the victims staged a demonstration on the steps of the Louisiana state capitol in Baton Rouge demanding that something more should be done. The task force's response was to tell the public that they should ignore the composites previously circulated. They were now looking for a man of any race or description. Nor should they only be on the look out for white pick-ups. The killer might be using a vehicle of any type as no white truck had been spotted in connection with Carrie Yoder's murder.

On 24 March, Melinda McGhee, a 31-year-old mother of two, disappeared from her home in Atmore, Alabama. She worked as a nurse in a nearby nursing home. She called her mother and her husband from there some time before 8.30 on the morning of her disappearance. In her home, there were signs of a struggle, but no evidence of murder and no DNA that could identify the perpetrator. Although Melina McGhee's home was some 220 miles from Baton Rouge, it was easy to get to up the Interstate and there were striking similarities between McGhee's disappearance and those of Kinamore and Yoder. However, no body has been found.

On 8 April 2003, another name was added to the list of victims. This was not a new case, but one that had been overlooked before. On 10 February 2002, the naked body of Lillian Robinson, a 52-year old prostitute from St Martin Parish between Lafayette and Baton Rouge, had been found in the Atchafalaya River, near Whisky Bay Bridge. She had gone missing the previous month. However, the body had been in the water for more than a week and was so badly decomposed it was impossible to obtain reliable DNA samples.

Possibly another woman had fallen victim to the Baton Rouge serial killer in May 2002, when the car of Christine Moore, a 23-year-old student at Louisiana State, was found abandoned near River Road in Baton Rouge. She had left home to go jogging at a park, but never returned. Her body was found on a dirt road in Iberville Parish in June. Like Trineisha Colomb, she had been bludgeoned to death. Despite its similarities to the other killings, her death was not formally attributed to the Baton Rouge serial killer.

The investigation then took a surprising turn on 23 May 2003 when Fox News reported that the task force were looking into three incidents in which a young black man attacked women in St Martin Parish, though none of them were killed. A composite was produced showing a light-skinned African-American male who said his name was Anthony and, initially, tried to charm his victims. Until then, it was assumed that the Baton Rouge serial killer was white.

On 5 May DNA swabs had been taken from a man who resembled the composite and were sent to the crime labs for analysis. They matched the DNA taken from the body of Carrie Yoder and linked the suspect to three more victims of the Baton Rouge serial killer.

The DNA belonged to 34-year-old Derrick Todd Lee, who lived in St Francisville in West Feliciana Parish, 20 miles north of Baton Rouge. He had given the sample voluntarily nearly three weeks earlier, but later that day his wife Jacqueline Denise Lee took their two children out of school, saying the family were moving to Los Angeles. Packing up their belongings, they left their brick-built ranch house at 4273 US 61 in St Francisville and fled, first to Chicago, then to Atlanta.

On 26 May a warrant was issued for his arrest. The following day he was arrested in a tyre store in Atlanta. For a week he had been living in Lakewood Motor Lodge, where other residents found him to be a "very nice man" who grilled ribs and chicken at a party and set up a Bible study class. He even charmed a number of women there, inviting them back to his room for a glass of cognac. Lee waived extradition proceedings and was flown back to Louisiana voluntarily the next day. Initially he was charged with the murder of Carrie Yoder. However, by early June he was also accused of the rape and murder of Gina Green, Charlotte Pace, Pam Kinamore and Trineisha Colomb.

What confounded the authorities was that Lee did not fit the typical profile of a serial killer, specifically not the profile they had drawn up in this case. Lee was black, with a wife and two children and was outgoing and charming to everyone he met, not a solitary white male who was awkward, introverted and a bit of a loner.

He did, however, have a criminal record that stretched back to 1984 when he was caught peeping into the window of a St Francisville woman's home at the age of 15. A string of arrests for peeping, stalking, as well as illegal entry, burglary, assault and resisting arrest continued until 1999. Then things got more serious. In January 2000, he was accused of attempted murder after severely kicking his mistress Consandra Green after an argument over Lee's advances towards another woman in a bar. While fleeing the police, he tried to run over the sheriff's deputy and got two years. After being released the following year, he was arrested for wife-beating, but the charges were dropped. It was said that his wife "lived in denial of her husband's transgressions, which include stalking, peeping into windows and infidelity". At one point, against his wife's wishes, he moved a mistress into the family home. The police in Zachary, Louisiana, ten miles north of Baton Rouge, also suspected Lee in the murder of 41-year old Connie Warner in 1992 and the disappearance of 20-year-old Randi Mebruer in 1998.

The police were particularly eager to trace Lee's wife Jacqueline. She was found by the FBI in Chicago in June with the couple's two children. They had received an anonymous tip-off that more bodies had been buried under a concrete slab at the couple's home and needed her consent to dig it up.

They also set about excavating the driveway at the former home of Lee's girlfriend Consandra Green as Lee had been seen pouring concrete to form a roadway there in the middle of the night only a couple of days after Randi Mebruer had disappeared from her home in Zachary, Louisiana, in 1998. A woman's bracelet was found, but the search for human remains drew a blank at both of the sites. However, in February, DNA evidence linked Lee to Randi Mebruer's disappearance. The police in Bolton, Mississippi, also tried to tie Lee to the slaying of four women found near a truck stop as he once been a truck driver.

Investigators were still puzzled by the white pick-up seen in the Kinamore murders. They impounded a truck from Consandra Green's uncle, said to have been sold to him by Lee, but no connection was established between it and the murders. As the witness had said that the driver of the truck was white, the pick-up she had seen might have had nothing to do with the murders. Then there was the rape victim who had been sexually assaulted by a white man in a white van.

On 24 September 2003, Lee was formally indicted with the first-degree murder of Trineisha Dene Colomb of Lafayette, Louisiana. However, the district attorney decided not to take that case to trial. Meanwhile DNA evidence failed to link Lee to the murder of Connie Warner.

The following Wednesday, Lee was charged with the attempted rape and murder of Diane Alexander, a nurse in Breaux Bridge outside Lafayette. She claimed that Lee had beaten her and attempted to rape and strangle her in her trailer in 2002 – and would have succeeded if her son had not come home and scared him off. Lee was also charged with the murder of 21-year-old Geralyn DeSoto, who was found beaten and stabbed in her mobile home at Addis, across the Mississippi from Baton Rouge, on 12 January 2002 – the day she registered as a graduate student at Louisiana State. This was a second-degree murder charge because the prosecution felt it could not prove an underlying felony, such as forced entry or rape, which is needed for the charge of first-degree murder in Louisiana.

Lee was found guilty of the second-degree murder of Geralyn DeSoto on 10 August 2004, after his 15-year-old son testified to seeing his father's bloody boots. The verdict brought a mandatory life sentence. On 12 October, Lee was found guilty of the first-degree murder of Charlotte Murray Pace after the prosecution was allowed to introduce evidence from other suspected Baton

Rouge serial killer cases to prove a pattern. He was sentenced to death. As he was taken from the courtroom he shouted: "God don't sleep." Then he cried: "They don't want to tell you about the DNA they took eight times."

While he has been found guilty in these two case, he has not been prosecuted in any of the others. No one has explained the discrepancies between Derrick Todd Lee and the serial-killer profile – or even the early evidence. So there could be a white male serial killer with a white pick-up still out there.

Charlotte, N.C.'s Killers

On 4 October 1996, the people of Charlotte, North Carolina were told that the police suspected a serial killer was at work and was possibly responsible for the murder of at least four African-American women since 1992. They speedily set up a task force to investigate the unsolved cases.

The authorities moved with such despatch in this case because of public reaction to their recent investigation of the murders committed by Henry Louis Wallace. Arrested in March 1994, after killing four in three weeks, Wallace admitted to murdering ten African-American women in Charlotte in a 22-month period.

Charlotte police were severely criticized for not making an arrest sooner. Initially they had not even admitted that a serial killer was at large. Black residents were particularly scathing, saying the police should have spotted similarities between the slayings. All the victims were attractive young black women who had been strangled, usually after being raped, in their own home. The police denied the allegation of racism, saying that Wallace, who is also black, did not fit the general profile of a serial killer. Unusually Wallace preyed on acquaintances, friends of his sister or former girlfriend, or colleagues in the fast-food restaurants where he worked. This is rare. Serial killers usually murder strangers.

Wallace was also outgoing and charming, not the archetypal brooding loner. He also varied his MO. Some victims were stabbed. In one case, he poured rum on one victim's body and set fire to her apartment to obscure the cause of death. Before he left the murder scenes, Wallace wiped off fingerprints and washed his victims. However, he could be slovenly. He would put incriminating articles in the stove to burn them, then forget to turn the stove on. He returned to the apartment of his final victim, Debra Slaughter, to smoke crack after he had strangled her and stabbed her 38 times. Then he put on her Chicago White Sox jacket, grabbed a beer from her refrigerator and left.

Of his killings he said: "It was like an out-of-body experience. It was like I didn't want to, but something or somebody was taking over my body, and I couldn't even stop when I tried to stop."

Despite being a confessed serial killer Henry Louis Wallace got married before he died. The ceremony took place on 5 June 1998 in a room next to the execution chamber where he was sentenced to die. The bride Rebecca Torrijas, a former prison nurse, wore a pale green dress covered with pink flowers and a pearl necklace; the groom a red prison jumpsuit and black tennis shoes. Wallace's court-appointed attorney, Mecklenburg County public defender Isabel Day, served as the witness and photographer. Also present was the manager of death row. The newlyweds were allowed to talk for some 20 minutes in the room where they were married. Then they were allowed another hour in a room separated by plastic glass and bars.

Despite the speed with which the police set up a task force to catch the new killer in 1996, they made little progress and a second task force was established in April 1999, when a fifth African-American woman was added to the list of victims. Like the others, she had been a drug user and prostitute.

On 14 May Charlotte police charged 58-year-old converted Muslim Jafar Abdul Talib, formerly known as Willie James Lynch, with one of the killings. He had already been in the Mecklenburg County Jail on an unrelated charge of assault with a deadly weapon with intent to kill. He had previously been charged with the murder of a woman in 1985. But that charge was later dismissed by the district attorney's office. However, police say they have not ruled out the possibility that the other women were the victims of an as yet unidentified serial killer.

Chicago's Crack-Head Killers

On 22 July 1999, the authorities in Chicago issued a city-wide warning confirming that some four separate sex killers were active in the city who were responsible for the murder of as many as twelve African-American prostitutes in and around the city's South Side over the previous four years. The murders centred on Englewood, between 51st and 59th Streets, and Halsted and Damen – an area ravaged by heroin and crack cocaine. The police said that the victims all lived the same "high-risk" lifestyle, selling sex to buy drugs.

Police Commander Frank Briggs of the Chicago PD said: "We are now dealing with four distinct patterns. We have four individuals involved in 11 homicides and in two criminal sexual assaults."

DNA samples collected from the victims linked one man to seven murders, another one to three, and two more men to one murder and two rapes. Many of the dead were found in burnt-out buildings in Englewood and the adjoining New City Area, and in Washington Park. The police believed that the killers picked out the locations during the daylight hours, then at night picked out their victims, lured them back there with drugs, then raped and murdered them.

By then, the police had already arrested two men in connection with the multiple murder of women in Englewood and New City neighbourhoods. However, the killings continued.

On 12 November 1997 Hubert Geralds Jnr, of 5601 South May Street, was found guilty of killing six women in Englewood in 1994 and 1995, along with one count of rape and attempted murder. The verdict came after an eight-day trial and some 12 hours of deliberation. All seven attacks occurred within a 15-block area over a six-month period.

Along with DNA evidence that linked Geralds to the rape of at least four of the victims, damning testimony came from 27-year-old Cleshawn Hopes, who tearfully described how she narrowly escaped becoming Gerald's seventh victim.

Hopes said she had been smoking crack cocaine with Geralds in her apartment before the attack. The two went out to buy more drugs, but parted company to make their score separately. As she walked by an alley near the intersection of 57th Street and Racine Avenue, she was grabbed from behind. Picked up off the ground in a chokehold, she passed out. When she came around she was in a wrecked van with Geralds on top of her, she said. A quick-thinking girl, she managed to convince him that he "could get it for free". When he relented, she made her escape, running from the van naked from the waist down. Prosecutors maintained that Geralds had taken drugs with all of the dead women. They also said that DNA evidence linked him to a seventh slaying.

The defence contended that Geralds was mentally retarded, with the brain of an eight-year-old and had a sexual deviation that compelled him to have sex with women while they were asleep or unconscious. Geralds had become obsessed after watching a film, during which a man strangled a woman during sex, while he was in prison on drug charges, and vowed to do the same when he was released.

The prosecution dismissed Geralds as "a fake" and brought witnesses to testify that, although Geralds had impaired intellectual functioning, this did not affect his ability to tell right from wrong. The jury recommended that he be sentenced to death by lethal injection. Two months later a judge confirmed the sentence.

But two years later, doubt was cast on the verdict. On 11 February 2000, the *Chicago Tribune* carried a story on its front page about the Geralds case, pointing out that his conviction of two of the murders were based solely on his confessions, despite the fact that he was mildly mentally retarded. One of those cases was that of the murder of Rhonda King. By then the Cook County State's Attorneys Office had come to believe that Rhonda King had been killed by Andre Crawford, who had recently been charged with 10 murders in the Englewood and New City neighbourhoods. Crawford confessed on videotape to King's murders and he provided more compelling detail than Geralds' confession did. The State had to move to vacate all six of Geralds' murder convictions, though it planned on retrying him in at least five of these cases.

Then there was the case of 32-year-old Gregory Clepper, of the 8300 block of South Carpenter Street, who was also charged with killing 13 women in the Englewood area between 1991 and 1996. When he went on trial in October 2000 for the murder of 30-year-old Patricia Scott, who lived on the 8300 block of South Halsted Street, four years previously, a Cook County judge ruled that prosecutors would not be allowed to tell jurors about 12 other first-degree murder charges Clepper was facing.

The prosecution maintained that Scott was killed in April 1996 at Clepper's home. They had been doing drugs together and were having a dispute over sex and money when she was killed. He then dumped her body in a dumpster at Calumet High School, prosecutors said.

The judge also approved a motion to allow defence attorneys and their expert witnesses to go to laboratories in Springfield and Chicago, where DNA tests were conducted on Clepper and the victims. The defence questioned the methods used and the validity of the test results. Outside the court Clepper's attorney said that prosecutors had DNA evidence linking Clepper to Scott, but he insisted that DNA evidence could prove Clepper was innocent in six or seven of the other cases.

As a result Cook County prosecutors dropped charges in 12 of 13 murder cases pending against killer Gregory Clepper because laboratory tests have failed to confirm his alleged confessions – indeed, in some cases the DNA specifically excluded him. Chicago police had said he admitted to killing 40 women, making him Chicago's most prolific serial killer since John Wayne Gacy, who was executed in 1994 for the rape and murder of 33 boys and young men.

The Clepper cases had began crumbling a year before when the Chicago police Cold Case Homicide Unit turned up evidence implicating another suspect in one of the killings. Clepper had been charged with the murder of an unidentified African-American woman whose body was found in an alley in the 4900 block of South Champlain Avenue on 24 May 1994 after detectives said he confessed. DNA evidence matched Earl Mack Jnr, who was arrested and gave a tape-recorded confession. The charge against Clepper in that case was then dropped. As a result the Cold Case Homicide Unit began an extensive re-examination of all remaining Clepper cases.

The question must be asked: if Geralds and Clepper are not responsible for these killings, who is? And why have they not been arrested?

Chicago's Tylenol Terrorist

In autumn 1982, seven people in the Chicago area collapsed and died after taking Extra Strength Tylenol. The capsules had been laced with cyanide. Those who died were the first victims to die from a new type of murder known as "product tampering".

The poisoned capsules had been placed on shelves in six different stores by a person intent on killing innocent people at random. One victim was a 12-year-old girl named Mary Kellerman of Elk Grove Village, who had a sore throat and a runny nose. On 29 September 1982, her parents gave her an Extra Strength Tylenol capsule to ease her symptoms. At 7 a.m. they found her lying on the bathroom floor. She was rushed to hospital where she was pronounced dead. The doctors initially thought that she died from a stroke.

Later that day, an ambulance was sent to the home of 27-year-old postal worker Adam Janus in Arlington Heights. He was found lying on the floor, his pupils fixed and dilated. His blood pressure was dangerously low and his breathing laboured. He was rushed to the emergency room at Northwest Community Hospital. The doctors attempted to resuscitate him, but it was too late. Adam died shortly after arrival of what the doctors thought was a massive heart attack.

But the tragedy was going to take more of a toll on the Janus family. That evening the grieving family gathered at his house to discuss funeral arrangements. The shock of the sudden bereavement hit hard at Adam's 25-year old brother Stanley and his 19-year-old bride, Theresa. They suffered headaches. On the kitchen counter, Stanley found a bottle of Extra Strength Tylenol. He took a capsule from the bottle, then handed one to his wife.

Soon after, Stanley and Theresa collapsed. Scarcely able to believe what was happening, other family members called an ambulance. When the paramedics arrived, they found the couple in a critical state. They were rushed to the hospital. Stanley died later that day; Theresa two days later.

The three sudden deaths of members of the same family can hardly be ascribed to natural causes. Dr Thomas Kim at the Northwest Community Hospital initially suspected that a gas leak in Adam's home had killed them. He consulted John Sullivan at the Rocky Mountain Poison Center, who said the symptoms suggested that their deaths might have been caused by cyanide. Blood samples were taken from the victims and sent to a lab for testing.

News of the deaths quickly circulated among the emergency services. By chance Elk Grove firefighter Richard Keyworth was talking to his friend Philip Cappitelli from the Arlington Heights station about the Mary Kellerman case. It was known that she had taken Tylenol before she died and Keyworth suggested the Janus deaths could also have been related to the tablets. So Cappitelli called the paramedics who had attended the Janus family. They confirmed that they too had taken Tylenol. The police were called and they went to the Kellerman and Janus homes to retrieve the remaining Tylenol.

The next day, Cook County's chief toxicologist, Michael Shaffer, tested the capsules and found that some had been tampered with. Instead of being filled with a harmless proprietary pain killer, they contained some 65 milligrams of deadly cyanide. Only five to seven microgrammes are needed to kill the average person. The victims had given around 10,000 times the lethal dose. Blood samples of all four victims then confirmed that they had all been poisoned with cyanide.

The authorities contacted McNeil Consumer Products, the subsidiary of Johnson & Johnson who made Extra Strength

Tylenol. They immediately warned pharmacists, established a crisis hotline and began a massive product recall which cost $125 million. But for other victims it was too late.

That day, a United Airlines stewardess Paula Prince, aged 35, was found dead in her suburban Chicago apartment. An open bottle of Extra Strength Tylenol capsules were found nearby. Meanwhile 27-year-old Mary Reiner was recovering at home in Winfield, Illinois, after the birth of her fourth child when she too turned to Tylenol for relief. She took two capsules and died soon after in the hospital where she had just given birth to her son. Thirty-five-year-old Mary McFarland of Elmhurst, Illinois was the seventh victim of the cyanide-laced Tylenol.

Nobody could be sure that seven would be the total body count of the "Tylenol Terrorist" and police drove through Chicago issuing warnings over loudspeakers and sending people rushing home to dispose of bottles. That evening the nightly news on all three US national television networks reported the deaths from the contaminated drug. A day later, the Food and Drug Administration advised consumers to avoid the Tylenol capsules, "until the series of deaths in the Chicago area can be clarified". This caused a nationwide panic. A hospital in Chicago received 700 telephone calls about Tylenol in one day. In Washington state, Seattle's Poison Control Center informed citizens that, if they had indeed been poisoned with cyanide, they would be dead before they were even able to make a telephone call to a hospital or the police. Nevertheless people in cities across the country were admitted to hospitals on suspicion of cyanide poisoning. Despite the panic, there were no further cases.

Officials at McNeil Consumer Products made clear that the tampering had not taken place at either of its plants, even though cyanide was available on the premises. Indeed, as the cyanide-laced Tylenol discovered so far came from different batches and in different shipments from both of the company's plants, the contamination had not happened at the factory. And as the poisoned Tylenol had only been found in the Chicago area, the authorities concluded that any tampering must have occurred after the product had reached Illinois.

The lot numbers of the tainted Tylenol capsules were MD 1910, MC 2880, MA 1801, and MB 2738. Clearly they had taken from different stores over a period of weeks or months. The culprit had then emptied out the painkiller, refilled the capsule with cyanide and returned them to the shelves of stores in the Chicago area. This was done relatively haphazardly. One of the bottles contained ten poisoned capsules; some five or less. One bottle each was left at the Walgreen Drug Store at 1601 North Wells, Chicago; Frank's Finer Foods on Winfield road, Winfield; and the Jewel Foods store at 122 North Vail, Arlington Heights, and Jewel Foods, 948 Grove Mall, Elk Grove Village. Two were left at the Osco Drug Store, Woodfield Mall, Schaumburg, and two more bottles were recovered from one other retail outlet that was not identified.

The choice of locations for placement suggested that the poisoner drove along Routes 90/94, 290 and 294. That way, it would have only taken him a few hours to distribute his lethal packages. He could have done this in the evening without even taking time off from his day job. There was little risk. After all, stores were on the look-out for shoplifters, not people putting products back on the shelves. He picked stores in more affluent residential areas where those who picked the fatal product from the shelves were likely to have been local residents.

Investigators had no evidence as to who might have committed the heinous crime and there was continuing fear that more deaths might occur unless they caught the Tylenol Terrorist. They had no idea how many bottles had been tampered with, or whether the culprit would strike again. Thousands of bottles of Tylenol removed from the shelves had to be tested. Then, on 2 October 1982, the police discovered another contaminated pack among a batch removed from a drug store in the Chicago suburbs. In an effort to put an end to the senseless deaths, Johnson & Johnson offered a reward for information leading to the arrest and conviction of the terrorist.

The poison used in the Tylenol Murders was the compound potassium cyanide, commonly used in metal electroplating, gold and silver extraction, fertilizer production, and the photographic and cinematographic film processing industries. The poison could have been obtained relatively easily there.

The killer emptied each of the capsules completely, then refilled them with the grey crystalline potassium cyanide. The capsules that were recovered all appeared deformed or bulky. This would have been obvious to a careful eye, but no one was anticipating such an act in 1982.

There was no clear motive for the murders as no demand for money was made by the perpetrator. The poisoner could have made money on the stock market as Johnson & Johnson stock dropped dramatically after the plot was discovered. However, one would have to have had a detailed grasp of stock market trading to make money when a stock is going down. The shoddy work done on capsules themselves hardly revealed that level of competence.

None of the victims seemed likely to be the possible target of a murder plot covered up by further six random murders. All the victims were relatively young. They were not wealthy and carried no large life assurance policies. The crime bought the killer no fame or fortune. He could hardly boast about what he had done.

The police could only speculate that the perpetrator had a grudge against Johnson & Johnson, society in general, or perhaps just the stores where he had placed the poisoned Tylenol. Perhaps he had been caught shoplifting in these stores. Unfortunately, this line of investigation led nowhere. The only clear clue was that the distribution of the tampered bottles suggested that the Tylenol Terrorist lived in west Chicago.

A month after the poisonings, a 48-year-old dockhand who worked at a warehouse that supplied Tylenol to two of the stores where the contaminated bottles were sold became the prime suspect. He was an amateur chemist and the police claimed that he had admitted to working on a project that involved the use of cyanide. According to an article in *Newsweek*, a search of his apartment turned up a book that described "how to kill people by stuffing poison into capsules", two one-way tickets to Thailand and a number of weapons.

Although there was no hard evidence connecting him with the poisoning, the police charged the dockhand with illegal possession of firearms. He went to jail, but was released on a $6,000 bond. Soon the focus of the investigation turned elsewhere.

Johnson & Johnson received a handwritten note, demanding $1 million to put an end to the poisonings. The police traced the note to a tax accountant and con artist named James W. Lewis who was already on the run after a jewel robbery and the murder of his boss in Kansas City. A warrant was issued and the FBI began a manhunt across four states for Lewis and his wife LeAnn.

In the last week of October, the *Chicago Tribune* received a letter from "Robert Richardson" – one of the many aliases used by Lewis. It claimed the he and his wife were not involved in the Tylenol murders and, should they be arrested, informed the police they were unarmed.

Meanwhile on 11 November 1982 – just six weeks after the first Tylenol poisoning – Johnson & Johnson put Tylenol back on the market, this time with a triple-seal tamper-resistant package. The product was advertised widely. A $2.50 coupon was given to purchasers and Tylenol quickly regained more than 98 per cent of its sales.

After a ten-week search, the FBI got a tip from a librarian in the New York Public Library who had recognized Lewis from a wanted poster the FBI had sent out. He was a regular reader. On 13 December 1982, the FBI agents surrounded the reading room of New York Public Library and arrested Lewis. His wife LeAnn turned herself into the Chicago police the following week.

Under interrogation, Lewis denied having anything to do with the poisonings. But he also denied writing the extortion letter to Johnson & Johnson, even though it was in his handwriting and his fingerprints were on it. According to *Newsweek* another extortion letter threatening more Tylenol deaths was sent to the White House demanding that Ronald Reagan changed his tax policies. Again this was in Lewis's handwriting. Again he denied writing it.

A New York hotel register showed that the couple had been checked in there when the poisoned bottles had been planted.

LeAnn Lewis worked in the city. She took no time off. Witnesses said that she had lunch with her husband every day and he met her after work. No train, bus or airline records put the Lewises back to Chicago during the time the bottles were tampered with. This ruled them out and the police had to admit the poisoner was still at large. Lewis was found guilty of extortion and six un-related counts of mail and credit-card fraud. He served 13 years of a 20-year sentence and was released on parole in 1995.

A second man, Roger Arnold, was investigated and cleared of the killings. However, the media attention caused him to have a nervous breakdown and he blamed bar-owner Marty Sinclair for fingering him to the police. He shot and killed a man he believed to be Sinclair, but who was in fact an innocent man named John Stanisha. Arnold wound up serving 15 years of a 30-year sentence for second-degree murder.

The crime remains unsolved and the $100,000 reward, posted by Johnson & Johnson for the capture and conviction of the Tylenol Terrorist, has never been claimed.

However, the Tylenol killings set off a wave of copycat product tamperings afterwards. In 1982 alone, the US Food and Drugs Administration recorded 270 incidents – 36 of them "hard core". A 14-year-old boy in Minneapolis named Marlon Barrow became ill after drinking chocolate milk that had been contaminated and 27-year-old Harry Browning in Florida was sick after drinking orange juice laced with insecticide. Neither died. But Congress was so worried that, in May 1983, it passed the "Tylenol Bill" that made the malicious tampering of consumer products a Federal offence.

Then in February 1986, 23-year-old Diane Elsroth was visiting her boyfriend in New York, where she took two Extra Strength Tylenol capsules from a new "tamper-proof" bottle. She was dead within minutes. Again the cause of death was cyanide; three more deadly capsules were found in the bottle.

A rapid recall located another bottle containing a poisoned capsule at a Woolworth's in Westchester County. It seems that even the new seals could not be trusted and the publicity sur-rounding the murder of Diane Elsroth sparked a new wave of copycat tamperings. There was another death just four months later.

Just after 6 a.m. on 11 June 1986, 40-year-old bank manager Sue Snow woke in the Seattle suburb of Auburn with a headache. She took two capsules of Extra-Strength Excedrin, a rival to Tylenol made by Bristol-Myers. Then she went into the bathroom to have a shower and fix her hair.

Her 15-year-old daughter Hayley went into the bathroom 40 minutes later to see what was taking her so long and found her mother sprawled unconscious on the floor. She called 911. Sue Snow rushed to hospital, where she died a few hours later without regaining consciousness.

An aneurysm in the brain was suspected, but doctors found no evidence of internal bleeding. The symptoms also suggested an overdose, but Hayley insisted her mother neither drink nor smoked – and certainly did not take drugs. With no obvious the cause of death, a post mortem was ordered.

During the autopsy, one of the pathologist's assistants noticed a faint odour of bitter almonds emanating from the body – the telltale sign of cyanide. Lab tests confirmed that cyanide was indeed the cause of death. The source was traced to the bottle of Extra-Strength Excedrin and Bristol-Myers organized a national recall.

Hysteria spread through Washington. Police stripped all non-prescription capsules from pharmacy shelves and the FBI was called in. They found two more bottles of contaminated painkillers, one in Auburn and one in the adjoining suburb of Kent.

The day after the highly publicized product recall had started, 17 June, Stella Nickell telephoned the police. The 42-year-old widow said she feared that her husband had been poisoned the same way less than two weeks earlier. On 6 June, 52-year-old Bruce Nickell, a heavy equipment operator who worked for Washington State, had collapsed and died after taking four capsules of Extra-Strength Excedrin. A post mortem had initially determined the cause of death to be complications resulting from emphysema and Bruce Nickell had already been buried. However, earlier he had volunteered to be an organ donor, so a sample of his blood serum had been kept. On 19 June a lab test on the serum showed cyanide to be present. By that time the police had discovered two bottles of contaminated Excedrin capsules in Nickells' home.

All five contaminated bottles were sent to the FBI crime lab in Washington, D.C. to be checked for fingerprints that might belong to the killer. During the examination, lab technician Roger Martz made an unusual discovery. He found that the cyanide in all five bottles contained tiny green crystals. Breaking the particles down chemically, he identified it as the substance that killed algae in fish tanks. He even came up with the brand name: Algae Destroyer. And he concluded that the killer had mixed up the cyanide in a container used earlier for crushing pellets of the algicide.

FBI agent Ron Nichols then spotted an anomaly. Of the 740,000 capsules from Washington, Oregon, Idaho and Alaska the FDA had examined, the capsules that contained cyanide were found in only five bottles – and two of them were found in Stella Nickell's home. If she had bought the two bottles in the same store at the same time, that might just be a case of bad luck. However, Stella Nickell said she bought them at different times in different stores. The odds against such a coincidence were infinitesimal.

Stella Nickell, a grandmother with two daughters, seemed an unlikely suspect. She worked as a security guard at the Seattle-Tacoma airport and lived a seemingly happy life with her second husband Bruce in a trailer on a large woody lot. Neighbours said she was cheerful and hard-working and seemed genuinely grief-stricken when Bruce suddenly died. But then FBI agent Jack Cusack, who was now heading the investigation, remembered something seemingly insignificant another agent had told him earlier – "Stella Nickell has a fish tank in her trailer."

Agents combed pet stores to see if anyone recalled selling Algae Destroyer to Nickell. On 25 August 1986, a clerk at a store in Kent identified Stella Nickell from a photo montage. She stuck out in his mind because she had a little bell attached to her purse and he called her "the woman who jingled". Intrigued, FBI agents began a background check on the grandmother who had now become their prime suspect.

Between 1968 and 1971, she had convictions in California for cheque fraud, forgery and child abuse. What's more the Nickells were chronically short of money, barely escaping bankruptcy recently and the bank had been moving to foreclose on their trailer before Bruce died.

The crisis had been averted when the state had paid out $31,000 in life-assurance, a policy that they maintained as Bruce Nickell's employer. However, they would have paid out $176,000 if his death had been "accidental" – under the policy being poisoned by a random killer would have qualified as accidental. The problem was that the doctor who examined Bruce had failed to detect the cyanide. The autopsy said that her husband had died of natural causes. Stella Nickells had called the hospital to question the post-mortem findings. She stood to make an extra $105,000 if the cyanide was found. That was why she had had called the police.

Furthermore, in the year before his death, Stella had taken out two $20,000 policies on Bruce's life. Now she had even filed a wrongful death suit against Bristol-Myers for "contributing to" her husband's death.

Up until this point, Cusack had been trying to find a link between the murders of Sue Snow and Bruce Nickell. Now he was faced with the chilling thought that Stella Nickell had put bottles of Excedrin laced with cyanide on drug store shelves – risking the lives of many others and taking one – to make the murder of her husband look like an accident.

On 18 November, Cusack asked Stella Nickell to come in for a routine interview at FBI headquarters in Seattle. As a dark-haired, middle-aged woman in a buckskin coat walked into his office sat down, Cusack heard a soft jingle from the bell on her purse.

First, he went over the details of her husband's death, then asked where and when she had bought the tainted bottles. Had she ever bought Algae Destroyer? he asked. She said no. Then he asked whether she had ever bought extra life assurance on her husband. Again, she said no.

Cusack had caught her out lying, twice. So he asked Stella Nickell if she would take a polygraph test. She refused, sobbing like a grieving widow and saying that she was not in a fit state to undergo any further questioning. Cusack let it go at that, but kept up the pressure in what he calls his "pebbles-on-the-roof" technique.

"The suspect gets the impression we're interviewing everyone they know. They begin to think we know about every mistake they make," he said. "It's like they're almost asleep at night and there it is again – ping, ping, ping on the roof."

Four days after the first interview, Stella Nickell called Cusack and agreed to take the lie-detector test. Once she was hooked up to the polygraph machine, Cusack asked if she put cyanide in Excedrin capsules. She calmly denied it, but the jump in the needles measuring her pulse rate and her breathing told a different story.

Unfortunately, polygraph tests are rarely admissible in court, so Cusack switched the machine off.

"Based on your physiological responses," he said, "I am positive you caused Bruce's death."

"I want to see my attorney," said Stella Nickell. It was plain that Cusack was not going to get a confession.

Cusack had already questioned Cindy Hamilton, Stella Nickell's 27-year-old daughter from a previous marriage. She had defended her mother but, hearing about the result of the polygraph test, she was beginning to have second thoughts. When Cusack questioned her for a second time, she said that her mother had talked about killing her stepfather for years. She was bored, but she did not want a divorce because she would lose half of their meagre property. She had even talked of hiring a hit man to shoot Bruce or run his car off the road. Once, she tried to poison him with foxglove seeds, but they only made him drowsy. Then, a few months before his death, Cindy said, Stella began talking about cyanide. When Bruce died, Cindy talked over the matter with her mother.

"I know what you're thinking," said Stella, "and the answer is no."

Cindy had allayed her suspicions until the polygraph results revived them.

"I knew my mother was capable of doing this," she said. "I just didn't want to believe it."

Slowly, a nine-hour interview with Cusack brought home to Cindy the enormity of what her mother had done. She had killed an unsuspecting victim to make the murder of her husband seem like the random act of a deranged poisoner. What if Sue Snow's daughter Hayley had taken the capsules that morning? What if the other two bottles had found their way into people's homes? How many people would Stella Nickell have killed for an extra $105,000?

Cindy agreed to testify against her mother as long as she did not have to face the death penalty. Cusack assured her that a Federal conviction for product-tampering conviction carried a maximum sentence of life imprisonment.

But there was still no smoking gun. Cindy had not seen her mother put the cyanide in capsules, administer them to her husband or place the contaminated bottles in stores. In court, her testimony could be dismissed as a feud between mother and daughter. Indeed, the maternal bond was strong and she might deny everything in court.

As the grand jury began hearing testimony in February 1987, the FBI team had shrunk to just three men – Cusack, Nichols and a rookie named Marshall Stone. Desperately they tried to put together the last link in the chain of evidence against Stella Nickell. But most of the leads they checked out went nowhere. Then Cusack remembered that Cindy had told him, in the months before her stepfather's death, her mother had been researching in libraries. Stone headed for Stella Nickell's local library in Auburn.

"Do you have a library-card holder by the name of Stella Nickell?" he asked the librarian. She searched the files and handed to Stone an overdue notice for a book Stella had borrowed and never returned. Its title: *Human Poisoning*.

Armed with the number Stella Nickell's library card, Stone combed the aisles for other books on toxicology. He found a volume on poisonous plants called *Deadly Harvest*. Stella Nickell's library number had been stamped twice on the checkout slip – and both dates were before her husband's death. The book was sent off to Washington, DC, where the FBI crime lab found 84 of Stella's prints in *Deadly Harvest* – mostly on the pages covering cyanide.

On 9 December 1987, Stella Nickell was charged with the murder of her husband and Sue Snow. When her trial began four months later, she pleaded not guilty. It took 31 witnesses to piece together a portrait of a woman whose unhappy marriage and financial desperation led to her to see random acts of murder as a solution. The prosecutor called her an "icy human being without social or moral conscience".

The jury found her guilty on 9 May. Saying her crimes exhibited "exceptional callousness and cruelty", Judge William Dwyer sentenced her to 99 years, with no consideration of parole for 30 years.

As a result of the case, the FDA tightened its regulations, setting national requirements of anti-tampering protection for over-the-counter medicines. The maker of Excedrin, Tylenol and other non-prescription drugs stopped using two-piece capsules that could easily be pulled apart, refilled and pushed back together. They were replaced with one piece "caplets" in an attempt to prevent tampering by crazed killers. It failed.

On the evening of 2 February 1991, Jennifer Meling collapsed in the apartment she shared with her husband Joseph in Tumwater, Washington, after taking the decongestant Sudafed. Earlier the couple had been separated and Jennifer had filed for divorce, but now they were now reconciled. When she lapsed into unconsciousness, her 31-year-old husband called 911.

Rushed to hospital, emergency room staff had trouble identifying what was wrong with her. Joseph Meling then suggested that they look for signs of cyanide poisoning. Cyanide was found in her blood, but Jennifer recovered. Unfortunately that was not the end of the matter. In attempting to murder his wife to cash in on a $700,000 life assurance policy he had taken out on her, he had tried to cover his tracks with more product tampering.

On 11 February, 40-year-old Kathleen Daneker died of poisoning in Tacoma. The Pierce County coroner found cyanide in her body on 1 March. In her home, the police found Sudafed capsules which they took to Seattle where they confirmed they had been tampered with.

By then 44-year-old Stanley McWhorter of Lacey, Washington, had died shortly after taking a Sudafed capsule on 18 February. Once the Pierce County findings came to light, the Thurston County coroner checked McWhorter's body and found cyanide.

The following day, nearly all of FDA's Seattle district's employees, along with investigators from the agency's offices in Spokane, Yakima and Portland, Oregon, started removing Sudafed capsules from store shelves. Over the next three weeks, district investigators worked around the clock collecting the drug from all stores along the 47-mile stretch of Interstate 5 from Olympia, Washington, north to South Seattle. Some 248,000 capsules were collected and screened.

One contaminated Sudafed capsule was found at a Pay 'n' Save Drug Store in Tacoma, about 30 miles from Tumwater. Two consumers returned packages each containing one cyanide-laced capsule that they had purchased at the Drug Emporium Store No. 6 and a K-mart Discount Store, both in Tacoma.

Although Jennifer Meling stood by her husband and testified for the defence at his trial, Joseph Meling was found guilty of two counts of murder, one attempted murder, six counts of product tampering and three counts of mail fraud. On 8 June, he was sentenced to two concurrent life terms plus 75 years in prison, with no possibility for parole.

The judge said that Meling's "planning and preparation for the crime was extraordinary, detailed and elaborate, and it was only through good fortune that more persons didn't die".

In addition, Meling was ordered to pay $3.5 million in restitution to Burroughs-Wellcome, the manufacturer of Sudafed, and $4,794.29 to Blue Cross for his wife's medical bills. Any money Meling earns through media contracts and book royalties will be used to make the restitution.

Many of the product-tampering cases that have resulted in death have, for the most part, led to the successful conviction of the perpetrator. Despite the pharmaceutical industry's best efforts to make their products tamper-proof, incidents of product tampering have continued all over the US, with a surprising concentration in the Chicago area. Some 53 threats of product tampering have been received by the FBI with a postmark from south Chicago or Gary, Indiana which is part of the Greater Chicago area. Other cases of tampering – in some cases using cyanide – have occurred in North Chicago, Lombard, Chicago proper and outlying areas.

Although some culprits have been brought to book, the man who started it all – the Tylenol Terrorist – is still at large. He had no simplistic motive like that of Stella Nickell or Joseph Meling. There has been another unsolved product-tampering cyanide poisoning in Detroit and one in Tennessee. The Tylenol Terrorist is still at large and could be at work, attempting to bypass the latest tamper-proof devices. If, as seems likely, he was in his 20s in 1982, he will only be in his 40s or 50s today.

The Cincinnati Carbon-Copy Killings

A serial killer seems to be stalking the Cincinnati area. Since 1996 numerous women have simply vanished and about a dozen female bodies have been found in the counties of Ohio, Kentucky and Indiana that surround the city. The victims all have a similar in age and appearance.

The disappearances began on 28 August 1996. That evening 22-year-old Carrie Culberson and two friends from Blanchester, Ohio went over to the town of Morrow, some nine miles away, to play in a volleyball march. After the game, Carrie rode around town with her friends looking for something to do, but it was a quiet Wednesday night in a small town in the Midwest and a neighbour saw Carrie being dropped off at around 11.30 p.m. at the home she shared with her mother, Debbie Culberson, and her teenage sister, Christina. A few moments later that same neighbour said they saw Culberson's 1989 red Honda CRX reverse out of the driveway and head down the block.

Debbie Culberson noticed her daughter's car was not in the driveway at around six o'clock the following morning and began driving around Blanchester looking for her daughter. First she checked out the house of Carrie's long-term boyfriend, 24-year-old Vincent Doan, but he was not home. Nor was Carrie's Honda in the driveway where it would normally have been if Carrie had spent the night away from home.

Debbie found Doan later that morning at the home of his father, Lawrence Baker. She said that Vincent first told her he had not seen Carrie for three days, but later he changed his story. He then said that Carrie had driven by his house at around 12.30 a.m., honking her horn. She had plainly been drunk, so he just closed his door and ignored her. However, Carrie's companions at the volleyball match said she only had one beer.

Debbie Culberson maintains that Doan changed his story a second time, when she went to see him again. This time, she said he told her that he had come out of his house wrapped in a towel to talk to her – and when he told her that he did not love her any more, she sped off.

Far from not loving her any more, Carrie's friends said that he was obsessed by her. He would call the beauty parlour where she worked as a nail technician at least five times a shift, co-workers said. Relatives, friends and acquaintances said that his obsession manifested itself in physical abuse. Some had witnessed the abuse; others saw injuries. A photograph of her taken in April 1996, showed Carrie with badly bruised, swollen face, allegedly the result of a beating. When challenged by Carrie's parents, they said that Doan blamed her injuries on a bumpy ride in a Jeep. Later, Debbie Culberson maintained, Doan told her he only slapped Carrie and never hit her with a fist. But Carrie told friends that scratch marks on her face were caused by her frantic efforts to pull Doan's hands away from her mouth and nose when he tried to smother her.

Friends said that on 28 July 1996 – one month to the day before she disappeared – he hit her on the back of the head with an electrical heater. The resulting wound needed five stitches, but Doan, they said, had told her to say that she had fallen on his front porch. Debbie Culberson was not having this, though. She took Carrie to the Blanchester police to file misdemeanour assault charges against Vincent Doan. These charges now had to be dropped when Carrie disappeared and there were no other witnesses.

Even though Carrie was pressing charges against Doan, she continued the relationship with him. Three days before Carrie disappeared, she spent the day with Doan at the beach. The next evening they went out to dinner together. But things did not go well. A friend named Tonya Whitten said that, the next morning, Carrie told her that Doan held her at gunpoint for around five hours out in the countryside. According to Whitten, Doan had said: "You think I'm a big joke. I'll show you how big a joke I am. I'm not going to jail."

He faced a maximum of six months' imprisonment on the assault charges.

Whitten said that Carrie eventually persuaded Doan to drive her home, promising to come to his house later. But Carrie reneged. She phoned Doan, telling him she had changed her mind. He got angry, threatening to kill her. She took the threat seriously, locking the windows and doors, and sleeping on the couch.

On 27 August 1996, Carrie went to the gym as usual. Soon after she got there, Doan phoned and they spoke briefly. Then he showed up in person. An argument ensured and he was verbally abusive. There was a further confrontation in the car park and, when Carrie drove off, Doan sped off after her. Tonya Whitten said that Carrie told her that Doan had tried to assure her there would be no repetition of what had happened the previous evening and he cried when he told Carrie he no longer had the gun and had given it to his brother.

Carrie went to the gym again on the morning of the 28th. Doan called her three times. Apparently he was appearing in court that evening over a traffic ticket and was angry Carrie was not coming with him for moral support. Instead she was playing volleyball with her friends. Later he turned up at the bar where the volleyball game was being played, offering to drive Carrie home. Her girlfriends said that Carrie did not want to be alone with Doan and claimed that she was the designated driver who had to drive her friends home after they had been drinking. He was insistent and she was seen repeatedly shaking her head and saying "no". He left the bar, only to come back almost immediately to ask her again. Again she refused to go with him. Eventually the scream of tyres were heard when he sped out of the parking lot.

Afterwards Carrie was reluctant to go home, so she and her friends drove around town for a while. She was particularly concerned about Doan's whereabouts and they drove past Doan's house several times. Finally, her friends dropped her home at about 11.30 pm. It was the last time they would ever see her.

Small-town America turned out for Carrie Culberson once news of her disappearance spread. The following weekend over 300 volunteers combed the surrounding counties, but found nothing. Debbie Culberson then took to the TV, appearing on *Inside Edition, The Montel Williams Show* and *Oprah Winfrey*.

Police sniffer dogs trained to find human remains showed a great deal of interest in a raised section of earth in the scrapyard belonging to Vincent Doan's father, Lawrence Baker. But when it was excavated all that was found was an old freezer filled with rotting meat that Baker had formerly used to feed a pet lion. The naked body of a woman was found in an abandoned farm cistern some counties away. But it was not Carrie. And a red Honda car dragged from the Ohio River turned out to be a 1985 model rather than a 1989.

Posters carrying Carrie's picture went up all over the state and a $10,000 reward brought in more reports. Some even claimed to have seen her alive. None panned out.

As months passed the missing person's case turned into a criminal investigation with Vincent Doan as the chief suspect. On 27 March 1997, a Clinton County grand jury indicted Doan on four counts of kidnapping. Doan turned himself in and, after a few days behind bars, he was released on bail set at $100,000.

The trial was scheduled for 9 June 1997, but on 4 June two murder charges were added. One alleged that Down had killed Carrie Culberson while effecting the kidnapping. The other accused him of deliberately killing her to stop her testifying against him on the assault charges. There would be no more bail. Doan was returned to a county jail and the trial postponed until 14 July 1997.

When the trial opened, the prosecution conceded that the case against Doan was circumstantial, but nevertheless it was solid and conclusive. They had witnesses to prove that Doan was not only controlling and physically abusive towards Carrie Culberson, he was caught up in an escalating spiral of violence that ultimately ended, they contended, with her death. They also conceded they could not prove that she was dead. However, there was no evidence that she was alive, even though witnesses claimed that they had seen her. There were regular sightings of Elvis, but that did not mean he was alive.

They contended that Vincent Doan murdered Carrie Culberson in the early hours of 29 August 1996. Doan's neighbour, Billie Jo Brown, said she had seen Doan chasing Culberson through her yard, cursing and threatening her. Then he had grabbed her, punched her in the face and shoved her into her car.

Another key witness was Lori Baker, the ex-wife of Doan's half-brother, Tracey, who still cohabited with him. She said that Vincent Doan had knocked on her door at about 3.15 a.m., asking for Tracey. This was corroborated by Vicki Watkins, Lori's twin sister, who was staying the night. Doan was dishevelled and covered in blood. He took a shower and changed into some of his brother's clothes. The two men left in Tracey's truck at around 4.30 a.m., carrying some garbage bags and a gun. When they came back at around six, Lori said both men had blood on them.

A few days later, Doan was at his brother's house when a report on Carrie's disappearance came on TV. He began rocking back and forth. He pulled his shirt over his head and told Lori she could not imagine "hurting someone and holding them until they died".

The prosecution then produced Mitchell Epperson, Doan's cellmate in the county jail. He said Doan had told him, that before he had murdered Carrie, he would "lie awake at night and think of a hundred different ways to kill her before he did it". Doan thought that Carrie was cheating on him.

"When they do that, you can't let 'em walk on you," Doan had said, Epperson testified, "you've got to make them pay."

Prosecutors said the circumstantial evidence was clear: whether motivated by obsession or a desire to keep Carrie quiet in the criminal case against him, Vincent Doan kidnapped and murdered Carrie Culberson on or about 29 August 1996.

In his own defence, Vincent Doan insisted that he knew nothing about Carrie's disappearance and denied kidnapping or murdering her. His attorney maintained that Doan could not have killed Carrie Culberson, because the evidence suggested that she was still alive. Dozens of reports had come in that Carrie or her car had been sighted since her supposed disappearance. The prosecution dismissed these as unreliable, saying that people were confused after seeing her picture on posters or on the television. The defence countered by showing that some of those who had claimed to have seen her had known her before she went missing. But even if Carrie Culberson was dead, the defence argued there was nothing concrete to indicate that Vincent Doan killed her. The prosecution had nothing – no body, no murder weapon nor any other scientific proof. Hundreds of samples taken from Doan's home and car, his brother's home and his father's scrap-yard had yielded not a single shred of evidence.

The defence also maintained that Doan's neighbour, Billie Jo Brown, was an ex-convict with a record of writing bad cheques and, thus, an unreliable witness. Doan's cellmate Mitchell Epperson had a long criminal history, with arrests for assault, theft, breaking and entering and violating probation. Lori Baker, they maintained, had a history of drug abuse and was a Satanist who repeatedly changed her account of what had happened on the morning of 29 August 1996. Her twin sister was a fantasist and a habitual liar who was not even there that night. Besides Doan had an alibi. Lawrence Baker and Doan's stepmother Betty Baker testified that they had visited Doan's home some time between 1.30 a.m. and two that morning. Lawrence Baker said he had found his son asleep on his living room couch. He then turned off the TV and lights without waking Doan and left the house.

The authorities had been frustrated that they had not been able to locate Carrie Culberson. They had failed to follow up on the sightings of her properly in a rush to pin unprovable charges on the defendant. During the trial itself, a woman claiming to be Carrie Culberson placed a 911 phone call in Cincinnati saying that an innocent man was on trial. A tape of the call was played to Debbie Culberson, who said the voice was not her daughter's. In fact, the report of another sighting came in while the jury was out. A woman who looked like Culberson ran out of a convenience store after seeing newspaper headlines on the trial.

The defence conceded that Carrie and the defendant had had what they called "spats" in their three-year relationship. But lovers' tiffs were far from evidence for murder. And it was ridiculous to imagine that Doan had killed Carrie to keep her from testifying against him. Although the assault charges carried a maximum penalty of six months' imprisonment, if found guilty he would probably have been given probation. Besides, he denied the charges.

On 7 August 1997, after four days of deliberation, the jury found Vincent Doan guilty of three of the four counts of kidnapping and one of two counts of aggravated murder. They determined that Doan had killed Culberson while effecting the kidnapping.

On his way from the courthouse, Doan protested his innocence and when asked if he would reveal what had happened to her body in exchange for a reduced sentence, he said: "If you don't know where anything is, how can you explain where it is?"

In mitigation of sentence the defence called 20 witnesses including peers, family friends and his grade school teachers who all testified that he was generous, helpful and polite. Former girlfriends said that he was never jealous nor abusive. Even the guards at the county jail testified that he was a model prisoner. However, several witnesses said that he had suffered both physical and mental injuries in 1992 during an accident involving a collapsing crane.

Doan's mother, Priscilla, begged the jury not to recommend the death sentence, saying: "He doesn't deserve it. He's innocent, and I would miss him." Then Doan himself made an impassioned plea for his life in a 20-minute unsworn statement.

"As her friend, and somebody who still loves her, I'm not going to give up hope that she's safe somewhere," he said. "I would still like to do anything that I could do to help out the Culbersons, and help out Carrie as much as I could . . . I miss her tremendously, even though we couldn't have a relationship . . . when she comes home, I still would not turn my back on her as a friend."

In response Debbie Culberson told the court: "By not knowing the truth of what really happened that night, we will be forever tormented." And she pleaded with Doan to tell the authorities where her daughter's body was so that she could have the "humane and Christian burial that she deserves". All Doan could do was protest his innocence once again.

After a further two days of deliberation, the jury agreed to spare his life, recommending instead that he served a life sentence without possibility of parole. The judge added another nine years for kidnapping.

Afterwards Tracey Baker was charged with the obstruction of justice, tampering with evidence and the gross abuse of a corpse. At his trial two strands of hair found in his truck and said to match Carrie Culberson's were introduced in evidence. Red paint was also found on his vehicle, said to have came from Carrie's Honda. His ex-wife Lori also testified against him. Tracey Baker himself took the stand and denied involvement. He was sentenced to eight years imprisonment on two counts of obstructing justice and one of tampering with evidence, but he was acquitted of the gross abuse of a corpse.

For fabricating his son's alibi, Lawrence Baker was charged with the obstruction of justice and tampering with evidence. In his trial, Lori Baker said that she had given her father-in-law incriminating items the police missed during an initial search. They were never seen again. She also testified Lawrence Baker encouraged her to lie to police, but the jury did not believe her and he was acquitted.

Blanchester police chief Richard Payton was also charged with obstructing justice and dereliction of duty – the allegation was that he had warned Doan and the Bakers that the pond next to Lawrence Baker's scrap-yard was about to be dredged. Payton pleaded no contest to two lesser misdemeanour charges of dereliction of duty. He received a suspended 90-day sentence, a $750 fine and one year of unsupervised probation.

On 24 October 1997, Carrie Culberson's family filed a wrongful death lawsuit in US District Court in Cincinnati against Vincent Doan, Tracey Baker, Lawrence Baker and Richard Payton, asking for punitive damages and demanding to be told where Carrie's remains were. The suit also alleged that the Blanchester authorities were also negligent for not securing the area around the pond next to Lawrence Baker's scrap-yard. They were awarded $3.5 million. As part of the settlement the village agreed to hang a photograph of Carrie Culberson in the Blanchester Police Department's lobby until her remains are discovered.

However, while Vincent Doan served life at the Southern Ohio Correctional Facility, a maximum-security prison located in Titusville, Ohio for the murder of Carrie Culberson, something strange happened. Twenty-three-year-old Alana "Laney" Gwinner from West Chester, just 22 miles from Blanchester, went missing in remarkably similar circumstances.

At about 1 a.m. on 10 December 1997, she was seen leaving Gilmore Bowling Lanes on Dixie Highway–Ohio 4 in nearby Fairfield in her 1993 black Honda Civic Del Sol. Her friends reported that she had scars on her arms from being abused by a former boyfriend. The police have interviewed several of her ex-boyfriends, as well as new friends she made playing pool at the bowling alley the night she vanished, but no arrests were made.

The Fairfield Police were struck by the similarities between the Gwinner and Culberson disappearances and checked for any possible connection. They found none.

Laney had gone to Gilmore Bowling Lanes the night of 9 December expressly to play pool. It was a game she excelled at and she took it seriously, said a friend. She came into the bowling alley with a male companion – not a boyfriend, just a good friend. They arrived in separate cars, though they had dined together at the BW–3 restaurant in Forest Fair Mall.

People remembered her. She was a beautiful woman and her arrival caused a stir, though no one remembered seeing her there before. At around 12.30 a.m. she called a boyfriend in Fairfield, saying she was coming over. Half-an-hour later she left alone, leaving the friend she had came with at the alley. What happened to her after she left is not known. The boyfriend she called said she never showed up.

Her whereabouts remained a mystery until 11 January 1998, when her body was spotted floating down the swiftly flowing Ohio River by a helicopter searching for a missing Covington police officer. Thirty minutes later and nearly three miles downstream, rescuers were able to pull the body ashore at Sugar Bay in Warsaw, Kentucky, some 65 miles from Fairfield. The Kentucky State Police said that she was not put in the water in the state. It is thought that she was dropped in the Great Miami River, a tributary of the Ohio River, some 40 miles upstream in Ohio.

She was easily identified as – clad in a blouse and jeans – she had her driver's licence in her pocket. There were no visible wounds on her body and the authorities had not revealed the cause of her death, except to say that the autopsy showed that her death was a homicide. But the condition of the body showed that she was in the river for a considerable time. Her car was not found.

The involvement of the police in Kentucky brought another similar case came to investigators' attention. Seventeen-year-old Erica Fraysure of Brooksville, Kentucky – some 40 miles south of Blanchester – went missing on 21 October 1997, while out driving her car. Her black 1988 Bonneville sedan was found the following day abandoned near Fronks Lane just outside Brooksville in Bracken County. Her purse, chequebook and other belongings were found inside. There were no signs of a struggle, though, later, the car keys were found lying among some leaves on the ground.

The last person to see her was 21-year-old friend Shane Simcox, who had been bar-hopping with friends and was "a little drunk" from beer. He was standing on a street corner in Brooksville when Erica pulled up. A girl got out and Erica asked Simcox if he wanted to ride around for a while. They rode around together alone together for ten or fifteen minutes, he said.

"She said she was talking to this boy, that she kind of liked him a little bit, just telling me about him," said Simcox.

When they did not see any friends hanging out on street corners or cruising around, Erica decided to go home and dropped Simcox on the way. That was around 9.30 p.m.

There was no reason to think that Erica Fraysure ran away from home and a $7,000 reward was posted. The possibility of a connection between the cases of this string of missing women appeared unlikely, police said.

Less than a week after the body of 23-year-old Laney Gwinner was recovered from the Ohio River, the body of 24-year-old mother Kimberley Sue Sipe was found on the banks of the Licking River in Covington, a suburb on Cincinnati on the Kentucky side of the Ohio. It was recovered by Covington police just after 4.30 p.m. on 17 January 1998 on the west bank of the river at Ninth and Prospect Streets.

She was last seen at about 8 am on 12 January, when she left her mother's home in Newport's West End, an adjoining suburb where she had been living temporarily, to catch a bus to visit her newborn daughter, Jaslin. The baby, who had been born five weeks prematurely six days before Kimberley went missing, was at St Elizabeth Hospital South in Edgewood. She also had a seven-year-old son named Tyrone.

Again Kimberley had ex-boyfriend problems. Two days before her body was recovered, her ex was arrested for violating probation on drug and trespassing convictions. Kimberly was a nurse's aide and was a generally upbeat, good-natured person whose primary interests were her children and work, her mother said. She had had her problems, but had put them behind her. Again the police said that they could find no connection with the other cases and no one has been prosecuted. Whether there is a serial killer operating in Cincinnati, no one can say. But it is hardly less disturbing to imagine that there are a series of copy-cat killers on the loose.

Cincinnati's Cumminsville Killings

The normally peaceful Cincinnati suburb of Cumminsville was home to a grisly series of killings in 1904 and 1910. Five women were mercilessly hacked to death within a mile of the intersection of Winton Road and Spring Grove Avenue.

The first victim was 31-year-old Mary McDonald, who had something of a reputation. After an ill-starred affair with the widower of her late sister, she had turned to drink. However, things seemed to have turned a corner for Mary. In the spring of 1904 she got engaged. On the night of 3 May, she had been out with her fiancé. Soon after 1.30 the following morning, they had left a local bar. He walked her to the nearest streetcar stop and put her on board an "owl car" that ran all night and would take her home.

At dawn, the switchman on a train near Ludlow Avenue saw a body by the tracks and called for help. It was Mary. She was still alive but incoherent. One leg had been severed and she had a fractured skull. A few hours later, she died from her injuries. At first, her death was thought to be accidental. A drunken woman had fallen in front of a streetcar. However, the police deduced that she had been beaten before she was pushed in front of a tram. This was clearly a deliberate act of murder.

On 1 October 1904, 21-year-old Louise Mueller went out for a walk. The following morning her body was found in a ditch beside some disused railway tracks. Her skull had been battered to pulp. Her killer had made some effort to conceal her body. In the soft earth nearby, he had dug a shallow grave. But the cadaver had not been put in it, suggesting that the killer had been disturbed before he could bury her.

Eighteen-year-old Alma Steinigewig was last seen alive when she left her job as an operator at the local telephone exchange at

9 p.m. on 2 November. However she never reached home. A streetcar conductor spotted her body the following morning in a vacant lot nearby. Ferocious blows had crushed her skull. In her hand was a streetcar transfer ticket. It had been stamped at 9.40 p.m. on the day she had gone missing. She had been dragged across the lot and her clothes were caked with mud. This time, the police discovered a clue that might help them identify the killer. In the mud of the lot, they found footprints that seemed to belong to the suspect. But, in the end, this took them no further forward.

In response to growing public concern, the police began dragging in suspects. Each, in turn, had to be released due to lack of evidence. However, there was one particular man that they wanted to talk to. He was stocky and heavily bearded, and he had turned up at the gully where Louise Mueller had been found. Seen wringing his hands, he cried out: "It was an accident!" According to other witnesses, a man of a similar description had been seen at the vacant lot where Alma Steinigewig's body was dumped. But he eluded the police and was never identified. The killer then took a six-year sabbatical and the murders were slowly forgotten.

The first victim of his second spree was 43-year-old Anna Lloyd. A secretary at a local lumber yard, she left work at 5.30 p.m. on New Year's Eve 1909. Her body was found a short distance from the office a few hours later. Her skull had been crushed and her throat slashed. It was clear that she had put up fierce resistance. The killer had gagged her with a cheap black muffler. Clutched in her fist, investigators found a single strand of black hair, but this was of little use in identifying the perpetrator, given the primitive state of forensic science in those days. At first, the police initially claimed that Anna Lloyd's murder was a contract killing, but no motive presented itself and it became clear that this was the work of the Cumminsville serial killer who had last operated in 1904.

There was another long hiatus until 25 October 1910. It was then 26-year-old Mary Hackney was found in her cottage on Dane Street. Her skull had been fractured and her throat slashed. The police initially suspected her husband, but they then established that his wife was still alive when he got to work. Although she was the only victim to get found indoors, the police concluded that she was another victim of the mysterious Cumminsville killer.

The police then received a series of letters from someone claiming to know about the murders. They were signed with the initials "S. D. M.", but detectives eventually dismissed them as a prank. The investigation then faltered.

However, in December 1913, the Burns Detective Agency were called in to investigate acts of violence associated with a recent strike by streetcar staff. Detectives from the agency told the mayor that they believed that a former conductor, now incurably insane and confined to an asylum was responsible for the death of Anna Lloyd. When searching his rooming house, they had found a menacing letter, addressed to persons "who saw him in the act of December 31". However, there was no evidence to tie him to the other murders and the Cumminsville murderer seems to have escaped justice.

Cleveland's Torso Murders

Kingsbury Run is a prehistoric river bed, some 60 feet deep in parts, that runs across the east side of Cleveland. It was once a beauty spot that ran down to the clear waters of the Cuygahoga River, a wooden area filled with secluded lakes. But as the city grew up it became home to a number of quarries that provided Cleveland's stone. Rapid industrialization in the 19th century polluted the river, which was lined by steel works and factories, and Nickel Plate and Erie Railroads ran eastwards out of Kingsbury Run.

During the Great Depression of the 1930s, when poverty drove farmers off the land, the freight lines brought itinerant workers into Cleveland in the slim hope that they would get one of the increasingly rare jobs in the mills. Most of them ended up in a squalid, shanty town next to an area called "The Roaring Third", home of bars, brothels, flophouses and gambling dens. This backed onto the hobo jungle of Kingsbury Run. It was there, at the height of the Depression, that a bizarre series of murders gripped Cleveland.

On the afternoon of Monday 23 September 1935, two teenage boys were making their way around the foot of an embankment where East 49th Street ends at Praha Avenue, known locally as Jackass Hill, when one of them saw something sticking out from the undergrowth. They went to investigate and found a headless corpse.

When Detectives Orly May and Emil Musil reached the crime scene, they found not one headless corpse, but two. According to the police report the victims were two white men. Both were naked though one retained his socks.

After an extensive search the heads of both men were found. One was 20 feet away from one body. The second was buried some 75 feet away from the other. Both men's penises had been cut off and were left near one of the heads. Searchers also found a pair of blood-stained long johns, a light cap and an old blue coat.

Both bodies had been washed and drained of blood, indicating that the murders had not taken place where they were found. The detectives noticed that the flesh appeared scorched, either by acid or some corrosive chemical, or oil had been poured over them in an attempt to set them on fire. A metal bucket containing a small quantity of oil and a torch had been found nearby. The attempt to destroy the corpses had been unsuccessful as the bodies had remained more or less intact. But as they had been there several days, they had begun to decompose.

In the County Morgue was it was discovered that the John Doe now known as Victim One had been dead between seven to ten days. He weighed 165 pounds, was around 5 feet 6 inches tall and had dark brown hair. It was determined that he was between 40 and 45 years old. One testicle was missing. The clean edges of the incision showed that a sharp instrument had been used. The muscles of the neck were retracted, indicating that the man had been decapitated while still alive and the cause of death was established as "decapitation, haemorrhage and shock".

According to the coroner's report the skin appeared leathery and tanned as if it had been treated with acid. On closer examination, it was "a reddish yellow colour" and hard "not unlike bacon rind". The hair had been removed and the tissue was dead.

A lab examination of the contents of the bucket revealed that it contained oil from a crankcase, along with human hair and partially decomposed human blood. The conclusion was that, after death, the body had been treated with a chemical preservative, then doused with oil and set on fire. But the oil only burnt well enough to scorch the flesh, rather than burn it. Coroner Arthur J. Pierce's verdict was: "Homicide by person or persons unknown." The advanced state of decomposition prevented fingerprints being taken and Victim One remained unidentified.

Victim Two had only been dead two or three days. He was in his 20s with brown hair and blue eyes. Around 5 feet 11 inches tall, he weighed approximately 150 pounds. He had eaten a meal of vegetables shortly before he died and was naked except for his black cotton socks.

Again the cause of death was decapitation. There were rope marks on his wrist, indicating that he had been castrated and beheaded while still conscious with his hands tied behind him.

Fingerprints identified him as Edward A. Andrassy of 1744 Fulton Road. He had been arrested several times for being drunk and had spent time in Warrensville Workhouse after being arrested for carrying a concealed weapon.

Tall, slim and handsome, he was 28 when he died. Earlier he had worked at Cleveland City Hospital as an orderly on the psychiatric ward. In 1928 he married a nurse from the hospital. They split up soon after, though she bore him a daughter some time after the separation.

Andrassy left the hospital in 1931 and sold magazines for a while. But when he died, he had no job or visible means of support and was know to associate with unsavoury company in The Roaring Third. A policeman who remembered him from the area called him "snotty punk . . . the kind of fellow gives a cop a lot of lip when he's questioned" and claimed that he had to knock him down once.

The Andrassy family were Hungarian immigrants, one of the many aristocratic families displaced by the collapse of the Austro–Hungarian Empire at the end of World War I. His father and brother John identified the body at the morgue. They had last seen Edward four days earlier. Helen Andrassy, the victim's mother, told detectives that a middle-aged man came to the house two months earlier and said he was going to kill her son for "paying attentions to his wife".

A strange story circulated about Andrassy. He had once claimed to be a gynaecologist and offered to examine a childless acquaintance's wife. Then he had used the opportunity to sodomize her. He then told them that, if he could go home and get his instruments, he could fix her problem so that she could have children. They declined his offer.

Others said that Andrassy was gay, or at least bisexual. It was said that he smoked marijuana and dealt in pornography. And there were rumours that he had fled Detroit briefly earlier that summer after crossing an Oriental gangster.

Before leaving home on the Thursday before the bodies were found, he was seen to be nervous at venturing out and he had told his sister that the Mob were after him because he had stabbed an Italian in a fight. He did not return that night. The post mortem report assumed he had been killed on Friday, but no one came forward to say where he had stayed on Thursday night.

The obvious conclusion was that the two men had been killed by the same individual. Victim One had been killed first, then preserved in some chemical solution until Andrassy had been caught and slain. The perpetrator must have been strong as they had carried the bodies at least 30 yards from the nearest road then down the steep embankment. This was presumably done at night and the slope would have been hard to negotiate in darkness. The murder weapon was thought be a sharp butcher's knife and detectives believed that a woman had played some part in the case. But, with no further clues, the investigation hit a brick wall.

It was only later that these two murders were related to an incident that had occurred a year before. On 5 September 1934, a young man had found the lower half of a woman's torso that had washed up near the Euclid Beach amusement park in Bratenahl just east of Cleveland along the shore of Lake Erie. The thighs were still attached to the pelvis, but the legs had been severed at the knees. Coroner Pierce had estimated that the remains had been in the water some three to four months. The skin was discoloured like Victim One's, suggesting that she, too, had been treated with the same chemical preservative. The upper half of her torso had been washed up 30 miles away, two weeks before, though it was so badly decayed it was not immediately identified as part of a corpse. The head was never found.

The woman had been about 30. She did not fit any missing person's report and she was never identified. The newspapers called her "The Lady of the Lake". It was only two years later that she was recognized as a victim of the same killer and became "Victim Zero". The question was then asked: had her body been dumped in Kingsbury Run, then floated down the Cuyahoga River into Lake Erie?

Located just across Lake Erie from Canada, during prohibition, Cleveland became a haven for bootleggers and mobsters, and police corruption was rife. In November 1935, Republican Harold Burton won mayoral election on the promise of cleaning up the city. His first act in office was to hire Eliot Ness, whose Untouchables had cleaned up Al Capone's Chicago, as director of public safety. After two years in Washington, heading the alcohol-tax unit of the US Treasury, Ness was raring to get back into action. He lost no time in launching a major attack on gambling and police corruption. But soon he was confronted with a case that he was not equipped to handle.

On Sunday 26 January 1936, Charles Paige, a butcher and the owner of the White Front Meat Market on Central Avenue, phoned to report a murder. An African-American woman had told him that there was a dead body on Central Avenue at East 20th Street. When he went to investigate he found parts of a woman's body wrapped in newspaper and packed into two half-bushel baskets. The police responded in force.

When Lieutenant Harvey Weitzel, Detective Sergeant James Hogan and Detectives Wachsman and Shibley arrived on the scene, they found further body parts in burlap sacks along with some white cotton underwear wrapped in newspapers outside the premises of Hart's Manufacturing Company. Soon after, Lieutenant David L. Cowles, head of the crime lab, arrived on the scene.

James Marco, who lived next door to the Hart's factory, said that he had heard dogs barking at around 2.30 a.m. and Acting Chief of Detectives Joseph Sweeney concluded that that was when the body was dumped. It was discovered some time later thanks to the insistent barking of a dog named Lady. The victim had been dead from two to four days so, again, she had been killed elsewhere before her body was dumped.

As before the cause of death was decapitation. The woman's head was found some ten days later in an empty lot nearby on Orange Avenue. Strangely, though, the killer had waited until rigor mortis had set in before he dismembered the rest of the body. Once again a sharp knife had been used and the killer seemed to be an expert at cutting flesh – indicating that the murderer was either a surgeon or a butcher.

Although her lower legs and most of her upper torso were missing, her right arm was intact and her fingerprints revealed that she was 42-year-old Florence Saudy Polillo, a waitress and barmaid, who had been arrested a couple of times in Cleveland and Washington, D. C., for prostitution. Her former husband, 40-year-old mail man Andrew Polillo, drove from the 180 miles from his home in Buffalo, New York, to speak to the police. He said that they had been married in the early 1920, but after six years Florence had begun drinking heavily and had left him ostensibly to get herself straightened out. Though everyone who met her liked her, due to her drinking, she slipped inexorably to the bottom of society. The men she took up with beat her up and, at the time she died, she was living in a rooming house at East 32nd Street and Carnegie Avenue, right on the edge of The Roaring Third. Her landlady said she was a kind woman, but she numbered among her acquaintances numerous prostitutes, whorehouse madams, pimps, bootleggers and bar owners. However none of them had seen her the weekend she died. There were few clues and the investigation stalled once again.

The coverage of the murders was quickly overshadowed in the press by Eliot Ness's purge of the police department and his systematic attack on organized crime. Meanwhile Mayor Burton was busy buffing up the city's image ready for the Republican National Convention, which Cleveland was hosting in the second week of June 1936.

On 5 June, the Friday before the convention began and as delegates came rolling into town, two young boys set off to go fishing and took a shortcut through Kingsbury Run. They saw a pair of trousers rolled up under a bush near the East 55th Street bridge. They poked the pants with their fishing rod and a man's head rolled out.

The next morning the body was found. The naked, headless corpse of a man in his twenties had been dumped almost directly in front of the Nickel Plate Railroad police building. The policemen there were hired by the railroad company to secure the area and keep hobos out of the freight cars. The killer seemed to be taunting them.

The victim was a tall, slender man with a handsome face – not unlike Andrassy. His fingerprints were not on file, but he had six distinctive tattoos on his body. The police thought he might be a sailor – one of the tattoos showed a cupid riding an anchor; another flags. The others depicted a butterfly, a cartoon figure called "Jiggs", a heart with an arrow through it and a dove with the linked names "Helen-Paul" over it, but these did not match the tattooed initials "W. C. G.". Nor did they match the initials "J. D." on a pair of undershorts found in a pile of bloodstained clothes nearby.

Although he had been found in Kingsbury Run, the victim was no hobo. The clothes were new and expensive. He was clean-shaven, well nourished. Again, the body had been drained of blood and washed clean. No blood was found soaked into the ground near where the head and body had been dumped. So, again, the victim had been killed elsewhere and his body brought to Kingsbury Run.

That Sunday, the day before the convention started, with news of the new killing filling the papers, Eliot Ness held a top-level meeting with his forensics chief Lieutenant David Cowles and the newly appointed head of the Homicide Division, veteran detective Sergeant James Hogan. Ness wanted to know if Hogan thought all four – possibly five – cases were connected.

Hogan said he did not. The men, he thought, were related. All three had been decapitated and their bodies dumped in Kingsbury Run. The women had been found elsewhere and their bodies more comprehensively dismembered.

The concept of a serial killer was not well understood in the 1930s and, in a homicide case, the standard method of investigation was straightforward. The detectives should first look for anyone who had a motive for the killing, then concentrate on those who had both the means and the opportunity. It had been assumed that sexual jealousy, or sexual deviancy, was the motive for the first two Kingsbury Run murders, which were clearly related. It was hard to extend this motive to include the other murders, particularly those of the women.

But Ness, Cowles and the coroner Arthur J. Pierce were convinced that all the killings had been committed by the same man. Like the three men, the cause of death in the Florence Polillo case had been decapitation, which was rare in homicide cases. The bodies were cleaned up and neat, and had been cut by the same expert hand. However, Ness gave very clear instructions that no one should get wind of the fact that they were looking for a single killer – particularly while the convention was going on. Otherwise, Ness wanted nothing further to do with the case. His job was to oversee the security of the Republican National Convention, then go back to cleaning up the police department and cracking down on organized crime.

Besides Ness had every confidence in his Homicide Division. The newest body had six unique tattoos, which meant that it should be easy to identify the victim and this might easily lead them to the perpetrator. Detectives circulated tattoo parlours and visited the bars where sailors hung out. Hundreds of people traipsed through the morgue to view the body, while the police checked missing-persons' files and tried to track down the source of the victim's clothes and the laundry marks in his underwear. Pictures of the tattoos and a plaster cast of the victim's head were put on display at the Great Lakes Exposition of 1936, which was visited by seven million people over the following two years. Despite everything, the so-called "Tattooed Man" was never identified. His death mask is now on display in the Cleveland Police Museum.

While the search for the "Tattooed Man" was underway, on 22 July 1936, a teenage girl stumbled across the headless corpse of a 40-year-old white man near a hobo camp in the woods to the west of Kingsbury Run near Clinton Road and Big Creek. Again the dead man was naked. His head, partly wrapped in his clothing, was found some 15 feet from the body. The body had been lying there for over two months and was very badly decomposed. The head was little more than a skull. He had died before the "Tattooed Man", but had only now been found.

Unlike the "Tattooed Man", he was a hobo. His hair was long and a pile of cheap bloodstained clothes were found near the corpse. This time a lot of blood had soaked into the ground, indicating that he was killed where he lay. Nevertheless it was plainly the work of the same man. Coroner Pierce pointed out that the head had been separated from the body precisely at the junction of the second and third cervical vertebrae. The ends of the bones showed no evidence of fracture. The expert hand seen in the other murders was at work again and Hogan was forced to concede that all the cases were linked. But the body was so badly decomposed that no fingerprints could be taken. The corpse could not be identified. That left him with precious little to go on. Fortunately, the press could be distracted from what they were now calling the Cleveland Torso Murders by Ness's high-profile raids on Mob-run gambling dens.

Cleveland had began to market itself as a convention town and the American Legion was due to hold its convention there in the middle of September. But on 10 September, a hobo tripped over the upper half of a man's torso while trying to hop a train at East 37th Street in Kingsbury Run. Police searched a nearby creek, which was essentially an open sewer, and found the lower half of the torso and parts of both legs. A search was made in the weeds along the creek and for the rest of the body. The fire brigade dragged the creek with grappling hooks. A small amount of flesh was found on a ledge above the point where the stream emerged from a pipe, indicating that the body had been dumped over the edge. A further search yielded the right thigh. In the surrounding woods a blue work shirt, covered in blood, was found wrapped in a newspaper, along with a dirty grey felt hat, rather dirty, which appeared to be spotted with blood and carried a label saying: "Laudy's Smart Shop, Bellevue, Ohio".

Divers were sent to search the garbage-strewn bottom of the creek and a high-pressure fire hose was used to flush it out in the hope of finding more key parts. All this activity could hardly escape attention and a crowd numbering over 600 watched the creek being scoured. The comprehensive dismemberment of this body linked the decapitated men's bodies with the women victims and the *Cleveland Press*, the *Cleveland News* and the *Cleveland Plain Dealer* now dubbed the perpetrator "The Mad Butcher of Kingsbury Run". They put pressure on Mayor Harold Burton to get the high-profile Eliot Ness more involved in the case and reported Coroner Pierce's calls for a "Torso Clinic" – a meeting of the city's top law officers to "profile" the fiend responsible for the killings.

Once again the victim had been dispatched by an expert decapitation, which had occurred a day or two before the body was found. It belonged to a white man aged between 25 and 30, of medium height and a muscular build. The head and hands were never found, so no identification from fingerprints could be made. However, the hair on the body indicated that the victim had light brown hair, but he matched no description in the missing-persons' files and could not be identified.

Hogan inadvertently told a reporter that he believed the murderer lived in or around Kingsbury Run. This created local hysteria, with residents afraid to go out. There was a huge increase in the population of guard dogs in the vicinity. To calm locals' fears, Eliot Ness was pulled off the largest corruption case in the history of Cleveland and he set about cleaning up Kingsbury Run. Every hobo in area was brought in for questioning and told that they had better find somewhere else to live.

Despite the paucity of clues, 20 detectives were permanently assigned to the case. They were inundated with tip-offs concerning anyone seen carrying a large package, or who had large knives, or kept irregular hours, or was in any way peculiar. Ness insisted that every tip, no matter how flimsy, was to be followed up. Detectives also visited hospitals for the insane and monitored recently discharged patients. Meanwhile the head of the Federal Narcotics Bureau urged the police seek out marijuana users as, he maintained, smoking induced "both the desire for a thrill and a homicidal obsession" and the weed grew wild in Kingsbury Run.

Among the detectives working on the case were Peter Merylo and his partner Martin Zelewski. Merylo used his position in the police department to persecute gay men – homosexuality was illegal in Ohio. It was said that he filled an entire jail wing with gay men he had arrested *in flagrante*. He brought the same zeal to the Mad Butcher investigation, roaming The Roaring Third, sometimes in his own time and often dressing the part. He amused his colleagues parading up and down Kingsbury Run in his long johns in an effort to entice the killer.

Merylo and Zelewski interviewed more than 1,500 people in what would be the biggest murder investigation in the history of Cleveland. These included a crazed giant who stalked Kingsbury Run carrying a large knife, a "voodoo doctor" who claimed to have a death-ray and "Chicken Freak", who hired prostitutes to strip naked and behead chickens while he masturbated. Merylo's adventures were a popular source of copy for reporters and his antics kept the Cleveland Torso Murders in the newspapers.

The *Cleveland News* offered a reward of $1,000 for information leading to the capture of the Mad Butcher. Cleveland City Council voted to match that amount. Newspapers right across the Midwest became obsessed with the killer. He was plainly a clever man, who never left the merest scrap of a clue. The police department now believed that he was taunting them by leaving the bodies in Kingsbury Run where they could be expected to be keeping a special look-out – just as he had mocked the Nickel Plate Railroad police, dumping the Tattooed Man within sight of their headquarters.

Newspaper speculation ran wild. Some thought that the killer was a religious nut who was bent on ridding the world of prostitutes, homosexuals, wastrels and hobos. Others thought he was a wealthy doctor who killed lower-class people for sport. Others still thought he was an outwardly normal person who occasionally lapsed into madness.

Elliot Ness knew that the man they were seeking was no ordinary one. Eventually he took Coroner Pierce's advice and held a "Torso Clinic". Those present included Police Chief Matowitz, County Prosecutor Frank Cullitan, Inspector Joseph Sweeney, Lieutenant Cowles, Sergeant Hogan and Dr Reuben Strauss, the pathologist who had performed many of the victims' post mortems, along with several outside medical consultants. They pieced together what they knew about the killer. Firstly, they agreed that one perpetrator working alone was responsible for all the murders. The murderer was strong to have overpowered his victims. To carry their bodies considerable distances over rough terrain meant that he was a large man – they pretty much ruled out the possibility that the perpetrator was a woman.

While the killer was clearly psychopathic, he was probably not obviously insane. The genital mutilation of the first two corpses might be an indication that the killer was a homosexual. However, in other cases there had been other non-genital mutilation. Some of this had been performed to thwart identification or to transport the body more easily. But some of the mutilation seemed to have been purely gratuitous.

Cutting the head off a living person is necessarily a messy business. Once the carotid artery and jugular vein are cut, blood spurts all over the place. That meant that the killer had private premises where the victims could be slaughtered, cleaned up and stored – perhaps even in preservatives – until they could be dumped. This could be a doctor's office, a butcher's shop or private home where unsuspecting victims could be lured by the promise of food, shelter or sex. This would be near Kingsbury Run and the killer had clearly an intimate knowledge of the area.

The killer also had specialist knowledge of anatomy. However, the medical men at the meeting were adamant that this did not necessarily mean he was a doctor. After all, a butcher or hunter who cut up game would have enough anatomical knowledge to decapitate and dismember the corpses.

He usually picked victims from the lower strata of society, perhaps on a crusade to rid the city of "undesirables". By and large he dumped their bodies in Kingsbury Run. Perhaps this was an attempt to ward off the hobos who lived there.

Selecting victims from the lower strata of society also meant they were more difficult to identify. And he was clearly getting more cunning. Only the early victims Andrassy and Polillo had been identified. Even the "Tattooed Man" had been picked with care as, despite all his distinguishing marks, the police were unable to discover who he was. Latterly, the heads and hands were missing or too badly decomposed to render fingerprints. Nobody came forward to claim these victims as missing persons. Plainly he picked his victims for their anonymity.

The Mad Butcher gave Eliot Ness a seven-month break, allowing him to return to his crack-down on corruption in the police department and go after organized crime. As a result, in November 1936, Harold Burton was returned to office as mayor. However, Arthur J. Pierce was replaced as coroner by the young Democrat Samuel Gerber. Qualified both in medicine and law, he was to make the Mad Butcher case his own.

His first opportunity to move the case forward came on 23 February 1937 when the upper half of a woman's torso washed up on the beach at 156th Street, east of Bratenahl, in virtually the same place as the Lady of the Lake had surfaced. She had only been dead for between two and four days and had been in the water not more than three. Three months later the lower half of her torso washed ashore at East 30th Street. Again the question was asked whether she had been washed down the Cuyahoga River into Lake Erie from Kingsbury Run.

Her head and arms had been removed with the murderer's usual expertise and her legs were amputated with two "clean sweeping" strokes of a heavy knife. However, the bisection of the torso was more amateurish and showed marks of hesitation. There was something else different about the corpse. She had not been killed by decapitation. The blood clots in the heart indicated that her head had been cut off after she was dead. And there was a bizarre new touch. Her anus was enlarged and the killer had inserted the pocket from a pair of trousers inside her rectum.

The woman's clothes were never found. Nor were her head and limbs. However, from the parts that reached the morgue, it was possible to ascertain that she was in her mid-twenties, had a light complexion and medium brown hair, and weighed around 100 to 120 pounds. She had been pregnant at least once and she had lived in the city as there was dirt in her lungs, causing moderate emphysema. But that was all that was known of Victim Seven. Her identity was never discovered.

Nevertheless the forensic work brought the new Coroner Sam Gerber a great deal of favourable publicity – oxygen for an elected official. Gerber then devoted his time to writing up his conclusion which he published in March 1937. Again he deduced that all the killings were the work of one man. The killer was right-handed and used a sharp, heavy knife rather than a medical instrument. As to motive, Gerber believed the killer to be a sexual psychopath, the first on record to murder both sexes. His knowledge of anatomy was also clear and Gerber pushed the idea he was a medical student, male nurse, surgeon or veterinary practitioner.

Gerber's report brought him into conflict with Eliot Ness. While Gerber aimed to hog the limelight with his theories, Ness asked the newspapers to scale down their coverage on the grounds that the exposure was inflating the killer's ego and might encourage him to kill again. The sensationalism surrounding the murders was also bringing in thousands of useless tips, everyone of which had to be followed up. Much to Gerber's annoyance, the newspaper editors agreed to curtail their coverage.

However, they could not keep a lid on public interest when, on 6 June 1937, Victim Eight appeared. A teenager named Russell

Lawer had been watching the Coast Guard boats on the Cuyahoga River when, on his way home, he found a human skull about 400 feet west of Stone's Levee under the fifth span of the Lorain-Carnegie Bridge. Next to it was a rotting burlap bag, containing skeletal remains, wrapped in a newspaper from June 1936. The lab agreed that the victim had been dead for around a year.

Although the arms and legs were missing, the victim's delicate bones showed she was a petite woman, less than five feet tall and around 40 years old. The skull showed extensive dental work – a several of her teeth had been crowned with gold. She had had a wide nose and a prominent mouth. Her hair was kinky and fastened to it with a rusty hairpin was a black wig. Gerber concluded that she was an African-American.

Although the skull was found separate from the rest of the skeleton, it was impossible to tell whether the cause of death had been decapitation. There was little cartilage and flesh left as the body had been treated with quicklime. However, there was "considerable hacking and cutting of the 3rd, 4th and 5th cervical vertebrae" – indicating that the perpetrator had not demonstrated the Mad Butcher's normal level of skill.

The skull's dental work led to the unofficial identification of the victim as a prostitute named Rose Wallace of Scovill Avenue who had disappeared in August 1936. A lengthy investigation led nowhere, leading Sergeant Hogan and Coroner Gerber to believe that the victim was not Rose Wallace at all, though Detective Merylo continued to believed that it was.

There were labour problems in the Cleveland in the summer of 1937 and the Ohio National Guard were called in to maintain order. On 6 July, a young guardsman on watch by the West Third Street bridge saw the upper part of a man's torso bobbing in the water in the wake of a passing tugboat. Over the next few days, police recovered most of the body parts from the waters of the Cuyahoga River, though the head was missing. The victim had been dead a couple of days when the first parts were found. The man was in his mid to late 30s. He was around five foot eight, weighed around 150 pounds and had well-groomed fingernails.

The cause of death was, once again, decapitation. But this time some of the surgery had been sloppy and some was very skilful. For the first time, the internal organs including the heart had been ripped out, indicating a new element of viciousness in the killer's modus operandi. None of the internal organs were ever found and the victim was never identified.

At Gerber's instigation, the investigation now began to concentrate on medics. Detectives combed the records for doctors that had a weakness for drink, drugs or illicit sex – particularly of a homosexual nature. They soon happened upon Dr Frank E. Sweeney, a physician who fitted the physical profile of the murderer that the Torso Clinic had come up with. Sweeney was very tall, large and physically strong. He had grown up in the Kingsbury Run area and, at various times, had practised there.

At one time Sweeney had been a resident surgeon at St Alexis, a hospital close to Kingsbury Run. But he had lost his job because of drunkenness. At the same time he had been separated from his wife and sons. He was violent when drunk and there were rumours that he was a bisexual. It seemed that, at last, the police had a suspect.

But soon the police dropped Dr Sweeney from their investigations because he had an alibi. He was often out of town at the Sandusky Soldiers' and Sailors' Home, a veterans' hospital 50 miles to the west of Cleveland, when the Mad Butcher was at work. And although Dr Sweeney was not related to Inspector Joseph Sweeney, the chief of detectives on the case, he was a first cousin to the outspoken US Congressman Martin L. Sweeney.

A Democrat, Martin L. Sweeney was a fierce critic of Mayor Burton and his Republican administration. Earlier that year he had launched a scathing attack on Mayor Burton's "alter ego, Eliot Ness" who, he said, spent all his time persecuting cops that took $25 bribes from bootleggers years before while doing nothing to catch major criminals such as the Mad Butcher of Kingsbury Run. This meant investigating Dr Sweeney would be politically embarrassing. With municipal elections in the offing, the Congressman was urging voters to "send back to Washington the prohibition agent who is now safety director". However, with the help of the Ohio National Guard, Ness chalked up a considerable victory against "labour racketeers". His job was safe, but he still had little time to devote to the Torso Murders.

In mid-March 1938, a dog found the severed leg of a man in a swampy area near Sandusky, just down the coast of Lake Erie from Cleveland. Desperate for a lead, Lieutenant Cowles drove out to Sandusky personally to see if there was any link between the leg and the Mad Butcher. However, it was soon discovered that the leg was part of hospital refuse not properly disposed of. It had been removed during legitimate surgery and had nothing to do with the Mad Butcher.

But while he was in Sandusky, Cowles recalled that one of the doctors who had been a suspect in the Mad Butcher case had been eliminated because he had been at the veterans' hospital in Sandusky when the Cleveland murders occurred. So Cowles decided to pay the hospital a visit.

He quickly confirmed that Dr Sweeney had voluntarily admitted himself to the Sandusky Soldiers' and Sailors' Home to treat his alcoholism at times when the Mad Butcher was at work, confirming his alibi. However, when Cowles enquired further, he discovered that patients were not watched closely and a voluntary patient who had checked in with a drinking problem would not really be watched at all. Security was nonexistent and, at weekends and holidays, there were so many visitors that it would be impossible for the nursing staff to keep track of a patient's movements. It was not unusual for alcoholics to disappear on a binge for a day or two, then return, without having been discharged. Cowles concluded that it would have been easy for Dr Sweeney to travel to Cleveland by train or car, commit the murders, dump the bodies and return without his absence being recorded.

Cowles also discovered that the veteran's hospital shared some of its facilities with the Ohio Penitentiary Honor Farm. In the farm, he met a convicted burglar named Alex Archaki, who had arranged a reciprocal deal with Dr Sweeney. Archaki supplied Dr

Sweeney with liquor, while Dr Sweeney wrote Archaki prescriptions for barbiturates and other drugs.

What's more, Archaki believed that Sweeney was the Mad Butcher and he told a strange tale. The two had met a few years earlier in a bar in downtown Cleveland. Archaki had been sitting alone when Sweeney came up to him. He bought Archaki drinks and asked a lot of personal questions. Where was he from? Was he married? Did he have any family in the city? At the time, he thought that such a detailed cross-questioning was peculiar. Later, he realized that Sweeney was sizing him up as a victim. This made sense to Cowles as the Mad Butcher would made sure that most of his victims remained unidentified by picking men and women who had no close friends or relatives in the area. Archaki also told Cowles that every time Sweeney got back from one of unexplained absences from the hospital, a new body turned up in Kingsbury Run.

When Cowles returned to Cleveland, he renewed the investigation of Dr Sweeney, discreetly. He discovered that Francis Edward Sweeney had been born in 1894 into a poor Irish immigrant family who lived on the edge of Kingsbury Run. His father had been crippled in an accident and, when Frank was just nine, his mother had died of a stroke, leaving him and his brothers and sisters in dire poverty. Nevertheless, Frank was intelligent and determined to make a success of himself. He graduated from high school and worked his way through medical school in St Louis while holding down a full-time job. His fellow students elected him vice president of his sophomore class and his professors commended him both in science and medicine.

In July 1927 he married a beautiful dark-haired young woman who produced two healthy sons. In 1928 he graduated from medical school and took a surgical post at St Alexis hospital near Kingsbury Run. While remaining the consummate professional, he was a deeply compassionate man who loved his family and would take time off to attend to his siblings and their children if they were sick. At St Alexis, he rose quickly through the ranks and seemed destined for great things. But then, in 1929, he began drinking heavily. There might have been a genetic cause for this.

Sweeney's father had been an alcoholic who had spent the last years of his life in mental hospital, after being diagnosed as suffering from "psychosis".

There might also have been a physical cause. Sweeney had been injured in the head in World War I so badly that he was awarded a disability pension, though he may merely have succumbed to pressure after years of overwork. He was admitted to City Hospital for alcoholism, but his condition seemed resistant to treatment. Drunk all the time, his health deteriorated, along with his career and his marriage. Impossible to work with, he was sacked by the hospital. At home he was abusive and violent. His wife left in September 1934 and, when she filed for divorce and sought custody of the kids two years later, she requested a restraining order preventing him "visiting, interfering, or molesting her". The break-up of the marriage coincided with the beginnings of the Torso Murders.

Certainly Dr Sweeney would have the knowledge and ability to expertly decapitate and dismember the victims. He was also strong enough and large enough to carry Edward Andrassy and his unidentified companion down Jackass Hill in Kingsbury Run. And his alleged bisexuality could possibly explain why the victims were both male and female.

Cowles was just putting the finishing touches to his case when, on 8 April 1938, a young labourer on his way to work saw what he at first thought was a dead fish in the Cuyahoga River. On closer inspection he saw that it was the lower half of a women's leg. Eliot Ness was reluctant to believe that this was Victim Ten, hoping that it might be a piece of hospital waste like the leg in Sandusky, a limb lost as the result of a boating accident or another piece of an earlier victim not recovered at the time. Then Gerber announced that the woman's lower leg was just a few days old. Ness insisted that Gerber hand over the leg for independent evaluation of the time of death. Gerber refused, saying that the voters had elected him as coroner to determine the time of death, not the director of public safety who had so conspicuously failed to catch the Mad Butcher.

A month later Gerber was vindicated when the police pulled

two burlap bags out of the Cuyahoga River that contained the nude torso of a woman that had been cut in half, along with the rest of her legs. The dead woman was between 25 and 30 years old, around 5 feet 3 inches tall, and weighed about 120 pounds. She was flat-chested and her hair was light brown. She had once had given birth by caesarean section and had suffered an injury to her cervix by an abortion or another birth. She had also had her appendix removed. The head was missing and she had probably died from decapitation.

For the first time Coroner Gerber detected drugs in the system, but it was impossible to tell whether the drugs had been used to immobilize the victim or she was an addict. The arms might have rendered a vital clue but they were never found. With no hands there were no fingerprints and the young woman was never identified.

This threw the investigation back on Cowles' new suspect, Dr Sweeney. But the police had to proceed cautiously. If they went after Dr Sweeney directly, they risked Congressman Sweeney launching a new attack on the Burton administration, claiming that Ness was vindictively trying to frame one of his family.

Cowles tried to put Dr Sweeney under surveillance, but Sweeney soon spotted he was being followed. Once he even introduced himself to his tail, before giving him the slip. But while Sweeney was out, the police searched his lodgings and his office. They even opened his mail, but unearthed no evidence linking the doctor to the murders.

Despite all the attention being paid to Dr Sweeney, the activities of the Mad Butcher did not stop. On 16 August 1938, three scrap-metal collectors were foraging in a rubbish dump at East Ninth Street and Lakeside – a location overlooked by Eliot Ness's office – when they found the torso of a woman wrapped in a man's double-breasted blue blazer and an old quilt. Nearby the legs and arms were discovered in a makeshift cardboard box, wrapped in brown paper and secured with rubber bands. The head had been wrapped up in the same way and, uncharacteristically, the hands were also present.

As the police continued searching the area, an onlooker spotted some bones nearby. Detective Sergeant James Hogan picked up a large tin can nearby to put the bones in, but when he looked inside he saw a skull grimacing back. More skeletal remains were found, some wrapped in brown paper.

Gerber estimated that the woman had been a Caucasian in her thirties, approximately 5 feet 4 inches tall, and weighing around 120–125 pounds. She had been dismembered, like the others, with a large, sharp knife. The body was so badly decomposed it was impossible to determine the cause of death. However, some parts of her body were remarkably well preserved and Gerber said they looked as if they had been refrigerated. He estimated that she had died sometime between the middle of February and the middle of April, possibly before the first week of April when the tenth victim had been killed. However, he thought that her remains had only been on the dump for a few weeks. Her left thumb was one of those parts still left intact and they were able to lift a fingerprint. But it did not match any on file.

The skeletal remains found nearby belonged to a white man who was also in his thirties. He was around 5 feet 7 inches and weighed around 135 to 150 pounds. His dark-brown hair was long and coarse. His corpse had also been dismembered with a long, sharp knife. But, again, the cause of death could not be determined.

There were some doubt that these two were the victims of the the Mad Butcher as they did not conform to his developing MO. He had not left the hands and heads with the bodies of his victims since 1936. Usually he dumped bodies in the Cuyahoga River or in Kingsbury Run, or somewhere else where they would be found easily. These two had been discovered by accident – though leaving them in plain sight of Eliot Ness's office smacked of the audacity he had exhibited before.

Although unofficially listed as Victims Ten and Eleven, as no cause of death had been determined, these two might not even have been victims of homicide. The man and woman might have died of natural causes then had their bodies mutilated either as a prank or by a necrophiliac. Such things were not uncommon.

Receiving an anonymous tip-off, the police investigated a man who ran an embalming college. Though no charges were ever brought against him, the man quickly moved out of town.

Whether the two new bodies were the work of the Mad Butcher or not, the people of Cleveland believed they were and radical action was required. Ness conferred with Mayor Burton and two days later, at 12.40 a.m. on 18 August, Ness and 35 police officers and detectives raided the hobo shantytowns bordering Kingsbury Run. Eleven squad cars, two police vans and three fire trucks descended on the largest cluster of makeshift shacks where the Cuyahoga River twists behind Cleveland's main Public Square. Ness's raiders worked their way south up the Run, arrested 63 men, fingerprinted them and sent them to the workhouse. At dawn, police and firemen searched the deserted shanties for clues. Then, on orders from Director of Public Safety Eliot Ness, the shacks were set on fire and burned to the ground. This backfired. It brought adverse reaction in the press as it did nothing to help catch the Mad Butcher. Now Ness had to solve the murders.

There was only one course open to him. He pulled in Dr Sweeney. But instead of taking him to police headquarters Sweeney was held discreetly in a suite at the Cleveland Hotel in Public Square. However, it was made clear to the doctor that if he did not co-operate he would be marched downtown surrounded by a howling mob of the reporters.

Sweeney was left to dry out for three days. Then, on 23 August 1938, the interrogation began. It was conducted by Ness, Cowles and Dr Royal Grossman, a court psychiatrist. In an adjoining room Dr Leonard Keeler, co-inventor of the polygraph, set up his equipment.

The first thing his interrogators noticed was what a large and powerful man Sweeney was. Cowles and Grossman cross-questioned him for two hours, while Ness listened intensely. They got nowhere, so Ness took him through to the next room where Dr Keeler was waiting. Sweeney was rigged up to the polygraph sensors, then asked a series of innocuous questions. Was his name Francis Edward Sweeney? Had he been born in Ohio? Did he have two sons? The machine registered that Sweeney was telling the truth.

Then Keeler turned to a list of questions prepared by Cowles. Had he ever met Edward Andrassy? Did he kill Edward Andrassy? Had he ever met Florence Polillo? Did he kill Florence Polillo? Had he ever met Rose Wallace? Did he kill Rose Wallace? The needles of the polygraph kicked as Sweeney made his denials.

Afterwards Dr Keeler told Eliot Ness: "He's your guy."

Dr Grossman agreed that Sweeney was a psychopath with a violent schizoid personality aggravated by chronic alcoholism. Ness was not so sure. He found it hard to reconcile the intelligent, articulate, educated man he saw with the homicidal maniac he knew the Mad Butcher to be. Ness then went through to the other room to interrogate Sweeney on his own.

"Well?" asked Sweeney asked. "Are you satisfied now?"

"Yes," said Ness. "I think you're the killer."

"You think?" said Sweeney then, with his face inches from Ness's, he hissed: "Then prove it!"

Ness was suddenly acutely aware of the size and strength of Sweeney. He called for Cowles and Grossman. There was no reply.

"Looks like they went to lunch," said Sweeney.

Ness quickly phoned down to the coffee shop and asked Cowles to return, immediately. Later, Ness said that he had never been so scared in his life.

That afternoon, Dr Keeler retested Sweeney repeatedly, each time with the same result. Keeler, Ness, Grossman and Cowles were all convinced of Sweeney's guilt. But there was nothing they could do about it. Polygraph tests were inadmissible and the only evidence they had against him – that he was absent from the Sandusky veterans' hospital at the times of the murders – was circumstantial at best and was provided by a convicted criminal who would be viewed by the court as an unreliable witness at best. However, the story then took a strange twist.

Two days after the interrogation Dr Sweeney checked back into the Sandusky veterans' hospital. A note attached to his records said that if he left the hospital grounds the police were to be informed. From 25 August 1938 until his death in 1965, Sweeney remained confined voluntarily to various veterans' and state mental hospitals. However, it is not clear whether Sweeney was the Mad Butcher or found a twisted pleasure in taunting the police. He sent a series of incomprehensible and jeering postcards to Eliot Ness from the veterans' hospital in Dayton, Ohio, where he was confined in 1955. Despite this, his brothers and sisters never believed that Sweeney was a man capable of violence. Indeed another man confessed to the crimes.

A few months after Dr Sweeney admitted himself to Sandusky veterans' hospital, the newly elected Cuyahoga Country Sheriff Martin L. O'Donnell moved in on the case. He was a political ally of Congressman Martin L. Sweeney – his son was married to the congressman's daughter. O'Donnell hired a private detective named Pat Lyons to investigate the Kingsbury Run murders. Lyons' investigation narrowed down the suspects to a 52-year-old alcoholic bricklayer named Frank Dolezal. Merylo had already investigated Dolezal and rejected him.

Nevertheless Sheriff O'Donnell had his men search a room Dolezal had previously rented. They found a knife and stains on the floor. Lyons' brother was a chemist who concluded the stains were human blood.

On 5 July 1939, Dolezal was arrested and after a rough night in the cells, he confessed to the murder of Florence Polillo. Apparently they had lived together for a while. He and Flo had a fight. Dolezal claimed that she attacked him with a butcher's knife. In self defence, he hit her and she fell against a bathtub. Assuming that he had killed her, he cut up her body and dumped it in the alley where she was found. Her head and other missing parts were thrown into Lake Erie.

Lyons also discovered that a tavern Dolezal and Polillo used was also frequented by Edward Andrassy and Rose Wallace. Another young woman claimed that Dolezal had come at her with a knife and she jumped out of a second storey window to escape him, but it seems that she was an alcoholic and the interview was conducted with the aid of a bottle of whiskey.

Dolezal's "confession" turned out to be a blend of incoherent ramblings, punctuated with precise details of the crimes which could have been planted by his interrogators. But before he could go to trial, Dolezal was found dead in his cell. Apparently five-foot-eight Dolezal had hanged himself from a hook that was only five feet seven inches from the floor. Gerber's post mortem revealed that he had six broken ribs, presumably obtained while in the Sheriff's custody. To this day no one thinks Frank Dolezal was the Torso Murderer. But was Sweeney the killer, or did the killer remain at large?

Although the Torso Murders officially ended in August 1938, that December Cleveland Police Chief Matowitz received a letter mailed in Los Angeles. It read: "You can rest easy now as I have come out to sunny California for the winter."

Between 1939 and 1942 there were five more torso murders across the state line in Pennsylvania. On 13 October 1939, the headless, decomposing corpse of a man was fished out of the swamp near West Pittsburgh. The victim's head was found nearby, in an abandoned box car, five days later. Charred newspapers surrounding the remains of the body included month-old copies from Youngstown, Ohio. This was intriguing as the railroad lines from Cleveland to Pittsburgh run through Youngstown. However, decapitated corpses had appeared in that area before. The headless body of a young man was found in a marshy area between New Castle and West Pittsburgh on 6 October 1925. This, again, lay on the railroad track from Cleveland to Pittsburgh. The man was naked and had been dead at least three weeks. His severed head was found two days later but, like the other victim, he remained unidentified.

Soon after, on 17 October 1925, a headless male skeleton was found in the same "murder swamp". Two days later, the skull was found, along with the skull of a woman killed at least a year before. Her body was never found and neither victim was identified.

Another headless corpse of a man was found dumped on a slagheap belonging to the Pittsburgh & Lake Erie Railroad at New Castle Junction on 1 July 1936. His head was never found, and he remains unidentified. However, newspapers spread under the body included editions from July 1933, from both Pittsburgh and Cleveland – tying the corpse to the Cleveland Torso Murders. Detective Merylo concluded that these were the work of the same killer, as were some 20 to 30 other murders, nationwide.

Working some 70 years later, criminologist William T. Rasmussen also tied the Cleveland and Ohio cases to the murders of Maoma Ridings, socialite Georgette Bauerdorf, the Red Lipstick Murders attributed to William Heirens and the famous Black Dahlia case.

On 28 August 1943, Maoma Ridings, the 32-year old daughter of a prominent Georgia family, checked into Room 729 of the Claypool Hotel in Indianapolis. She was a corporal in the Women's Army Corps, but before the war she had been a physiotherapist for Franklin D. Roosevelt in her hometown of Warm Springs, where the president had a summer home.

Stationed at Camp Atterbury, Indiana, she just had arrived in Indianapolis by bus on a weekend pass. On her way from the bus depot, she had bought a fifth of whiskey and went directly to her room in an isolated corner of the seventh floor, flanked by two stairwells.

At 5.30 p.m. she called down to room service for ice and a soft drink. A bellhop came within ten minutes. Later he told police, a woman dressed in black was lying on the bed smoking a cigarette. She had changed out of her uniform apparently. She told him to take a quarter from the dresser. He did so, thanked her and left.

Around an hour later there was another order for ice from Room 729. This time the bellboy saw no one, but a woman's voice from the bathroom told him to put the ice on the dresser and take 25 cents for his trouble. Again, he did so, thanked her and left.

Meanwhile Corporal Emanuel Fisher, who was also stationed at Camp Atterbury, arrived at the Claypool. He called up to Room 729 from the lobby. Getting no reply, he said, he left the hotel.

At 8 p.m., the housekeeper knocked on the door of the Ridings' room and called out: "Linen for 729." There was no answer, so she opened the door to find Maoma Ridings lying dead on the floor near the bed in a pool of blood. A quarter was found next to the body.

She was partially dressed and had just had sex, though the authorities could not determine if this was consensual or she had been raped. The cause of death was a blow to the head with the whiskey bottle, though the body had been slashed repeatedly. Gashes around the neck severed the jugular vein. There were more cuts on her wrists. The body was still warm when she was found. Only 43 cents were found in the room. Fisher was ruled out as a suspect because he called again after the body had been discovered. When a man answered the phone, he hung up. The murder remains unsolved.

Eighteen hundred miles away in Los Angeles, 20-year-old oil heiress Georgette Bauderdorf was doing her bit for the war effort by dancing with enlisted men at the Hollywood Canteen. After lunching with her father's secretary on 12 October 1944, she planned to fly to El Paso to see her boyfriend. The following morning the maid found Bauderdorf's partially clothed body face down in the bathtub in her apartment. She had been strangled. It was thought that a man was awaiting her when she returned home that night. She put a up a tremendous struggle but was overwhelmed. The case remains unsolved.

In Chicago, 43-year-old Josephine Ross was found dead on 5 June 1945; as was 30-year-old Frances Brown on 10 December 1945; and six-year-old Suzanne Degnan on 7 January 1946 in the so-called "Red Lipstick Murders". Said to be the victim of the "Mad Butcher of Kenmore Avenue", Degnan was strangled and her body was cut into seven pieces. Six months later, 17-year-old University of Chicago student William Heirens was arrested for burglary and became a suspect in the Red Lipstick Murders. Throughout his interrogation he maintained his innocence but, after being charged with the crimes, he agreed to plead guilty to avoid the electric chair. Sentenced to four terms of life, he protested his innocence ever since. Rasmussen maintains that there was another Red Lipstick Murder in Los Angeles on 10 February 1947. The victim: Jeanne Axford French. That links to the Black Dahlia Murder, where the body of 22-year-old aspiring actress Elizabeth Short was found in a vacant lot in Leimert Park in Los Angeles on 14 January 1947, less than a month before. Like the women in the Cleveland Torso case, Elizabeth Short's body had been cut in two. It was said that Short was "terribly preoccupied with the details of the Degnan murder". The murders of both Jeanne Axford French and Elizabeth Short remain unsolved, though Merylo believed that the Cleveland Torso Killer was responsible for Short's death.

Rasmussen has placed Jack Anderson Wilson in Indianapolis and Los Angeles at crucial times. He spent his early years in Canton, Ohio less than 50 miles south of Cleveland. He was at Cleveland for the Great Lakes Exposition in 1936, during the Cleveland Torso Murders. He was in Los Angeles at the time Cleveland Police Chief Matowitz got the letter from the killer saying he was in sunny California and when Elizabeth Short and Jeanne Axford French were killed, and he was in Indianapolis when Maoma Ridings was slain. Los Angeles Detective John St John – aka "Jigsaw John" – was convinced that Wilson was the killer in the Black Dahlia case and was about to arrest him in 1982 when Wilson's hotel in downtown Los Angeles burned down.

The Connecticut River Valley Killings

In the late 1970s and early 1980s, two serial killers stalked the scenic Connecticut River Valley between New Hampshire and Vermont. One, Gary Schaefer, was captured. The other remains at large.

The unknown slayer's first victim was probably 26-year-old Cathy Millican. Her body found on 25 September 1978, in a wetlands preserve near New London, New Hampshire. She had been viciously stabbed to death. A hitchhiker named Mary Elizabeth Critchley disappeared from Interstate 91 in Massachusetts in 1981. Her body was found in New Hampshire. By then Gary Schaefer had got to work.

A native of neighbouring Vermont, Schaefer was a member of the fundamentalist Christadelphian Church. He first fell foul of authority while serving in the US Navy, where he was charged with arson and possession of illegal drugs. He entered a plea of insanity, but the Navy psychiatrists found him competent to stand trial. Discharged, he managed to convince his family and friends that he was both sane and responsible. However, under his quiet exterior, he was seething with violent sexual obsessions.

In 1979, Schaefer kidnapped, raped and murdered 13-year-old Sherry Nastasia, whose family lived in a Springfield apartment complex managed by Schaefer's brother. Theresa Fenton suffered the same fate in 1981. However, in 1982, 17-year-old Deana Buxton survived an attack in Brattleboro on the border with New Hampshire. The description of her attacker she gave focused police attention on Schaefer, but there was little hard evidence.

On 9 April 1983, Schaefer abducted young Catherine Richards in Springfield. He drove to a remote spot where he forced her to perform oral sex, then crushed her skull with a stone. The body was found at noon the following day. Descriptions of Catherine's abductor given by an eyewitness matched that Deana Buxton had given the year before.

The police put a case together against Schaefer and were preparing to arrest him in September 1983, when Catherine Richards' mother wrote an open letter to Schaefer, accusing him of murder and challenging him to confess his sins, in accordance with the precepts of his church.

Schaefer cracked. In custody, he confessed to the murders of Theresa Fenton and Catherine Richards, and the rape of Deana Buxton. In December 1983, he pleaded guilty to kidnapping, sexual assault, and second-degree murder in the Catherine Richards' case. The charges in the Fenton case were dismissed as part of a plea bargain. A month later, Schaefer was sentenced to a term of 30 years to life in the federal penitentiary in Leavenworth, Kansas.

Schaefer was safely in jail when the Connecticut River Valley Killer struck again. On 30 May 1984, 17-year-old nurse's aide Bernice Courtemanche disappeared while hitch-hiking in Claremont, New Hampshire, on her way to see her boyfriend eight miles away in Newport. Her remains were found by a fisherman in Newport on 19 April 1986, almost two years after her disappearance. A post mortem revealed that she died from stab wounds to the neck.

Two months after Bernice Courtemanche disappeared, another nurse went missing. Twenty-seven-year-old Ellen Fried, who was a supervising nurse at Valley Regional Hospital in Claremont, stopped late at night on 10 July 1984 outside Leo's Market, a Claremont convenience store. It was on Main Street, five miles from I–91 and not far from where Bernice Courtemanche was last seen. Ellen Fried regularly used the payphone there to call her sister who was out of town. They talked for almost an hour. Then, something spooked Fried.

"That's strange," she said.

"What?"

"A car just drove through."

There was a pause. Then Ellen spoke again.

"Hold on a minute," said

Her sister heard an engine turn over. When Fried returned to the phone, she said she wanted to make sure her car would start. They talked for a few more minutes, then hung up.

Fried was never heard from again. Her skeletal remains were found in 19 September 1985 near the spot where Bernice Coutermanche's remains were discovered. A post mortem failed to determine exactly how she died. But, like Bernice Courtemanche, she showed signs of knife wounds to the neck.

Single mother Eva Morse was last seen hitch-hiking in Charlestown, New Hampshire, after leaving her place of work on 10 July 1985. A logger found her body on 25 April 1986. The remains still showed signs of knife wounds. Then, on 15 May 1986, housewife Lynda Moore was stabbed to death in her home outside Saxtons River over the state line in Vermont.

Another nurse was murdered in January 1987. Thirty-six-year-old Barbara Agnew disappeared on her way home from a skiing trip. Her car was found abandoned at a Vermont rest stop, but her body was not recovered until 28 March. She too had been killed by vicious stab wounds to the neck and lower abdomen. Investigators now recognized this as the Valley Killer's signature. However, two more murders, one dating back to 1968, are also considered as possible victims of the Valley Killer, despite the fact that both victims had been not stabbed but strangled.

Then detectives got a break. On the night of 6 August 1988, Jane Boroski was cornered by a man outside of a rural store near Keane, New Hampshire. The attacker pulled the pregnant 22-year-old from her car and stabbed her repeatedly. But she was saved when another vehicle approached and scared her assailant away. Jane Boroski survived the ordeal to give birth later to a healthy baby daughter.

The police now had a good description of the man they were looking for. An artist produced a sketch which was circulated, but this led nowhere. The killer did not strike again – at least not in the Connecticut River Valley.

The trail then went cold for nearly 30 years until a murder-suicide on New Year's Eve 2005 caught the attention of a private investigator in St Petersburg named Lynn-Marie Carty. When she opened the newspaper on New Year's Day, she recognized the name of the killer, Michael Nicholaou, who had attacked his estranged wife, Aileen, in her home the day before.

According to the *St Petersburg Times*, Nicholaou had "slipped into the West Tampa home on New Year's Eve. It was daylight. He wore a black suit and tie and carried a guitar case full of guns.

"He found his estranged wife at the dining room table.

"'You didn't think you were ever going to see me again,' he said.

"When it was over that day on Walnut Street, blood stained a floral bedspread and a beige and pink dresser. Nicholaou, 56, killed his wife and fatally wounded his stepdaughter before shooting himself in the mouth."

Five years earlier, a Vermont mother had hired Carty, a detective who specialized in reuniting families, to find her daughter, Michelle Ashley, who had had two children by Nicholaou before she disappeared in 1988.

"If I ever go missing," she had told her mother beforehand, "he killed me, and you need to track him down and find the kids."

After a few minutes at the computer, Carty found a phone number for Nicholaou and called it.

"How did you find me?" she remembered him asking.

Carty asked about Michelle Ashley. At first, Nicholaou denied knowing her, but when she pressed, he said Michelle was a slut who was taking drugs and had run off, abandoning the children. Carty then asked about the children. Nicholaou said he had them and they were fine. The conversation was curtailed at this point, but when Carty called back the next day, Nicholaou's phone line was disconnected.

Reading of the murder-suicide of Michael Nicholaou, Aileen Nicholaou and her daughter Terrin Bowman in 2006 stirred up old memories. Carty began wondering what had happened to the children, Nick and Joy. After a bit more digging, Carty found a new phone number. This time she got Nick Nicholaou, now 18, on the phone and told him she did not think their mother had abandoned them. Nick said that he and his sister had never believed it. He cried as he described the hard life they suffered being dragged around the country by their father, who was still traumatized by his service in the Vietnam war that had ended more than three decades before.

Nicholaou had flown helicopters with the 335th Aviation Company, known as the Cowboys, in Vietnam. His comrades remembered Nicholaou as a brave man always prepared to do his duty. He earned a Distinguished Flying Cross, Bronze Star and Air Medal, among other honours, flying into combat zones to drop supplies and recover the wounded. But he had a dark side. A least once, he had left camp on his own, carrying only a knife and bent on hand-to-hand combat with the enemy. His solo efforts became a legend in the company.

Then in May 1971 Nicholaou and seven other helicopter crewmen were charged with murder for strafing innocent civilians while on a flight in the Mekong Delta the previous year. But the charges were dropped due to insufficient evidence. A few days later, Nicholaou was stood down from active duty. He returned to the United States, but his homecoming celebration was short. The war had already become unpopular at home. He worked doing odd jobs and moved from place to place, never staying anywhere for long. Friends soon spotted the symptoms of post-traumatic stress disorder. He later sought treatment in Miami and Tampa.

By 1977, Nicholaou was living off and on in Virginia. Police in Charlottesville busted him for dealing drugs, then used him as an informant. For years afterward, Nicholaou told people he was a cop, or that he worked for the CIA.

In 1983, he opened a porn shop called the Pleasure Chest in Charlottesville. At that time, he was living with his business partner and the partner's wife. Two weeks after the porn shop opened, Nicholaou and his partner were charged with selling obscene materials. A jury convicted them. Months later, police raided again. This time another jury returned a not guilty verdict.

"Evidently the police don't have enough serious robberies, murders and rapes to occupy their time," he said told a local newspaper. The story was published on 22 May 1984.

Eight days later, 500 miles away, Bernice Courtemanche set off hitch-hiking in Claremont. For Carty, Nicholaou's residence in Virginia is no alibi. He would often leave town alone, later telling friends he been in New York or Miami. And he had plenty of reasons to drive north. He spent Christmas in Vermont some years and his ex-wife Susan lived in Connecticut.

Michelle Marie Ashley grew up in the Connecticut River Valley. She was a tomboy who built tree forts with her cousin in the thick woods. Then, with her teens, she became interested in fashion and men. She met one and ran away with him. The next time the Ashleys saw Michelle, she had had a baby, but had left the child with its father. It was 1984, not long before she had met another man – Michael Nicholaou.

Her family were not impressed with her new beau. He was her mother's age and they found him unsettlingly quiet and creepy when the couple visited Michelle's mother and grandmother in Vermont. He had a deep voice and a thick New York accent. Her aunt, Chicki Merrill said that he would not let Michelle shave her underarms. He was possessive and seemed to follow Michelle about everywhere.

Undeterred, Michelle was soon pregnant again. She told her family they were married, though this could not be confirmed through public records. The couple moved in together in an apartment in Holyoke, Massachusetts, about 110 miles away from the family home down the I-91.

Michelle gave birth to Joy in August 1986 and Nick in January 1988, keeping detailed notes in their baby books. She wrote regularly to her cousin Julie Virgin, enclosing baby pictures. But then her letters slowed. At times she acted as if she wanted to confide in her family, Virgin said, but Nicholaou was always within earshot.

Finally, she told her mother that she was afraid of Nicholaou. She said that she planned to leave him after her sister's wedding in November 1988. Nothing happened. Worried, her mother walked into the couple's Holyoke apartment at the end of December 1988, looking for Michelle. The Christmas tree was up, but the presents were unopened and the refrigerator was full of spoiled food. The baby books were left incomplete. Michelle's mother never saw her daughter again.

Carty tracked Nicholaou's movements. In the years that followed, he visited his mother in Virginia, friends in Florida and Army buddies across the country, with the kids in tow. He told some that Michelle was dead; others that she had run off with a drug dealer. In the late 1990s, he met Aileen through a newspaper personal ad and they married.

A few days after reading that Nicholaou had killed his second wife and her daughter, Carty was on the Internet when she came across the unsolved Connecticut River Valley murders and noticed that all the victims had been dumped beside back roads along the I-91 in a stretch that straddled Vermont and New Hampshire.

Cary also noticed that several of the victims were nurses. She remembered hearing that Nicholaou's first wife had been a nurse and that his mother had worked at a hospital. A note in one of Michelle's abandoned baby book place her and Nicholaou at a hospital in Hanover, New Hampshire, hospital on Thanksgiving in 1986. A nurse from that hospital disappeared in January, a few miles from the Vermont home where the Nicholaous spent Christmas and the few weeks that followed.

Carty tracked down a phone number for Susan Nicholaou, who was a nurse in Connecticut when Nicholaou married her in 1978. The two divorced in 1982, a year after the first valley victim, Elizabeth Critchley, disappeared off I-91. Little was known of their short marriage, but Nicholaou took off with their daughter soon after she was born, infuriating his wife.

When Carty called, Susan was guarded.

"I'm not going to talk to you," she said in a voice that shook. "I'm not going to talk about him."

But Carty pressed on. What kind of cars did he drive? she asked. Susan said she barely saw him.

"I got away from him," she said.

Had she been afraid of Nicholaou? Carty asked.

"What do you think?" Susan screamed.

Nicholaou's mother denied knowing him until she learned that her name and phone number were noted in a Tampa Police Department homicide report.

"I threw him out years ago," she said. "He stole my car and took off. I haven't seen him or heard from him since."

While she heard little from Nicholaou, FBI agents had contacted her three times in the past 15 years looking for him, she said. Once, they asked about Susan Nicholaou's baby. The other times, they did not say why they wanted him.

Nicholaou had claimed that his mother molested him when he was young. His mother insisted that Nicholaou was never sexually abused, but admitted that her second husband, Rudy, had hit him. Nicholaou's birth father, Edward Stafford, is a registered sex offender in South Carolina. He was a child molester. His mother divorced Stafford on grounds of "extreme cruelty" when Nicholaou was three years old. Otherwise Nicholaou had a relatively stable childhood on Long Island, New York, riding a motorcycle to high school in Farmingdale, in Nassau County, where he distinguished himself as a wrestler. He enlisted in the Army in Brooklyn in 1968.

When Cary studied the testimony of Jane Boroski, the pregnant woman who survived the attack, she discovered that the killer had used a martial arts grip during the attack. Nicholaou had a black belt in karate. Nicholaou also wore dark-framed glasses like those that appeared in the composite sketch of the Connecticut River Valley killer.

Michelle Ashley's relatives had told Cary that they remembered taking Christmas gifts out of a station wagon with wood-panelled sides in the mid 1980s. Jane Boroski had told police her attacker drove a wood-panelled Jeep Wagoneer. This last attack was only four months before Michelle disappeared and Nicholaou left the area.

Carty contacted criminal psychologist John Philpin who, in the 1980s, had helped police profile the serial killer. He agreed Nicholaou could be the killer. She called New Hampshire State Police, who had not heard of Nicholaou before, but soon made him one of their three strongest suspects – the other two are still alive, so little more could be done in their cases without showing probable cause. However, the introduction of Nicholaou has now meant that the investigation can be opened up again.

Denver's Down-and-Out Destroyer

Five homeless men have been found beaten to death in downtown Denver in 1999 in what was thought to be a murder spree by a thrill killer. Although police did not officially link the five deaths, the circumstances in the five killings appear too similar and they happened over too short a time to be coincidental. All five men were bludgeoned to death in September and they were all found within a six-block radius of Coors Field.

On 7 September the bodies of 62-year-old George Worth and 51-year-old Donald Dyer were found under a loading dock at 2460 Blake Street. Forty-seven-year-old Melvin Washington was found the following day on 18th Street. He had been severely beaten and died from his injuries in hospital a week later. On 26 September the battered body of 51-year-old Milo Harris was found in the South Platte River. The body of the fifth man, 42-year-old Kenneth Rapp, was not found until 22 October, when municipal workers cutting weeds in a field at Lipan and 19th Streets northwest of Coors Field stumbled across it. Investigators believe Rapp had lain there undiscovered for four to eight weeks – putting his murder in September. Like the others, he had died from blunt trauma to the head.

"However, not all the trauma has been the same," said Denver Police Captain Tim Leary. Some of the victims appeared to have been beaten with a weapon, others with fists. Indeed Rapp had been completely decapitated, though his head was found.

Police have not been able to determine a motive.

The killings have scared many of the homeless who would normally spend their nights on the street into seeking shelter. In a survey in June 1998 there were 5,800 homeless people, but the city only had about 3,200 beds available. Due to the increased demand, the city advanced its winter policy allowing shelters and the rescue missions to take in more people than they are normally licensed for, and the Colorado Coalition for the Homeless began putting people up in motels. The Denver Rescue Mission was overflowing and continued to put up makeshift beds in the chapel. And an anonymous donor put up a reward of $100,000 for information leading to the apprehension of the killer.

Three homeless youths were charged with the murder of Melvin Washington and two of the suspects, along with four other homeless youths, have been charged with attempted first-degree murder in the beatings of two other homeless men.

Michael Leathers, aged 18, was charged with robbing and a non-fatal assault on a transient on 25 September. Leathers, who is from Littleton, to the south of the city, also is a suspect in the attack on another homeless man on 26 September. But blood samples did not connect him to any of the murder scenes.

But then on 18 November, more than a week after the suspects had been jailed, two more bodies were found in a field behind

Union Station in the LoDo section of Denver. They had been beheaded. Their heads were never recovered and the bodies had lain dead for around a week. They were later identified as Harry Redden, aged 46, and Joe Mendoza, 50. The new discoveries sparked fears that a serial killer was at work, or that the original thrill killer had spawned a copycat. FBI profilers were called in.

On 16 November Denver police had arrested Rodney Donald Polk, aged 37, for beating a transient sleeping in the doorway of a building on Welton Street in the 16th Street Mall with a board.

Another Denver homeless man, 41-year-old Charles "Stoney" Sanbourne, told journalists that he was the victim of an unprovoked attack by two teenagers.

"The young punks hit me on the head with a two-by-four," he said. "Why they tried to get me I don't know."

Sanbourne, a newspaper seller, said he was hanging out at the corner of California and 16th streets around 7 p.m. He already had a broken leg in a cast and was leaning against a wall next to his wheelchair when two teenagers sneaked up behind him. He said they struck him on the head with a board three times, inflicting injuries to his head and bruising his nose. They then ran off with the case of a Braille machine he used to write his blind mother.

He was standing near a Taco Bell on the 16th Street Mall, a prime hangout for homeless young people. The beating may have been retaliation for intruding on their turf, he said. Living on the streets, homeless teens and older homeless men often came into conflict. Sanbourne said he was an easy mark because of the cast.

"I was also kind of intoxicated," he admitted.

Drinking kept him out of the shelters where he would not be able to take his "medication". Others go off to remote areas to drink to avoid getting arrested for intoxication. This leaves them vulnerable. An ex-con, Sanbourne did not want to report the incident to the police – a 1995 survey in Denver showed an under-reporting of crimes by the homeless – and said he may resort to carrying a gun.

However, his assailants are unlikely to be responsible for the decapitations. Former FBI profiler Gregg McCrary said the beatings and the beheadings were probably not linked, though he would surprised if more than one person were involved in the beheadings.

"The likelihood that you've got more than one killer is pretty small because this is such bizarre pathological behaviour," he said.

Meanwhile, the "mall rats" – the homeless youths who hang out in the 16th Street Mall – complained that they had been unfairly targeted in the wake of the killings of homeless men.

"Since all this really got started, like the last two or three weeks, I've had probably 30 friends arrested down here," said a young man who called himself "Animal".

The parents of Tommy Holden, who has been charged earlier, said they are sure of their son's innocence, particularly in light of the discovery of the new bodies.

"Tommy's got the best alibi he can have," said his mother Denise. "He was in jail."

David Kadans, an organizer with the homeless outreach program Stand Up for Kids, said the mall rats were "being railroaded . . . There's definitely the potential there for violence, but I can't see any of them being driven to serial killing."

The fact that the latest two bodies were found near the railway station led suspicions to fall on the Freight Train Riders of America, thought to have been responsible for some 300 similar murders.

The gang was formed in a Montana bar in 1984 by a small group of Vietnam veterans who were then transients riding trains across the western United States, according to a report by the Placer County Sheriff's Department in Salem, Oregon. Three years later, the group formed a "goon squad" to keep its members in order and beat up other transients who did not want to join.

The FTRA is divided into various factions such as the Wrecking Crew, who use violence to steal clothing and food from other hobos, and the Stone Tramp People, who are heavy drug users. Although FTRA members claim that it is a loosely knit group of homeless people who gang together for mutual support, alumni have been associated with drug trafficking, theft, food stamp fraud and hundreds of assaults and murders committed on other transients. Some also leave racist graffiti with Nazi emblems, leading the authorities to believe that they are affiliated to white supremacist organizations.

Because of FTRA members' use of multiple aliases and the nomadic nature of the gang, it is hard to know exactly how many riders there are. Estimates range from 600 to 2,000, according to Walt Copley, a criminology professor at the Metropolitan State College of Denver.

"They have a shifting membership and short-term leadership," Copley says.

Another FTRA expert is retired Spokane police officer Bob Grandinetti who studied the riders when tracking a drifter suspected of killing a young girl in the early 1980s. He spent years developing informants within the group and likens them to outlaw motorcycle gangs, such as the Hell's Angels.

"They're hard-core druggies who prey on the weak," he says.

Riders identified themselves by coloured bandanas around their necks, held in place by silver clasps known as conchos. Blue bandanas are worn by those from Northern states, red by those from the South and black by those from the Midwest. According to Grandinetti, a new rider is initiated by having three current members urinate on his bandana. After they have ridden over a million miles, they get a gold concho.

Its most notorious member is Robert Joseph Silveria Jnr – aka "Side Track" and the "Boxcar Serial Killer" – who has confessed to nine murders in seven states from Florida to Oregon, though he is thought to have stabbed and bludgeoned at least 14 transients to death and maybe as many as 100. He is currently serving three life sentences in Oregon State Penitentiary. If he is ever paroled, he faces another life sentence in Florida for robbing another drifter and beating to him death with a metal post.

Silveria boasted of killing at least 50 others and claimed he learned his craft from another unidentified, multiple-murdering rider, who Silveria says is still at large.

In the wake of the Denver killings, Bob Cote, former street person and long-time director of Step-13, a shelter and substance abuse rehabilitation centre in Denver, sought an interview with Silveria, as the riders pass through Denver on their way south during the autumn. Cotes believed that they may have stayed on longer that year because of the unusually warm weather. However, when he eventually got to meet Silveria, he found that the 39-year-old Californian was "as crazy as they come".

"He made Charles Manson look like an altar boy," Cote said.

However, Denver, Colorado, has recently had some success at catching a serial killer. On 29 November 2004, Richard Paul White was sentenced to two consecutive life prison terms. He had pleaded guilty to first-degree murder in the deaths of 27-year-old Annaletia Maria Gonzales and 32-year-old Victoria Lyn Turpin. The bodies of both women were found last year, buried in the yard of a home White once shared with a girlfriend.

He was sentenced to another 144 years after pleading guilty to three counts of sexual assault and assault with a deadly weapon for attacks on three women who survived. As part of his plea bargain, prosecutors agreed not to ask for the death sentence provided White co-operated in the search for the bodies of his other victims. He admitted to murdering five women and burying them around the state. Another victim had been discovered, but the remains have not been identified.

In a separate case, White pleaded guilty to first-degree murder of his friend, 27-year-old Jason Reichardt, shooting him dead while trying to rob his truck. It was after his arrest for Reichardt's death in 2003 that White told detectives he had killed five women since 1998 and buried their bodies around the state. The bodies of Gonzales Turpin and were recovered. Authorities also searched sites in Costilla and Otero counties. One of those sites near Mesita, yielded the skeletal remains of a woman. White said he had picked her up at a bus stop and killed her later.

Detroit's Babysitter Killer

There was a spate of child-killings in the Oakland County area of suburban Detroit, Michigan in 1976 and 1977, but the authorities are not sure that they are the work of one man. However, they are certain that there was a connection between four of the victims.

The first was 12-year-old Mark Stebbins, who was abducted while walking home from the American Legion Hall in Ferndale on 13 February 1976. His body was found six days later in a parking lot behind an office building nine miles away in Southfield. He had died approximately 36 hours before his body was discovered. The child had been sexually assaulted with an object and smothered to death, but his corpse was meticulously cleaned and laid out where it would be discovered easily.

On 22 December, 12-year-old Jill Robinson disappeared from her home in Royal Oak after having an argument with her mother and threatening to run away. Her body was found four days later six miles away in Troy on the other side of the I–75. She had been killed by a shotgun blast to the face. There was no evidence of sexual assault. Again, her body had been scrubbed clean and redressed in her own clothes – even her backpack was replaced – before being laid out neatly on a roadside snow bank. The care he lavished on the corpses of his young victim earned the killer the sardonic nickname "The Babysitter".

The next victim was 10-year-old Kristine Mihelich, who disappeared on her way to a 7-Eleven in Berkley on 2 January 1977. Her body was found days later seven miles away at the roadside in Franklin Village. She had been smothered. Her body had been cleaned, like the others, and laid out in the funerary position.

The last certain victim was 11-year-old Timothy King, who went missing on 16 March 1977 in Birmingham after skateboarding to a local drug store. His mother made a TV appeal, promising him his favourite meal – a chicken dinner – if he returned home safely.

A woman said she had seen a boy with a skateboard talking to a man in a parking lot of the store that Timmy had told his parents he was going to. A composite drawing of the suspect was released. He was thought to have been driving a blue AMC Gremlin with a white side stripe.

A week after he went missing, Timothy King was found dead in a ditch 12 miles away near Livonia. He been sexually assaulted with an object before being smothered, but his body had been scoured clean, his nails manicured and his clothes freshly washed and ironed. The post mortem revealed that he had eaten chicken before he died.

It was clear that these killings were related. All victims were snatched off the street in seemingly safe areas and held captive for several days before being murdered. They showed signs of being well cared for and bathed. All the victims were re-dressed in their own clothing with most of their belongings intact. And there was evidence of sexual trauma on both boys, none on the girls. But there was no obvious connection between the kids, other than that they lived relatively close together in a small area of the same county.

Other killings that occurred in that part of Michigan around the same time may have been tentatively linked. On 15 January 1976, 16-year-old Cynthia Cadieux was abducted from Roseville. Her naked body was found 15 miles away lying on a rural road in Bloomfield Township the following day. She had been raped. Her corpse had apparently been dragged over a snow-covered pavement and her clothes were left in a pile 15 feet from the body. However, she was a little older than previous victims, the only one found naked and the killer had not paid the meticulous attention to the body exhibited in the other cases.

Just five days after Cadieux's disappearance, Sheila Shrock was raped and shot dead at her home in Birmingham. All the other victims had been abducted before they were killed.

Thirteen-year-old Jane Allen was murdered by carbon monoxide poisoning after hitching a ride in Royal Oak on 8 August 1976. Her body was found three days later 200 miles away in Miamisburg, Ohio. None of the others had been killed in this manner and all their bodies had been dumped locally.

The 1972 slaying of teenager Donna Serra in Ray Township has also been mentioned as possibly being connected to the string of slayings. However, that took place nearly a hundred miles from the other murders.

Though the body count is disputed, at least one serial killer was at work in Oakland County and Detroit psychiatrist Dr Bruce Danto wrote an open letter to the Babysitter. After it was published, a caller told Danto: "The article was wrong. You better hope it doesn't snow any more." However, when it snowed the following winter, there were no more killings.

A task force of over 300 officers and support personnel was formed and appeals for information made in the media. This brought in some 100,000 calls and over 20,000 were investigated seriously. At one point a priest with a dubious reputation became a serious suspect. It was noted that the children had gone unprotestingly with their murderer and it was thought that a dog collar would have lulled them into a false sense of security. After a thorough investigation, the priest was cleared. Schools started a "Nay Nay, Stranger Stay Away" program, featuring a little pony who warned children of the danger of strangers.

As, in the original four murders, both the boys had been sodomized after death, while the girls had been left unmolested, the police began putting proactive ads in gay magazines and frequenting gay hangouts. This too drew a blank.

Suspicion fell on autoworker David Norberg. He had driven a blue Opal, which looked very similar to a blue Gremlin like that seen in the parking lot when Timothy King had disappeared. Soon after he had stopped driving it. Then he moved from southeast Michigan to Wyoming where he resumed driving it. He was apparently a violent man who physically and sexually assaulted both his wife and his sister. There was speculation he had killed two girls other than the two known victims of the Oakland County Child Killer, as the Babysitter has become known in the literature. He died in a car accident not long after moving.

After he died, his widow said she found a silver cross inscribed "Kristine" among his belongings. Kristine Mihelich had owned such a cross, according to her aunt. Mrs Norberg also said she had found a St Christopher's medal – Timmy King wore one that was never recovered – and a green worm pin like the one Jill Robinson wore. But Mrs Norberg said she had given these away after her husband died and could not remember who she gave them to. However, when Norberg's DNA was compared to genetic material found the hair of one of the suffocated children, he was cleared. The case then went on the back burner.

Then, following the 2005 arrest of Dennis Rader for the BTK – Bind, Torture, Kill – murders in the 1970s, Michigan police revived the investigation into the unsolved Oakland County killings, using the advanced computer databases and forensic techniques now available. As part of this, they announced that they were to open a new hotline for information on the Oakland County Child Killer. In the first two weeks, there were more than 200 calls.

"We're inundated," said Detective Sergeant Garry Gray, head of the new task force. Calls, he said, came from psychics and profilers, ex-wives and relatives who said their cousin was "acting strange". Some callers were in prison, others mentally ill.

A man in his late 30s called in to say the renewed interest in the case had rekindled memories of when he was 11. He said he and a friend were on Evergreen when a reddish van passed them, turned around, passed again and suddenly stopped. Another man, now in his 40s, recalled hitch-hiking in the 1970s and being picked up by a "weird person" whose "car smelled horrible, like maybe a dead person was in the trunk". And a woman called in to say that her old boyfriend would joke about being the Oakland County Child Killer. He had an AMC Gremlin and moved to Wisconsin, might have since married, and "was just very creepy".

Michigan police zeroed in on a man named Todd Warzecha, who had moved to Texas. Warzecha had long been suspected in the unsolved murder of two boys in Bay County, Michigan. In June 2005, Michigan police flew to Texas, but when they arrived at 53-year-old Warzecha's home, they found him hanging in a storage shed on his property. He had committed suicide. However, DNA samples sent to the FBI laboratory in Quantico, Virginia, cleared him. At the same time, the lab also tested another sample from 71-year-old John McRae, who had died recently in Jackson Prison, where he was serving a life sentence for killing a 15-year-old from Harrison, Michigan.

Then in December 2006, the police in Parma Heights, Ohio,

arrested 65-year-old Ted Lamborgine, a retired autoworker who had left Detroit for Ohio in 1978, in connection with the Oakland Country murders. He was also thought to be a "person of interest" in the unsolved abduction and murder of 10-year-old Amy Mihaljevic, in Bay Village, Ohio, in 1989. Like the children from Oakland County, Amy was abducted in a supposedly safe district – the Bay Square Shopping Center in Bay Village, Ohio – and seems to have gone willingly with her kidnapper. And, like the children from Oakland County, Amy's body was left just a few feet from a country road, in a place it would be found easily.

Wayne County prosecutor Kym Worthy said that the arrest and conviction of Lamborgine's friend, Richard Lawson, had drawn attention to him as a suspect. Lawson was found guilty of first-degree murder and armed robbery in March 2006, He had shot and killed 67-year-old Exavor Giller, the owner of a cab company where Lawson once worked, outside his Livonia home in 1989.

Lawson and Lamborgine have been charged with assaulting 12 juveniles between the ages of 10 and 15 during the 1970s and 1980s in Detroit's downtown Cass Corridor. They were running a child-porn ring. However, the charges were unrelated to the deaths of the four Oakland County children.

The two men had worked together as sexual predators, Worthy said, but were charged separately. The two men allegedly lured the victims to motels, hotels and homes with soft drinks, drugs, food and cash.

"These suspects knew that there were a lot of poor kids living in that area," said Livonia police Detective Sergeant Cory Williams. "It didn't take too much for them, the suspects, to figure out they could take the kids a case of pop, some drugs or cash."

Lawson and Lamborgine face maximum penalties of life in prison if convicted of the sexual assaults.

While Lawson was not a suspect in the Oakland County Child killings, he had provided authorities with information about Lamborgine related to the Oakland County case, said Garry Gray, the head of the Oakland County Child Killer Task Force.

However, the testimony of a convicted killer might not stand in court. Indeed, Lawson may have fingered Lamborgine in an effort to save his own skin. There had been false leads before. That would mean that the Oakland County Killer is still at large.

The Fiend of Flint, Michigan

On 24 October 1999, a task force was set up in Flint, Michigan to try to determine if a serial killer was at work. The bodies of seven African-American women – all involved with drugs and prostitution – had been found in or near abandoned houses, a situation disturbingly similar to the Chicago crack-head killings that were going on at the time.

However, the police stressed that there were no similarities between the girls, nor were the murders confined to a specific area of the city. A man convicted of kidnap and rape who lived in Grand Blanc Township outside the city was listed as a suspect in three of the killings, but no charges were brought.

Another serial killer was at work at the time, though. On 9 November the body of Margarette Eby was found in her home in Flint. The 55-year-old music professor was a former provost at the University of Michigan-Flint. She had been raped and murdered. For a year, detectives made little progress with the case.

Then on 18 February 1991, 41-year-old Northwest Airline stewardess Nancy Jean Ludwig was found with her throat slashed in a room at the Hilton Airport Inn near Detroit Metropolitan Airport in Romulus, Michigan. She had been bound, gagged and raped. Ludwig, from Minnetonka, Minnesota, had flown into Detroit from Las Vegas the previous night and had checked into room 354 of the Hilton. That night the killer entered her room and attacked her with a knife. The injuries to her body show she resisted, but her attacker slashed her throat with such force that he nearly decapitated her.

Nancy Ludwig was tied up and raped during this horrific attack, police said. The killer cleaned up the room and left, taking her clothes and personal property with him.

A witness saw a man loading burgundy airline luggage into a

bronze or brown Monte Carlo outside the hotel in the middle of the night.

Romulus police collected DNA from the scene of the killing, but Michigan did not have a database to compare samples against at that time.

Police Lieutenant Dan Snyder and his team continued their dogged search, hoping that other evidence would bring them to a suspect.

In the summer of 2000, Lynne Helton, a forensic specialist for the Michigan State Police, who was building the DNA database, retested the sample from the Ludwig murder at the Northville crime lab and entered it. It sat there for about a year until DNA from the Eby case was entered.

"Within a matter of a few minutes it matched the evidence on the Ludwig case," Helton said. "It was just an incredible day."

On 15 August 2001, the police investigators announced evidence linked the murders of Ludwig and Eby. From then on, Romulus, Flint and the Michigan State Police worked together closely, merging their investigations. A latent fingerprint found at the scene of Eby's murder matched from a case in Florida. In May 1983, 20-year-old Jeffrey Wayne Gorton broke into a house near Orlando and stole a woman's underwear. He was convicted and imprisoned. In 1985, he was released and headed to Michigan.

The police tracked him down to Clio, Genesee County, five miles north of Flint, where he worked as a sprinkling-service employee. Then in February 2002, they began trailing him. On 7 February, Romulus Police Officer Mike St Andre picked up a cup Gorton left behind. DNA taken from the cup matched semen found in both the Ludwig and Eby cases. Two days later, Gorton was arrested. The following day he was charged with the murder of Margarette Eby in Genesee County.

During a search, police also found a 1982 gold Monte Carlo similar to one seen leaving the Hilton Airport Inn near Detroit Metropolitan Wayne County Airport on 18 February 1991. Inside the car, police found luggage similar to that used by Northwest Airlines employees. And on 11 February he was charged with the murder of Nancy Ludwig. He was arraigned in Romulus District Court on five felony counts of murder and criminal sexual conduct. Convicted in the Ludwig case, he pleaded no contest to the rape and murder of Margarette Eby.

Wayne County Assistant Prosecutor Michael Cox promised that detectives would be doing a thorough follow-up.

"There are a lot of things here that are very disturbing that we've uncovered," Cox says.

Homicide investigators in Orange County, Florida, contacted Michigan authorities about the disappearance of a 14-year-old Vickey Willis in April 1983, when Gorton was living nearby in Orlando.

The investigation goes much wider than that. A total of 800 pairs of women's panties labelled with dates and places were found in Gorton's house. But that takes investigators no closer to the killer of the seven African-American women in Flint.

The Florida Lady Killer

On 17 February 1981, the body of a young African-American woman was found in a vacant lot on the outskirts of Fort Lauderdale's ghetto area. She could not be identified and the medical examiner could not determine the cause of death, describing it as a "homicide committed by unspecified means".

On 1 June 1981, the skeletal remains of a black girl were found on the same patch of rough ground. She was roughly 13 years old, but she was carrying no form of ID. Again she could not be identified and a post mortem revealed no cause of death.

A third victim was identified. She was 30-year-old Eloise Coleman, a resident of the neighbourhood. Her corpse was found in the same lot on 10 June 1981, roughly 100 yards from where the first body was found. She had last been seen alive three days before when she left home on the evening of 7 June. This time the medical examiner could also determine the cause of death. It was described as blunt trauma to the victim's head, caused by a powerful blow.

Despite the fact that all the bodies had been dumped on the same patch of waste ground, the police were reluctant to call the murders the work of a serial killer and the killer, or killers, remain at large.

The Fort Lauderdale Lacerater

Florida police found themselves investigating another series of unsolved murders in the Fort Lauderdale area, after the mutilated body of Delia Lorna Mendez was found in a dumpster on Federal Highway in nearby Hollywood on 21 May 1999. They sought to connect her death with the murder of four Fort Lauderdale prostitutes who worked the highway at one time or another.

At least three of the women had strawberry-blonde hair and a slender figure. Three were last seen strolling along US 1 in Fort Lauderdale and, when their bodies were found, they had been strangled. The fourth was mutilated and dumped near a Palm Beach highway.

Boston police flew to Florida, looking for connections between Mendez's death and the murder of 20-year-old Swedish nanny Karina Holmer living in Dover, Massachusetts. She was last seen outside Zanzibar, a nightspot near Boston Common, between 3.30 and 4 a.m. on 22 June 1996. Her body was found in dumpster the next day by a man rummaging through the trash. She had been strangled and her torso was cut in half with surgical precision. The two halves of the body had been washed and placed in a garbage bag under a pile of rubble in the dumpster.

The Grand Rapids Grim Reaper

The murder of 11 women in the area around Grand Rapids, Michigan, remains unsolved. The police said that they were not sure that they were the work of a serial killer, though they assigned a task force of 15 to investigate.

The first victim was 25-year-old Lesa Otberg of Grand Rapids, whose body was found some 35 miles away in Muskegon in March 1994. Eight months later, another body was discovered to the south in neighbouring Ottawa County. The victim has not been identified. The remaining victims have been found in Grand Rapids itself, except for 29-year-old Victoria Moore. Her badly decomposed body was discovered by a squirrel hunter 20 miles north of the city.

Nine of the victims were prostitutes and at least five of them had contacts with the Rose Haven Ministry, a sanctuary for sex workers. By and large they were young white women with dark hair. Other than that, there are few clues and their killer remains at large.

The I–10 Long-Distance Lorry Driver of Death

Police in San Diego have been looking for a serial killer responsible for a string of murders along Interstate 10, the 2,500-mile highway running across eight states in the lower United States from California to Florida.

The investigation was instigated by a woman who accused a truck driver of a 1981 murder in San Diego's Balboa Park, along with a string of slayings across the southern States. The unidentified female informant described how the 1981 killing was committed and took detectives to the spot, providing details that only someone who had witnessed the murder or who had been told about it by the killer could have known.

The woman said the truck driver had killed up to 20 people, largely prostitutes and hitch-hikers. Many were killed in Texas and their bodies deposited hundreds of miles away.

Law enforcement agencies all along I–10 had unsolved cases that might correspond to the trucker's movements. They were afraid that the I–10 had struck again when the Baton Rouge serial killer began dumped his victims along the same Interstate some 1,800 miles to the east.

The I–35 Killer

The I–35 had been the hunting ground of a serial killer – or killers – before. Between 1976 and 1981, there were at least 22 murders along the 420-mile stretch of the I–35 in Texas. The victims were largely hitchhikers and motorists in trouble.

The killer's first "official" victim was 21-year-old Lesa Haley, who was hitch-hiking from Texas to Oklahoma City. She was last seen climbing into a van outside Waco. Her body was found dumped on the hard shoulder of the eastern branch of the I–35 two miles north of Waxahachie, Texas, on 23 August 1976. She had been stabbed in the neck with an awl.

On the night of 5 November 1978, Rita Salazar, aged 18, and Frank Key, 19, were out on a date in the state capital Austin, Texas, when they ran out of gas. The next morning, Frank Key's body was found north of Georgetown. He had been shot nine times with a. 22-caliber pistol, including four shots in the back of the head after he was dead. Rita Salazar's body was discovered 70 miles further on, dumped on a frontage road near Waco. She had been shot six times with the same gun.

On 3 September 1979 – Labor Day – 27-year-old Sharon Schilling was found 125 miles to the south of Austin on a street in San Marcos, Texas, just a few blocks from I–35. She had been shot once in the abdomen with a .410-gauge shotgun. She died ten days later without regaining consciousness.

Sandra Dubbs was driving from St Louis to San Antonio when her car broke down on the I–35 on 8 October 1979. She was abducted from the disabled vehicle. Her body was discovered near Austin in Travis County, Texas. She had been stabbed 35 times.

On 31 October – Halloween – the body of a woman, naked except for a pair of orange socks, was found near Georgetown in a culvert under the I–35. She had been strangled and has never been identified. Henry Lee Lucas confessed to her murder but work records and a cheque he cashed indicated that Lucas was somewhere else and Texas Attorney General Dan Morales con-cluded that it was "highly unlikely" that Lucas was guilty in the "orange socks" case.

On 23 June 1980, the body of Rodney Massey was found in a field near Temple, Texas, 60 miles north of Austin. He had been shot four times. Then on 9 July, the body of an unidentified Hispanic woman was discovered near Pflugerville, 13 miles north of Austin. Although her pants had been pulled down, there was no evidence of sexual assault. She had been stabbed 27 times with a screwdriver. In May 1981, the body of another unidentified female was found near New Braunfels, 25 miles outside San Antonio. She had been shot in the head six times with a .25-caliber pistol.

It was now clear that a serial killer was at work and the authorities involved met in Austin on 30 October 1981. They decided to pool their resources but even there they could come up with no solid suspects.

In 1983, the prolific serial killers Henry Lucas and Ottis Toole confessed to most of the I-35 murders and Lucas was convicted and sentenced to death in the "orange socks" case. But it was later demonstrated that Lucas was working as a roofer in Florida in October 1979. Work records and cheque-cashing evidence show that he could not have done it. Subsequently it has been shown that Lucas and Toole were not guilty in many of the 350 murders they confessed to. It seems that the police were merely trying to clear their books of troublesome cases. The "orange socks" case and the other I-35 returned to the "unsolved" list. Many believe that the I-35 killer is still at large.

The I-70 – "America's Sewer Pipe"

The I-70 has been the killing ground of so many serial killers that it has become known as "America's Sewer Pipe". One killer who used the stretch between Indianapolis and Columbus, Ohio in the 1980s and has never been caught became known simply as the "I-70 Killer". The killer dumped the bodies of nine gay men within a few miles of the highway. No suspect has ever been apprehended, despite the widespread publicity the murders have generated, including their being featured several times on the television show *America's Most Wanted*.

In October 1998, authorities announced that they strongly suspected that Indianapolis businessman and serial killer Herb Baumeister could have been the I–70 Killer. Baumeister was a closet homosexual. A married man with three children, he secretly frequented gay bars in Indianapolis. In the summer, when his wife and kids were away at his mother's lakeside condominium, he took young men back for a "cocktail and a swim" to their $1-million Westfield estate, known as Fox Hollow Farm.

In May 1993 gay men began disappearing in Indianapolis. Ten went missing over two years, but the killer left no clues. Then in the autumn of 1994, a man told the police that he had been picked up by a man who called himself Brian Smart. They had gone to Smart's sprawling estate and engaged in autoerotic asphyxiation. Smart was a devotee and admitted that, sometimes, there had been accidents. A year later the man spotted Brian again and, aware of the disappearances, took down his licence-plate number. The car belonged to Baumeister.

Although the police lacked the necessary evidence to obtain a search warrant, in November 1994, they turned up at Fox Hollow Farm and ask for permission to search the grounds. When Baumeister refused, they petitioned his wife Julie. They told her that her husband cruised gay bars and that they suspected him of being a serial killer. He was a devoted husband of 20 years standing and she refused to believe them.

"The police came to me and said, 'We are investigating your husband in relation to homosexual homicide,'" she recalled. "I remember saying to them, 'Can you tell me what homosexual homicide is?'"

It was only when their 13-year-old son found parts of a skeleton in the woods that she gave her permission. Then, when her husband was away in June 1996, the police began their search. The remains of seven men were found. They had been strangled. All the victims used the same bars that Baumeister did and disappeared at times when his wife and kids were away. Meanwhile, 49-year-old Baumeister disappeared. On 3 July

1996, campers discovered his body lying beside his car in Ontario's Pinery Provincial Park. He had a bullet hole in his forehead and a .357 Magnum in his hand.

An FBI profiler said that Baumeister's cavalier manner of openly dumping his victims' corpses in his back yard indicated that he had killed many times before. Baumeister insinuated to a potential victim that he had killed 50 to 60 people. He was known to have travelled on the I–70 from Indiana to Ohio around the time of the highway killings, which stopped in 1990, around the time that Baumeister bought Fox Hollow Farm.

In 1998, investigators concluded that Baumeister probably killed 16 men in all after linking him to nine other men whose bodies were found dumped along rural roads in Indiana and Ohio between 1980 and 1990. Baumeister's wife provided credit card receipts, phone call records, and even gave the police the use of the car that her husband had used on those business trips.

Baumeister's photo matched the police sketch drawn from descriptions provided by witnesses who thought they had seen the I–70 Killer. One eyewitness identified Baumeister's picture as the same man who had given his friend Michael Riley a lift home from a bar one evening in 1988. Riley was found dead the next morning.

"We'll never know for sure, of course, if he was indeed the same man," said Virgil Vandagriff, a private investigator employed to look into the disappearance of some of the missing men. "Everything points to him – even the fact that the roadside killings ended at the same time he bought his house and now had a place with plenty of room to dump his bodies with a lot less hassle."

However, Vandagriff complained that, as a private detective, he did not always have the freedom or the money to follow his suspicions to the limit.

"I would have taken the Baumeister case a lot further than I feel the police did," he said. "While there were many fine moments in the investigation . . . I think there were certain loose ends that should have been tied up."

For example, while Baumeister was active in Fox Hollow Farm, his older brother in Texas was found dead in his pool.

However the killings along I–70 did not stop with the death of Baumeister. On 4 May 2006, the body of 24-year-old Dusty Shuck was found by a motorist on I–70 near a truck stop in Frederick County, Maryland. Last seen in New Mexico on 24 April, she had died from a combination of blunt force trauma to the head and a slit throat. Her head was wrapped in blood-soaked cloth and, although fully dressed, she had no shoes.

The I–70/I–35 Shootist

During a 29-day killing spree running from 8 April to 7 May 1992, a man in his mid-to-late-twenties or early thirties killed five women and one man along the I–70, which runs from Utah to St Louis, and I–35 which branches off at Kansas City and heads south through Wichita, Oklahoma City and Dallas to Laredo on the Mexican border. The victims were shop assistants in stores within two miles of the two Interstates. The one male victim had long hair and an earring and the authorities believe that the killer mistook him for a woman. The killer also robbed his victims, but seemingly as an afterthought.

The perpetrator was five foot seven inches tall and thin. He had sandy blond hair with a reddish tint and designer stubble. After a month, his killing spree stopped, leading the police to believe that he was in jail for some other offence. Then in 1993 he started killing again in Texas, where he shot three more women using the same .22 automatic pistol.

Kansas City's Independence Avenue Killer

A serial killer has been killing women from Kansas City's red light district around Independence Avenue and dumping them in the Missouri River, earning him the name the "Independence Avenue Killer" or the "Missouri River Killer".

The hunt began on 10 October 1996 when the body of 21-year-old Christy Fugate, aged 21, was pulled from the waters of the

Missouri River near Dover in Lafayette County, Missouri, some 50 miles downriver from Kansas City. She had gone missing the previous month. Since then, nine more bodies of Kansas City women have been found downstream.

On 29 March 1997, the body of Sherri Livingston was spotted in the river near where Christy Fugate had been found. She had been reporting missing in February. Three weeks later, on 22 April 1997, Connie Wallace-Byas's body was recovered. She had been reported missing the previous October. The following day, the body of Linda Custer was found near Dover. She had gone missing in February. Two weeks after that, on 7 May, the body of Chandra Helsel was found 80 miles further on near Booneville. She had been missing since 17 April. On 31 July 1997, Wilmalee Manning's body was recovered from the river. Then on 31 August, Lana Alvarez's body was found. In March 1998, Maria Woods' body was found in the river. On 2 April 1998, the mutilated body of Tammy Smith was found in the river near Sibly, just 25 miles downstream from Kansas City.

All the victims were thought to be prostitutes working in the Independence Avenue area of Kansas City, Missouri. For once the police were quick to admit that a serial killer was at work as all the women were of approximately the same height and weight. They issued a warning that a serial killer was on the prowl, but few heeded it.

Four more missing women are thought to have been the victims of the mysterious Missouri River Killer. They are 18-year-old Jennifer Conroy, who was last seen on 14 December 1993; 41-year-old Jamie Pankey, last seen 30 July 1996; 33-year-old Connie Williams, last seen 16 October 1996; and 20-year-old Cheresa Lordi, last seen 14 February 1997.

The La Crosse Drownings

At the end of September 1997, 28-year-old Chuck Blatz, a student at the University of Wisconsin's Platteville campus, travelled from his home in Kiel, Wisconsin, to La Crosse for the annual Oktoberfest. He was five foot ten inches tall, weighed 130 pounds and had recently been honourably discharged from the military. On the night of Saturday, 27 September 1997 he was at Sneakers, a popular downtown bar and left some time after midnight. Five days later his body was pulled from the Mississippi River, that flows through La Crosse, by a fisherman. One of his socks was missing along with one of his black sneakers. Blatz was known to be a strong swimmer and a keen scuba diver. He was an unlikely victim of drowning.

Two days after Blatz's body was found, 19-year-old Anthony Skifton disappeared. Skifton was last seen alive at 2.30 a.m. on 5 October 1997, when he left a party carrying a case of beer. Five days later he was found floating in Swift Creek, not far from a gay cruising area. His bladder was empty and his flies unzipped. This led the authorities to believe that he had been urinating in the river when he slipped and fell into the freezing waters. However, Skifton was not a good drinker. He had a reputation for getting drunk and passing out early. Everyone would pounce on him with magic markers and he would wake up with writing all over his face. When his body was recovered the case of beer was missing. His death could easily have been accidental – had it not fitted into a disturbing pattern.

On 22 February 1998 Nathan Kapfer, a 20-year-old baseball player who was attending nearby Viterbo College on an academic scholarship, went missing. At 5 foot 10 inches and weighing 150 pounds, he bore a striking resemblance to the other two missing boys. But the night he went missing, he turned up at a downtown pub called Brother's Bar after having DJ'd at a local party. He was drunk and the bartender refused to serve him. When the bouncer was called to escort him out of the bar, Kapfer cursed. The police were called and he was arrested. At the police station he was given citations for underage drinking, disorderly conduct, possessing false identification and being in a bar under the age of 21. Then, at around 2 a.m., he was released. Soon after, his hat, wallet and the four tickets he had been given were found laid out neatly on the deck of a riverboat gift shop. His body was fished out of the water downstream six weeks later. A post mortem revealed that his blood alcohol level was 0.22 percent – above 0.15 percent you are considered drunk when driving. According to the authorities the evidence suggests that Kapfer had committed suicide. His death could have been an accident, or he could have been pushed.

Then on 10 April 1999 Jeffery Geesey went missing. A 20-year-old student at the University of Wisconsin-La Crosse, he did not return to his dorm that night. He was last seen in a bar on Third Street. Forty-one days later, on 22 May his body was found in the Big Muddy by two fishermen. The medical examiner classified the manner of death as "undetermined". But unofficially, the police considered it a suicide as there were four shallow self-inflicted scars on his arms. But Geesey's father said that, after an overnight stay in hospital visit, a psychological evaluation had determined. that when Jeff cut himself, he was upset – but not suicidal.

There was other evidence to suggest that Jeff Geesey did not kill himself. The bloodhound used to search for him hit on a scent that indicates Geesey experienced trauma in several locations. At the Niedbalski Bridge, around a mile from Third Street, the dog found Geesey's blood.

"She was licking the pavement," said Penny Bell, the dog's handler. "But there was no forensics follow-up."

La Crosse police chief Ed Kondracki was sceptical.

"Things she said those dogs could do, dogs can't do," he said.

Like the other young men the river had claimed, Jeff Geesey was young and fit – 6 foot 2 inches tall and 200 pounds. And he was a little drunk when he went missing. However, for four strapping young men to drown in the river in the space of two years seemed like too much of a coincidence. The theory circulated that a serial killer was at work.

The police, however, dismissed it. The deaths were classified as "exceptional clearance", meaning that they were not witnessed and there was no evidence to suggest that a crime had been committed. Consequently, they must have been accidents or self-inflicted and the trail went cold.

Then on the night of 9 April 2004, Jared Dion and his brother Adam went out with their friends. It was a cold night, in the low 40s, and a chill wind blew through La Crosse. But it was a Friday night and the students from the University of Wisconsin went out drinking. Jared Dion was a 21-year-old sophomore, 5 foot 9 inches tall and weighing 172 pounds. And he was fit. An outstanding athlete at high school, he was a member of the college wrestling team. That night he was drunk, but no more drunk than the other college revellers and few took any notice when he staggered out of the bar. Five days later, his body was fished out of the Mississippi.

Authorities said his death an accident. The post mortem found that he had drowned and his blood-alcohol level was a massive 0.28 percent, nearly twice the level at which the law considers a person to be intoxicated. The police maintain that he was drunk, wandered too close to the river and fell in.

However, there was one inconvenient fact that spoiled this picture. Dion's white Boston Red Sox baseball cap was found neatly hanging from a post on the riverbank near to the spot the police assumed he fell in. Did he take it off and hang it there before he plunged into the water? Police Chief Kondracki said that a group of joggers passing by had seen it on the ground and one of them had picked it up and put it there. However, the joggers say that the cap was already on the post and they did not touch it.

The fact that five muscular young men had all died in the same way was, the police maintained, a coincidence. La Crosse was a college town with a culture of heavy drinking. And when young men are drunk, accidents happen. But long-time residents wondered why it had never happened before. Others asked why other riverside college towns, such as Winona, Minnesota – 25 miles upstream – did not suffer from a similar string of drownings. The idea that a serial killer was at work began to circulate again.

Everyone had their own theory. Perhaps La Crosse had its own cold-weather version of Aileen Wuornos, the prostitute in Florida who took her revenge on men by killing her clients. Maybe the killer was a taxi driver who offered his drunken victims a ride home, or a homicidal cop was prowling the streets at night.

Talk of a serial killer on the loose became so pervasive that Kondracki took the unprecedented step of calling a town meeting which was broadcast live on local TV. One of those fielding the questions was Police Lieutenant Dan Marcou, who was also the uncle of one of the five boys who died in the river and "fought back tears as he chastised the crowd," a reporter said.

"The La Crosse Police Department investigated all of these [deaths] thoroughly," Marcou insisted. "I have to listen to people applaud at the thought that my nephew was killed by a serial killer. This community is like an alcoholic. It would rather think that a killer is on the loose than admit that it's got a drinking problem."

However critics pointed out that the police had dismissed the idea that a killer or killers were responsible for some or all of the deaths too readily and had failed to investigate any of the deaths as possible homicides.

The University of Wisconsin was also eager to crush the idea that a serial killer was at work in their seat. The chair of the psychology department Betsy Morgan, who has taught at the university for ten years, did not buy it. She and the criminal-justice professor Kim Vogt wrote an open letter to students called "Why We Are 99.9 Percent Sure It Is Not A Serial Killer", pointing out that students and the local brewing industry would rather believe that a serial killer was at large than examine their own penchant for excessive drinking. It concluded with a homily on Occcam's razor: "When you hear hooves behind you, you should expect to see horses, not zebras . . . In the case of Jared Dion and other students who have drowned in the past several years, the 'horse' diagnosis is 'alcohol' while the 'zebra' plays the part of the 'serial killer.' It was a plain old tragic accident that took the life of [Jared Dion] and the others who drowned."

Vogt also dismissed it fact that all the victims shared specific physical characteristics. While it is true that serial killers are often drawn to victims who were similar in looks and age and occupation, the population of northern Midwest is unusually homogeneous. College towns attract a disproportionate number of young men who go out at night and get drunk.

"The coincidence that people always pull up is that they're all college-age, they all have brown hair and they're all white," Vogt said. "Well, that describes 95 percent of our population . . . a serial killer would have to really hunt to find a young man who didn't match the profile of the victims."

She also pointed out that, statistically, young men are ten times more likely than young women to die by drowning.

Vogt searched the records and found no incidence of a serial killer who drowned their victims. True, there were killers who intentionally drowned their victims. In rare cases they had used drowning as a method in multiple murders – for example, Andrea Yates, the psychotic Texas mother who drowned her five young children one by one in the bathtub in 2001. But serial killers, who plan their attacks and get a kick from the execution, were different.

"Serial killers," she said, "want to see people die."

As psychotherapist and profiler John Kelly dismissed the idea that a serial killer was responsible for the La Crosse drownings was "pretty weird".

"They could have been murdered, but the person was just so good at doing it that they didn't leave any physical evidence," he told *Stuff* magazine. "If a serial killer is involved, they're going to make sure that person is dead before they throw them in the river. They're not going to take any chances that they could be identified in court. I suppose the killer could sedate the victim and drown him in a tub or something like that and then throw him in the river."

Such a scenario seems unlikely. But some experts are not so sure. Reviewing the cases for *Stuff* magazine, criminal psychologist Dr Maurice Godwin said: "The probability is virtually zero that five intoxicated students just happened to walk similar or even different routes and end up on the river bank."

Indeed, even to get to the bank, a drunken student would have to make his way down a concrete stairway and across several feet of loose rocks.

Pat Brown, an expert on sexually motivated homicide, concurs.

"More people are killed by serial killers than we realize," she says.

True, it is not easy to lure a victim to a convenient body of water.

"So you have to bring somebody back and try to get them into your bathtub which is not the easiest thing in the world," she says. "Unless you're Jeffrey Dahmer."

But then there are people who fantasize about becoming the next Jeffrey Dahmer and get sexually aroused by the act of drowning. She even has a candidate, though his name has been withheld as the man has never been charged with related offences, nor has been named as a formal suspect in the case. She says she first came across the man when she was investigating a similar case.

In 2002, 21-year-old University of Minnesota student Chris Jenkins drowned 120 miles upstream in Minneapolis after being kicked out of a Halloween fancy-dress party at the Lone Tree Bar & Grill at 528 Hennepin Avenue minutes before midnight on 31 October.

Although his car was parked just south of the Warehouse District bar, he was last seen walking north, clad in an American Indian costume. Chuck Loesch, a private detective hired by the family, believed that Jenkins intended to walk to his apartment near Dinkytown, which would involve crossing the Mississippi River.

A senior in the business school, his disappearance sparked a communitywide search. Numerous University of Minnesota students and hundreds of other volunteers scoured the area but found nothing. Then, in late February 2003, Jenkins' body was pulled from the Mississippi River near the St Anthony Falls in downtown Minneapolis.

The medical examiner spent seven hours on the post mortem, but did not find any obvious indication of foul play. Nor was there any reason to believe that he had died from natural causes. So the exact manner of Chris's death had been listed officially as "undetermined". However, while the blood-alcohol level in his heart was only 0.12 percent, tests found a high level of the date-rape drug known as GHB in his system – though medical examiners maintain the body could produce this substance naturally.

At that time, the coroner did not classify the death as a crime. However, others were not so sure. One clue that it was a homicide was that Jenkins was outside without his coat, wallet or cell phone.

In November 2006, the death of Chris Jenkins was reclassified as a homicide. But police in La Crosse dismissed any connection with the drownings there and continued to consider the Wisconsin deaths as accidents.

Brown's suspect came to her attention after he walked into the police station in St Charles, Missouri, in the late 1990s and announced that he was going to be the next Jeffrey Dahmer. Of course, neither the cops or the FBI believed him, on the grounds at if somebody says they are going to be a serial killer, they are not.

"But it's not true," says Brown. "We have a history of exactly that sort of thing, where they do claim it and they are it. They're trying to practice the concept . . . people say, 'I want to be something, so let me go out and say (I am) something, and then after a while I get comfortable with the concept, then I can be it.'"

The man was so persistent that the police even got a restraining order to stop him harassing them. However, one St Charles' detective did take the man's claims seriously, particularly when he revealed his obsession with a sexual fantasy of forcing young boy-next-door types underwater and watching them panic and struggle until they drowned. It was then he contacted Brown.

The private eye Chuck Loesch also came across the unidentified man when he was working on the Jenkins case. He lived in Minneapolis at the time of Jenkins' death, just a few blocks from where he disappeared. Brown says that the man has also spent time in Wisconsin.

The man worked in a funeral parlour – the perfect job for a man fascinated with death. At night he was a part-time male prostitute and was a regular on a website called manunderwater.com for gay men who have a fetish about having sex underwater. The St Charles' cop asked Brown to see if she could contact the man via the website.

Posing as a 15-year-old boy who had seen his own brother die in a back yard pool years before, Brown role-played with the man via the website's message boards. She quickly noticed a sadistic bent to the man's fantasy.

"Some people will present online as one who will share going under water, 'You drown me then I'll drown you' that type of thing," Brown says. "He's not like that at all. He doesn't like being drowned. He just lies about that so he's not really sharing with you. Once you get to the fantasy with him, he wants to do all the drowning. I mean he'll play at it one time or so to pretend that you get your turn, but it isn't that way . . . It is more about 'I'm holding you under the water. You're struggling. You're struggling. I watch the bubbles come up . . .' That's his whole thing. To watch you drown, to watch your eyes when you're drowning."

His emails were disturbing and graphic.

"He would take me under water in various forms of nudity or non-nudity, in different water settings and he would watch me struggle and die. That's when he would have an orgasm," Brown recalls.

The man was also cold and calculating, and Brown believes that he confines his activities to Minnesota and Wisconsin as they do not have the death penalty.

"He said he'd never kill in Missouri," Brown recalled, "because it's a death-penalty state."

Meanwhile, the suspect was up to no good in the real world. He made sexual advances towards the teenage son of the owner of the funeral home and, when the father confronted him, he threatened to murder the funeral director's entire family. When a detective interviewed him, he concluded: "The defendant is a danger to the community . . . because he goes for white males between 16 and 25 . . . spoke of bondage and putting Saran Wrap over a victim's face . . . and has serial-killer tendencies."

The police then issued a warrant, but when they tried to arrest the man he drove into their squad car and led them on an hour-long car chase. He was jailed for seven months for resisting arrest. The problem was that he was in jail at the time of Jared Dion's death. Nevertheless Brown believes that he was involved in the four earlier deaths, or that someone with a similar tendency is out there at work.

"There are more serial killers out there than we know about," Brown says. The La Crosse fatalities are not necessarily all the victims of the same killer. "It could be one guy who maybe killed two of them."

The detective in St Charles agrees and would like a chance to investigate.

"I think if I had all those cases, he'd be a great lead to eliminate," he said.

When *Stuff* magazine told the police in La Crosse police of Brown's suspect, Captain Mitch Brohmer said that he knew nothing about him. Caroline Kelly, a detective with the Wisconsin Division of Criminal Investigation, admitted that the state police, as well as the local department, had not heard of him.

A former FBI profiler told *Stuff* that, at 40 years old, Brown's suspect "has probably done more than just watch. If I had to vote, I'm voting killer."

While Brown concedes that the man from St Charles may not be the killer in the La Crosse drownings, his existence demonstrates that such a killer may exist.

Los Angeles' South Side Slayer

Homicide Detective Jeffrey Steinhoff was moved by the death of Princess Berthomieux. On 9 March 2002, her naked body was found dumped in bushes in an alley in the 8100 block of South Van Ness Avenue in Inglewood. She had been strangled. In her short life the runaway from Hawthorne had been in and out of foster homes. The 14-year-old was working as a prostitute when she was killed. There were no further clues to her murderer and she seemed destined to be just one of the dozens of young women in her profession who died at an unknown hand in that area of Los Angeles.

For over two years the case remained cold. But in December 2004, the sheriff's crime lab linked traces of the DNA found on her body to those taken from the bodies of two other slain women. The first was 26-year-old Mary Lowe who was found on 1 November 1987 in an alley in the 8900 block of South Hobart Boulevard. Last seen at a Halloween party at a club the night before, she had been shot in the chest. In 1979, she had been arrested for prostitution though, at the time of her death, she was working as a receptionist and was living at home with her parents. The second was 35-year-old Valerie McCorvey. Like Princess Berthomieux, she had been strangled. Her body was found on 11 July 2003, dumped near the corner of 108th Street and Denver Avenue.

Valerie McCorvey had dropped out of high school and by her late teens she had a drug habit. She went into rehab and at one time she had a job helping other addicts kick the habit. But the lure of drugs was too powerful, even though she had strong family ties to her father, who had divorced from her mother, and her aunt Mary Taylor. Four months before she died, Valerie left a message on her aunt's answering machine, saying she was okay. She was found just one block away from her regular hang-out on Figueroa Street. She had been sexually assaulted, though she was still wearing her familiar brown pants and blue leotard.

Initially the police thought an ex-boyfriend was responsible as he was less than forthcoming when they interviewed him. But then the DNA evidence connected her to the murderer of Princess Berthomieux and Mary Lowe.

The following year, another match was made to DNA found on the body of an earlier victim. This was 25-year-old Bernita Sparks, whose body was found on 16 April 1987, covered with garbage, inside a dustbin in an alley in the 9400 block of South Western Avenue. The night before, she had told her mother that she was going out to buy a packet of cigarettes. She was found fully clothed and had no arrests for prostitution. There was evidence that she had been sexually assaulted. She had also suffered blunt-force trauma to the head, been strangled and shot in the chest. The bullet came from the same .25-calibre handgun that had shot Mary Lowe. Ballistics linked the bullets with six other handgun killings in the 1980s.

Twenty-nine-year cocktail waitress Debra Jackson was last seen leaving a friend's home in Lynwood to take a bus back to her apartment in South-Central. A few days later, on 10 August

1985, her decomposing body was found fully clothed and covered with a carpet in an alley in the 100 block of West Gage Avenue, west of South Vermont Avenue. She had been shot twice in the chest.

A year later, 35-year-old Henrietta Wright was also killed by two shots to the chest. On 12 August 1986, her body was found in the 2500 block of West Vernon Avenue. She was fully clothed, though her shoes were missing. Her body wrapped in a blanket and covered with a mattress. In 1982, Wright had been arrested for prostitution at 47th Street and Figueroa Street in 1982. Again she had been sexually assaulted.

On 14 August 1986, the body of 36-year-old Thomas Steele, a resident of San Diego, was found dumped in the road near 71st Street and Halldale Avenue in Los Angeles. He was fully clothed and had been shot once behind the right ear. He seems to have been in L.A. for the day to visit his sister and detectives believe that his death was drug related, but in 1978 he had been arrested in Sacramento on prostitution and pimping charges. He was the only male victim.

The body of 23-year-old Barbara Ware was found fully clothed in an alley in the 1300 block of East 56th Street on 10 January 1987. A plastic bag was draped over her head and upper torso, and she was covered with rubbish. Five years before, she had been arrested for prostitution.

Lachrica Jefferson, aged 22, was found by LA County Sheriff's deputies in an alley in the 2000 block of West 102nd Street in Lennox on 30 January 1988. She died from two gunshots to the chest and was fully clothed.

The body of 17-year-old Alicia Alexander was found naked in an alley in the 1700 block of 43rd Street at Western Avenue on 11 September 1988. Again she died from two gunshots to the chest and was covered with a mattress.

There were now ten related victims. The police had to ask themselves: was there a serial killer on the loose? If there was, they were going to have a hard time catching him. The DNA matched none on any criminal database and the investigation ground to a halt.

The 1980s cases were lodged with the LAPD's cold-case unit hat was formed in 2001 and had begun to work its way through more than 9,000 unsolved murders. But with the current Berthomieux and McCorvey cases now under investigation, it seemed that the same killer had been going about his business unimpeded for 18 years.

At the time, the early killings were thought to be the work of the "Southside Slayer" who was credited with at least 14 murders between September 1983 and May 1987 and had never been caught. The victims had been black women, largely prostitutes. They had been tortured with superficial cuts before being strangled or stabbed. As in the case of Bernita Sparks he exhibited a "pattern of overkill". Again bodies were dumped in alleyways, on residential streets and in schoolyards. At least three others are considered possible victims, and three women managed to survive the predations of the slayer.

The first on the list attributed to the slayer was Loletha Prevot, whose body was found in Los Angeles on 4 September 1983. Then on 1 January 1984 the body of Patricia Coleman was dumped in Inglewood. The third victim, Sheila Burton – aka Sheila Burris – was found on 18 November. Then the murder rate increased. Frankie Bell was killed on New Year's Day 1985. The mutilated body of Patricia Dennis was found on 11 February. On 20 March Sheily Wilson was murdered in Inglewood. Lillian Stoval joined the list on the 23rd. Patsy Webb was murdered on 15 April and Cathy Gustavson on 28 July. Only one victim survived, but she suffered a vicious beating that left her in a coma.

On 6 August the slayer's next intended victim managed to escape by jumping from his moving car. She told detectives that her attacker was a black man in his early thirties, who wore a baseball cap and had a moustache. His description and sketch were circulated, but brought no new leads. Nor did their publication discourage the attacker. On 15 August, the body of Gail Ficklin was found. On 6 November the killer moved a little further south to dump Gayle Rouselle's body in Gardena, but on 7 November he returned to his regular stamping grounds to dump Myrtle Collier's corpse in LA proper. Twenty-three-year-old

Nesia McElrath's body was found on 19 December. Three days later the mutilated corpse of Elizabeth Landcraft was found. Then on 26 December, Gidget Castro's body was found to the east in Commerce.

On 5 January 1986, the Southside Slayer despatched Tammy Scretchings. Then on 10 January, a 27-year-old prostitute was viciously beaten. A male acquaintance who tried to protect her was stabbed. Their descriptions of the man matched that given by the women who had leapt from his car on 6 August.

On 11 February, Lorna Reed's body was found in San Dimas, 30 miles to the east of Inglewood in the foothills of the San Gabriel Mountains. On 26 May, the body of known prostitute Verna Williams was found in the stairwell of a Los Angeles elementary school, and on 3 November Trina Chaney's body was found in Watts. It was then that those killings officially attributed to the Southside Slayer stopped, though in January 1988 police added to the list Carolyn Barney. She had been killed on 29 May 1987.

Three other killings were thought to have been the work of the Southside Slayer, but were not officially on the list. There was 22-year-old Loretta Jones, whose body was dumped in an alley on 15 April 1986. She had no criminal record. Three weeks later, an unidentified white woman, aged between 25 and 30, was found in a dumpster. She had been strangled. Then on 24 July, the body of 22-year-old Canoscha Griffin was found in the grounds of a local high school. She had been stabbed.

By early 1988, police were backing off their initial body count, when Charles Mosley was convicted for one of the 1986 murders. Los Angeles County Sheriff's Deputy Ricky Ross was arrested in connection with the slayings. He was cleared, but his career was ruined by the press coverage. Then the cases of Sheila Burton, Gail Ficklin, Nesia McElrath, Gidget Castro and Caroline Barney were "closed" with the arrest of two other serial killers thought to be responsible. However, these and other suspects were cleared of the remaining 15 cases, leaving at least one vicious killer still at large – and probably two.

During the lull between 1987, when the police had first closed the Southside Slayer's victim list and 2002 murder of Princess Berthomieux, the killer may have simply moved his operation to Pomona, California, just five miles from San Dimas where the Southside Slayer dumped the body of Lorna Reed in 1986. In the early 1990s, a serial killer was murdering African-American prostitutes there. In 1993 alone, four women who worked Holt Avenue, the local hooker strip, were found dead. The deaths of three more women over the next two years were thought to be the work of the Pomona Strangler. Although the police were reluctant to attribute them to a serial killer, in April 1994 the FBI were called in, but could do little to help.

The police were overwhelmed at the time. In the 1980s, the Los Angeles County Sheriff's office alone had the murders of some 50 black women on their books. No one was ever charged, but there were reams of suspects.

"We have three books of people they were interested in," says Sergeant Cliff Shepard. The problem was the advent of crack cocaine. "It took hold all over the city. It was an explosion down here, and the murder of women suddenly increased and gangs really started taking off."

Then there seemed to be a breakthrough. On 3 August 2005, Detective Jeffrey Steinhoff, who was still working on the Berthomieux case, got a call from a Fresno County District Attorney's Office investigator. He had in custody a 65-year-old repo man named Roger Hausmann, who had been accused of kidnapping two teenage girls. Around 15 years before, he had been a suspect in a spate of prostitute killings. The two girls who accused him of abduction said that he had boasted of going to LA to kill whores.

Interviewed in jail by *LA Weekly*, Hausmann denied the allegations. He said that the police had it in for him because he was a converted Jew who liked black women. But then he had little respect for women. Divorced at least three times, he referred to his exes as "hos", calling one "Peanut Butter" because she "spread so easily".

Despite Hausmann's denials, Steinhoff believed that he was a strong suspect.

"Hausmann admitted that he has killed people and wrapped them in carpet in the Los Angeles area," said Steinhoff. "One victim was covered with a carpet, one covered with a blanket, one covered with a trash bag, and three were covered with debris."

Hausmann also got a traffic ticket in Inglewood three months before Princess Berthomieux's death and in the kidnapping case, it was said, he exhibited violent tendencies. Hausmann had been at work, driving around Fresno looking for cars to repossess, when he offered to give the 17-year-old girlfriend of his son Dana and her 16-year-old friend a lift home. After taking them to McDonald's, he said that he would drop off the older girl first. But the younger one did not feel safe with him and insisted on being taken home first. Hausmann lost his temper and punched her in the face, then he said that he was going to drive out on the highway and kill them both.

They tried to flee, but Hausmann pulled the younger girl back into the truck by the hair. Eventually she escaped by jumping from the vehicle, which was doing over 30 miles an hour, and suffered cuts and bruises. He was caught four days later hiding in the closet in a friend's flat. When he refused to come out, the police Tasered him. Then, he claimed, the police had beaten him up.

He also accused the two girls of beating him up and robbing him. The older girl, he said, also made it clear that she wanted to have sex with him, even though she was under age. She was involved in a ring of prostitutes, he said, and tried to extort money from him.

A native of Santa Rosa, some 200 miles to the north of Fresno, Hausmann had a record of having sex with minors. His first wife was 15 when he married her; he was 19. Twenty years later, in 1979, he was arrested in Fresno for having sex with a minor, but escaped prosecution when he married her. According to Steinhoff, Hausmann was also arrested in Lynwood, South LA, in 1976 on suspicion of committing lewd acts against a child. He was arrested again in 1982 in Bakersfield for pimping and enticing an underage girl into prostitution.

Steinhoff also unearthed a series of weapons offences. In 1968,

1972 and 1979, Hausmann was arrested for carrying a concealed weapon; in 1971 and 1976 for exhibiting a deadly weapon; in 1981 and 1982 for carrying a loaded firearm; and in 1985 for assault with a deadly weapon in Los Angeles.

Then in 1991, Hausmann came to the attention of Fresno Police Department. The local sheriff's office had set up a joint task force to investigate the deaths of 25 black women, aged 18 to 30, over a period of 13 years. Some of them were known prostitutes and their bodies were found dumped in fields, empty lots, abandoned houses and irrigation canals.

According to the police, Hausmann knew some of the women.

"He admitted that he dated some of the girls," said Detective Doug Stokes.

A prostitute also accused him of hitting her with a steam iron and saying: "You're harder to kill than the other ones." A witness also said that he had heard Hausmann say: "This one is hard to kill."

Hausmann claimed that the prostitute had hit him with the steam iron first. He also accused her of hitting him over the head with a bronze ashtray and stealing jewellery from him. According to Hausmann, it was a male friend who had knocked her out, tied her up and suggesting rolling her body up in a carpet and dropping her in a lake. Hausmann claimed that he had gallantly rescued the woman. In court, though, he pleaded no contest to false imprisonment and assault with a deadly weapon and served two and a half years in jail.

Detective Stokes said that of all the suspects the Fresno police task force investigated in the case of the murders of the 25 black women, Hausmann was "probably the one we looked at closest or the longest". Nevertheless, the investigation was disbanded after ten weeks. No arrests were made. However, DNA testing was not available at time. Evidence in the cases is now being reviewed.

Released in November 1993, Hausmann's pattern of violence continued. Stivette Street, the mother of Hausmann's son, accused him of grabbing her by the throat when he thought he was cheating on her and beating her head against the wall on another occasion. She also said that he had kidnapped the boy and took him to Los Angeles. Another ex-wife said that he had tried to choke her when she refused to have sex with him and threatened to kill one of her friends. Again, Hausmann denies ever using violence, though he claimed to have ridden with the Hell's Angels for eight years, but quit because they "used to talk trash about my black women".

He also claimed to have been a drug dealer and a pimp, both in Fresno and LA. He boasted to *LA Weekly* that he hung out at now-defunct restaurant at Florence Avenue and Figueroa Street. His stable of girls worked out of bars and hotels along the Miracle Mile and in Beverly Hills. From 1960 to 1995, he sold cocaine out of a "rock house" on 19th Street in LA and in Fresno. But then he became a Christian and, he says, flushed two kilos of cocaine "still in the Medellin Cartel wrappers" down the lavatory. That year, he was arrested once again for assault with a firearm and Steinhoff maintains that his arrest record shows that he travelled frequently between Fresno and Los Angeles.

In his defence Hausmann maintains that he had been beaten and victimized by the Fresno police because he stopped supplying the cops with drugs. One local officer also called him a "nigger-lover Jew-boy slave" because of his predilection for black women. In May 2003 he claims he was molested by the police and dropped on his head in the street when he tried to repossess a pick-up truck legally. The police failed to come to his aid, he said, when he was hit over the head with a large kitchen pot and robbed. The police laughed at him when he turned up at the station to report the matter and complained to a judge about his treatment.

Steinhoff sought a court order to take a DNA sample from Hausmann as a suspect.

"There is a link between each of the homicides," Steinhoff wrote in his affidavit. "Based on my training and experience, I believe that Hausmann is a suspect in these homicides. Hausmann admitted that he killed people and wrapped them in carpet in the Los Angeles area."

However, when a sample of Hausmann's saliva was tested it did not match the DNA taken from the body of Princess Berthomieux.

LA County coroner's office has now set up a special serial homicide team consisting of a criminologist, two pathologists and four investigators specially trained by the FBI's Behavioural Science Unit who study serial killers, their traits and profiles. The coroner's office also hooked up to the FBI's Violent Criminal Apprehension Program (VICAP), a computer database that seeks to identify similarities in violent crimes that have been committed by the same violent offenders.

Using the latest computer techniques, investigators have begun sorting through 800 autopsy and investigative reports involving the deaths of women in Los Angeles since 2002. They made separate lists of those who had been dumped in fields, alleys or on the sides of roads. Some women had been strangled or stabbed. Others had been bound and gagged. In some cases their bodies had been covered with plastic bags. Some had been prostitutes; others drug users – quite often both. They came up with a list of 38 that could possibly be the victim of a serial killer or killers. Then the FBI came in, concentrating on the first 18 cases involving African-Americans.

"Nobody had ever looked at them all because of the sheer number we get," said Captain Ed Winter, head of the coroner's serial homicide team. "When you start looking at them, there are similarities. There is no one else tracking this. The goal of this unit is to track possible serial-related homicides and supply law enforcement with data to help solve the murders."

The list was circulated to police agencies in the area and detectives were asked to investigate whether there were any similarities between cases on the list and those they were working on. An investigator from the coroner's special unit now turns out every time a body is dumped in LA County.

Another weapon in the investigators' armoury is Proposition 69, which was approved by California voters in 2004. It allows authorities to collect DNA samples from anyone convicted of a felony and from all adults arrested on suspicion of murder and sex crimes. In 2009, the law will be extended to include any person arrested on suspicion of any felony and some misdemeanours, regardless of whether they are convicted.

Meanwhile the Figueroa corridor, a 30-block span of one of South LA's most dangerous territories that runs from Vernon Avenue to 120th Street, will continue to provide plenty of victims for the serial killers at large. It is peppered with $15-an-hour hotels, crack houses, liquor stores and used-car lots, along with Gospel, Baptist and Evangelical churches. The prostitutes lean on fences, hang out in phone booths or strut down the sidewalks, waving to catch the eye of eager Johns who drive slowly by. Some of the prostitutes are local; others come in from outside or bounce back and forth between LA and Las Vegas. Most are African-American, aged range between 14 and 50. Some are "strawberries" – a women who turn the occasional trick to feed a drug habit. Rates are low. A blow job costs $20 to $40. Oral stimulation followed by full sex costs about $50. The LAPD's Southeast vice unit gets regular calls from residents complaining about prostitutes blowing Johns in cars outside their homes.

There is less prostitution in the area than there was in the 1980s, when the Southside Slayer was at work. Then dozens of girls could be seen hanging out on corners with their pimps. Now things have changed. Most of the women work on their own without pimps. They stand on the corners alone, away from other girls. There is less competition that way, but it also makes them more vulnerable. Some of the women carry pocket knives, screwdrivers or box cutters. Most don't.

"These girls think they are good judges of character," says Southeast Division Sergeant Roy Gardner. "But these guys don't have on their foreheads that he is a serial rapist killer."

And there are no shortage of them. The LAPD cold-case unit has gone back to processing the 1980s cases. Recently they have added another possibly related case to the list – that of 21-year-old Diane Johnson, whose partially clothed body was found by two passing motorists on 9 March 1987, in a roadway construction area west of the Harbor Freeway at 10217 South Grand Avenue. She had been strangled.

But some progress has been made. Shepard says that DNA evidence now possibly links two of the Southside Slayer victims with two suspects who are currently in custody on unrelated charges. Whether either one will ever be charged depends on the results of months, possibly years of investigation.

In November 2004, 38-year-old pizza deliveryman Chester Turner was charged with the murders of 13 women between 1987 and 1998, ten of them in the Figueroa Street area. Victims were largely homeless women, prostitutes or drug users. He sexually assaulted them before strangling them and dumping their bodies in alleys, vacant buildings or, in one case, a portable toilet. Among them was Diane Johnson. Intriguingly, cat hair was found on some of the victims, as it had been on some of the victims of the Southside Slayer.

Turner was caught after being required to supply a sample to California's Combined DNA Index System after he was sentenced to eight years in prison for sexually assaulting a 47-year-old woman in March 2002. DNA may yet help track down the killer of Princess Berthomieux – and the killers of all the other victims in South LA, Pomona and Fresco who are still at large.

Madison's Capital City Murders

On a May evening in 1968, the body of 18-year-old Christine Rothschild was found hidden behind some shrubbery outside Sterling Hall, the mathematics building on North Carter Street in the campus of the University of Wisconsin at Madison. The discovery was made by a male student and it was thought that she had been killed that morning while out jogging. She had been stabbed 12 times in the chest.

Christine had enrolled at the University of Wisconsin the year before after having graduated with honours from Senn High School in Chicago, where she had lived in a modest home on the North Side with her father – the president of a brokerage company – her mother and her three sisters. A good student, Christine enjoyed her classes and hoped to become a journalist when she graduated. She was good-looking, with long blonde-brown hair and earned money in the summer as a model for department store catalogues.

The murder weapon was never found and, throughout the summer, one suspect after another was discounted. At one point a $5,000 reward was offered for information relating to Christine's murder. This solicited no new leads.

Any further progress in the Rothschild case was then overtaken by events. At around 3.29 a.m. on 29 June 1969, a massive explosion rocked the Capital City campus. Two sticks of dynamite had been detonated outside the Administration Building. More than 700 windows were shattered. The blast created a four-foot crater in the reinforced concrete floor of the entranceway and the ceiling of the room underneath fell down. Fortunately, the late hour meant that the area was deserted and there were no casualties. No one claimed responsibility for the explosion and, even though the faculty offered a reward of $10,000, no one was ever arrested for the crime.

Just over a year later, on 24 August 1970, Sterling Hall – where Christine Rothschild's body had been found – was also bombed. A 33-year-old researcher died in the blast. This time there suspects and warrants were issued, charging four men with conspiracy, sabotage and destruction of government property. Three of them were arrested and convicted of the bombing, but it has never been established if the two bombings were connected.

By then Christine Rothschild's murder was forgotten about, except by those who were close to her. It languished in the "cold-case" file for eight years until 21 July 1976. Then memories were jogged when the charred and decomposed remains of a young woman were found by real estate assessors in a gully beside Old Sauk Pass Road some 14 miles northwest of Madison.

A post mortem revealed that the woman had been dead for at least ten days, but the corpse was in such a bad state that the cause of death could not be established. However, dental records and a fractured collarbone allowed her to be identified. She was 20-year-old Debra Bennett. She had been staying in the Cardinal Hotel downtown Madison after being evicted from her apartment. A native of Ridgeway in Iowa County, she had only been in the area a short time. This left detectives with little evidence and no suspects. Then mysteriously, three weeks after Debra's body had been discovered, her room key was mailed back to the hotel. Tantalizing though this was, it moved the case little further ahead. There was no note with the key, no return address on the envelope, nor any other identifying marks. The murder of Debra Bennett then joined Christine Rothschild's in the "cold case" file.

In the summer of 1978 the body of another young woman was found in a shallow grave on Woodland Road in Waunakee, a small town nine miles north of Madison. She had been killed by a blow with a blunt object to the head and had been dead for more than three days. After two days the body was identified as that of 18-year-old Julie Ann Hall, who had close ties to the University of Wisconsin. On 1 May 1978, she had got a job as a library assistant on the campus. She was last seen on a Friday night at the Main King Tap, a bar near Capital Square in Madison. Again, there was little evidence and no suspects.

Julie Speerschneider, aged 20, spent most of the evening of 27 March 1979 at the 602 Club, a bar at 602 University Avenue. Then she decided to hitch-hike to a friend's house, but she disappeared on the way. Soon after, a man called the police and told them that he had given Julie a lift. He had recognized her from her description in the newspapers and on the media. She had been with a male companion, he said, and he had dropped off at the corner of Brearly and Johnson. He gave a detailed description of the man, but detectives were unable to identify him, even though Julie had many friends at the time of her disappearance. She had worked at the Red Caboose Day Care Center, where she was described her as friendly and reliable. Relatives and friends clubbed together to offer a reward and they even consulted a psychic in hope of finding her.

Julie Speerschneider had still not been found when, in April 1980, the dead body of Susan LeMahieu, aged 24, was discovered lying in the weeds near the Madison Arboretum. Six years before she had graduated from Madison's East High School, though she was physically handicapped and mildly retarded. When she had

gone missing on 15 December 1979, police di~~~
play, believing that she might have grown cont~~~
dered off because of her mental incapacity. Like Chr~~~
child, she had died of multiple stab wounds to the ch~~~

One year later, 16-year-old Charles Byrd was hiking al~~~
Yahara River when he came across the remains of Julie Speer~~~
neider. She had been missing for over two years and her body was
so badly decomposed that it was impossible to establish the cause
of death. In July 1981, the body of Shirley Stewart, a 17-year-old
who worked at the Dean Clinic, was found dumped in woodlands
to the north of Madison. She had been missing for over 18
months and, again, her body was so badly decomposed that
the cause of death could not be determined.

Another year passed. Then on 2 July 1982, 19-year-old student
Donna Mraz was on her way home from a diner on State Street,
where she worked as a waitress to pay for her tuition. Behind
Camp Randall Stadium, she was attacked and stabbed repeatedly. She never regained consciousness. According to the police
was "to all intents and purposes . . . dead when she hit the
ground". There was no evidence of sexual assault and her pay
cheque, money and keys were left on the body. Again the police
was confronted by a motiveless killing with no witnesses and little
hope of any promising leads.

Over two years later, Janet Raasch, aged 20, went missing after
a friend had dropped her off on Highway 54 in the town of Buena
Vista on 11 October 1984. She was a business major in her third
year at the University of Wisconsin and also worked at the DeBot
Center on campus. Five weeks later, her partially clad body was
found by deer hunters in woods southeast of Highway 54, around
two miles from where she was dropped. Once again decomposition made it impossible to ascertain the cause of death. But
although the coroner was unable to specify the exact time of
death, he said she could have died between a week and 10 days
before her body was found. She had been missing for over five
weeks.

There the murders ended. It is thought that they were committed by the same hand. In each case there was no clear motive

or the attack. All the victims were young women, who wore their hair long and parted it in the same way. This was reminiscent of the victims of the notorious serial killer Ted Bundy, who went to the electric chair in 1989. They were all associated in some way with the University of Wisconsin either attending classes there, or living or working on campus. Their bodies were found in and around Madison and concealed in wooded areas a little way from a road.

In 1984, America's most prolific serial killer Henry Lee Lucas confessed to several of the murders, but later recanted. Lucas had a long history of random slayings, but he also had a reputation for making false confessions. Given that he was in prison when several of the murders were committed, it seems unlikely that he was involved.

Although the cases are reviewed periodically, Captain James Lamar of the Sheriff's Department Operations Division in Portage County, Wisconsin, pointed out: "There's not much investigators can do without new information."

Although everyone was relieved that the series of killings seems come to an end, without the arrest and conviction of the culprit, no one knows whether he has actually stopped, or moved on to some other area or found some better way to conceal his activities. Of course he could be dead or incarcerated. Serial killers rarely give up of their own volition.

Massachusetts' Murderers

The towns of Marlborough, Massachusetts and neighbouring Hudson appear to have a serial killer on their hands.

On 24 September 2003, pupils from the Hillside School in Marlborough were clearing a track for a cycle path in a wooded area behind the school when they discovered the remains of an unidentified woman. She was white, aged between 20 and 35, and between 4 foot 11 inches to 5 foot 1 inch tall.

The woman had been in her shallow grave for up to three years before her discovery and her body was badly decomposed. But the police deduced that she had been wearing blue plaid flannel pyjama pants from "B-Time", a black and red long-sleeved "Guess" shirt made in 2000 and, over it, a dark greenish blue zip-front shirt with blue and white stripes on the sleeves. On her wrist, she wore a gold bracelet with "#1 Mom" engraved on it.

Investigators began searching the area for further clues and on 29 September they found a second shallow grave around 100 yards from the first. This time the remains could be identified. They belonged to 29-year-old Carmen Rudy, who had last been seen at her sister's home 15 miles away in Worcester the previous September. Although the bodies had not been buried at the same time, they were clearly related.

Then on 3 March 2004, a contractor was clearing the undergrowth in the same wooded area, just over the city line in Hudson, when he found the decomposed remains of 33-year-old Dinelia Torres, a resident of nearby Worcester. Forensic examination determined that her body had been buried there three to nine months before. She had been reported missing on 1 November and was identified by dental records. Because of the advanced state of decomposition no cause of death could be established in any of the three slayings.

However, in the case of Torres, the police had a suspect. A year before her body was discovered, she had taken out a restraining order against her ex-boyfriend Robert Toupin, who she claimed had beaten her and threatened to kill her. According the records of Worcester District court, Torres claimed that Toupin had entered her home the morning of 11 March. In the application for a restraining order filed later that day, Torres wrote: "I asked him to stop, he . . . started to punch me all over and I fell to the floor. He started to kick me all over. He would not let me talk. He just continued to hit me all over. After he was done hitting me, he damaged my house. He told me if I called the cops, he will [expletive] kill me."

Toupin was married to a woman who he had been married to since high school and was said to be living with her in Oakham. But records show that Torres and Robert J. Toupin had shared a house on Prospect Street in Worcester, owned by one of Toupin's relatives, and Torres' family maintain that the couple had a romantic relationship.

However, Dinelia Torres was a known drug user with convictions for prostitution. Carmen Rudy lived a similar high-risk lifestyle. The victims were all of roughly the same height, weight, age and appearance and, while Dinelia Torres' body was found 1¼ miles from the other two, both sites were just off Interstate 495.

"We're operating on the theory that they may be related," said Middlesex District Attorney Martha Coakley. "It's just too much coincidence . . . I have to say that that increases our concern that the killings are related, and that we may be dealing with someone who fits that description of a serial killer."

The Boston FBI office offered the DA's office the services of America's top serial-killer hunters at the bureau's National Center for the Analysis of Violent Crime in Quantico, Virginia. Meanwhile the Worcester Police Department began reviewing its four adult and twelve juvenile missing-person cases. Investigators then looked into possible connection with other murders in Massachusetts, such as that of 37-year-old Sheila Cormier of Leominster who was missing for years before her body was pulled from a swamp in Lunenberg in 2001. That same year, 17-year-old Latasha Cannon was found with her throat slashed on the grounds of the Raytheon Company in Bedford. And the following year, 19-year-old Melissa Doherty was found bound and burned in Andover. Authorities were also checking out missing person reports and unsolved cases throughout the state.

Three weeks after the discovery of Dinelia Torres, the police established the identity of the first body. She was 29-year-old Betzaida Montalvo, a drug addict and mother of five. She had been last been seen in late spring of 2003. Investigations had been hampered by the fact she had never been officially reported missing, but her body was finally identified from dental records. All three women were known drug users and were connected to prostitution in the South Main Street area of Worchester.

Then two prostitutes claimed that they were driven out along the I–290 which leads from Worchester to Marlborough by a client in a pick-up who pulled a cut-throat razor and attacked them. The women said they fought the man off and escaped.

In May 29-year-old Manuel Bonillawas arrested for three attacks on prostitutes in Worcester in March and April. He allegedly slashed two women and attempted to strangle the third. However, the authorities made no connection between him and the murders.

On 13 September 2004, the body of another prostitute was found 80 miles away in York County, Maine. Forty-two-year-old Wendy Morello had been stuffed in a trash can in a wooded area. She was from Millbury, two miles outside Worcester, and had been missing for a week. A drug addict, she was a mother of two and the police initially believed that she was murdered locally before being transported to Maine and dumped there. Later, it was concluded that her slaying murder was not connected with the other killings.

The police in Massachusetts had had similar cases before. From April to September of 1988 a serial murderer haunted New Bedford, Massachusetts, some 60 miles from Worchester. He also picked on drug addicts and prostitutes, dumping the bodies of his victims along the highways outside the city. He clocked up some 11 victims, though two of the bodies are still missing.

The first victim found was 30-year-old Debra Madeiros. She was last seen when she walked out on her boyfriend on 27 May 1988. On 2 July 1988, a motorist stopped to relieve himself near an exit ramp on I–140 and found a partially clothed skeleton. The remains were identified at those of Debra Madeiros in February 1989.

Thirty-six-year-old Nancy Paiva went missing on 11 July 1988. Nineteen days later, a body was found near an exit ramp from I–195, but her remains were not identified until December, by which time her killer had moved on. Both the I–140 and the I–195 connect to the I–495, which runs past Marlborough and Hudson.

Deborah DeMello, aged 34, also went missing on 11 July 1988. Her body was found on 8 November, near the exit ramp on I–195 where Nancy Paiva's remains were discovered. Three days later a road crew working on the I–195 found the body of 25-year-old Dawn Mendes. She had gone missing a week before.

On 1 December 1988, the fully clothed skeleton of 25-year-old Deborah McConnell was found just off the I–140. She had been missing since May. Police came upon her fully clothed skeleton during an extensive roadway search prompted by the other killings. Then the body of 28-year-old Rochelle Clifford was found on 10 December 1988 by hunters in a quarry near the I–195, close to where Nancy Paiva and Deborah DeMello had been dumped. She had been missing since April.

The body of Robin Rhodes was discovered on 28 March 1989, directly across the I–140 from the spot where Debra Madeiros had been found ten months before. Three days later, the body of Mary Santos was found, but not along an interstate. She was found along Route 88 which runs from Fall River to Horseneck Beach several miles outside New Bedford, but the other similarities between her murder and the others led the police to conclude that it was the work of the same man. She had been missing since July 1988. The last body to be found was that of Sandy Botelho, aged 24, whose remains were recovered along I–195. She was found on 24 April 1989, after going missing the previous August.

The police concluded that two other women were victims of the same killer. They were 19-year-old Christine Monteiro, who was last seen in May 1988, and 34-year-old Marilyn Roberts, who went missing in June.

At that time the population of New Bedford was less that 100,000 and, unsurprisingly given their similar lifestyles, several of the victims knew each other. Marilyn Roberts and Christine Monteiro were neighbours. Rochelle Clifford was last seen in the company of Nancy Paiva's boyfriend, though he was cleared of both killings. Robin Rhodes also knew both Rochelle Clifford and Nancy Paiva, as well as Mary Santos and Dawn Mendes.

The police pursued two suspects. One was Tony "Flat Nose" DeGrazia. He was arrested in May 1989 for the violent rape of several New Bedford prostitutes. He was released on bail in January 1990 after the authorities could find no evidence linking him to the murders. DeGrazia was later arrested again for raping another prostitute. He committed suicide soon after posting bond a second time.

In August 1990 a grand jury indicted attorney Kenny Ponte for the murder of Rochelle Clifford. Earlier there had been an incident involving Ponte, Clifford, another man and a gun. Ponte was a known drug user who had other run-ins with the law. In September 1988 – around the time the killings stopped – Ponte shut his law office and moved to Florida. However, in March 1991, special prosecutor Paul Buckley dropped the charges against Ponte on the grounds that he had found no evidence on which to proceed.

There is speculation that the New Bedford serial killer is the same man as Portugal's "Lisbon Ripper", who began killing drug-addicted prostitutes in Portugal, the Netherlands, Belgium, Denmark and the Czech Republic around the time the New Bedford killings ended. New Bedford has a sizable Portuguese immigrant population. Because his victims in Europe are so widely dispersed, it is thought that he works as a long-distance lorry driver. This would explain why the New Bedford victims were all found near interstates or other main roads – and it may also connect him to the I–495 killings in Marlborough and Hudson. Neither the I–495, the New Bedford slayer nor the Lisbon Ripper has ever been identified.

Newark's Nixings

In April 1998, Essex County set up a task force to re-examine the cases of 14 African-American women murdered over the previous five years. The women's bodies were all found in abandoned buildings or vacant lots within a few miles of one another. The women were aged between 19 and 37. Most were prostitutes. However, the method of murder varied. Some were stabbed, while others were strangled or suffocated.

Nine of the 14 were killed in Newark, two in nearby East Orange and three in Irvington. In neighbouring Union County, the country prosecutor appointed a homicide detective to determine if four unsolved slayings of black female prostitutes between 1988 and 1994 could be linked to the Essex County slayings.

New Haven Homicides

Eleven-year-old Diane Toney was last seen alive as she was watching the "Freddy Fixer" parade in the Hill section of New Haven, Connecticut on 18 May 1969. Five months later her fractured skull was found in a wooded area off Route 80 in North Guilford. It was clear that she had been beaten to death with a rock. The rest of her skeleton was later found in the same woods, wrapped in the green polka-dot dress she had been wearing when she disappeared.

By then 10-year-old Mary Mount was abducted from New Canaan, Connecticut. She was last seen on 27 May 1969, chasing her kitten. Her body was found on 17 June in the woods by the Norwalk Reservoir in Wilton, less than five miles away. She had also been beaten to death with a rock.

Three days after Mary Mount went missing, 14-year-old Dawn Cave had a fight with her sister and stormed out of her home in Bethany, some 35 miles away. Her body was discovered in a meadow northwest of New Haven two weeks after Mary Mount's. Again she had been beaten to death with a rock. Post mortem examinations revealed that the girls had been killed shortly after they had been kidnapped.

New York City police became involved on 9 July, when nine-year-old Wanda Waldonada was raped and strangled in Brooklyn. Witnesses recalled seeing a white car near the scene of the crime. In Connecticut, a white car with New York licence plates had been seen in both New Canaan and Bethany. Its driver had been reported for attempting to lure children away from their homes. But this tantalizing "lead" took homicide investigators nowhere in their search for suspects.

Then in September 1970, 5-year-old Jennifer Noon went

missing as she walked home from her school in New Haven, Connecticut, to her home to have lunch. Eight days later her body was found dumped in the woods in the Evergreen Avenue section of Hamden, Connecticut, less than five miles away. She too had been beaten to death with a rock.

Lorry driver Harold Meade was the prime suspect in all four Connecticut murders. He was sentenced to life in prison in 1972 for beating three mentally retarded residents of the Greater New Haven Regional Center with rocks. After his arrest Meade is said to have told police that the mentally retarded people were not his only victims. Some of the witnesses to the girls' abductions identified him in photo line-ups as well. However, Meade protests his innocence in these cases. He has never been charged with the girls' murders. Nothing connects him to the murder of Wanda Waldonada in Brooklyn or the white car.

Diana Toney remained unburied for 27 years as some of her family refused to believe that the body was hers and her remains were never claimed. They sat in the evidence room until 1996 when the police raised the money to bury her.

Meanwhile, there were more unsolved murders in Connecticut. Between 1975 and 1990, more than a dozen young women were the victims of an unknown killer or killers in the New Haven area. Authorities believe that at least seven were killed by one man. Detectives received a tip-off that a man named Roosevelt Bowden was responsible. A violent man, he fatally stabbed his one-year-old daughter Tabitha. Prosecutors agreed to a plea bargain for manslaughter carrying a maximum of 15 years in prison. In July 1986, Bowden was paroled.

The New Jersey Sea-Shore Slayings

Between September 1965 and August 1966, there were a series of unsolved murders along the Atlantic shore of Monmouth and Ocean Counties in New Jersey. There were indications that, in each case, the killer was the same man – though 40 years later detectives seem no closer to identifying him.

At 9 p.m. on 15 September 1965, 18-year-old high school senior Mary Klinsky left her home in West Keansburg to mail a letter to her fiancée in the post box at the end of her street. Seven hours later, her naked, battered body was discovered by motorists 60 miles away near the entrance to Garden State Park. The police said that she had been the victim of an "especially vicious attack".

On 11 February 1966, the body of 17-year-old high-school dropout Joanne Fantazier found on the ice of Yellow Brook in Colt Necks Township. She was fully clothed and there was no sign of sexual assault. Again she had been fatally beaten. Her body was thrown over the side of a road bridge there, but the impact had failed to break the ice as the killer clearly intended.

A month later, Catherine Baker, aged 16, left her home in Edison Township, heading for the local bakery, just a block away. On 14 May, her partially clad body was found in a branch of the Metedeconk River, which ran through a remote area of Jackson Township. The cause of death was a vicious beating, resulting in multiple skull fractures.

The killer then changed tack. The naked body of Paul Benda, aged five, was discovered on 21 June. It was hidden in the high grass along an unmetalled road near Raritan Bay. The boy had been sexually abused and tortured with lighted cigarettes, before being killed with five strokes of an ice pick. The child's clothes were found nearby.

On 7 August 1966, 18-year-old Ronald Sandlin was abducted from his job at a Lakewood service station. His body was dumped in a ditch in Manchester Township. He had been beaten to death with a tyre lever.

Three days later, the car of Dorothy McKenzie, aged 44, was found mired in the sand near a diner on Route 9, which runs through Lakewood. She had been shot. Her body was fully clothed and her pocket book lay untouched beside her on the seat. Although this murder seems unlike the others, the killer had already shown his versatility in the age and sex of his victim and whether he had sexually assaulted his victim or not. He had also used a variety of murder methods and could easily have swapped his ice-pick or tyre lever for a gun. Perhaps we will never know as the killer – or killers – remain at large.

New Orleans' Mad Axeman

In 1918, New Orleans was thrown in a panic when a mad axeman stalked the streets. He has never been convincingly identified, much less caught.

It began early in the morning of 23 May 1918, after New Orleans barber Andrew Maggio returned home drunk. The previous day he had received the papers drafting him into the Army. He was off to fight in World War I and he was not keen to go. As a result, he went out drinking. It was nearly two o'clock when he got home to the rooms he shared with his brother Jake. He noticed nothing untoward, but then he was not in much of a condition to notice anything.

Andrew and Jake's rooms were next door to the home of their married brother, Joseph Maggio and his wife of 15 years, Catherine. The two of them lived behind the small grocery store and bar they ran on the corner of Magnolia and Upperline Streets.

Jake was woken at about 4 a.m. by groaning. The sound was coming through the adjoining wall. Jake got up and knocked on the wall, but got no response. With some difficulty, he managed to wake Andrew. Together they went round to Joseph's house. There was evidence of a break-in. A wooden panel had been chiselled out of the kitchen door. It lay on the ground with the chisel on top of it.

Entering the house through the kitchen, they headed for the bedroom, where they found Joseph lying on the bed with his legs hanging over the side. Catherine lay next to him. When Joseph saw his brothers, he tried to get up, but faltered. His brothers caught him. There were deep gashes on his head and he was barely alive. Quickly checking, they found that Catherine was already dead. She had suffered numerous blows to the head. Her throat was cut from ear to ear and the bed was soaked with her blood. The brothers called an ambulance. But it was too late. By the time it arrived, Joseph was dead.

The first policeman on the scene was Corporal Arthur Hatener. In an initial search of the premises, he found a pile of men's clothing in the middle of the bathroom floor. An axe stood inside the cast-iron bathtub, leaning against one side of it. There was blood on the blade and in the bathtub, as if some attempt had been made to wash the murder weapon. In other accounts, the axe was found on the rear doorstep or under the house. In the bedroom, Corporal Hatener found a straight razor, lying on the bed. It too was covered in blood.

It was obvious that the killer had broken in through the rear door. In the bedroom, he struck Joseph and Catherine on the head with the axe. Then he had gone to work on Mrs Maggio's throat with the razor, almost detaching her head. He had also used the razor on her husband's throat before casting it aside. Perhaps he had been disturbed.

When the coroner arrived, he examined Catherine's body and estimated the time of death to be between two and three in the morning. As the victims were removed, a crowd gathered outside to gawp. A woman who lived nearby stepped forward to tell detectives that she had seen Andrew Maggio outside in the early hours of the morning hours. Andrew and Jake were taken to the police station for questioning. Jake was released the next day, but Andrew remained in custody as the police learned that the razor used on Joseph and Catherine Maggio belonged to him. One of the employees at his barbershop at 123 South Rampart Street had seen him take it when he left the day before. Andrew Maggio said that he had taken it home to repair a nick in it. Although he had not mentioned it before, he then said that he had noticed a man going into his brother's house at around 1.30 a.m., when he had got home. The police did not believe him and he remained their prime suspect.

Other evidence implicated Andrew Maggio. The police had established that the axe had belonged to Joseph and believed that the killer was familiar with the layout of the house. The door to the safe was open and the safe empty. A black cash box which was also empty was found in one corner of the room. The brothers said that Joseph always kept the safe locked. However, there was no indication that the door had been forced. Money in drawers and under Joseph's pillow had not been taken, and Catherine's jewellery, which had been wrapped up and hidden beneath the safe was still there.

Despite their suspicions, the police did not have enough evidence to hold Andrew Maggio and released him.

"It's a terrible thing to be charged with the murder of your own brother when your heart is already broken by his death – when I'm about to go to war, too," he told the *Times-Picayune* newspaper. "I had been drinking heavily. I was too drunk even to have heard any noise next door."

The paper had already caused a sensation by publishing a grisly photograph of the Maggios' blood-stained bedroom.

The story then took a bizarre twist. About a block away from the Maggios' small grocery store, the police found a strange message, written on the pavement in chalk: "Mrs Maggio will sit up tonight just like Mrs Toney."

Although the handwriting was childish, it seemed significant, though no one was sure what it meant. Then a retired detective named Joseph Dantonio came forward. Seven years before, in 1911, he had investigated a series of axe murders in New Orleans. The victims had been Italian grocers. They had been killed in bed and, in each case, the murderer had broken in through a panel in the back door. The first victim had been a man named Cruti, who had no wife. The second, Rosetti was killed with his wife, as was the third, Schiambra. Schiambra's first name was Tony and the police wondered if his wife was the "Mrs Toney" of the chalk message. Perhaps it was the women, not the men, who were the target of the killer.

The buzz in the Italian community was that the Mafia were responsible. Like the 1911 victims, the Maggios were Italian. Perhaps they had not paid their "dues" – the protection money extorted by the crime gang operating in the city. Perhaps they had borrowed money from a Mafioso and had not paid it back. There was only one way the Mafia dealt with defaulters. A number of Italians asked for police protection.

Organized crime had long been a force in New Orleans. In 1890, Police Chief David Hennessy had arrested a Mafia leader and his henchmen, and threatened to expose other Mafiosi in the forthcoming trial. But jury members were bribed and threatened, and the Mafiosi walked free. Finally, when Chief Hennessy was gunned down by Mafia assassins, the citizens of New Orleans became incensed. A mob marched on the prison and lynched 11 mobsters, as a warning to others. After that organized crime went underground.

However, in 1911, a gang known as "The Black Hand" was thought to have been responsible for axe murders. This was a spin-off from Midwestern mob whose activities there had been curtailed by a series of trials in 1907. It got its name from the black-hand symbol that appeared on notes threatening those who did not comply with its demands. Italians were expected to hand over a proportion of their wages to the mobsters. If they did not, they risked harassment, injury and even death. Since the 1911 killings, there was thought to have been a resurgence of organized crime in New Orleans. There were even rumour that the Black Hand had set up a crime school where they taught potential mobsters the finer points of intimidation and murder.

New Orleans had only just recovered from the shock of the Maggios' murders when, two weeks later, the axeman struck again. On the morning of 6 June, John Zanca was delivering bread to a grocer named Louis Besumer. When he reached Besumer's store on La Harpe and Dorgenois, he found it still closed. This was peculiar as 59-year-old Besumer usually opened early and was waiting for his bread.

Zanca went around to the side door and knocked. He heard movement inside and Besumer opened the door. His face was covered in blood. Besumer said he had been attacked and pointed with a quivering hand toward the bedroom. When Zanca went to look, he found Anna Harriet Low lying on the bed under a blood-soaked sheet. She had a terrible head wound and was barely alive. Bloody prints of bare feet led from the bed to a piece of wig – as a Jewish woman, Anna would have kept her real hair covered.

Zanca wanted to call the police, but Besumer tried to stop him. Instead he said he would call a private physician. But Zanca took charge and called the police and an ambulance.

Again the attacker had got in by prying out a panel of the back door with a wood chisel. The murder weapon was a rusty hatchet that belonged to Besumer. Again it was found in the bathroom. However, Besumer was not Italian, but Polish, and he had lived in New Orleans for just three months. Despite the fact that he survived the attack and was conscious and alive, Besumer was unable to give a description of the attack or a coherent account of the attack.

Anna Lowe died of her injuries some time later in Charity Hospital. But before she died, Anna said that she had been attacked by a "mulatto". A black man who Besumer's had employed the previous week was immediately arrested. Although the story he told was inconsistent, he was released when Anna changed her story. She then accused Besumer of attacking her with an axe and of being part of a German conspiracy. He was, she said, a spy. At the time, with a war on, this accusation was explosive. The newspapers ran stories saying that Besumer's grocery store was merely a front for espionage. In his home, there were trunks filled with secret papers, they said, written in German, Russian and Yiddish. The Department of Justice in Washington, D.C. sent agents to investigate, but the allegations were found to be without foundation. Stories also circulated that drugs had been found in Besumer's store. A neighbour said that he and the woman they took to be his wife were opium addicts.

After Besumer left the hospital, he admitted that Anna was not his wife. He then made a peculiar request. He asked to be allowed to investigate his own case. But Besumer was a grocer, not a police officer. Clearly, he had something to hide. The police began to believe that the couple's injuries were the result of a private domestic quarrel that had turned violent and bloody. This theory was supported by the bloody footprints on the floor – both Lowe and Besumer said that they had walked across the floor after the "attack". When the police were called, they had simply concocted the story of an attack to cover their tracks. At first, Lowe had colluded as she was just as culpable as Besumer, but when it became clear that she was going to die, she sought to damage Besumer as much as possible by accusing him of being a spy.

There were some extraordinary holes in the investigation. Although fingerprinting had been used in criminal investigations since 1901, no one dusted in the Maggio or Besumer homes for prints. That, as least, would have indicated if someone else had been present. Nevertheless, Besumer was arrested and charged with murder, though he was clearly not responsible for the attack on the Maggios, or the murders in 1911. But whoever had killed the Maggios was still very much in business, as he demonstrated two months later.

On 5 August, a businessman named Edward Schneider worked late at his office. When he returned home, he expected his wife, who was eight months pregnant, to meet him at the front door. She was not there. When he opened the door, the house was quiet. He called out to his wife, but there was no reply. He began to search the house. In the bedroom, he found his wife, lying on the bed covered in blood. She had a gaping head wound and some of her teeth had been knocked out, but she was alive. Schneider called an ambulance and the police.

Rushed to Charity Hospital, Mrs Schneider lay in critical condition for a few days. But then, slowly, she returned to consciousness. However, she could not give a description of her attacker. When the attack took place, she had been taking a nap, she said. She awoke to see a dark figure standing over her. Then the axe came down repeatedly. That was all she remembered. Happily, the attack did not affect her pregnancy. Three weeks later she gave birth to a healthy baby girl. Meanwhile a newspaper ran headline: "IS AN AXEMAN AT LARGE IN NEW ORLEANS?" They soon got an answer.

Just five days after the Schneider attack, the axeman struck again. On 10 August, Pauline and Mary Bruno were awoken early in the morning by the sound of loud thumps that seemed to be coming from the room of their elderly uncle Joseph Romano. Pauline sat up and saw the tall, dark figure standing right over her bed. She screamed. The man fled. The girls found their uncle with gashes to his head and face, his nightshirt soaked with blood. His room had been ransacked

"I don't know who did it," he said and told Pauline to call Charity Hospital, before lapsing into unconsciousness. He died in hospital soon after.

Detectives discovered that the door panel had been chiselled out and an axe was left in the yard. Romano was Italian, but he was a barber not a grocer. The best description his nieces could give was that the attacker was "dark, tall, heavy-set, wearing a dark suit and a black slouch hat". And he was extremely agile. Pauline said later said that he flew as if he had wings.

"He was awfully light on his feet," she told a journalist.

Panic spread. No one could sleep easy in their bed as that was the very place that the axeman might attack them. With the populace sleepless and alert, there were sightings all over the city. Stories of chisels and axes abounded, and some people claimed they had scared an intruder away. A grocer found a wood chisel on the ground outside his back door. Another said he had found an axe lying in his yard and a panel gouged out of his door. A third, hearing scraping sounds, shot through the door. When police arrived, they found signs of someone chiselling at the wood. There was even a story that "the Axeman" had been seen, strolling around dressed as a woman.

The police were stumped. The attacker left no clues and the victims seemed to have been picked at random. Some were grocers; others were not. All any witness could remember was that he had an almost supernatural ability to get in and out of their homes. No survivor had even seen him well enough to recall a single clear detail and it was not possible to go and arrest a "dark, looming figure". The police did not know whether the attacks were the work of a Mafia assassin, a single madman or a bunch of different people. This was of little help to the newspapers. They fell back on Joseph Dantonio, the retired detective who had investigated the axe murders in 1911. He said: "Students of crime have established that a criminal of the dual personality type may be a respectable, law-abiding citizen. Then suddenly the impulse to kill comes upon him and he must obey it."

This idea had come from Robert Louis Stevenson's 1886 novel *The Strange Case of Dr Jekyll and Mr Hyde* which had made a great impression in the world of criminal detection after it was cited regularly in coverage of the Jack-the-Ripper case two years after publication.

Dantonio believed that the perpetrator of the 1918 attacks was the same man that he had been pursuing seven years before. In the meantime, he thought the man had lived quite respectably before he had suddenly suffered the impulse to kill again. Dantonio speculated that the culprit could live and work alongside his victims and still remain practically invisible.

For seven months, the killer lay low. World War I ended and people got on with their lives. Then he struck again; this time it was across the river in the immigrant suburb of Gretna. On the night of 10 March 1919, screams were heard emanating from the Cortimiglia residence behind their grocery store on the corner of Second Street and Jefferson. A neighbour named Iorlando Jordano went to investigate and found the badly wounded Rosie Cortimiglia kneeling beside her husband Charles, who lay on the floor with a gaping hole in his torso. She was cradling a dead child.

Again, the attacker had broken in by chiselling a panel out of the kitchen door. It also appeared that the attacker had piled timbers by the fence ready to make his escape. Mrs Cortimiglia had been asleep with her two-year-old daughter Mary in her arms when she was attacked. Her husband had grappled with the attacker but had been injured himself. The neighbours said they had heard nothing. A bloodstained axe was found under the step to the kitchen. This time the police looked for fingerprints, but found none. As usual there were no clues, or anything that might help identify or locate the killer. But one thing stood out. Money that had been left out in the open was not taken, so the motive was not robbery. It was the act of a maniac, the coroner said.

Rosie Cortimiglia sustained five wounds to the head, but survived the attack, physically at least. When she recovered, she accused Iorlando Jordano and his son Frank of the attack. They were business rivals who operated from the premises next door.

They were arrested. Unfortunately, Iorlando had told the coroner's court a few days earlier that he had had a premonition that something bad was about to happen to the Cortimiglias.

The water now becomes murky. Newspapers at the time said that Charles had said that he had been attacked by a white man named Frank Jordano. Other accounts say that he disputed his wife's accusation and even left her over it. Still others say that he died of his wounds in hospital. According to one witness, after the attack, Rosie had stated directly that her own husband had done it – though it is unlikely that he inflicted such grievous wounds on himself. Nevertheless, Frank and Iorlando Jordano were convicted – even though Frank's 24-stone frame could hardly have squeezed through the hole in the kitchen door. Frank Jordano was given the death sentence and his father got life imprisonment.

Not everyone was convinced. Three days after the Cortimiglia attack, the editor of the *Times-Picayune* had received a letter that said it was from "Hell". This echoed the letters from Jack the Ripper in 1888 which also said that they were "From Hell".

The letter to the *Times-Picayune* was dated, "Hell, March 13, 1919," and read:

Esteemed Mortal:
They have never caught me and they never will. They have never seen me, for I am invisible, even as the ether that surrounds your earth. I am not a human being, but a spirit and a fell demon from the hottest hell. I am what you Orleanians and your foolish police call the Axeman.

When I see fit, I shall come again and claim other victims. I alone know who they shall be. I shall leave no clue except my bloody axe, besmeared with the blood and brains of him whom I have sent below to keep me company.

If you wish you may tell the police not to rile me. Of course I am a reasonable spirit. I take no offense at the way they have conducted their investigation in the past. In fact, they have been so utterly stupid as to amuse not only me but His Satanic Majesty, Francis Josef, etc. But tell them to beware. Let them not try to discover what I am, for it were better that they were never born than to incur the wrath of the Axeman. I don't think there is any need of such a warning, for I feel sure the police will always dodge me, as they have in the past. They are wise and know how to keep away from all harm.

Undoubtedly, you Orleanians think of me as a most horrible murderer, which I am, but I could be much worse if I wanted to. If I wished, I could pay a visit to your city every night. At will I could slay thousands of your best citizens, for I am in close relationship to the Angel of Death.

Now, to be exact, at 12:15 (earthly time) on next Tuesday night, I am going to visit New Orleans again. In my infinite mercy, I am going to make a proposition to you people. Here it is:

I am very fond of jazz music, and I swear by all the devils in the nether regions that every person shall be spared in whose home a jazz band is in full swing at the time I have mentioned. If everyone has a jazz band going, well, then, so much the better for you people. One thing is certain and that is that some of those people who do not jazz it on Tuesday night (if there be any) will get the axe.

Well, as I am cold and crave the warmth of my native Tartarus, and as it is about time that I leave your earthly home, I will cease my discourse. Hoping that thou wilt publish this, and that it may go well with thee, I have been, am and will be the worst spirit that ever existed either in fact or realm of fantasy.

It was signed: "The Axeman."

No one knew whether this was really from the Axeman or was a hoax. Nor is it plain whether people took it seriously or simply made it an excuse for a party. But the following Tuesday, although it was in the middle of Lent, New Orleans staged what seems to have been one of the biggest parties in its history. One party-giver issued the Axeman a macabre invitation, promising him "four scalps". However, the Axeman was to come in through the bathroom window, which would be open. He was not to go tampering with the kitchen door. Even so, the Axeman did not fulfil his promise. No one was murdered that night – though perhaps everyone was out listening to jazz.

In April, Louis Besumer went on trial for the murder of Anna Lowe, but the war had ended five months before and the spy scare was over. The coroner testified that it would take a man much fitter and more powerful than Besumer to inflict the wounds on himself Besumer had sustained. After ten minutes deliberation, the jury returned a verdict of not guilty.

Although the Axeman had not attacked again in March, as the letter had said, he was still at large. On 10 August Italian grocer Steve Boca was at home asleep in bed when he was hit with an axe. He survived the attack and manage to stumble to a friend's house to get help. He recovered but had no memory of the attack. Again, nothing had been taken, the Axeman had gained entrance by chiselling through the back door and he had left the bloodied axe in the kitchen.

On 3 September, 19-year-old Sarah Laumann was found unconscious in her bed with multiple head wounds. She died later in hospital. No door panel was tampered with to gain entrance, but a bloody axe was left outside an open window. She had been alone in the house and there were no witnesses. The attacker was as elusive as ever.

On 27 October, Mrs Pepitone heard the noise of a scuffle in the bedroom of her husband Mike, which was next door to her own. When she went to find out what the trouble was, she bumped into a man who was making his escape. In his room, Mike Pepitone's head was split open and he lay in a pool of his own blood.

The Pepitones' daughter ran to get the police. First on the scene was Deputy Ben Corcoran. He found Mrs Pepitone standing over her injured husband.

"It looks like the Axeman was here and murdered Mike," she said.

Mike Pepitone was rushed to Charity Hospital, where he died soon after.

Once again, a panel had been cut from the back door and the axe was left on the back porch. However, Mrs Pepitone claimed she had seen two men in her home. They had fled, taking nothing.

Strangely, Mrs Pepitone had not screamed when she had happened upon the scene. There were eight people in the house at the time and her screams would have alerted them. Plainly the attacker, or attackers, was not afraid of being caught. The police also noted that Mrs Pepitone showed no sign of grief when she was questioned.

Since the letter from "Hell", there had been three more attacks and the police were no closer to identifying the killer. All the newspapers could offer was frenzied speculation. They picked up on the idea that the door panels removed at the crime scenes were too small for a grown man to get through. Nor could the Axeman have reached in to unlock the doors. Besides the doors were always found locked. Consequently, he cannot have been human.

Such ideas are not uncommon in Louisiana, which is a place full of superstition. In the late 19th century, a voodoo scare swept New Orleans and people began killing others who they thought had put a spell on them. There was a widespread belief in "Black Bottle Men" who killed hospital patients to sell the cadaver to anatomy students. Then there were "Needle Men," who stabbed women and carried them off unconscious. The "Gown Man" rode around in a black car, wearing a long black gown, searching for girls on their own, who some thought was a malevolent ghost. In the suburb of Gentilly, his cousin, the "Domino Man", wore a white robe with a hood, who sprang in the middle of a group of girls and sent them fleeing. Taking their cue from Pauline Bruno, other purported eyewitnesses said that the Axeman had wings – plainly he was a vampire. More prosaically he might have been a sinister development of "Jack the Clipper" who went about cutting off locks of schoolgirls' hair in 1914. Or that Mike Pepitone was the son of Pietro Pepitone who had killed "Black Hand" extortionist Paulo Marchese some years before, raising again the spectre of the Axeman murders being Mafia slayings.

But perhaps the Axeman was identified and killed. On 2 December 1920, Mrs Pepitone, dressed in her widow's weeds, stepped from a darkened doorway in Los Angeles and accosted New Orleans resident Joseph Mumfre and shot him dead. He was, she said, the man she had seen fleeing from her husband's bedroom the night he had been killed.

Mumfre was a career criminal. Intriguingly, between the last murder in 1911 until the Maggios' murder in 1918, he had been in jail. He had been in jail again during the hiatus between the murder of Joseph Romano on 10 August 1918 and the Cortimiglia attack on 10 March 1919. Then right after the Pepitone murder in October 1919, he left New Orleans. At the times of the murders, he had been at large and in New Orleans. However, apart from Mrs Pepitone's testimony, there is no evidence that directly links Mumfre to any of the attacks. There has been some speculation that Mumfre was a Mafia hitman. However, the victims were not confined to the Italian community. Besides, the Mafia has its own strict code of conduct. It does not murder women.

Mrs Pepitone was sentenced to ten years for the killing, but was released after three years, then disappeared.

The mystery deepened on 7 December 1920 – just five days after the killing of Joseph Mumfre – when Mrs Cortimiglia came down with smallpox. Perhaps fearing the wrath of her maker, she claimed that a saint had visited her and ordered her to redeem her sins. Publicly, in a newspaper office, she retracted her accusation against the Jordanos, admitting she had lied because she had a grudge against the two men and begging their forgiveness. Both men were released.

There were no more axe murders in New Orleans after the slaying of Joseph Mumfre. But as no one truly knows who the Axeman was, he may simply have moved on.

New Orleans' Waterside Slayings

In August 1995, the authorities in New Orleans announced that another serial killer was on the loose in the Big Easy. He is thought to have slain 24 people, mostly prostitutes and drug users. Most were black women, though the victims included men and transsexuals. They had been abducted from Treme and

Algiers, two of the poorest neighbourhoods of the city, and had died by strangulation or drug overdoses. Their naked bodies were dumped around New Orleans itself, in Jefferson parish and in the swamps to the west of the city.

The first suspect was New Orleans police officer named Victor Gant. Curiously, though, he was only connected to two of the deaths – the body of his 28-year-old girlfriend Sharon Robinson and that of a friend were found floating in a swamp on 30 April 1995. A 15-year veteran, Grant denied any wrongdoing and remained on duty during the investigation, although he was reassigned to a desk job. Later, though, after a domestic fracas involving his new girlfriend, he was suspended from the force.

Then on 2 March 1998, another suspect emerged. Taxi-driver Russell Ellwood was arrested in connection to two of the killings. Ellwood, a former cab driver, is suspected in six more of the killings. However, authorities have four more suspects, including Gant.

"We never thought, from the beginning, that this was the work of one person," said a spokesman.

Ellwood was charged with the murder of Cheryl Lewis and Delores Mack. The body of Cheryl Lewis had been found in a canal near Hahnville 30 miles up the Mississippi from New Orleans on 20 February 1993. Initially it was thought she had drowned while under the influence of amphetamines and cocaine. The next day, the body of the other woman, Delores Mack, was found 350 yards away. She had been strangled and suffocated, and there were traces of cocaine in her bloodstream. The following year, a police officer found Ellwood in the area of the crime scene in the dead of night. He said he was changing his cab's oil in that remote spot near a canal off the state highway because he did not want to be caught by the Department of Environmental Quality dumping the dirty oil.

The officers were satisfied at the time and Ellwood was released. However, when a murder task-force was formed, he became a suspect on the grounds that serial killers often return to the scene of their crimes. They tracked him down to a Florida state penitentiary where he was serving time on a cocaine conviction and violation of the condition of his probation. When New Orleans detectives contacted him, he was co-operative and he told them that he had dreamt that the serial killer task force wanted to talk to him.

In October 1997, a fellow inmate in Florida told the police that Ellwood had told him that he liked sex with men and women who were drugged into insensibility. Ellwood apparently had boasted that "he enjoyed the fun of having sex with people who were not in control of their bodies . . . He said if they were high on cocaine or heroin, the heroin would put them in a state of mind as if they were paralyzed and he could take advantage." Another inmate said that Ellwood had confessed to some of the New Orleans murders.

Months later, after Ellwood had been released and had gone to Ohio to stay with relatives, he was questioned again by the police. It was then that Ellwood allegedly told the task force's head, Sheriff's Lieutenant Sue Rushing, and a former Cincinnati homicide detective that he had dumped the body of a woman in the water beside a rural road.

In January 1998 Ellwood agreed to return to Louisiana in an effort to clear his name and help solve the cases. Once he was in the state, he was jailed on outstanding traffic charges. But once behind bars in St Charles Parish, Ellwood rescinded his earlier admission, saying that he had been badgered to the point he would have said anything as long as he was returned to New Orleans, where he could see his long-standing attorney Ross Scaccia, who represented him in a marijuana possession case three decades before.

According to Scaccia, Ellwood was a serial loser, who grew up in Massillon, Ohio, and later moved to New Orleans. He worked as a freelance photographer then turned to driving a cab. A loner, Ellwood never had a girlfriend, Scaccia said, and constantly thought of get-rich-quick schemes that failed. He inherited $15,000 from his mother but lost it all investing in penny stocks. He frequently slept in his cab as he could not afford to rent a room.

In Ellwood's defence, Scaccia said that Ellwood had helped police at first because he craved attention and the detectives told him he could help them solve the case. The lawyer also claimed that Lieutenant Rushing had coached key witness Sharon Jones to say that Ellwood took her to the canal where Cheryl Lewis and Delores Mack were found to smoke crack cocaine and see a "surprise". According to a police affidavit, Jones said that Ellwood had showed her one body in the canal with an arm and hand showing and another body that was almost submerged.

Ellwood maintained he was in Ohio at the time and had had receipts to prove it, but they had been taken by Lieutenant Rushing who had destroyed or was concealing them. The 1993 receipts seized by police have a mysterious two-week gap in February, Maria Chaisson, another of Ellwood's lawyers, said.

In November 1998, Lieutenant Rushing failed a lie detector test when asked if she destroyed or lost receipts that could place Ellwood in Ohio February 1993 when the two women were murdered. The polygraph also indicated Rushing was "not telling the truth" when she denied persuading Jones to say that Ellwood showed her the two bodies in a canal. The FBI investigated these and other allegations made against the task force and Ellwood has filed a federal lawsuit against task force investigators, asserting that they had violated his civil rights when falsely claiming that he had confessed under relentless interrogation.

"It's clear they have deprived him of his right to a fair trial," said Maria Chaisson. She believed that the police were desperate to prove they had caught the serial killer. "They wanted to get a conviction, but whoever did this is certainly still out there."

Prosecutors admit they have no physical evidence to connect Ellwood to the place the bodies of Cheryl Lewis and Delores Mack were found in February 1993. On 24 February 1999, they dropped one of two murder charges against Ellwood after Jefferson Parish Sheriff Harry Lee admitted that Ellwood was in Ohio when Dolores Mack was murdered and could not have committed the crime. This completely undermined Sharon Jones' testimony and left the prosecution with only Ellwood's disputed confession, the tales of jailhouse snitches and the testimony of a prostitute who sold drugs to Ellwood and claimed that, when she got in his car, he suddenly became very angry and said to her: "You know what I do to bitches like you? I kill them."

"This is the biggest railroad case ever in the state of Louisiana," said Ellwood.

Despite four years work by the task force made up of the FBI, New Orleans' police and four sheriff's departments, it seems the killer remained at large. The task force eventually disbanded, leaving the perpetrator free to kill again.

Oklahoma City's OKC Serial Killer

The dismembered bodies of at least four women found in Oklahoma City between 1976 and 1995, are thought to belong to victims of the mysterious "OKC Serial Killer". Missing body parts made identification of the victims impossible.

The pieces of the first body were found scattered over several blocks near the Capitol in 1976. The fourth body was found during the ground work in preparation for the construction of the Centennial Expressway in 1985. None of the victims matches women who have been reported missing.

On 22 April 1995, the body of a female Native American and Hispanic was found in a shallow grave on an abandoned stretch of highway 50 miles west of Oklahoma City. The head, feet and hands were missing, again making identification almost impossible. The authorities believe that the perpetrator could be re-activated the "OKC Serial Killer" as the method of dismemberment is similar.

Oradell, N.J.'s Doctor X

Publicity surrounding the suspicious deaths of patients in the Michigan Veterans' Administration Hospital in Ann Arbor, Michigan, discussed above, reopened a ten-year-old case in New Jersey. Over a ten-month period, beginning in December

1965, some 13 patients died in similar circumstances at Riverdell Hospital, a small osteopathic facility in suburban Oradell, just eight miles from Manhattan. Most of them had had routine surgery and were well on their way to recovery when they died of unrelated causes. A doctor was suspected, but an investigation in 1966 failed to produce enough evidence to bring charges.

Then in 1976, prompted by what he said were "post-Watergate pangs of conscience", a well-informed source, thought to be a member of the hospital's staff, became "Deep Throat" to *New York Times* reporter Myron Farber. Armed with inside knowledge, Farber began questioning survivors, doctors and other interested parties. He found inconsistencies in the testimony of the surgeon originally suspected and compiled 4,000 pages of notes on the case. But because the man had never been charged and still practised medicine in New Jersey, when the *New York Times* ran the story he was referred to as "Doctor X".

The Ann Arbor case also stirred the interest of Bergen County Prosecutor Joseph C. Woodcock and he was impressed by the evidence Farber had unearthed. However, he knew that to press charges against Doctor X he would need a much stronger case than had been established in 1966. Back then several staff physicians had noted that Dr X had been on duty near many of the victims around the time they died, though none of the 13 was his patient.

Nine cases attracted particular suspicion. The first involved 73-year-old Carl Rohrbeck, who was admitted for a hernia operation on 12 December 1965 and died the next day due to "coronary occlusion" – a blockage of the coronary artery. Four-year-old Nancy Savino was admitted on 19 March 1966 to have her appendix removed, and died two days later due to "undetermined physiological reaction". Twenty-six-year-old Margaret Henderson died on 23 April, after exploratory surgery which proceeded satisfactorily. Edith Post, aged 62, was admitted for surgery on 15 May, dying two days later of undetermined causes. Sixty-four-year-old Ira Holster underwent gall bladder surgery at Riverdell on 12 July and died without apparent cause seventeen days later. Fifty-nine-year-old Frank Biggs was suffering from an ulcer when he entered Riverdell on 20 August. A week later he was dead. Mary Muentener, aged 80, underwent surgery on her gall bladder on 25 August. She died seven days later. Seventy-year-old Emma Arzt also also had gall bladder surgery on September 18, dying five days later. And 36-year-old Eileen Shaw gave birth by Caesarean section on 18 October, but died on the 23rd.

Hospital administrators had launched an investigation on 1 November 1966, after a Riverdell surgeon found 18 vials of curare – most of them empty – in Dr X's hospital locker. Dr X told Guy W. Calissi, the County Prosecutor in 1966, that he was using the muscle relaxant for experiments on "dying dogs" in his spare time and claimed that other doctors were trying to frame him. But Calissi had been told that it was impossible to detect curare in tissue long after death, so he dropped the case.

However, forensic science had moved on by 1976. Prosecutor Woodcock got permission to exhume five of the bodies and sent tissue samples to specialists who used new detection techniques that could identify toxins in amounts weighing only a trillionth of a gram. Traces of curare had definitely been found in the body of four-year-old Nancy Savino and possibly in two others.

The Bergen County authorities then named Dr X as 48-year-old Dr Mario E. Jascalevich, who had immigrated from Argentina ten years earlier. In May 1976, he was charged with five counts of murder and was forced to surrender his medical licence pending the resolution of the case. Meanwhile, Farber secured a book contract with Doubleday for an advance of $75,000.

Dr Jascalevich hired Raymond Brown, then one of the most well-known trial lawyers in the US, to defend him. Brown went after Farber, calling him "greedy and ambitious", and repeatedly citing Farber's advance. He then attempted to subpoena Faber's notes. Farber and the *New York Times* refused to hand them over, saying that they owed a duty of confidentiality to the journalist's source. Farber insisted that he had no information of crucial bearing on the case, nothing that could be used to establish Jascalevich's innocence or guilt. But the judge said he would be the judge of that and demanded that the notes be handed over to the court, so he could read them *in camera* before deciding whether they should be turned over to the defence. Farber refused to comply and The *New York Times* was fined $100,000 for refusing to obey a court order, plus another $5,000 a day until the notes were handed over. Farber still refused to part with his notes. In consequence, he was jailed for a day in July 1978, then for another 27 days in August, and once again in October. As the reporter languished behind bars, the doctor went on trial for the murder of Rohrbeck, Savino, Henderson, Biggs and Arzt.

The prosecution maintained that Jascalevich had committed the murders to discredit his colleagues whose abilities he had little time for. The animosity, it seems, was mutual. The defence maintained that medical experts had conspired with the prosecutor to bring the case. Brown maintained that the patients had, in fact, died of natural causes and general malpractice by other doctors at the hospital. The trial lasted for 34 weeks.

The trial judge directed an acquittal on two of the five murders as the prosecution had failed to prove the presence of curare in those two bodies. The jury was then asked to decide on the three victims. After just three hours' deliberation, the jury found Jasccalevich not guilty of all charges.

The case had cost the *Times* more than $1 million, including $250,000 in fines. New Jersey's legislature, appalled at the imprisonment of a reporter, toughened its shield law to protect journalists. However, Farber's case divided journalists. The executive editor of the *New York Times*, A. M. Rosenthal, maintained: "The First Amendment guarantees the right to print the news, but without the right to gather the news, the right to print has very little meaning." Others pointed out that the case pitted the First Amendment's freedom of the press against a defendant's Sixth Amendment right to evidence for his defence. Carl Bernstein, one of the two journalists responsible for unearthing the Watergate scandal, pointed out that, when someone was on trial for their life, freedom of the press was not absolute.

At the end of the trial, Mario Jascalevich returned to his native Argentina, where he died of a cerebral haemorrhage in September 1984. But if he was not the killer, whoever was responsible for those 13 mysterious deaths in Riverdell Hospital in 1966 is still at large.

Philadelphia's Frankford Slasher

The Philadelphia district of Frankford is older than the city itself. First settled by Swedes in the 1660s, the village became known for its main road, King's Highway, which later served as the primary route between Philadelphia and New York. Horse-drawn carriages transported members of the Continental Congress along it in pre-Revolutionary days. The Jolly Post Inn served as a popular way station. George Washington is said to have slept there and legend has it that it was at the Jolly Post that the founding fathers decided to let Thomas Jefferson write the Declaration of Independence. Later Frankford became the home of the local mill-owners. It had its own symphony orchestras and a football team – the Frankford Yellowjackets, which eventually became the Philadelphia Eagles. And travelling circuses wintered there.

Then in 1922, the elevated railway – the El – arrived, turning Frankford into a suburb. At first this only served to increase the area's prosperity, but by the 1970s, Frankford had become the run-down, crime-ridden inner-city area chosen by Sylvester Stallone as the backdrop for his 1976 movie *Rocky*. Then came a series of murders that would taint the name of Frankford to this day.

The story began on 19 August 1985, when 52-year-old Helen Patent was last seen by her ex-husband Kermit when she left the house they still shared 12 miles from Frankford in Parkland, in neighbouring Bucks County, Pennsylvania. A well-known habitué of Frankford, few people knew that she lived outside town.

A week later the body of a middle-aged woman turned up in the rail yard of the Southeast Pennsylvania Transportation Authority. Railway workers found the dead woman around 8.30 a.m. on 26 August 1985. She was naked from the waist down. Her legs were opened so her genitalia were exposed and her blouse was pulled up to show off her breasts. She had been stabbed in the head, chest and right arm numerous times. There was also a deep gash across her abdomen, exposing her internal organs. Her body was identified the following day by her ex-husband. A post mortem revealed that she had been sexually assaulted, but she had been stabbed so many times it was impossible to discover which wound had actually killed her. The motive for her murder was not immediately obvious. A regular in local bars and, the newspapers later speculated, possibly a casual prostitute, she might easily have been picked up by a stranger who raped and murdered her.

On 3 January 1986, 68-year-old Anna Carroll was found dead in her apartment in the 1400 block of Ritner Street. It was a cold winter's day, but the door to her apartment was found open. She had been stabbed six times in the back and was left lying on the floor of the bedroom with the kitchen knife still in her. The body was naked from the waist down and there was a gaping Jack-the-Ripper-style gash from her groin to her breast-bone made after death, as if the killer intended to eviscerate the corpse.

Although Anna Carroll's apartment was ten miles from the rail yard where Helen Patent's body had found, they were both regulars in bars in the Frankford area – particularly the Golden Bar, known to one and all as "Goldie's", near the El station on the 5200 block of Frankford Avenue, as King's Highway had become known. Both murders seem to have happened at night. Both involved numerous stab wounds. Both women were naked from the waist down and both corpses were opened with a post-mortem gash. This lead the authorities to believe that they had both been struck down by the same killer – whom the newspapers would soon dub the Frankford Slasher.

The next victim was 64-year-old Susan Olszef, who was also found in her apartment. She lived on Richmond Street, just three miles from the SEPTA rail yard. She, too, had been stabbed six times in the back. And she was also a regular at Goldie's.

The problem was that Frankford was an area teeming with nightlife. It was full of strangers who turned up during the hours of darkness and were, perhaps, never seen again. It was an area where it was hard to track witnesses and where it was easy to commit an anonymous murder. The police came up with no positive lead and, as the murders had all occurred in different parts of the city, they began to doubt that they were related.

Then at 7.30 a.m. on 8 January 1987, the body of 28-year-old Jeanne Durkin was found by a restaurant employee under a fruit and vegetable stall on a Pratt Street lot west of Frankford Avenue, just a block from the rail yard where Helen Patent had been found. In and out of mental institutions, Durkin was homeless and lived on the streets, sheltering most nights in the doorway of an abandoned bakery just two doors from Goldie's, even dropping in for a little warmth on a cold night. Found lying in a pool of her own blood, which had been splattered up the side of the fruit stand and a nearby fence, she had been stabbed 74 times in the chest, back and buttocks. Her body was naked from the waist down and her legs spread. The post mortem showed that she had been sexually assaulted.

It was now clear that a serial killer was at large in Philadelphia and the newspapers began demanding that the police catch the Frankford Slasher. Unfortunately, the Slasher's murders were quickly upstaged. On 24 March 1987, a young black prostitute named Josefina Rivera turned up at a Philadelphia police station, claiming that she had escaped from a filthy basement on North Marshall Street owned by Gary Heidnik, where he had kept her and a number of other women as sex slaves. He had already killed two of them by maltreatment. The police obtained a search warrant, released the women and arrested Heidnik, who was convicted of the two murders in 1988. He died by lethal injection in 1999.

Then, on a hot August day in 1987, Harrison "Marty" Graham was evicted from his north Philadelphia apartment because of the terrible smell coming from it. Before leaving he nailed the door to one of the rooms shut. The landlord's son looked through the keyhole and called the police, who found the decomposing corpses of six women, along with parts of a seventh. Graham was also convicted, but was found to be mentally incompetent, so could not be executed.

Despite having other work to do, officers canvassed the Frankford Avenue neighbourhood for clues. A barmaid at Goldie's told them that she had seen all the women in the bar. She believed that they had been murdered by a man who had dropped in and picked them up. She even pointed out a suspect, but could provide no evidence to substantiate her suspicions.

The police came to believe that the victims had known their killer. Jean Durkin had been homeless for five years. She was strong and streetwise. Once, when six policemen had tried to arrest Durkin, she put up such a fight that they gave up. She could not be overwhelmed easily so her killer must used have cunning, rather than strength, to put her in a vulnerable position. Helen Patent was also independent and savvy. People who knew her did not believe that she would have gone into the rail yard with a stranger. But that took the police little further.

The neighbourhood held a candlelight vigil for the dead woman and a task force was formed. Meanwhile, the killer seemed to lie low for over a year, then he struck again. On 11 November 1988, 66-year-old Margaret Vaughan was found lying in the entranceway of an apartment block in the 4900 block of Penn Street, just three blocks from where Jean Durkin had been found. Vaughan had lived in the building, but had been evicted that day for not paying the rent. She had been stabbed 29 times.

A bartender reported that Vaughan had drinking with a middle-aged white man the evening before her death. He had a round face, wore glasses and walked with an obvious limp. A police artist drew a sketch, which was circulated. But no one came forward to identify him.

On the evening of 19 January 1989, 30-year-old Theresa Sciortino was found dead in her apartment, where she lived alone, on Arrott Street, three blocks from where Margaret Vaughan had been found and a block and a half from Frankford Avenue. Lying face up in a pool of blood in the kitchen, she was naked except for a pair of white socks. The attacker had used a sharp knife to slash her 25 times in the face, arms, and chest. He left the bloodstained weapon leaning against the sink and a bloody footprint on the floor. He had also used a three-foot piece of wood to sexually assault her. The attack seems to have happened the night before. It was then that a neighbour had heard a struggle, followed by a loud thump as if a large object had been thrown to the floor. Indeed Sciortino had put up quite a struggle. All the rooms in the apartment showed signs of the disturbance and blood was spattered everywhere.

Like Durkin, Sciortino had been an inmate of several psychiatric institutions and was currently an outpatient under treatment. Like the other victims, she was seen regularly along the Frankford Avenue strip, often with male companions. One neighbour said she enjoyed "a lot of company". She had last been seen alive at 6 p.m. in the Jolly Post at the corner of Griscom and Arrott Streets in the company of a middle-aged white man. This was shortly before her neighbour heard the scuffle in her apartment.

The medical examiner Paul Hoyer dismissed the idea that a serial killer was on the prowl, on the erroneous grounds that serial killers kill much more frequently. But detectives were convinced. All of the victims were white women. Though their ages differed dramatically, they lived similar lifestyles. They all frequented the same area and drank in the same places. All had been viciously stabbed. In each case, the killer had left little evidence and there were no witnesses. Miraculously, no one had ever noticed the killer fleeing the scene, even though he must have been covered with blood after inflicting multiple stab wounds.

Consequently, the detectives looked back in their files to see if they could find any other unsolved murders that could have been perpetrated by the same killer. They came across the case of 29-year-old Catherine Jones, whose partially clad body had been found on a sidewalk in the Northern Liberties neighbourhood of the city on 29 January 1987, frozen and covered in snow. She worked as a waitress in Frankford and had been a patron of the bars there. However, she had not been stabbed but bludgeoned to death. Her jaw had been broken and her skull crushed, so she was never officially added to the Frankford Slasher's tally.

While detectives were reviewing the Catherine Jones case, a foot patrol called to investigate a burglary stumbled across the naked body of 46-year-old Carol Dowd at 2 a.m. on 29 April 1990 in an alley behind Newman's Sea Food market at 4511 Frankford Avenue. Like Catherine Jones, she had been beaten around the face and head. And like the Slasher victims, she had also been stabbed 36 times to the chest, back, face and neck. She also had cuts to her hands, showing she had tried to fend off her attacker. As in earlier murders, her torso had been cut open and her intestines spilled out of the long wound. One report also says that her left nipple was removed. The medical examiner determined that Carol Dowd had been murdered between midnight and 1.40 a.m.

A few hours before she had been killed, Carol Dowd had been seen walking with a middle-aged white man. Her clothes were found not far from her body. Her purse was also found in the alley. It was open and some of its contents had spilled out on the ground. But nothing was missing and, for the time being, robbery was ruled out as a motive. It seemed clear that the Frankford Slasher had struck again.

Like Jean Durkin and Theresa Sciortino, Carol Dowd had a history of mental illness. When her brother died in the late 1960s, she began hearing voices. Diagnosed as a paranoid schizophrenic, she was institutionalized. Then she was released into a community-based programme and moved into an apartment, where she was raped. But lately, she had been moved into a hostel near where she had been found and seemed happy.

During their investigation the police came across a black man named Leonard Christopher, who worked in the fish market and lived nearby. He had seen the police in that alley that night. The store had been broken into several times before and he told reporters that he thought the market was being burgled again. He concluded that they were busting someone for selling drugs or prostitution, both of which went on in the alley, and moved on. However, when the police questioned him, he admitted to knowing one of the earlier victims, Margaret Vaughan.

Christopher claimed that he was with his girlfriend the night Carol Dowd was killed, but his girlfriend said she had been at home alone. A prostitute who initially denied seeing Christopher that night, later said that she had seen him with Carol Dowd outside a bar. Another said she had seen him coming out of the alley, sweating, with a large knife in his belt.

When the police searched his apartment, they found clothing with blood on it. Christopher said that he had been told by his boss to clean up the blood in that alley – that's how it had got on his clothes. Workmates and friends vouched for his good character. Even his landlord stuck up for him, though he complained that Christopher sometimes made too much noise. And it was plain that Christopher was black, not the middle-aged white man seen with other victims. Nevertheless on 5 May 1990, Christopher was arrested and charged with the murder of Carol Dowd, the abuse of a corpse, theft and possession of an instrument of a crime. He was refused bail and jailed.

At a preliminary hearing on 20 June, the prosecution presented their case. Emma Leigh, who knew Christopher, said that she had seen him walk into the alley behind the fish market at around 1 a.m. Then she heard a woman scream. But then Leigh left with a man – a date or, perhaps, a client – in a car. Linda Washington, who also knew Christopher, said she had seen him leaving the alley, with his shirt over his arm and a large knife in a sheath hanging from his waist.

Christopher's defence attorney, Jack McMahon, challenged the prosecution's case, saying that in key detail the two witnesses had contradicted each other and their testimony would never stand up at the trial. He also contested the theft charge on the grounds that, while Carol Dowd's purse had been open, there was still money in it. The purse had simply been dropped during the attack. Nevertheless Leonard Christopher was bound over to stand trial.

Even though Christopher had only been charged with one of the murders, the residents of Frankford breathed a sigh of relief – but not for long. While Christopher was safely locked away in the county jail on 6 September 1990, the body of 30-year-old Michelle Dehner – aka Michelle Martin – was found in a fourth-floor studio apartment on Arrott Street, not far from Frankford Avenue. She had been stabbed 23 times in the stomach and chest.

Once again, there was no sign of forced entry. Her apartment was on the same street as the one where Theresa Sciortino had been murdered 18 months before and was only three blocks from the alley where Carol Dowd had been slain. She had even been an early suspect in the murder of Jean Durkin as, the night before Durkin died, the two of them had fought over a blanket.

Like Jean Durkin, Theresa Sciortino and Carol Dowd, she had a history of mental instability. A hard-drinking, paranoid loner who was less than fastidious about personal hygiene, she was called "Crazy Michelle" by people in the neighbourhood, who saw her traipsing from bar to bar dressed in jeans and a sloppy sweatshirt. Considered eccentric and anti-social, she sometimes barricaded herself in her apartment or flung things out the window, endangering people below. Streetwise and single, she frequented the same bars as the other victims. When she was not selling pretzels on the street, she spent all day drinking. A blowsy blonde, she often took men home with her. She was last seen the day before her body was found leaving a Frankford Avenue bar with a middle-aged white man. There was little doubt that Michelle Martin's death was the work of the Frankford Slasher.

All those who had vouched for Christopher, insisting that he was a decent and friendly man, now seemed vindicated. He had been falsely accused and the real killer was still at large. Once again, the residents of Frankford took to the streets, insisting that the police catch the Slasher. On 27 October, 50 of them marched in the rain along the routes they believed the killer had taken with his victims. The *Philadephia Inquirer* reported that the procession went "past the fish market, behind which one body was found butchered with a knife, past a bar that four of the dead had patronized, and along Arrott Street, where the latest victim was found stabbed to death early last month". Again, they lit candles and commemorated "the women who couldn't be here".

Detectives also took to the streets again, watching for men who picked up women in bars in Frankford. They had two men under constant surveillance and leads on a third suspect. They even tracked down the owner of the shoe that had left the bloody shoe print on the floor of Theresa Sciortino's apartment. It turned out to be one of Sciortino's boyfriends, but he was eventually cleared as a suspect.

The public phoned in, naming fresh suspects. Psychics were called in. A local witches' coven was accused, but excluded.

Calls were made for the release of Leonard Christopher. But even with the murder investigation still in full swing, on 29 November 1990, his trial in the Court of Common Pleas began. Christopher appeared in a grey suit and black horn-rimmed glasses, looking, the newspapers said, "studious" – a mile away from the public image of the demented killer who had been raping and killing women in Frankford for the last five years. Nevertheless in her opening statement, Assistant District Attorney Judith Rubino insisted that the mild-mannered Christopher was a vicious killer who used a "Rambo-style knife" to slash and kill Carol Dowd in the alley behind the fish market where he worked.

She admitted that while she had no witnesses to the actual murder, she did have testimony that would provide sufficient circumstantial evidence to prove the defendant's guilt. Christopher had been seen with Carol Dowd going into the alley, and a witness heard a woman scream. He had also been seen leaving the alley. Dowd had been found dead in the alley immediately afterward. He had been seen with a knife, and his clothes had blood on them. What's more, Christopher had lied about his whereabouts that night.

Defence attorney Jack McMahon told the jury that Christopher had no history of violence. The police were under pressure to solve the case, he said, and they had rushed to judgment. When the prosecutor objected, Judge George Ivins cautioned McMahon to stick the facts and not offer opinions. However, McMahon stuck to his guns. He pointed that there had been at least six murders before Carol Dowd's that were so similar that they were thought to be the work of a serial killer. But Christopher had only been charged with one of the slayings. The prosecution objected to this line of reasoning as McMahon could plainly infer that, as another similar murder had occurred while his client was in custody, he could not have killed Carol Dowd. When attorneys for the prosecution and defence approached the bench, the argument became heated.

McMahon continued by pointing out that prosecution were relying on evidence that in a stronger case would have been discarded. Their witness were, by and large, drug users and prostitutes, who had nine aliases between them and long rap sheets. Emma Leigh had even admitted to lying to the police to start with. She was plainly an unreliable witness. Could any jury believe such witnesses "beyond reasonable doubt"?

No physical evidence connected Christopher to the crime scene. No murder weapon had been found – certainly not a "Rambo-style" knife. When Christopher had been arrested less than a week after the murder, there were no marks on him – no bruises or abrasions as you would expect from a woman fighting for her life. In short, there was no reason to view Leonard Christopher as a murderer.

However, the prosecution did have a reliable witness. It was Christopher's boss Jaesa Phang. On the morning after the murder, Christopher had said that a white women about 45 years old had been murdered in the alley, Phang testified. Those details had not been released by the police, the prosecution maintained. Phang said that, few days later, Christopher had said: "Maybe I killed her." Although he quickly recanted, Phang maintained that he had seemed quite serious at the time. He was also inordinately interested in the details of the crime and, when he talked about it, he mimed disembowelling the body. Christopher also claimed to have seen a white man on the street at around 1 a.m. However, no one else had reported seeing him, while others had said they had seen Christopher.

About five days after Carol Dowd's death, Christopher told Phang that he could not sleep well because he had witnessed a murder. His speech was rambling and his manner agitated, Phang said. Christopher then said that he thought a white man was trying to kill him. The man knew that he had seen the murder and Christopher believed that he would get into his apartment and would hide in the closet.

The prosecution presented the bloodstains in evidence. But the spots of blood found on Christopher's trousers were too small to type at that time. A bloodstained tissue was found in the driveway next to Christopher's apartment building. DNA analysis was in its infancy at that time and was still being challenged in many courts. But the blood was Type O, matching Dowd's. In Christopher's statement to the police, he said that when he was at his girlfriend's apartment that night he had seen a white man in his 40s outside wiping his hands on what looked like a handkerchief or tissue. But this was the wrong apartment.

The trial lasted less than two weeks. McMahon ended by emphasizing Christopher's good character. Violence was completely out of character for him. The prosecution had no weapon, no motive, no weapon and no solid evidence.

But Rubino asked what motive the witnesses had for lying. Some of them had been his friends, including Emma Leigh who had initially lied on his behalf to the police. There was no reason for her to change her story unless she was now telling the truth. Christopher had no alibi for that night and had lied about being with his girlfriend. She ended with a vivid description of what Carol Dowd must have gone through in her last few moments. The following day Christopher was convicted of the first-degree murder. According the *Inquirer*, Christopher "showed no visible reaction". The prosecution asked for the death sentence, but Christopher was sentenced to life imprisonment. He maintained that he had been railroaded by "pipers" – that is, prostitutes pressured into testifying by the police. McMahon simply said: "The real killer may still be out there."

While the police considered Christopher a suspect in some of the other murders, there are other suspects as well. At least seven of the Frankford Slasher murders remain unsolved and Christopher certainly could not have done one of them as he was in jail at the time. And no one ever found the middle-aged white man seen with a number of the victims shortly before their deaths.

The Phoenix Baseline Killer

In 2005 and 2006, the police in Phoenix, Arizona figured they had two serial killers on their hands. The most pernicious was the so-called Baseline Killer – aka the Baseline Rapist – who committed countless crimes, including 27 murders, along Baseline Road, a long stretch of highway running east-west across southern Phoenix, and the neighbouring towns of Tempe and Mesa. The other was Serial Shooter, who was involved in 38 random shootings north of the Salt River, resulting in at least six deaths.

The Baseline Killer sought out victims who were blue-eyed blondes, preying on them in secluded areas. He appeared to spend some time stalking his victims and initiated contact before the attack.

The attacks began in September 2005, when two men, aged 19 and 27, were sexually assaulted at gunpoint behind a church. At the time the police did not link these crimes to the murder of 34-year-old barmaid Georgia Phompbon around midnight on 16 September. She was shot sitting in the parking lot outside her apartment block on South Boulevard Avenue after returning home from work. Later it was seen to be the work of the same man.

Then at 9.30 p.m. on 20 September 2005, the suspect jumped through the take-out window of a fast-food restaurant on South Central Avenue, snatched an employee's purse, then jumped out again. He then hijacked a car, forcing the mother to drive while he sexually molested her daughter in the back seat. Then he forced the mother to park and sexually assaulted her too. Later that evening, he robbed a man with an infant outside a chemist in West Baseline Road.

At 8 p.m. on 3 November, a man with a moustache, dreadlocks and a fisherman's hat walked into a lingerie shop on North 32nd Street brandishing a gun and robbed the store of $720. This provided the enduring image of the Baseline Rapist who, less than ten minutes later, abducted a woman from outside a grocery store across the street and sexually molested her in her car. The perpetrator was a black or Hispanic man, about 5 foot 10 inches tall and weighing around 170 pounds. It later became clear that he wore disguises and the dreadlocks were possibly a wig.

On 7 November 2005 the suspect robbed four people at gunpoint inside Las Brasas, a Mexican restaurant on North 39th Street. Then he went to a Little Caesar's Pizza restaurant next door and robbed three people there. Outside on the street he robbed four more people. Pocketing $463, he fired a round into the air as he fled.

Later he sexually assaulted a 21-year-old woman. She told the police that the man first approached as she was tossing a bag of clothes into a donation bin in central Phoenix.

"I thought he was just asking for a ride," she said. "He started saying that he needed me to take him down the corner, and I was just like in shock."

He said he had just robbed a place. According to her description, the man was wearing a fisherman's hat, a wig and big round plastic glasses without lenses.

"He was telling me just to drive at the speed limit so not to cause attention," the woman said. He told her to calm down and threatened to kill her if she tried anything stupid. Then he told her to stop the car and turn off the engine. He forced her to put the seatback down, then told her to take off her clothes. He said it would give him more time to get away. But then he started molesting her. She asked him to stop, but he would not. When he had finished, he took money from her wallet and left.

At 6.55 p.m. on 12 December 2005, he killed 39-year-old Tina Washington, a single mother of three, behind a fast food restaurant on South 40th Street. She was a teacher at Cactus Preschool who had moved from Missouri 13 years before and was last seen waiting for a bus home. Gunfire alerted the police and a witness saw a man standing over her body with a gun drawn. She had been shot in the head.

Tina had previously told co-workers that two African-American men wearing hooded sweatshirts had been harassing her at the bus stop recently. The day after Tina was killed a black man walked into the gas station across the street from the crime scene and claimed to be a relative of Tina Washington. He asked to see the CCTV footage from the crime scene the night before. Police described him as a person of interest at the time. They said they were looking for a 140-pound man between 5 foot 7 inches and 5 foot 9 inches wearing a dark blue hooded sweatshirt, black baggy pants, and possibly glasses. At 8 p.m. that day, the suspect robbed a woman on East South Mountain Avenue.

At 7.38 p.m. on 20 February 2006, the bodies of 64-year-old Mirna Palma-Roman and 98-year-old Romelia Vargas were found in their snack truck at Lower Buckeye Road and 91st Avenue. They had been shot. Initially, police thought the killings were drug-related and only connected the crime to the Baseline Killer in July.

On 14 March 2006, there was another double homicide. At 9 p.m. two employees of Yoshi's Chinese restaurant at Indian School Road and 24th Street set off home together. The body of 20-year-old Liliana Sanchez-Cabrera was found in a car in the parking lot of a Burger King in the 2200 block of East Indian School Road. Employees saw the car at 5 a.m. but did not spot the body inside until 8 a.m. At 11.45 a.m. 23-year-old Chao "George" Chou was found dead about a mile away. Both had been shot in the head.

Soon after a local businessman noticed blood in the gravel of a parking lot on North 14th Street and there were marks as if a body had been dragged across it. He called the police, who searched the area. A week later, the businessman noticed a bad smell in the area and turned up the decomposing body of Kristin Nicole Gibbons, who had been shot in the head.

At 9 p.m. on 1 May 2006, a man in a Halloween mask abducted a woman at gunpoint outside Las Brasas restaurant and sexually assaulted her on North 32nd Street.

One woman displayed what the police called "heroic actions" and escaped the suspect's predations. She had just walked out of a check-cashing business when she saw a man in a mask pushing a shopping trolley. She was opening her car door when he ran up to her, pointed a gun and told her to give him a ride, the police said. He forced her to drive to a secluded area, then ordered her to make the seat lie flat and told her to take off her clothes.

"I am going away for a long time," he said, "and you are the last woman I am going to be able to touch."

However, the woman refused to perform oral sex, even after he threatened to kill her.

"Would you rather die?" he asked.

"Yes, kill me," she said. "You're not going to violate me."

She took the car keys and ran.

At 8.30 p.m. on 29 June 2006, 37-year-old Carmen Miranda was abducted from a carwash while she was on her cellular phone. She was found dead from a gunshot to the head behind a barber shop at the corner of 32nd Street and East Thomas about 100 yards away. The abduction was captured on CCTV.

By August 2006, the number of major crimes attributed to the Baseline Killer had risen to 23. The reports show the sexual assaults have ranged from fondling to rape. In many cases, victims had conversations with the man before they were attacked. He appeared always to have a gun, and often threatened to shoot and kill victims – and sometimes did. The varying descriptions of the attacker and his mannerisms show that he is "apparently clever with disguises," said Sergeant Andy Hill. Some victims said he appeared smart; other victims the opposite. One woman said the man smelled of old beer. One said he appeared handsome at first; another told police he appeared to be a "crazy transient" asking for money.

While being interviewed by police in Kentucky on a burglary matter, James Dewayne Mullins claimed responsibility for the murder of Georgia Phompbon. Having been charged with second degree murder, he publicly maintained his guilt, then changed his story when the police linked the homicide to the Baseline Killer. Since then, he has told police that he acted with two other men, one of whom he is unable to identify. The police still hoped that Mullins could help them discover the identity of the Baseline Killer. But on 3 August 2006 the homicide charge against Mullins was dropped. Authorities angrily stated that he had caused a significant diversion of resources during the hunt for the genuine killer.

Police have, as of late, given a more detailed description, citing that he is most likely in his late twenties to early thirties, and wears a baseball hat backward or a beanie, along with his fisherman's cap. His hair may now be short.

On 4 September 2006, Phoenix police arrested 42-year-old construction worker Mark Goudeau for an attack on two sisters, aged 21 and 24, as they were walking in a Phoenix park at night. He allegedly forced them to disrobe and put a gun between the legs of the older sister, who was pregnant, while he repeatedly raped the younger woman. The press immediately announced that he was the Baseline Killer, although the police have not charged him with any of the other attacks.

According to Arizona prison officials, Goudeau is an ex-convict who served 13 years for aggravated assault. Goudeau's wife and friends insist the police have the wrong man.

Meanwhile two men – Dale S. Hausner, aged 33, and Samuel John Dieteman, 30 – were under arrest for Serial Shooter's crimes. The police believe the men took turns shooting random victims late at night and early in the morning.

Pittsburgh's Prostitute Killer

In 1999, the police in Pittsburgh began to suspect that a serial killer was at work in their city. Twelve women who had taken to prostitution to support a drug habit had been killed and their bodies dumped in suburban or rural areas.

Jessica Freeman of North Braddock was a ward of the county and a runaway who worked as a prostitute at Penn Avenue and Ninth Street, Downtown. She was just 15 when she was found beaten to death in the early morning hours of 26 July 1992 on the railroad tracks in a remote section of Willis Road off Horning Road in Bethel Park.

The severed arms and legs of Faye Jackson – aka Faye Norris – of Garfield were recovered from a creek off Route 286 in Monroeville on 13 October 1994. She was identified from her fingerprints. The cause of death could not be determined. Jackson was last seen three days before in Garfield, where she worked as a prostitute. The previous August, she was rescued by police after her boyfriend kept her shackled to a gas line for 52 hours and raped her repeatedly in his Lawrenceville home. However, her boyfriend was not considered a suspect in her death.

Twenty-nine-year-old Dorothy B. Siemers was originally from North Carolina but had moved to Allegheny West and was working as a prostitute in the area of Cedar Avenue, East Ohio Street and at the north end of the Ninth Street Bridge. Her body was found embedded in the ice of Pine Creek in Shaler on 15 January 1997. The cause of death could not be determined, but drowning was suspected.

The body of 32-year-old Leah J. Hall of Oakland was found by a track inspector just after 11 a.m. on 28 February 1997 near Conrail tracks in Carnegie. The mother of three, she worked as a prostitute in the Uptown section of the city. She had been strangled. The police suspected that there was a connection between the murders of Dorothy Siemers and Leah Hall.

The skeleton of 45-year-old Cherida Oden Warmley of Garfield was found on 10 October 1998, on a steep, wooded hillside along the Triboro Expressway just west of the former Westinghouse Electric plant in North Versailles. She had last been seen alive over a year before, on 10 June 1997, by her live-in boyfriend. Like the other victims, she had worked as a prostitute in Pittsburgh. Her remains had been thrown over the hillside and had landed just 28 feet from the road. The cause of death could not be determined and she could only be identified from her dental records.

Then on 28 June 1999 the skeletal remains of a young women were found in a vacant house in Wilkinsburg and on 6 October the skeletal remains of 27-year-old Angelique Morgan, a known prostitute and drug addict, were discovered in an abandoned house in Shadyside. The cause of death could not be determined, but police believed she had been killed because she was found under a carpet and a mattress with her sweatshirt wrapped around her head.

Although there is no hard evidence linking the cases, Pittsburgh police Commander Ron Freeman thinks it improbable that so many similar deaths – perhaps as many as 18 – would be the work of different people.

Rapid City's Creek Killings

Eight homeless men were found drowned in a stream that runs through a park in downtown Rapid City, South Dakota, over the course of 16 months in the late 1990s. In a typical year, just one corpse is fished from the creek.

When the first few bodies turned up in the stream on the edge of the Black Hills, police thought nothing of it. As more men died, however, law officers became suspicious. And after 49-year-old Timothy Bull Bear Snr, of the town of Allen on the Pine Ridge Reservation, was found in the creek on 8 July 1999 they realized they had a problem on their hands.

"There's just too many of them to say it's coincidence," said Police Chief Tom Hennies.

Authorities have no witnesses and no motive for the killings. There are no bullet holes, stab wounds or evidence of foul play. Police do not even know where most of the men entered the stream. What investigators do know is that six of the eight dead were Native Americans, and all but one had been drinking heavily just before they died.

The homeless people who live under the bridges along the creek say they believe someone is pushing unconscious or helpless drinkers in the water. Chief Standing Elk says the killers are racist skinheads and that the creek people have banded together to chase some of them away. However, the rumours reported to police include accusations that the "creek people" are being killed by a fellow homeless man, members of a Satanic cult and a big white man on a bicycle. One report even accused a police officer.

Homeless people and others complain that the police are doing little to investigate the deaths because most of the victims are

Native Americans. The two men who lead the task force investigating the deaths say they have asked themselves whether they would do anything differently if the dead men had been affluent whites. Chief Sheriff's Deputy De Glassgow says he believes the investigation is being conducted the same as if all the victims had been white. A $4,000 reward has been offered.

Rochester, N.Y.'s Alphabet Murders

Between 1971 and 1973 a serial murderer terrorized Rochester, New York. He raped and murdered three Rochester girls, before dumping their bodies in nearby towns. These were dubbed "The Alphabet Murders" because, in each case, the victim's first and last name and the town where their body was found began with the same letter.

The killings began when 11-year-old Carmen Colon disappeared on 16 November 1971. Her body was found 12 miles away in Churchville two days later. Her uncle Miguel was suspected of killing her and remained a suspect until he committed suicide in 1991.

Then about 5.15 p.m. on 2 April 1973, 11-year-old Wanda Walkowicz left her Avenue D home to get a few items for her mother at a delicatessen in Conkey Avenue. She reached the store, bought the groceries and was last seen heading home. She did not make it.

When she did not return promptly, her family and neighbours began searching the streets for her, and when they could not find her, they called the police. At 10.15 a.m. the following day, a New York State Trooper on patrol found Wanda Walkowicz's body at a rest area off of State Route 104 in Webster, New York, seven miles from Rochester.

"Wanda was a tomboy," said her sister Rita, who was ten at the time. "She loved to play baseball and ride bikes. She had lots of friends."

After the murder, the Walkowiczes lived for another five years in the same Avenue D home.

"I was scared to go outside," said Rita, "but we still had to go to the store and things."

The final victim was 10-year-old Michelle Maenza, who went missing on 26 November 1973. Her body was found in 15 miles away Macedon two days later. Each girl showed evidence of being raped before death.

Other connections were made. Curiously, C, M and W are the third, 13th and 23rd letters of the alphabet, but no obvious inference can be drawn from that. All three victims were from poor Roman Catholic families in Rochester and were reportedly in trouble at school. This sparked speculation that the three homicides were committed by some sort of counsellor who had access to all three girls. It did not pan out. However, there was another suspect in town that the time. This was serial killer Ken Bianchi who later came to fame as one of the Hillside Stranglers who terrorized Los Angeles in the late 1970s.

Kenneth Alessio Bianchi was born in Rochester on 22 May 1951. His mother was a 17-year-old alcoholic prostitute who gave him up for adoption at birth. He became the only child of the Bianchi couple. His adoptive father worked for the American Brake-Shoe Factory. His adoptive mother's sister was the mother of Angelo Buono, his accomplice in the Hillside Stranglings, who was also born in Rochester.

When he was three, his mother took him to hospital because he could not sleep and wet the bed. A doctor noted: "Mother needs help."

At five, he lapsed into trances, daydreaming with his eyes rolled back, and he was known at school for his inattentiveness. He idolized the Arthurian comic-strip hero Prince Valiant, but did not emulate his idol and become a compulsive liar in early childhood. He was also quick to anger and threw temper tantrums. His mother consulted a doctor again. He was diagnosed with petit mal epilepsy, but the doctor thought he would grow out of it. However the symptoms did not subside. At the age of eight he was treated at a psychiatric centre for mental problems. At nine, due to his inability to control his bladder, his mother forced him to wear sanitary napkins and he was taken to the DePaul

Psychiatric Clinic to be treated for "involuntary urination, tics, absenteeism, and behaviour problems". There he underwent the minor procedures for the urination problem, but his behavioural problems continued. At 11, he was moved from two schools because he could not get along with his teachers. His mother felt the teachers made him nervous, but his IQ was 116 and his teachers thought he was working well below his capacity and he was falling behind in his school work. He was lazy, inattentive and prone to temper tantrums at school and at home.

At 12, he pulled down a six-year-old girl girl's panties and, at 13, showed no emotion when his adoptive father died. Sent to a high school outside of Rochester, he suddenly changed. He became a clean-cut all-American boy, respectful of elders and dates. But afterwards he joined a motorcycle gang and he got a tattoo that read: "Satan's Own M. C." He married briefly at 18 but dated other women throughout the marriage.

At 19, he enrolled at Monroe Community College to be trained to become a police officer. The following year he remarried but his wife left him after eight months. At 20, he wrote to a girlfriend, claiming he had killed a local man. She dismissed this as part of his incessant macho posturing. This was when the Alphabet Murders started.

The following year, his application to join the sheriff's office was turned down. And by 1973, he was certain police suspected him of the Alphabet Murders. At that time he was working as a security guard and over the next four years he was frequently charged with theft by his employers. He proposed to his childhood sweetheart, but she turned him down because he did not have a steady job. So in January 1976, Bianchi pulled up sticks and moved to Los Angeles, teaming up with his adopted cousin, Angelo Buono, in an amateur white-slave racket.

Born at Rochester in October 1934, Buono came from a broken home. At five, he was transported across the country by his mother. By 14, he was stealing cars and displaying a precocious obsession with sodomy. Sentenced for auto theft in 1950, he escaped from the California Youth Authority and was recaptured in December 1951. Buono hero-worshipped "Red

Light" rapist Caryl Chessman, who achieved fame for his literary output on death row. His books became bestsellers. Noted writers, including Aldous Huxley, Ray Bradbury, Norman Mailer and Robert Frost, wrote to the governor appealing for clemency and Chessman became a major figure in the campaign to abolish the death penalty that was gaining ground at the time. Nevertheless he went to the gas chamber in San Quentin on 2 May 1960 and died the very moment a fresh stay of execution arrived.

Despite his simian appearance, Buono attracted scores of women. He fathered several children, violently abusing several wives and girlfriends along the way. He also worked as a pimp, recruiting a "harem" of prostitutes through rape and torture.

The sadistic Buono introduced Bianchi to perverse sex and even encouraged Bianchi to sleep with one of his son's girlfriends. Things seem to be looking up for Bianchi when he took a job with the California Land Title Company and his mother sent him enough money to buy a 1972 Cadillac. He moved out of Buono's home into his own apartment briefly before he moved in with Kelli Boyd, a girlfriend he met at work, though Bianchi already exhibited a violent temper. He lost his job after marijuana was found in his desk.

In 1977, his applications to join the Los Angeles Police Department, Los Angeles Police Reserves and the nearby Glendale Police Department were rejected. After that he bought a fake psychology degree and credentials and rented an office space from a legitimate psychologist, but he did not get much business. Then he faked cancer as an excuse for not working. Meanwhile Kelli became pregnant. Bianchi proposed. She turned him down but they continued to live together.

Bianchi then decided to go into the prostitution racket with Buono. They bought a list of Johns from Deborah Noble and her friend 19-year-old Yolanda Washington, a part-time waitress and prostitute who worked on Sunset Boulevard. The list turned out to be fake and Yolanda disappeared on 17 October 1977. Her naked body was found on a hillside near Universal City several days later. A cloth was tied around her neck and she had died of strangulation. The post mortem showed she had sex with two men before she died, but as she was a prostitute this was not considered significant.

Bianchi had long cherished an ambition to be a cop and fell in line with Buono's suggestion that they emulated Caryl Chessman, who had impersonated a policeman so that he could rob and rape his victims. But this couple would go further than Chessman, who never murdered. Armed with fake badges, they would stop female motorists or nab prostitutes, then subject their victims to an ordeal of rape, torture, sexual humiliation and brutality, before garrotting them.

On 31 October, police retrieved the body of 16-year-old Judith Miller. Wrapped in a tarpaulin, it had been dumped in a flowerbed in La Cresenta, a residential neighbourhood north of downtown Los Angeles. There were marks of ligatures on her ankles, wrists and neck. The slim teenager had been trussed up, raped and strangled.

Twenty-one-year-old Hollywood waitress Elissa Kastin was abducted on 5 November, raped, strangled and sodomized. Her naked body was found near a Glendale Country Club and showed ligature marks similar to those on Judith Miller's body. Three days later, 28-year-old aspiring actress and model Jane King was kidnapped, raped and smothered. Her body was dumped on an off-ramp of the Golden State Freeway, where it lay undiscovered until 22 November.

So far, the police had not taken much notice of these crimes as the victims were considered to have lived a high-risk lifestyle. But then the killers turned their murderous attention on young girls. On 13 November 1977, classmates at junior high Dolores "Dollie" Cepeda, aged 12, and Sonja Johnson, 14, disappeared after they got off their school bus. A week later a nine-year-old boy cleaning up trash found their naked bodies in Elypsian Park. The schoolgirls had been raped and there were ligature marks on their bodies. In picking these young girls, was Bianchi reliving the Alphabet Murders?

That same day, 20 November, the naked body of 20-year-old art student Kristina Weckler was found by hikers on a hill near

Glendale. She had been sexually assaulted and had ligature marks on her inner arms and neck. Bianchi later recounted Kristina Weckler's last moments: "She was brought into the kitchen and put on the floor and her head was covered with a bag and the pipe from the gas stove was disconnected, put into the bag and then turned on. There may have been marks on her neck because there was a cord put around her neck to make a more complete sealing." Bianchi and Buono kept her in there for 90 minutes before she died of asphyxiation.

By the time the decomposing body of Jane King was recovered on the 22nd, female residents of Los Angeles were in uproar. Then on 29 November, the police found the naked body of 18-year-old Lauren Wagner. Again she had been strangled and there were ligature marks. But this time there were electrical burns on her palms that indicated she was tortured.

A task office of 30 officers was established. The police now knew that they were looking for two suspects, based on the testimony of eyewitnesses, including one prospective victim – the daughter of 1940s screen villain Peter Lorre – who had managed to escape the stranglers' clutches.

On 9 December, prostitute Kimberly Diane Martin – who worked under the name "Donna" – answered her last call-out in Glendale. The following morning her naked body was found on a hillside in Echo Park. Then on 16 February 1978, a helicopter spotted an orange Datsun that had run off a cliff in Angeles National Forest. In the trunk was the naked body of 20-year-old Cindy Hudspeth. She had been raped and her body showed the marks of ligatures.

In May 1978, Bianchi moved to Bellingham in Washington State to be with his girlfriend Kelli Boyd, and newborn son. Finally he got the position he craved with the police and was taken on by the Whatcom County Sheriffs Reserve. He also worked as a security guard at a number of properties, including a house whose owners were in Europe. On 11 January 1979, he told college roommates Karen Mandic and Diane Wilder that a burglar alarm needed repairing, and gave them $100 to house-sit for a few hours. While showing them around the house, Bianchi attacked Karen Mandic on the stairs to the basement, raped and strangled her with a ligature. Then he raped and killed Diane Wilder the same way. He put both bodies in their car and dumped it in a heavily wooded area, though it was found soon after. When the police investigated the murder of the two women, they discovered that they had last been seen when they went for the house-sitting job. This led them to Bianchi. A search of his home turned up items stolen from sites he was paid to guard, evidence that linked him to the murders of Karen Mandic and Diane Wilder, and jewellery belonging to Yolanda Washington and Kimberly Martin. In June 1979, he was indicted for five of the Hillside murders.

In custody, Bianchi at first denied everything. Then he began to manufacture a complex insanity defence. He had just seen the movie *Sybil*, about a schizophrenic suffering from multiple personalities triggered by childhood abuse. He claimed one of his multiple personalities committed the crimes and pretended to have large gaps in his memory when talking to his attorney Dean Brett. Brett asked a memory expert, Dr John Watkins, to look at his client. Bianchi then feigned to submit to hypnosis and introduced the evil personality, Steve Walker. Walker admitted killing in the Bellingham and Hillside murders, implicating Angelo Buono. In the process, he convinced Dr Watkins that he suffered from multiple personality syndrome.

But LA Detective Frank Salerno was not so easily taken in. When he watched video footage of the hypnosis, he noticed that "Steve" referred to himself as "he", instead of "I". Salerno persuaded the court to find a second expert, Dr Ralph Allison. But Allison was also convinced and even seemed afraid of Steve. A third psychologist, Dr Martin Orne, was called in. He tricked Bianchi. Orne explained to Bianchi that that type of schizophrenia usually involved more than just two personas. Under hypnosis session Bianchi duly produced a third persona, named Billy, and two others emerged as well. Clearly Bianchi was a fake.

Having been found out, Bianchi agreed to testify against Buono if he was spared the death penalty in Washington State. He told his interrogators how the prostitutes were easy prey. Posing as police officers, they found it easy to persuade the girls to get in their car on the pretext that they were going to be taken downtown and booked for soliciting. With other victims they asked for directions, or pretended to have some trouble with their car, before bundling them into the vehicle. The victims were tied up, raped, in some cases tortured, strangled and dumped. He pleaded guilty to five counts of homicide.

In October 1979, Angelo Buono was arrested and indicted on ten counts of first-degree murder. After ten months of preliminary hearings, Buono was ordered to stand trial on all counts.

Meanwhile in June 1980 Bianchi received a letter from Veronica Lynn Compton, a 23-year-old poet, playwright, and aspiring actress, who sought his advice on her new play which dealt with a female serial killer. She visited him in jail. Their ongoing conversations and correspondence revealed her bizarre masochistic obsession with murder, mutilation and necrophilia. This encouraged Bianchi to suggest a bizarre defence strategy. With barely a second thought, Veronica Compton agreed to go to Bellingham, strangle women there and sprinkle some of Bianchi's sperm on their bodies. Bianchi was a non-secretor – that is, a person with A or B type blood whose body secretions do not contain the identifying A or B substances. This was before the development of DNA fingerprinting. So if Compton mimicked Bianchi's MO, it could possibly lead police to believe that the real killer was still at large.

On 16 September 1980, Compton visited Bianchi in prison, where he gave her a book. Inside was part of a rubber glove containing his semen. She flew to Bellingham and checked into the Shangri-la Motel. Picking out a potential victim, a woman who worked in a bar, she invited her back to the motel. But the woman was too strong. When Compton tried to murder her, she fought her off and escaped. Arrested in California on 3 October, Compton was convicted in Washington in 1981 and sent to prison with no hope of parole before 1994.

At Buono's trial, Bianchi admitted faking multiple personality disorder. This undermined his testimony. Veronica Compton also took the stand and admitted that she had conspired with Bianchi to kill women in the manner of the Hillside Strangler. The defence implied that Bianchi and Compton had intended to frame Angelo Buono and let him take the heat. This brought reasonable doubt to the case, which the defence then moved to have thrown out. However, the judge refused. A new prosecution team was brought in and in November 1983, Buono was convicted on nine counts of murder – Yolanda Washington's murder was excluded. He was sentenced to nine terms of life without parole.

Buono also found love in prison. In 1986, Buono married Christine Kizuka, a mother of three, who met him through another inmate. He left her a widow when he died in Calipatria State Prison on 21 September 2002 from "unknown causes".

In jail in Washington, Bianchi married serial killer groupie Shirlee Book in 1989 after a three-year correspondence. He was just one of many prisoners she had written to – even Ted Bundy was on her list. It is said that Book had bought her wedding gown and had invitations printed before she had even met Bianchi.

Slighted, Compton turned her attentions to "Sunset Strip Slayer" Douglas Clark, who had shot his victims in the head while they were giving him oral sex, then had sex with the dead body or just the severed head. To win her, Clark sent Compton a red rose when she was convicted for attempted murder and, as a Valentine, a photograph of a decapitated female corpse. Compton wrote back to Clark: "Our humor is unusual. I wonder why others don't see the necrophiliac aspects of existence as we do." She also admitted under oath that she and Clark planned to buy a mortuary together so that they could have sex with the dead bodies, once he was free. Their plan was that Compton should testify on his behalf at Clark's trial, which, by coincidence, took place across the hall from the trial of the Hillside Stranglers. Carol Bundy, Clark's accomplice who had lured his victims into his car, was in the same jail as Compton and Compton was to say that she had heard Bundy admit to the murders.

The affair ended when Compton lost her bottle in court and pleaded the Fifth Amendment, which allows witnesses to refuse to give testimony that would incriminate them. Clark then married a woman named Kelly Keniston, who crusaded to prove his innocence while he awaited execution at San Quentin. Carol Bundy was sentenced to 27 years to life and 25 years to life – the equivalent of two life sentences in the UK. The terms were to run consecutively. She died in the Central California Women's Facility in Chowcilla on 9 December 2003 at the age of 61.

Although Bianchi was suspected of the Alphabet Murders in Rochester, no evidence was ever found to connect him with the killings. A film was made about *The Alphabet Killer* and is due for release in 2007.

Veronica Compton wrote a book about her prison romances called *Eating the Ashes*. Then on 27 July 1988, she escaped from the women's prison at Gig Harbor, Washington. She remains at large.

The San Diego Strangler

When prostitute killings began in San Diego in the summer of 1985, the police feared that the Green River Killer had moved down the coast from Washington State. But as the body count climbed towards ten, they realized that another, but just as elusive, serial killer was on the loose. Then almost exactly three years after he had started, he stopped, leaving the police baffled. He has neither been identified nor caught.

His first victim was 22-year-old Danna Gentile, who was last seen alive on 22 July 1985. Her naked, lifeless body was found three days later. Gravel and rocks had been forced into her mouth and she had been strangled.

A year after Danna Gentile had gone missing, the naked body of an unidentified woman was found. She had been strangled. Then on 3 August, Theresa Brewer was found dead. She had been tied up and strangled. The following April, the naked body of 29-year-old Rosemarie Ritter was found. And on 22 June, the body Anne Varela was discovered. Like the others, she was naked and had been strangled.

In 1987 three more women – Diana Moffitt, Sara Gedalicia, and Sally Moorman – had been killed, the murderer using the same MO. In April 1988 the body of another unidentified woman was found. The following month, the body of Melissa Sandoval was found just 30 yards away. Sandoval had been last seen eight days earlier driving off with a customer.

Then, for no discernable reason, the killings stopped. Two men who were later convicted of prostitute killings in the San Diego area during 1988 were suspects, but nothing linked them to these killings. There was a great deal of speculation about another one-time suspect, who has since died. Again there was no hard evidence linking him to these killings. The murders of these ten women remain unsolved.

San Francisco's Zodiac Killer

An unidentified killer terrified the Bay Area in the late 1960s. Dubbed the "Zodiac Killer", he killed at least six people, though his body count may have been as high as 37, or even 49.

His reign of terror began on a chilly, moonlit night around Christmas in 1968, when a teenage couple pulled up in an open space next to a pump house on Lake Herman road in the Vallejo hills overlooking San Francisco. This was the local lovers' lane and David Faraday and Bettilou Jensen were indifferent to the cold. They were so wrapped up in each other that they did not even notice when another car pulled up about ten feet away. They were rudely awoken from their amorous reverie by gunfire. One bullet smashed through the back window, showering them with glass. Another thudded into the bodywork. Bettilou threw open the passenger door and leapt out. David tried to follow. He had his hand on the door handle when the gunman leant in through the driver's window and shot him in the head. His body slumped across the front seat. Bettilou's attempt at flight was futile. As she ran screaming into the night, the gunman ran after her. She had run just 30 feet when he fired five shots into her. She collapsed and died. Then the gunman calmly walked back to his car and drove away.

A few minutes later, another car came down the quiet road. Its driver, a woman, saw Bettilou's body sprawled on the ground, but did not stop. Instead, she sped on towards the next town, Benicia, to get help. On the way, she saw a blue flashing light coming towards her. It was a patrol car and she flashed her lights frantically to attract the driver's attention. The car stopped and she told the patrolmen what she had seen. They followed her back to the pump station, arriving there about three minutes later. They found Bettilou Jensen dead, but David Faraday was still alive. He was unconscious and could not help them with their enquiries. They rushed him to hospital, but he died shortly after arriving there.

There was little to go on. The victims had not been sexually assaulted, nor was anything missing. The money in David Faraday's wallet was untouched. Detective Sergeant Les Lundblatt of the Vallejo county police investigated the possibility that they had been murdered by a jealous rival. But the police could find no jilted lovers or any other amorous entanglements. The two teenagers were ordinary students. Their lives were an open book. Six months later, Bettilou Jensen and David Faraday had just become two more of the huge number of files of unsolved murders in the state of California.

Then, on 4 July 1969, their killer struck again. Around midnight, at Blue Rock Park, another romantic spot just two miles from where Jensen and Faraday were slain, Mike Mageau was parked with his girlfriend, 22-year-old waitress Darlene Ferrin. They were not alone. Other cars of other courting couples were parked up there. Again Mike and Darlene were too engrossed in each other to notice when a white car pulled up beside them. It stayed there just a few minutes, then drove away. But it returned and parked on the other side of the road.

Suddenly, a powerful spotlight shone on Mike Mageau's car. A figure approached. Thinking it was the police, Mike reached for his driver's licence. As he did so, he heard gunfire and Darlene slumped down in her seat. Seconds later, a bullet tore into Mike's neck. The gunman walked calmly back to the white car, paused to fire another four or five shots at them, then sped off, leaving the smell of cordite and burning rubber behind him.

A few minutes later, a man called the Vallejo county police and reported a murder up on Columbus Parkway. He told the switch-board operator: "You will find the kids in a brown car. They are shot with a 9 mm Luger. I also killed those kids last year. Goodbye."

When the police arrived, Darlene Ferrin was dead. Mike Mageau was still alive, but the bullet had passed through his tongue and he was unable to talk. However, there were some other leads. Four months earlier, Darlene's babysitter had spotted a white car parked outside Darlene's apartment. Suspicious, she asked Darlene about it. It was plain that the young waitress knew the driver.

"He's checking up on me again," she told the baby-sitter. "He doesn't want anyone to know what I saw him do. I saw him murder someone."

The baby-sitter had had a good look at the man in the white car. She told the police that he was middle-aged with brown wavy hair and a round face. When Mike Mageau could talk again, he confirmed that the gunman had brown hair and a round face. But after that clues petered out.

Then, on 1 August 1969, almost two months after the shooting of Ferrin and Mageau, three local papers received handwritten letters. These began: "DEAR EDITOR, THIS IS THE MUR-DERER OF THE 2 TEENAGERS LAST CHRISTMAS AT LAKE HERMAN & THE GIRL ON THE 4TH OF JULY . . ." Like the "Son of Sam" letters written by David Berkowitz, they were printed and contained basic errors in spelling and syntax. But the author gave details of the ammunition used and left no doubt that he was the gunman. Each letter also contained a third of a sheet of paper covered with a strange code. The killer demanded that the papers print this on the front page otherwise, the writer said, he would go on "killing lone people in the night". The letter was signed with another cipher – a circle with a cross inside it which looked ominously like a gunsight. All three newspapers complied and the full text of the coded message was sent to Mare Island Naval Yard where cryptographers tried to crack it. Although it was a simple substitution code, the US Navy's experts could not break it. But Dale Harden, a teacher at Alisal High School, Salinas, could. He had the simple idea of looking for a group of ciphers that might spell the word "kill". He found them and, after ten hours' intense work, he and his wife decoded the whole of the message.

It read: "I like killing people because it is so much more fun than killing wild game in the forrest [sic] because man is the most dangerous of all to kill . . ." The killer went on to boast that he had already murdered five people in the San Francisco Bay area. He said that when he was born again in paradise, his victims would be his slaves.

The killer's cryptic message brought with it a tidal wave of information from the public. Over a thousand calls were received by the police. None of them led anywhere. So the killer volunteered more help. This time he gave them a name – or, at least, a nickname that would attract the attention of the headline writers. He wrote again to the newspapers, beginning: "DEAR EDITOR, THIS IS ZODIAC SPEAKING . . ." Again he gave details of the slaying of Darlene Ferrin that only the killer could have known. But although this increased the killer's publicity profile, the police were no nearer to catching him.

On 27 September 1969, 20-year-old Bryan Hartnell and 22-year-old Cecelia Ann Shepard – both students at the Seventh Day Adventist's Pacific Union College nearby – went for a picnic on the shores of Lake Berryessa, some 13 miles north of Vallejo. It was a warm day. They had finished eating and were lying on a blanket kissing at around 4.30 p.m. when they noticed a man coming across the clearing towards them. He was stocky and had brown hair. He disappeared for a moment into a copse. When he emerged he was wearing a mask and carrying a gun. As he came closer, Bryan Hartnell saw that the mask had a symbol on it. It was a circle with a white cross in it. The man was not particularly threatening in his manner. His voice was soft.

"I want your money and your car keys," he said.

Bryan Hartnell explained that he only had 76 cents, but the hooded man was welcome to that. The gunman then began to chat. He explained that he was an escaped convict and that he was going to have to tie them up. He had some clothes-line with him and got Cecelia to tie up Bryan. Then he tied Cecelia up himself.

The gunman talked some more then calmly announced: "I am going to have to stab you people."

Bryan Hartnell begged to be stabbed first.

"I couldn't bear to see her stabbed," he said.

The gunman calmly agreed, sank to his knees and stabbed Hartnell in the back repeatedly with a hunting knife. Hartnell was dizzy and sick, but still conscious when the masked man turned his attention to Cecelia. He was calm at first, but after the first stab he seemed to go berserk. He plunged the hunting knife into her defenceless body again and again, while she twisted and turned frantically under him in a futile attempt to escape the blows. When she finally lay still, the man grew calm again. He got up and walked over to their car. He pulled a felt-tip pen from his pocket and drew something on the door. Then he walked away.

A fisherman heard their screams and came running. Bryan and Cecelia were both still alive. The Napa Valley Police were already on their way, alerted by an anonymous phone call. A gruff man's voice had said: "I want to report a double murder."

He gave a precise location for where the bodies were to be found, then left the phone hanging.

Cecelia Shepard was in a coma when the police arrived. She died two days later in hospital without regaining consciousness. Bryan Hartnell recovered slowly and was able to give a full description of their attacker. But the police had already guessed who he was. The sign he had drawn on the door of their car was a circle with a cross in it. The police found the phone that the man with the gruff voice had left hanging. It was in a call box less than six blocks from the headquarters of the Napa Valley Police Department. And there managed to get three good fingerprints off it. Unfortunately, there was no match on record.

Two weeks after the stabbing, on 11 October 1969, a 14-year-old girl was looking out of the window of her home in San Francisco and witnessed a crime in progress. A cab was parked on the corner of Washington and Cherry Streets and a stocky man, in the front passenger seat, was going through the pockets of the driver. She called her brothers over to watch what was happening. The man got out of the taxi, leaving the cab driver slumped across the seat. He wiped the door handle with a piece of cloth, then walked off in a northerly direction. The children called the police, but they did not give their evidence clearly enough. The telephone operator who took the call, logged at 10 p.m., noted that the suspect was an "NMA" – negro male adult. An all-points bulletin was put out and a patrolman actually stopped a stocky man nearby and asked whether he had seen anything unusual. But as he was white, the police officer let him go.

Later a stocky man was seen running into the nearby Presidio – a military compound that contains housing and a park area. The floodlights were switched on and the area was searched by patrolmen with dogs. In the cab, the police found the taxi-driver, 29-year-old Paul Stine, dead from a gunshot wound to the head. The motive, they thought, was robbery.

Then, three days later, the *San Francisco Chronicle* received a Zodiac letter. It read:

THIS IS THE ZODIAC SPEAKING. I AM THE MURDERER OF THE TAXI DRIVER OVER BY WASHINGTON ST AND MAPLE ST [sic] LAST NIGHT, TO PROVE IT HERE IS A BLOOD STAINED PIECE OF HIS SHIRT.

San Francisco criminologists managed to match the piece of cloth in the letter exactly with the shirt of the murdered taxi driver. The bullet that had killed Stine was a. 22 and fired from the same gun that had been used in the murder of Bettilou Jensen and David Faraday.

The letter went on to say:

I AM THE SAME MAN WHO DID IN THE PEOPLE IN THE NORTH BAY AREA.
    THE S.F. POLICE COULD HAVE CAUGHT ME LAST NIGHT,

it taunted, concluding,

> SCHOOL CHILDREN MAKE NICE TARGETS. I THINK I
> SHALL WIPE OUT A SCHOOL BUS SOME MORNING.
> JUST SHOOT OUT THE TYRES AND THEN PICK OFF
> ALL THE KIDDIES AS THEY COME BOUNCING OUT.

The letter was signed with a circle with a cross in it.

The description given by the children and the policeman who had stopped a stocky white male leaving the scene of the crime matched those given by Darlene Ferrin's babysitter, Mike Mageau and Bryan Hartnell. A new composite of the Zodiac killer was drawn up and issued to the public by San Francisco Chief of Police Thomas J. Cahill. It showed a white male, 35 to 45 years old with short brown hair, possibly with a red tint. He was around five feet eight inches tall, heavily built and wore glasses. The wanted poster was plastered around town.

But the Zodiac killer's appetite for publicity seems to have been endless. At 2 a.m. on 22 October 1969, 11 days after the murder of Paul Stine, a man with a gruff voice called the police department in Oakland, which is just across the bay from San Francisco. He introduced himself as the Zodiac and said: "I want to get in touch with F. Lee Bailey. If you can't come up with Bailey, I'll settle for Mel Belli. I want one or other of them to appear on the Channel 7 talk show. I'll make contact by telephone."

The men he was asking for were the two top criminal lawyers in America. F. Lee Bailey has been seen more recently defending O. J. Simpson. But he was not available on such short notice and Melvin Belli agreed to appear on the Jim Dunbar talk show at 6.30 the next morning. The show's ratings soared as people throughout the Bay area got up the next morning and tuned in. At around 7.20 a man called in and told Belli that he was the Zodiac, though he preferred to be called Sam. He said: "I'm sick. I have headaches."

But the two police switchboard operators who talked to the Zodiac when he reported the murders said his voice was that of an older man. The mystery caller was eventually traced to Napa State Hospital and proved to be a mental patient.

The real Zodiac continued his correspondence. He wrote to Inspector David Toschi of the San Francisco homicide squad, threatening to commit more murders. In another letter, he claimed to have killed seven people – two more than the official Zodiac body count so far. Later he claimed to have killed ten, taunting the San Francisco Police Department with the scoreline: "ZODIAC 10, SFPD 0." He gave cryptic clues to his name and fantasized about blowing up school children with a bomb.

The following Christmas, Melvin Belli received a card saying:

DEAR MELVIN, THIS IS THE ZODIAC SPEAKING. I WISH YOU A HAPPY CHRISTMAS. THE ONE THING I ASK OF YOU IS THIS, PLEASE HELP ME . . . I AM AFRAID I WILL LOSE CONTROL AND TAKE MY NINTH AND POSSIBLE TENTH VICTIM.

Another piece of Paul Stine's bloodstained shirt was enclosed and forensic handwriting experts feared that the Zodiac's mental state was deteriorating.

On 24 July 1970, the Zodiac killer wrote a letter which spoke of

THE WOEMAN [sic] AND HER BABY THAT I GAVE A RATHER INTERESTING RIDE FOR A COUPLE OF HOWERS ONE EVENING A FEW MONTHS BACK THAT ENDED IN MY BURNING HER CAR WHERE I FOUND THEM.

The woman was Kathleen Johns of Vallejo. On the evening of 17 March 1970, she had been driving in the area when a white Chevrolet pulled alongside her. The driver indicated that there was something wrong with her rear wheel. She pulled over and the other driver stopped. He was a "clean-shaven and neatly dressed man". He said that the wheel had been wobbling and offered to tighten the wheel nuts for her. But when she pulled away, the wheel he had said he had fixed came off altogether. The driver of the Chevrolet then offered her a lift to a nearby service station, but drove straight past it. When she pointed this out, the man said, in a chillingly calm voice: "You know I am going to kill you."

But Kathleen Johns kept her head. When he slowed on the curve of a freeway ramp, she jumped from the car with her baby in her arms. Then she ran and hid in an irrigation ditch. He stopped and, with a flashlight from the trunk of his car, started searching for her. He was approaching the ditch when he was caught in the headlights of a truck and made off. An hour later, she made her way to a police station to report what had happened to her. When she looked up and saw the Zodiac's wanted poster, she identified him as the man who had threatened to kill her. And when the police drove her back to her car, they found it burnt out. It seemed he had returned and set it alight.

Despite the new leads Kathleen Johns provided, the police got no nearer to catching the Zodiac killer. Police in Vallejo believed that the man they were after was now the driver of a new green Ford. He had stopped and watched a Highway Patrolman across the freeway. When the Highway Patrolman decided to ask him what he was doing and cut around through an underpass, he found the green Ford was gone. It was now sitting on the other side of the freeway where the squad car had been moments before. This cat and mouse game was played every day for two weeks.

Detective Sergeant Les Lundblatt became convinced that the Zodiac killer was a man named Andy Walker. He had known Darlene Ferrin and Darlene's sister identified him as the man who had waited outside Darlene's apartment in a white car. He also bore a resemblance to the description of the man seen near Lake Berrylessa when Cecelia Shepard was stabbed to death. And he had studied codes in the military. However, his fingerprints did not match the one left in Paul Stine's cab and his handwriting did not match the Zodiac's notes. But the police discovered that Walker was ambidextrous and believed that the murder of Paul Stine had been planned so meticulously that the Zodiac may have used the severed finger of a victim they did not know about. He was also known to suffer from bad headaches and he got on badly with women at work.

The police decided that they had to get his palm prints to see if they matched those on the telephone that had been left dangling after the Paul Stine killing. An undercover policeman asked Walker to help him carry a goldfish bowl. Walker obliged, but the palm prints he left were smudged. Walker realized what was going on and a judge issued a court order forcing the police to stop harassing him.

Zodiac letters threatening more murders were sent. Some of them have been authenticated, but rendered few new clues. The only thing that detectives could be sure of was that the Zodiac was a fan of Gilbert and Sullivan. He taunted them with a parody of "The Lord High Executioner", listing those people he intended to kill and using the refrain "titwillow, titwillow, titwillow". And there were no letters or criminal activity that could have been ascribed to the Zodiac killer during the entire run of the Mikado in San Francisco's Presentation Theatre.

There may have been more Zodiac murders, too. On 21 May 1970, the naked body of Marie Antoinette Anstey was found just off a quiet country road in Lake County. Traces of mescaline were found in her body. She had been hit over the head and drowned. Her clothes were never found. The murder of Marie Antoinette Anstey followed the pattern of the Zodiac killings. It took place at a weekend, in the same general area around Vallejo, and near a body of water. Although she was naked, there were no signs that she had been sexually molested.

The Zodiac had some curious connection with the water. All the names of all murder scenes had some association with water – even Washington Street. In one of the Zodiac letters, he claimed that the body count would have been higher if he had not been "swamped by the rain we had a while back". The police deduced that he lived in a low-lying area, susceptible to flooding. Perhaps he had a basement where he kept the equipment to make the long-threatened bomb.

A K-Mart store in Santa Rosa, California was evacuated after a bomb threat by a man identifying himself as the Zodiac killer. Two months later, the Zodiac wrote another letter to the *San Francisco Chronicle* claiming to have killed 12 people and enclosing the map with an X marking the peak of Mount Diablo – the Devil's Mountain – in Contra Costa Country across the bay from San Francisco. From there, an observer could see the entire panorama of the area where the murders had taken place. But when detectives checked it out more closely, the spot marked was within the compound of a Naval Relay Station, where only service personnel with security clearance could go.

The letters continued, demanding that people in the San Francisco area wear lapel badges with the Zodiac symbol on it. When they did not, he threatened Paul Avery, the *Chronicle*'s crime writer who had been investigating the story. Journalists, including Paul Avery, began wearing badges saying "I am not Paul Avery". But Avery, who was a licensed private eye and a former war correspondent in Vietnam, took to carrying a. 38 and put in regular practice at the police firing range.

An anonymous correspondent tied the Zodiac slayings to the unsolved murder of Cheri Jo Bates, a college girl in Riverside, California, on Halloween 1966. The police could not rule out a connection, but could not prove a concrete link either. But when crime writer Paul Avery checked it out he discovered that the police had received what they considered to be a crank letter about the murder, five months after the killing. It was signed with the letter Z.

Cheri Jo Bates was an 18-year-old freshman, who had been stabbed to death after leaving the college library one evening. In a series of typewritten letters, the killer gave details of the murder only he could have known. He also said that there would be more and talked of a "game" he was playing. But there were also handwritten letters, where the handwriting matched the Zodiac's and Avery managed to persuade the police to re-open the Bates case in the light of the Zodiac murders.

During 1971, there were a number of murders that could have been committed by the Zodiac. Letters purporting to come from him confessed to them, but he could easily have been claiming credit for other people's handiwork. However, on 7 April 1972, 33-year-old Isobel Watson, who worked as a legal secretary in San Francisco, alighted from the bus at around 9 p.m. in Tamalpais Valley and began walking home up Pine Hill. Seemingly out of nowhere, a white Chevrolet swerved across the road at her. The car stopped. The driver apologized and offered to give her a lift home. When Mrs Watson declined, he pulled a knife on her and stabbed her in the back. Her screams alerted the neighbours. The man ran back to his car and sped off. Mrs Watson recovered and gave a description. Her assailant was a white man in his early 40s, around five foot nine inches and he wore black-rimmed reading glasses. The police said that there was a better than fifty-fifty chance that this was the Zodiac killer.

As time went on, other detectives dropped out of the case, leaving only Inspector David Toschi. The FBI looked at the files, but even they could take the case no further.

The correspondence from the Zodiac ceased for nearly four years. Though psychologists believed that he was the type who might commit suicide, Toschi did not believe he was dead. Toschi reasoned that the Zodiac got his kicks from the publicity surrounding the killings, rather than the killings themselves. Surely he would have left a note, or some clue in his room, that he was the Zodiac. Then on 25 April 1978, Toschi got confirmation. The *Chronicle* received a new letter from him. This time it mentioned Toschi by name. The author wanted the people of San Francisco to know he was back. Now the police had a new opportunity to catch him.

Robert Graysmith, author of the book *Zodiac*, deduced that the killer was a movie buff. In one of his cryptograms he mentioned "the most dangerous game" which is the title of a film. In another, he called himself "the Red Phantom", the title of another movie. And he frequently mentions going to the movies to see *The Exorcist* or *Badlands*, a fictionalized account of the murderous spree of Nebraskan killer Charles Starkweather. The police used this information and the Zodiac killer's obvious love of publicity to try and trap him. When a movie about the Zodiac killings was shown in San Francisco a suggestions box was left in the lobby of the cinema. The audience were asked to drop a note of any information or theories they may have in it. The box was huge and a detective was hidden inside it. He read every entry by torchlight as it fell through the slot. If any looked like they came from the Zodiac killer, he was to raise the alarm. None did.

The Oakland police thought that they had captured the Zodiac killer. They arrested a Vietnam veteran who had seen the movie three times and had been apprehended in the lavatory at the cinema masturbating after one particularly violent scene. The Oakland PD was soon proved wrong. His handwriting did not match the Zodiac's. Soon there was a welter of recrimination. Toschi was transferred out of homicide after baseless accusations that he had forged the Zodiac letters for self-promotion. The police in the Bay area began to believe that the Zodiac killer was either dead or in prison outside the state for another crime. Or it could have been, after the close call with the killing of Paul Stine, that he figured that his luck was running out.

But Robert Graysmith was not convinced. He managed to connect the Zodiac killings with the unsolved murder of 14 young girls, usually students or hitch-hikers in the Santa Rosa area in the early 1970s. Most of them were found nude, their clothes were missing but largely they had not been sexually molested. Each of them had been killed in different ways, as if the murderer was experimenting to find out which way was best. Graysmith reckons that the Zodiac's body count could be as high as 40.

The Zodiac's symbol, a cross in a circle, Graysmith believes, is not a stylized gunsight but the projectionist's guide seen on the lead-in to a movie. Through a cinema in San Francisco which has the constellations painted on the ceiling he traced a promising suspect. The man, Graysmith was told, filmed some of the murders and kept the film in a booby-trapped film can.

Another Graysmith suspect was a former boyfriend of Darlene Ferrin's. He had also been a resident of Riverside when Cheri Jo Bates had been murdered. He lived with his mother, whom he loathed, and dissected small mammals as a hobby. During the crucial 1975–78 period when the Zodiac killer was quiet, he was in a mental hospital after being charged with child molesting at a school where he worked.

Although he had two promising candidates Graysmith could not pin the Zodiac murders on either of them. He published the story of his investigation in 1985.

But then, in 1990, a series of strange murders began in New York. The perpetrator claimed to be the Zodiac. The killer's description does not match those given by the witnesses in California. But a man can change a lot in twenty years.

The Sonoma County Slayings

Between 1972 and 1975 fifteen females were murdered around Sonoma County in northern California. The first victims were thought to be 12-year-olds Yvonne Weber and Maureen Strong, who vanished on their way home from the Redwood Ice Skating Rick in Santa Rosa at around 4 p.m. on 4 February 1972. Their remains were found at the bottom of a 60-foot embankment near a country road in the Franz Valley area, east of Sonoma County on 28 December. Forensic examination indicated that they had been killed elsewhere and simply dumped there. The killer had removed their clothes and taken a single gold earring from each girl – a practice he would continue in the future.

On 4 March 1972, 19-year-old Kim Wendy Allen, a student at Santa Rosa Junior College, was travelling home when she vanished. She was last seen at 5 p.m., hitch-hiking northbound along Highway 101. Her naked body was found on the bed of a creek. She had been strangled with a clothesline. There were rope burns on her ankles and wrists, as if she had been tied spread-eagled, and superficial cuts on her chest. Again her clothes and a single earring were missing. The killer had also taken her handbag and other possessions including a small barrel of soy sauce which had a Chinese character on it that resembled the character drawn by the Zodiac killer in one of his letters.

Then on 21 November, 13-year-old Lori Jursa was abducted from the U-Save market in Santa Rosa. She found with a broken neck three weeks later in a ravine near Calistoga Road. Again she was naked and, although the wire loops were still in her ears, the body of her earrings were missing.

Less than 100 yards from where Lori Lee Jursa's body had been dumped, the skeletal remains of 20-year-old Jeannette Kamahele were found in a shallow grave on 6 July 1979. A student at Santa Rosa Junior College, she was last seen hitch-hiking near the Cotati on-ramp of Highway 101 and was travelling north to Santa Rosa on 25 April 1972. Her hands and ankles had been together with white clothesline that was then wrapped around her neck four times.

The killer then moved to San Francisco. On 29 May 1973, the body of Rosa Vasquez of 834 Bush Street was found in Golden Gate Park. She had been strangled and was, at one time, thought to be one of the Zodiac victims. The body of Yvonne Quilantang of 140 Delta Street was found in a vacant lot in the Bayview district on 10 June. She had also been strangled and the 15-year-old was seven months pregnant. Again she was thought to have been a Zodiac victim. The body of 16-year-old Angela Thomas, originally from Belton, Texas, was found at Benjamin Franklin Junior High School on 2 July. She had been smothered. Then on 15 July, 24-year-old Nancy Patricia Gidley went missing from the Roday Inn motel at 895 Leary Street and was strangled. Another possible Zodiac victim, her body was dumped in the parking lot of George Washington High School, near where the taxi driver Paul Stine was killed. An X-ray technician from Mountain Home, Idaho, she was visiting San Francisco to be maid of honour at the wedding of Collete Mrozek, of Novato, California, at Hamilton Air Force Base in Marin County. She also had ambitions to be a freelance writer for the San Francisco *Chronicle*. All four were naked.

There was a strong military connection between these victims. Nancy Gidley served four years in the Air Force and had been discharged at Hamilton Air Force Base early the previous year. Rosa Vasquez was a keypunch operator at Letterman General Hospital at San Francisco's Presidio. Angela Thomas was the daughter of an Army sergeant who was once stationed at the

Presidio. In San Francisco for a visit, she was last seen in the area of the Presidio, where she had gone to look up old friends. And Yvonne Quilantang was engaged to a soldier who was stationed in Missouri, though she was pregnant by another man.

By now an established trend was obvious. Only the location changed. Four young women were strangled and dumped naked in San Francisco in the spring and early summer of 1973 before hitch-hiker Caroline Davis was poisoned and dumped in a ditch near Santa Rosa in July. It was the same spot that Strong and Weber's remains had also been discovered.

Fifteen-year-old Carolyn Nadine Davis was last seen leaving her grandmother's house in Garberville on 15 July 1973. A runaway from Anderson in Shasta County she went missing while hitch-hiking south on Route 101. On 31 July 1973, her naked body was found 2.2 miles north of Porter Creek Road on Franz Valley Road in the same spot as Yvonne Weber and Maureen Strong had been dumped seven months earlier. She had been poisoned by strychnine and the police discovered that Carolyn had bought a one-way ticket to fly from Redding to San Francisco. On the embankment above her body, twigs were placed in strange design to form two interlocking squares. This was thought to be a witchcraft symbol designating "the carrier of spirits". Again the Zodiac killer was interested in such symbols.

The next body turned up near Redding on 22 July. It belonged to Nancy Feusi. Practically naked, it was so badly decomposed the cause of death could not be determined.

Back in San Francisco, the naked body of Laura O'Dell was found on 4 November. She had been strangled.

On 22 December 1973, 22-year-old Therese Dian Walsh disappeared while hitch-hiking on 101 from Malibu Beach to her home in Garberville. She had been hog-tied with a one-quarter-inch nylon rope, raped, strangled and thrown into a creek near the spot where Kim Wendy Allen's body was found. Some believe that there is an occult significance that she went missing on the winter solstice.

The police believe the same killer stabbed Brenda Merchant in Marysville on 1 February 1974, dumping her naked body in a ditch alongside a rural road. Then on 29 September, the naked body of Donna Braun was discovered floating in the Salinas River near Monterey. The 14-year-old had been strangled. She was thought to have been the last of the killer's victims.

The idea that these murders might have had occult significance was put forward by Sergeant Erwin Carlstedt of the Sonoma County Police. He cited the "witchcraft symbol" found on the embankment in the Caroline Davis case, though they could have been just a piece of childish art. He also pointed out that the bodies had all been dumped on the east side of a road. At the time he tied the California killings to those of seven women in Washington state, between January and July 1974, who had all been abducted in the waning – or sacrificial – phase of the moon. His 1975 report stated that the killer was "familiar with witchcraft or the occult, because of a witchcraft symbol found during the Caroline Davis case and the possible occult involvement in the missing females in the states of Oregon and Washington". However, the Washington killings were later attributed to prolific serial killer Ted Bundy, while Bundy's known movements preclude involvement in the California murders.

Serial rapist and murder Harvey Carignan was a suspect in the unsolved murders, when it came to light that he had been given a speeding ticket he collected in Solano County, east of Santa Rosa, on 20 June 1973. But no solid evidence ties him to any of the murders. One week later, he attacked Marlys Townsend at a bus stop 1,500 miles away in Minneapolis. Clubbed unconscious from behind, she woke in Carignan's car, still groggy from the blow. But when he tried to make her masturbate him, she found strength enough to leap from the speeding vehicle and save herself. This ultimately led to his arrest in September 1974 and he was already in jail when Donna Braun was murdered. Besides none of the crimes showed Carignan's MO. He beat his victims with a hammer.

In his book *Zodiac*, published in 1986, author Robert Graysmith ascribes these and other unsolved murders to the elusive "Zodiac" killer. But as he has not been caught, then it is impossible to say whether one or more serial killers are at large in the Golden State.

Southern California's Original Night Stalker

While "The Night Stalker" Richard Ramirez, who terrorized southern California in 1985, languishes on death row in San Quentin, "The Original Night Stalker" is still at large. He started out as the "East Area Rapist", then became the "Orange Coast Serial Killer", before being dubbed "The Original Night Stalker" because his MO closely resembled Ramirez's, raping and killing his victims in their own homes.

As the East Area Rapist he committed 50 rapes in northern California between 1976 and 1986 and killed at least ten – Orange County Sheriff's Office says 12 – in southern California. We know the grand total because an enterprising Orange County criminologist matched DNA samples from the crimes in northern and southern California in 2001.

The Stalker began by raping women that were at home alone, then gradually moved on to couples, targeting "low-risk" victims – lawyers, medical professionals, computer programmers – people without a great deal of physical strength who were unlikely to fight back. He stalked upper-middle-class neighbourhoods looking for victims who lived in single-storey homes. He broke in late at night, then pulled a handgun. Always well-prepared, he brought pre-cut lengths of rope and cord with him to bind his victims. When attacking a couple, he would sometimes force the man to lie on the floor with perfume bottles or plates stacked on top of him while he raped the female, threatening to kill them both if the man moved enough to tip the bottles onto the floor or rattle the dishes.

The first 15 victims in late 1976 and early 1977 were women at home alone – though one attack was in the parking lot. Victims included a 16-year-old girl and an 18-year-old youth in East Sacramento who was shot in the stomach when he confronted and chased the prowler. The perpetrator escaped even though a police cordon was thrown around the neighbourhood. In one case, he seems to have waited until a woman's husband left the house before he attacked.

At the beginning of November 1976, a reward of $2,500 was offered for information leading to his arrest. That was later increased to $25,000, with a local dentist adding $10,000 to the $15,000 offered by the *Sacramento Bee*'s Secret Witness programme.

The *Bee* said that the perpetrator entered houses though a window like a "cat-burglar" and gave a description. He was white with a pale complexion, between 5 feet 8 inches to 6 feet tall, 25 to 35 years old, with a medium build and dark hair that hangs over his ears and collar.

Later descriptions make him younger – between 18 and 25 – of a slighter build. Though muscular, it was thought he weighed 140 to 180 pounds and was extremely agile.

"He has worn a mask, but descriptions are vague as to what kind," the newspaper said. He also wore gloves, so left no fingerprints. "He has worn military type boots and black tennis shoes. His weapons have included a revolver, knife, a stick and a club. He has cut and beaten his victims, but none severely."

The *Bee* added chillingly: "He frequently commits repeated attacks on individual victims over a period of three hours."

This was a serial killer waiting to happen.

The suspect attacked a single-storey, single family dwelling in a middle- or upper-middle-class neighbourhood. Nearby there was usually a drainage ditch, vacant field, new construction, park area or one of the levees of the American River that runs through Sacramento, so he could approach and make his exit with little chance of being spotted. He entered a residence in the night time through an unlocked sliding glass door or window, though he pried open doors and windows if necessary. Once inside he threatened the victim with a knife, gun or club. He tied her with the ligatures – often shoelaces – he brought with him. Then he used strips of towelling and electrical cord found in the house to further bind, gag and blindfold his victims. He usually cut the telephone cord and covered a lamp to dim the lighting.

He spent between one and three hours in the house, sexually assaulting the victim several times. In between the assaults, he would wander about the house, eating and drinking. Sometimes he would even go out. Beverage containers were found outside where the suspect apparently stood, watching for anyone approaching the house. He would also look through photograph albums and lingerie drawers, stealing small items of costume jewellery, class rings, an earring and items of little value.

Because of the way he moved in and out of the house, the victim rarely knew when her attacker had left the premises. It would usually take her between 30 minutes and an hour before she was able to free herself. Sometimes she would be unable to do so and had to await assistance.

After April he began attacking couples, though he varied his pattern slightly when teenagers were involved. In one case, he raped two sisters who were at home alone together. He also molested a 13-year-old girl while her mother was tied up, and raped a 15-year-old babysitter in front of her eight-year-old ward.

On 7 May 1977, while attacking a couple in Carmichael, the rapist said that he would kill his next two victims. This was what the police had long feared. But he stayed his hand when he attacked a couple on the South Area of Sacramento, near the office of the dentist who had put up the $10,000 reward. Gun and lock sales soared.

It became plain to the police that the attacker had detailed knowledge of his victims. He knew that the father of one victim was out of town for the weekend and that another's father was on vacation. The rapist knew families' habits and work hours. He caught one victim when her sister was visiting friends and her parents were at a Christmas Party; another when her parents were out; another when her parents were away for the weekend.

He knew the schedule of spouses, catching one woman when her husband had relocated to the Bay Area where she was to follow; another when her husband was on a business trip; another when her husband had just left for work; and a fourth when her husband had started on the night shift just two days before the attack. And he attacked one woman who was separated from her husband when her son was visiting his father.

He knew the purse of one victim was in her car. In another attack he knew where the garage door opener was. In another case where the outside lights were on a timer, he knew how to turn them off.

During one attack, the assailant said that he had seen the victim at Mather Officer's Club and knew her husband was a captain in the Air Force. However, his intelligence was not always 100 per cent accurate. In one case, he mentioned that his victim attended American River College. She did not, but a neighbour, who strongly resembled the victim, had attended American River College. It was thought that the offender had been in the other woman's home as well.

It was clear how he got this information. Old footprints from herringbone-pattern tennis shoes were discovered under the bathroom window in numerous cases where he could have overheard conversations. He also returned to the same area repeatedly, making maximum use of the intelligence he had gathered.

The police almost caught the attacker on 12 December 1977, when officers spotted a man wearing a ski mask on a stolen bicycle on the Watt Avenue bridge in the East Area of Sacramento. He was seen again two hours later by city patrolmen near an apartment complex on La Riviera Drive near Watt, a place where he had struck three times before.

As his career as a serial rapist lengthened, he got more violent, cruel, abusive and threatening. He made nine more increasingly savage attacks before he finally lived up to his word and became a killer on 2 February 1978, when he shot dead Brian K. Maggiore, a sergeant at Rancho Cordova Air Force Base, and his wife of 18 months Katie. They confronted a prowler when walking their dog down a quiet residential street. Katie was shot in the head. Brian was pursued into the backyard of a home on La Alegria Drive where he was shot fatally in the chest. The suspect was spotted by residents as he fled the scene. He was described as white, in his mid twenties, 6 feet to 6 feet 2 inches tall with dark hair and wearing a brown leather coat with a large stain on the back and dark pants and shoes. He may have been with an accomplice. A pair of shoelaces were found at the crime scene. Two weeks later composite drawings of the suspects were published in the *Sacramento Bee*. After that, the East Area Rapist never struck in the Sacramento area again.

He moved on to Stockton, Modesto, Danville, Fremont, Concord, San Ramon, Davis and Walnut Creek, and attacked couples and, occasionally, women on their own. A student at UC Davis was attacked in her apartment with extreme physical violence on 7 June 1978. A month later another woman was attacked in Davis and raped in front of her two sons. And on 25 June 1979, a 13-year-old girl was attacked while her parents were at home asleep.

On 1 October 1979, a man in a ski mask entered the home of a couple in Goleta, Santa Barbara County. They were awakened, a flashlight shining in their eyes. The woman was ordered to tie up her boyfriend with pre-cut lengths of cord that the attacker had brought with him. While the masked intruder ransacked the house supposedly looking for money, the woman managed to get out of the house and scream for help. The intruder pulled her back inside. While he was doing this, the man escaped into the backyard. While the intruder pursued the man, the woman escaped again, running into the arms of a neighbour who had been alerted by her screams. Having lost control of the situation, the intruder fled. He was seen escaping on a bicycle and he disappeared down a creek bed.

After this couple escaped, the attacker turned to killing in earnest. Two months later, on 30 December 1979, another couple was attacked a few blocks away. Dr Robert Offerman and Alexandria Manning were found shot to death. Both of them were tied up and Manning had been raped. Examination of the crime scene led detectives to believe that Offerman had managed to loosen his bindings and lunge at the intruder before he was shot and killed. Neighbours who heard the gunshots thought that they were firecrackers.

On 13 March 1980, the Stalker moved just 35 miles down the coast to Ventura, where he killed Lyman and Charlene Smith.

Charlene was raped and both were bludgeoned to death with a log from their fireplace. The Smiths were found still bound in their bedroom by their 12-year-old son. Their wrists and ankles had been tied with drapery cord and an ornate "Chinese knot" was used on their wrists. Though there were similarities to the attacks in Goleta, the Smiths' murder was not immediately linked to the others. Ventura Detectives suspected Joe Alsip, a former business partner of Lyman Smith, who was later exonerated.

Keith and Patrice Harrington were the next to die, also bludgeoned to death in their home in Dana Point on 19 August, as the killer moved south of Los Angeles for the first time. This time the murderer untied his victims before leaving, but left some cord lying on the bed. He took the murder weapon with him when he left. A single burnt match was found in the home by investigators. Patrice had been brutally raped before her death. Law enforcement agencies theorized that the male victims were bludgeoned to death first. Then the terrified female victims were raped before they too were killed by bludgeoning.

Next the killer attacked 28-year-old Manuela Witthuhn on 5 January 1981, while her husband was in the hospital ill. Her killer entered her home in Irvine, Orange County. He raped her and beat her to death, then disappeared, taking with him the bindings along with the murder weapon and, curiously, Witthuhn's answering machine, a lamp and a crystal curio. As in the Smith's case, burnt matches were found in Witthuhn's home.

Cheri Domingo and Gregory Sanchez were killed on 27 July 1981 back in Goleta, just half-a-mile from the scene of the Offerman-Manning murders. Sanchez had been shot once in the face and then bludgeoned to death. Cheri Domingo was bludgeoned. Again, the killer took the ligatures he had used to bind his victims and the murder weapon with him. The attacker's familiarity with the area lead police to believe he lived near the San Jose Creek.

Then for five years, the killer lay low. He struck one last time on 4 May 1986, killing Janelle Lisa Cruz only a mile from Witthuhn's home in Irvine. Her family was away on vacation in Mexico at the time. Cruz was raped and beaten to death like the previous victims. The murder weapon was thought to be a pipe wrench that was found to be missing from her home. Cruz was slain soon after a male friend left her house. The man told police he had heard strange noises outside Janelle's bedroom window before he had left, but she said they came from the washing machine.

Then the killer vanished completely, though it is thought that he made a telephone call to one of his victims in 1990 or 1991.

It was actually not until 2001 that his murders as the Original Night Stalker in the later part of his career and his rapes as the East Area Rapist earlier were definitively linked by DNA evidence. It is also thought that this prodigious criminal committed many other crimes, including two other home-invasion attacks where couples were killed in Goleta, California, from 1979 to 1981. In these crimes, a gun and bludgeoning were used and the victims were bound, but no sexual assault took place and there is no DNA evidence to link the Goleta crimes to the unsolved rapes and murders of the Original Night Stalker.

The killer has never been caught or identified, and is probably out here now. Younger victims put his age as middle to late twenties, while older ones said he was only 18 or 19. That means that in 2007, he would only be in his forties or fifties.

He had blue or hazel eyes. Type "A" blood was found after he cut himself with a knife – this victim's blood was type "O". He wears size nine shoes. Victims saw him wear brown lace-up boots, black high top military boots, ankle-high brown lace-up shoes, brown leather desert boots, black square-toed boots, black tennis shoes and red, white and blue tennis shoes. Impressions left by the prowler outside victims' home and footmarks left within show a herring-bone pattern.

The hair protruding from his ski mask was described variously as dark, medium brown and dirty blonde. The pubic hair he left behind at the scene of his rapes was medium brown.

His height was narrowed down to between 5 feet 10 inches and 5 feet 11. His build was athletic, not heavily muscled like a weightlifter, more like a runner or swimmer.

His voice was higher in pitch than the average male, though he made it husky or gruff when he talked to younger victims. He often talked through clenched teeth, possibly trying to disguise his voice. He had no hint of an accent. He favoured dark clothing, particularly army green, and was seen wearing fatigue pants with baggy pockets.

He had a large collection of ski masks, wearing a different one for each attack. Usually they were store-bought knitted masks, but sometimes they appeared to be homemade. On one occasion he wore a leather hood. Another time he wore a hood made out of army green canvas or heavy denim material which left his nose as well as his eyes and mouth exposed.

He also had a wide range of gloves, which he only took off during the sexual assault – though on one occasion he kept them on throughout. At first, the gloves were usually made of black leather, but later he wore brown gloves made out of heavy cotton with heavy stitching. Latent fingerprints have been found at the scene of the crimes, but no match has been made.

It is thought he lived in the Sacramento Area between 1976 and 1979, and frequented or lived in Rancho Cordova, possibly near Paseo Drive, up to 1976. He frequented Costa Contra County in 1979, and frequented or lived in Goleta from 1979 to 1980. Possibly he had relatives or friends living there at the time. And he frequented or lived near Ventura County or Orange County in southern California from 1980 to 1986.

As several of the neighbourhoods the suspect targeted had homes on the market or homes recently sold, he is thought to have posed as a realtor, building inspector or prospective home-buyer. He may even had studied plans of the homes where the attacks later took place.

In two cases there were two nearby homes for sale. In another case, there was a development directly opposite the victim's house. A neighbour of another victim had put his own home up for sale. About two weeks before to the attack, the house was inspected by a prospective purchaser, who said he was transferring from Las Vegas to McClellan Air Force Base. He was described thin, blond and in his twenties with a short haircut and blue eyes. Two signs from an real estate company were in the backyard of another victim. It appeared the house had been shown earlier.

Another victim had recently bought their house. The previous owner said that, while the house was in process of being put on the market, a very unusual realtor called. He paid no attention to the interior of the house, but inspected the south and west exteriors. He asked her where her husband worked and why her daughter was not at home. She said he was extremely well-dressed, with light brown hair, a darker complexion and a medium frame.

In the vicinity of another victim, there were several newly constructed and unsold homes. There was a vacant condominium for lease near another victim's home. The garage window at this location was opened. Yet another victim had recently moved into their house, which still bore a "SOLD" sign at the time of the attack. A neighbour of another victim had her home on the market. Another victim's home had just been sold and the victim was planning to join her husband in the Bay Area, where he had already moved. A new home was being constructed next to the home of yet another victim.

The killer was proficient at tying ornate knots and probably engaged in bondage-oriented fantasies with his female sexual partners. He would also have collected violent pornographic material that included bondage.

The killer had access to a large collection of knives and handguns – specifically, .38, .357 Magnum and .45 Calibre handguns. He also had a large collection of flashlights.

It seems that he made a practice of parking his car some way from his intended attack. No licence plate was ever linked to the attacker. Tracker dogs followed his path down the drainage ditches, fields and park areas where he made his escape to a place where one would expect a car to be left.

However, from 1977, it is thought he drove an older VW Bug of a nondescript colour. Seen under different lighting conditions, it was variously reported as dark green, grey or silver blue. It is also thought to have wide wheels and a large, customized rear bumper. While in southern California, he seems to have had access to a white 1970s model Pontiac. A bright yellow, 1952 or 1953 Ford or Chevrolet side-step pick-up was seen parked near the scene of a rape for three days before the attack.

It is also thought that the killer had some law enforcement or military police training, and that he was possibly stationed at McClellan or Mather Air Force Base in the early to mid-1970s. He may have been a student at American River College or California State University at Sacramento in the late 1970s, possibly attending school on the GI Bill. He may have tried to get into University of California, Davis around 1979, and was possibly a student at a college in Santa Barbara or Irvine in the early 1980s.

The Southern Pacific Railroad Axeman

Between January 1911 and April 1912, a homicidal maniac slaughtered 49 victims in the states of Louisiana and Texas. Victims were viciously hacked to death with an axe while they slept. In each case, the dead were mulattoes or black members of families with mulatto members. Both the police and leaders of the African-American communities believed that the perpetrator was a dark-skinned Negro who aimed to purge their mixed-race or "tainted" blood.

The first attack took place in early January 1911, at Rayne, Louisiana, when a mother and her three children were hacked to death in their beds. In February, at Crowley, six miles to the west, all three members of the Byers family were slaughtered in identical fashion. Two weeks later, the scene shifted to Lafayette, 15 miles east of Rayne, where a family of four was massacred in the small hours of the morning.

The murders shifted 400 miles to San Antonio, Texas, where five members of the Cassaway family were butchered by the axe murderer in April. As before, the victims died in their sleep and there was no sign of robbery or other "rational" motive for the crime.

On Sunday 25 November 1911 six members of the Norbert Randall family were butchered in the their beds back in Lafayette.

Each had been despatched with a single blow of the axe behind the right ear. The police arrested Clementine Bernabet, a black woman who they suspected was involved in the crime. But while she was in jail throughout the spring of 1912, the carnage continued.

The killer moved back to Crowley again in 19 January 1912, killing a mother and her three children as they slept. Just two days later, 50 miles away at Lake Charles, Louisiana, Felix Broussard, his wife and three children were slain. Again each was killed with a single blow behind the right ear. This time, the killer left a message that read: "When He maketh the inquisition for blood, He forgetteth not the cry of the humble – human five."

Armed with this quasi-Biblical quotation, police turned their attention to a small sect named the Sacrifice Church, arresting two members. There were rumours connecting the Sacrifice Church to a voodoo cult in New Orleans and the sect's leader, the Reverend King Harris, had spoken at a meeting in Lafayette on the night of the murder of the Randall family there. But still the killing did not stop.

On 19 February a mulatto woman and her three children were hacked to death in their sleep in Beaumont, Texas. Then on 27 March, another mulatto woman, her four children, and a male friend who staying overnight were butchered in Glidden, Texas. The police then noticed a geographical pattern in the crimes. They all took place along the Southern Pacific Railroad that ran from Louisiana to California. Since November 1911, the killings had been moving slowly westwards, striking at stops on the Southern Pacific Railroad line. Indeed the next massacre in the early hours of 12 April took place further west in San Antonio, when five members of the family of William Burton were butchered in their beds. But then the killer doubled back. Two nights later, the axe murder killed three more mulatto victims in Hempstead on another branch of the line.

Meanwhile, Clementine Bernabet surprised everyone by confessing. She admitted attending meetings of the Sacrifice Church, but that was not the inspiration for the killings. She had bought a *candja* or voodoo charm from a local witch doctor. The charm allowed Clementine and her friends to do anything they pleased and would never be found out. And what they pleased was to commit a series of axe murders. This sounded rather far-fetched and Clementine Bernabet never stood trial.

The axe murderer finally missed his mark in San Antonio on 6 August 1912, when the wife of mulatto James Dashiell was woken by an axe shearing through the flesh of her arm. Her screams woke the rest of the family and the attacker fled. All she could tell police was that her attacker was a lone man, but could not provide a useful description.

The killer had struck again, leaving the police without a single piece of solid evidence. Those who had been arrested had to be released. Informants from the Sacrifice Church pointed to the Gospel according to St Matthew, chapter seven, verse 19 in the New Testament which reads: "Every tree that bringeth not forth good fruit is hewn down, and cast into the fire." But that did not take the investigation any further forward and the killer, or killers, remained at large.

St Louis' Slayings

An unidentified man raped and killed more than five women in the South Side of St Louis during late 1999. It is not clear whether he is the same man who went on to terrorize East St Louis on the other side of the Mississippi.

Things came to a head in October 2001 when two women were found dead in East St Louis within a day, bringing the number of women slain in the same general area in the previous two years to eight.

The first victim was 41-year-old Lolina Collins, a mother of three who had worked at a state hospital and was planning to become an elementary school teacher. Clad only in a bra, she was found with trash bags over her arms and legs. She had been strangled.

The next day motorist found the naked body of 33-year-old Brenda Beasley lying on the sidewalk beside a fire hydrant. A mother of four, she worked full-time at a fast food restaurant. Her ankles and wrists were bound with duct tape and she had died from a blow to the head.

Police denied that these two killings were related to the earlier murders, most of whom were found in neighbourhoods frequented by drug users and prostitutes. However, police officials in East St Louis had repeatedly turned down the offer of help from the FBI's serial killer unit. They explained that they were under-staffed, lacked the resources, and that the murders did not seem to fit the pattern of a serial killing.

Journalist Earl Ofari Hutchinson maintained that the real reason was that the women were black, poor, and some had histories of prostitution and drug use.

"These are not the type of women that reflexively ignite police and public outrage," he said.

However, in November 2001, the East St. Louis police finally agreed to let the FBI join the hunt.

Texas' "Highway to Hell"

A series of serial killers seem to have been at work on the Gulf Coastal Plain since 1970. Over the three decades up to the year 2000, the FBI has filed the cases of at least 32 murdered women along the 50-mile stretch of Interstate 45 between Houston and Galveston in Texas known as "America's Highway to Hell". The *Encyclopedia of Unsolved Crimes* put the number of abductions of young women along that stretch between 1982 and 1997 at 42. In the general area, there have been around 200 unsolved murders of young women and police believe that up to a dozen serial killers may be at work.

Although the murders seem to have been going on since 1971, the situation was confused because 11 police forces have jurisdiction in the area and it was only with two well-publicized crimes in 1997 that anyone spotted a pattern. On 3 April 1997 12-year-old Laura Kate Smither disappeared while jogging near her home in Friendswood, Texas, five miles west of the I–45. Over 6,000 people took part in a massive search that covered over 800 square miles. Her headless corpse was found on 20 April dumped in a pond ten miles away in Pasadena. She was naked except for one sock and a ring. A dark coloured pick-up was observed in the same area as where she was last seen and a composite sketch was issued of the person in the truck.

"We thought we lived in a really safe town," her mother said. "And that at nine o'clock in the morning, to go for a run on a little private road, that she would be fine."

Investigators noted some obvious similarities between Laura Smither's murder and the abduction of nine-year-old Amber Hagerman in Arlington, Texas, three months before. She had been riding her bike with her brother Ricky near her grandmother's home in Arlington on 13 January 1993 when a neighbour heard a scream. In broad daylight, the neighbour saw a man pull Amber off her bike, throw her into the front seat of his black pick-up truck and drive away at high speed. She was found four miles away at the bottom of a creek bed at the Forest Hollow apartment complex on Green Oaks Boulevard a short distance west of Highway 360 in north Arlington. Her throat had been gashed numerous times and she had been sexually assaulted. Both girls' bodies were dumped in waterways, naked except for their socks. It could not be conclusively determined if the two cases are related or not. Amber's abduction lead to the Amber Plan, where local radio stations – initially in the Dallas area, then further afield – repeat news bulletins concerning missing children. In April 2003, President George W. Bush signed legislation making the Amber Alert system mandatory across the country. In 2006, a movie called *Amber's Story* aired on the Lifetime channel.

On 17 August 1997, 17-year-old Jessica Lee Cain disappeared. She was last seen at Bennigan's, a nightspot, in Clear Lake, Texas. She left the restaurant at approximately 1.30 a.m. to return to her home in Tiki Island, Texas. Her empty pick-up truck was found abandoned on the side of the I–45 between Exits Seven and Eight in La Marque near Highland Bayou Park. Several witnesses reported seeing a red Isuzu Amigo tow truck parked behind it.

Her wallet was found on the seat of her truck, but her keys were missing. Jessica Cain has not been seen since.

"Before Laura Smither and Jessica Cain, each one of us was in his own little world, investigating our own individual cases," said Lieutenant Tommy Hansen of the Galveston County Sheriff's Department. "We would have no way of knowing that some fellow we wanted to question in one murder, and had been a top suspect, had already been questioned in a very similar murder just a few miles down the highway."

Sex offender William Lewis Reece was suspected of involvement in the murders of Laura Smither and Jessica Cain. Convicted of rape in Oklahoma some years before, Reece worked at a construction site near the Smither home and left his work as a bulldozer operator because it was raining and too wet to work, around the same time Laura Smither disappeared. Later he was arrested for the abduction of Sandra Sapaugh.

On 16 May 1997, the 19-year-old Sapaugh was fixing a flat tyre on NASA Road 1 in Webster, across the I–45 from Friendswood, when Reece stopped. But instead of helping her he pulled a knife on her and forced her into his truck. As he drove at 70 miles an hour down I–45, he ordered her to undress. Instead she opened the passenger door and jumped out of the fast moving truck. She was rescued by another driver. Pregnant at the time, she sustained serious injuries but both she and the baby survived. Five months later she picked Reece out of a police line-up. She believed that he was responsible for her flat tyre in the first place.

Reece was convicted of aggravated assault and sentenced to 60 years imprisonment. He appealed on the grounds that there was a conspiracy to arrest him for the abduction of Sandra Sapaugh because there was no probable cause to arrest him in the Laura Smither case. But on 20 July 2000, his appeal was rejected and the conviction and sentence upheld.

Reece admitted he drove down the street where Smither was jogging but returned to the job site and his boss saw that he was alone in his truck. According to Reece, he then went home and did laundry. After a search of his home and truck turned up nothing, a lie detector test proved inconclusive. Reece's pick-up truck was examined for possible fibres, blood or other clues. But problems with the post mortem also surfaced. The medical examiner's report indicated that African-American hairs found on the girl's body were contaminants and that they did not come from the crime scene. The police even went as far as to dig up a pile of horse manure at the Diamond B Ranch. Reece was boarding a palomino at the stables there and occasionally shoed horses for other owners there.

Jessica Cain's disappearance was quickly related to that of Sondra Kay Ramber, who disappeared from her home five miles away in Santa Fe, Texas, on 26 October 1983. The door to her home was left open and and biscuits were baking in the oven. It was first thought that she had gone to the store, but she had left her purse and coat in the house. It was only when she had not returned the following morning that her father filed a missing person report. The authorities initially classified her as a runaway. She had just completed modelling school and wanted to becoming a model.

There was another suspect in the Jessica Cain case – Jonathan David Drew. On 29 November 1998, Drew attended a birthday party at a bar in Seabrook, Texas. He was introduced to 23-year-old blonde waitress Tina Flood at the party. He bought her drinks, and they were seen kissing. When the bar closed and the party ended at 2 a.m., several people went to a Holiday Inn hotel. Because Tina was too drunk to drive to the hotel, she and her friend Justin Chapman rode there with other people. Her car was left in a parking lot next to the bar. When they attempted to check into their room, Chapman, who was a Holiday Inn employee, realized he had left his employee discount card in Tina's car and they decided to go back and get it. Outside they saw Drew sitting in his pick-up truck in the hotel parking lot and accepted his offer to take them back to the bar. Tina sat in the middle next to Drew, who was driving, while Chapman sat in the passenger's side of the front seat. When they arrived at the parking lot next to the bar, Chapman got out of the truck and held Tina's purse while she got out as well. But as Tina attempted to scoot across the front seat to the passenger door, Drew grabbed hold of her and drove away.

Chapman was between the open door and the body of the truck and held onto the door as the truck drove away. He heard Tina screaming for Drew to stop. As the truck pulled out of the parking lot, the door slammed shut, knocking Chapman into a ditch. He picked himself up, ran to the bar and began beating on the front door.

At 2.52 a.m., Seabrook Police Officer Marc Hatton was on patrol when he saw Chapman beating on the bar's door and stopped. Chapman's trousers were covered in mud and he was hysterical. He told Hatton that his friend had just been kidnapped. He gave a full description of Drew's maroon, full-sized, single-cab Chevrolet truck. The description of the appellant's truck was broadcast to other officers in the area.

At 3.49 a.m., Harris County Deputy Constable Sean Kitchens spotted Drew's truck and pulled him over for failing to maintain a single lane of traffic. Deputy Kitchens asked Drew for his licence. But when he leant over to retrieve his licence from the glove compartment, Kitchens noticed a bloody foot lying on the seat. When Kitchens asked who it belonged to, Drew said: "That's my friend Tina. She's knocked out over there."

Investigating further, the deputy found Tina Flood lying unconscious in the foetal position against the passenger's door. She was naked except for her skirt, which was bunched around her waist. Her panties and blouse were later found in Drew's truck. She was bloody, bruised and scraped, and there were abrasions on her leg, buttocks and arms.

Kitchens called for back-up. When it arrived, Drew was asked to step out of the truck. Deputy Kitchens noticed a scratch on Drew's right arm, three scratches on the back and side of his neck, and what looked like blood on his shirt collar.

Tina Flood was rushed to the Clear Lake Regional Medical Center. Emergency Room nurse Christine McFall conducted a sexual assault examination. According to McFall, Tina repeatedly cried out: "Please help me. Please help me. Don't hurt me." And Emergency Room nurse Mary Jane Heady heard Tina say: "Please don't rape me."

A CAT scan showed that Tina had sustained a skull fracture,

which caused her brain to swell and haemorrhage. She was rushed into surgery. Tina died a day and a half later because of swelling in her brain.

The medical examiner found at least two distinct fractures to Tina's skull, the result of one or possibly two separate acts of blunt trauma. A considerable amount of force was required to cause those fractures. There was an abrasion on the back of Tina's head and a bruise on the back of her brain immediately below the point of impact. On the opposite side of her head, there was a massive amount of bleeding, but no external bruising on her skin. Such an injury is typically found where a moving head strikes a stationary object. Tina's ear was swollen and there was a bruise behind the ear. This bruise could be related to the skull fracture, but the swelling of the ear indicated the injury was probably caused by a separate impact. The medical examiner said that the injury to Tina's ear was more consistent with something striking her or her head striking something on that side.

The abrasions and contusions on Tina's shoulder, shoulder blade, elbow, lower back and buttocks were consistent with being dragged on a rough surface, such as concrete. The wrinkling or crumpling of the skin on Tina's back was consistent with the skin having been stepped on. The abrasions were not consistent with those that might result from jumping out of a moving vehicle. Further, there were small oval contusions on Tina's lower legs, ankles, and upper right arm, consistent with finger impressions. There were also abrasions on Tina's knuckles and the meaty part of the thumbs of both hands, suggesting defensive injuries. Drew had scratches on his right arm and neck.

The medical examiner also found bruising in the soft tissue of both sides of Tina's neck. This, he said, was caused by direct external compression often seen in manual strangulations. The anal swabs taken during the sexual assault examination contained Drew's DNA. While there were no obvious abrasions or tears in the vagina and anal area, the area was a little darker than normal, which suggested trauma.

The State tried Drew for capital murder, but the jury found him only guilty of felony murder and he was sentenced to life in prison. He appealed, but on 14 February 2002 both the conviction and the sentence were upheld.

Drew was also suspected of several sexual assaults and possibly the murder of Jessica Lee Cain. A search of his former home in League City, where his parents still lived, unearthed a vial containing several human teeth. League City was the home of the famous "killing fields" murders, but Drew would have been too young to have committed them, though it is thought that he did rape other women in the area.

Another case bore a similarity to Jessica Cain's disappearance. It involved 17-year-old Michelle Doherty Thomas, who was last seen leaving her family's home in Alta Loma, Texas, less that two miles from Santa Fe, on 5 October 1985. She was planning to meet friends at a nightclub on Galveston Island later in the evening, but she never arrived and has not been heard from again. Her family reported her missing on 7 October 1985, two days after her disappearance. She had served as an informant during a drug bust in 1985 and the police believe that she could have been abducted and murdered as a result.

Another young woman went missing from Galveston County in 1988. Twenty-two-year-old Suzanne Rene Richerson was a student at Texas A & M University in Galveston and was employed as a night clerk at Casa Del Mar Condominiums on Seawall Boulevard. She was last seen at work at around 6 a.m. on 7 October by the resort security guards. Another employee who was sleeping in the room above Richerson's office woke up to hear a woman scream shortly after the guards left the vicinity. Then came the sound of a car door being slammed shut, accompanied by another scream, and the sound of a car racing from the parking lot shortly after. A guest arrived at Richerson's office to check out at about 6.30 a.m. and discovered the desk unattended. There were no signs of a struggle and Suzanne's purse, school books and car were left at the resort. One of her shoes was found in the parking lot later that morning, but Suzanne Richerson has never been seen again. There was a suspect in the Richerson case named Gabriel Soto. But he died on 31 July 2002, aged 39, from a drug overdose. Soto was charged with intimidating witnesses in the case, though never charged for the abduction. However investigators believe he played a role in Richerson's disappearance.

The FBI set up Operation HALT – standing for Homicide-Abduction Liaison Team – to investigate the disappearances. At first, they thought they were looking for a single serial killer and were hopeful that they could put him behind bars. But they soon realized that they were looking for a number of killers whose crimes overlapped. Typically victims have disappeared while out alone, only to be found dead in a remote spot weeks or months later, leaving no hint as to their attacker's identity or motive.

The small towns and country roads in that part of Texas have proved an easy place to hunt victims. The patchwork of jurisdictions makes it easy for killers to hide their activities. Over the past 40 years a huge influx of people have settled in this fast-growing corner of Texas. The refineries and ports draw transients. And the bayous shrouded with long-leafed pine, beech and oaks have served as a dumping ground for killers from Houston as well as local predators. In some cases the victim is unknown. In early 1999 a small boy went out for a walk with his dog in some marshy woods. The dog found a bone, and then the boy saw a skull. Nearby, the police would later find earrings, shreds of clothing and a belt tied around a tree. Investigators believe the killer used it to bind the young woman while she was sexually assaulted.

Evidence pointed to a serial killer long ago when two girls disappeared from the same convenience store in the 1970s. Then four bodies were found between 1984 and 1991 in a overgrown patch of land next to Calder Road near League City off I–45 dubbed the "killing fields". In the 3000 block of Calder Drive was the abandoned League City Oil Field, tucked away between houses, strip joints, a few rundown businesses and Star Dust Trail Rides, run by retired NASA engineer Robert Able. All four victims were laying nude on the ground, face up and under trees with their arms crossed. They had been sexually assaulted and were placed within a hundred-yard radius of each other. One investigator who studied the scene thought the killer had used a footpath to view the bodies. The metal gates across one part of Calder Drive and adjacent Ervin Street are locked blocking access by automobile. Clearly the killer had had prior knowledge of this secluded area.

FBI profiler Mark Young said that there were at least four serial killers working the I–45 corridor. The picture was further confused by killers who only claimed a single victim. Few cases can be definitively linked as the method of abduction, cause of death and dumping ground often varies wildly. It is possible that a smaller number of killers is at work, who constantly change their modus operandi. However, it is very unusual for so many "low-risk" victims – that is, women not involved in drugs, prostitution or other illegal activity – to be murdered or go missing in such a relatively small geographic area without a number of serial killers being responsible for the majority of the crimes. Computer analysis of the evidence also indicates multiple murderers are at work. One killer has a preference for slim, short brown-haired women. Another killer has distinctive habits in the way he disposes of bodies.

Of particular interest were the "killing field" murders, which were the only cases publicly linked together by authorities. The first body to be discovered was that of 23-year-old cocktail waitress Heidi Villerial Fye, who vanished on 10 October 1983, after leaving her parents' home to use a payphone in a convenience store at Hobbs and West Main Street in League City. Her remains were found on 4 April 1984 when a dog carried her skull to a nearby house. She had been beaten with a club. She had several broken ribs and probably died from blunt force trauma to her head.

Then on 2 February 1986 four boys riding dirt bikes across the area smelled a foul odour. This led them to the skeletal remains of a female about 50 yards from where Heidi Fye had been found. They called the police. Never identified, she had died between six weeks and six months before she was found. She had been shot in the back by a .22 calibre weapon. But the post mortem also revealed healed fractures of the ribs. She was about 25 years old, weighed between 140 to 160 pounds and was between 5 feet 5 inches to 5 feet 8 inches tall. She had light reddish-brown shoulder length hair and had a distinct gap between her upper front teeth. But no one answering that description was listed as missing.

Later that day the police searching the area found a second body just 20 yards from the first. This was identified as Laura Lynn Miller, aged 16, a Clear Creek High School sophomore. She went missing on 1 September 1984, shortly after the Miller family had moved to League City. Their phone had not been connected, so she had gone out with her mother find a payphone to call her boyfriend. The one she found was the payphone in the same convenience store where Heidi Fye had last been seen. Her mother wanted her to come home, but Laura insisted on finishing her call, saying she was old enough to walk home by herself. When she did not turn up the police said that she was a runaway. But when her father heard about the discovery of Heidi Fye's body, he insisted that the police check the same area for his daughter. At that time nothing was found. It was only when they were looking for clues to the Jane Doe murder that they stumbled across her. She had been shot in the head.

For over five years there were no new discoveries at Calder Drive. Robert Abel continued to rent the property for his Stardust Trail Rides, then bought a lot at 3001 Calder Drive to stable his horses. His stepdaughter was riding on 8 September 1991 when she came across another set of skeletal remains a hundred yards from where the other bodies had been found.

This second Jane Doe died between a month and four months before her remains were found. She was too badly decomposed to determine the exact cause of death. There was a possibility that she had been strangled using a curtain cord found nearby. However she had also been beaten with a club and this was the most likely cause of death. Interestingly, she had two poorly healed fractured ribs like the first Jane Doe. She had been about 31 years old, between 5 feet and 5 feet 3 inches tall and weighed about 100 to 130 pounds, with a small frame and long, fine, light brown hair. All four women were left lying on their backs with their arms folded across their chests. Although there is not an exact match between the four "killing fields" murders – two had been shot, two beaten to death – the positioning of the bodies, along with the fact that the two identified victims had disappeared from the same payphone in the same convenience store, indicated that the murders were all the work of the same man.

Robert Abel, who has since died, was one of a raft of suspects, as was his one-time employee, Mark Stallings. After being fired by Abel, Stallings ended up in jail. There, in 2001, he confessed to some of the I–45 murders. However, the police could find no physical evidence to connect Stallings to the murders and could not substantiate his claims. Indeed he would only have been 15 or 16 at the time of the first murders. Investigators consider it unlikely that he is involved and only made his claims to improve his reputation in jail, where he is currently serving 489 years for aggravated assault and attempting to escape.

A search of Abel's property turned up nothing. Tim Miller, Laura's father, conducting his own search, used trained dogs and heavy equipment to dig up the sector where the victims had been found. Even a small retention pond in the old oil field was drained, but only the remains of a purse and some rotting clothes were found.

In an attempt to clear his name, Abel took a polygraph test on a national news show and passed. The FBI eventually eliminated Abel from their investigations, though some League City cops still have their doubts. But with only scant physical evidence and no eyewitness, the police were stymied. They even resorted to putting a billboard up on I–45 asking for help with the case. No new information came in and the case seemed dead.

Then in December 2005, Tim Miller received a letter from someone claiming to be the man who killed his daughter and others.

"Tim Miller, boo," it read. "It's me you're looking for, but I'm the last man your Laura saw and many more."

It was composed from words cut out of newspapers and magazines, like a ransom note. When Miller first opened the enveloped, he dismissed the contents as a messy newsletter. Then he spotted the Corvette Concepts' logo.

On 2 November 1983, someone had entered the business office of Corvette Concepts garage at 595 West Main Street in League City and stabbed Beth Wilburn over 100 times, killing her. When Tommy McGraw arrived at work he was stabbed multiple times. The implement used to stab him was left impaled in the dead man's spine. Then James Oatis, an electrician working at the rear of the business, was shot several times. He, too, died. The triple murder remains unsolved.

The letter boasted about the I–45 deaths and its author bragged that he was too smart for the police to catch. After receiving the letter Miller was so angry that he went out to the spot where Laura's body had been found. After it had been removed by the police, he had put up a wooden cross in her memory. The cross had been knocked down and broken apart, though he later repaired it. Nearby he found some pornographic videos. One featured a 16-year-old girl. Laura was 16. Miller believes that whoever sent the letter left these as a calling card for him to find and, in 2006, he had a public appeal for the man who wrote the letter to contact him again.

However, the police remain sceptical. It came just five months after Robert Abel died and it may have been sent by a friend or relative of Abel who was seeking to clear his name. Nobody has ever been charged with these murders.

The Occult and Violent Ritual Crime Center, Inc., have ana-lyzed the I–45 murders and believe that four serial killers are at work. The first offender was responsible for the abduction of 13-year-old Colette Wilson. She went missing on 17 June 1971 after the leader of the band she was in dropped her at a bus stop in Alvin, Texas, some ten miles from the I–45. Her naked body was found five months later in November 1971, 40 miles away near Addicks Reservoir in West Houston, on I–10 and Highway 6. The cause of death was a gunshot to the head. Her musical instrument was never found.

Next came 14-year-old Brenda Jones, who went missing two weeks later. She disappeared on 1 July 1971 while walking to

Galveston hospital to visit an aunt. The hospital was close to I--45. Her body was found the next day floating in nearby Galveston Bay, close to the Seawolf Parkway, which was also near the I–45. The cause of death was a head wound and a slip stuffed into her mouth.

On 28 October 1971, 19-year-old Gloria Gonzales went missing near her home in Houston. Her body was found in November 1971 near Addicks Reservoir, 35 yards from where Colette Wilson's body had been found. Again the cause of death was blunt force trauma to the head. However, the Occult and Violent Ritual Crime Research Center think this is the work of a second killer, possibly the same man who killed Heidi Fye in 1983.

On 9 November 1971, 12-year-old Alison Craven's mother had to go out to run an errand. She was away for about an hour. When she returned to their apartment near the I–45, her daughter was missing. Two hands, the bones from an arm and some teeth were found in a nearby field. On 25 February 1972 the rest of her skeleton was found in a Pearland field, five miles from I–45 and ten miles from where she had last been seen. Her murder does not make the OVRCRC list and may have been a one-off.

Then came a double murder which the OVRCRC ascribe to the first killer. On 11 November, two 15-year-olds went missing in Galveston. Ball High School students Debbie Ackerman and Maria Johnson left Ball High School to shop for Thanksgiving gifts at a Galveston mall. Two days later, fishermen saw their bodies floating in Turner's Bayou in Texas City, close to I–45 and Highway 3, and ten miles from where they had disappeared. Both girls were shot twice in the head before being dumped in the water. Their hands and feet were bound and both were partly naked.

Sixteen-year-old Kimberly Pitchford was last seen at a driving school in Pasadena, Texas, near I–45 on 3 January 1973. She was supposed to phone home to get picked up, but the call was never made. Two days later, her body was found two days later in a ditch on Highway 288 near Angleton, some 30 miles south of where she had last been seen. She had been strangled. Her uncle Ray Pitchford maintained a suspected serial killer was known to have attended the driving school about the same time. The

OVRCRC believe that Kimberley's murder was the work of a third serial killer, who went on to kill again in the 1980s.

The OVRCRC link the first killer to another unidentified woman, whose body was found in a wooded area on the east side of Houston on 19 September 1989. She had been dead for between one and three months. She was a brunette aged between 14 and 19, weighed between 110 and 130 pounds and between 5 foot 2 inches and 5 foot 5 inches tall. The cause of death was a gunshot wound to the head.

The same killer was thought to be responsible for the abduction and murder of 14-year-old Lynette Bibbs and 15-year-old Tamara Fisher. The two friends disappeared from a teen club in Houston on 1 February 1996. Two days later their bodies were found on the side of a rural road near Cleveland, Texas, some 40 miles to the north. Lynette was partially clothed and shot twice in the back of the head and once in the thigh. Tamara was fully clothed and died from a gunshot wound to the head.

None of these victims seems to have been sexually assaulted and the use of a gun by a serial killer is unusual. They usually prefer to strangle, bludgeon or stab so that they can savour their victim's pain, panic and death throes close up. Guns kill from a distance. They can kill quickly. They make a lot of noise and can be traced easily. In this case, the killer clearly had somewhere private where he could take his victims to kill them.

It is thought that the killer got his pleasure from hunting his victims. There is even a theory that he is some type of law enforcement officer, some other authority figure, or someone posing as one. The OVRCRC believe that he may have stopped killing because he no longer found hunting his victims fun.

On 6 September 1974, 12-year-old Brooks Bracewell and 14-year-old Georgia Geer skipped school. They were last seen in a convenience store in Dickinson, just four miles down the I–45 from League City. Both had been beaten to death and their bodies were found in a swamp near Alvin.

Other profilers connect these two killings to those above. All the victims were 19 years old or younger. They were all dumped in or near bodies of water, and all had died from either a gunshot to the head or some sort of head trauma. And the killer showed a distinct preference for pairs. Only Brenda Jones was abducted alone and found alone.

There was even a link between these cases and those found in the "killing fields". Brooks Bracewell and Georgia Geer were last seen at a convenience store pay phone, just like Heidi Fye and Laura Miller. Both sets of victims show the same mixture of murder methods – some being beaten to death or shot. However, the method of body disposal is quite different. In the "killing field" they were laid out on land. The others were dumped in or near water. The "killing field" victims were naked and had been sexually assaulted. The others were fully or partially clothed and showing no signs of rape.

The OVRCRC tie three other murders to the killer of Kimberly Pitchford, as strangulation was the method of murder. On 1 November 1980, a truck driver found the naked body of an unidentified brunette aged between 14 and 17 dumped on I–45, about five miles north of Huntsville. She had been strangled with pantyhose and there were human bite marks on her body. She was 5 foot 4 inches tall and weighed 110 pounds. On 7 June 1987, 14-year-old Erica Ann Garcia went missing from a teen club. This showed a similarity with the abduction of Lynette Bibbs and Tamara Fisher. However, they had been shot. When Erica Garcia's body was found, she had been strangled.

Another victim of strangulation was 13-year-old Krystal Jean Baker, the great niece of Marilyn Monroe, aka Norma Jean Baker. On 5 March 1996, the dark-eyed blonde disappeared after making a call from a payphone in a convenience store in Texas City, ten miles from Dickinson and 14 miles from League City. She had phoned to get a lift to a friend's house in Bayou Vista, four miles away on the I–45. Her body was found a few hours later under the I–10 Bridge over the Trinity River near Galveston Bay in Chambers County. Her face was pulverized. She had been beaten, sexually assaulted and despatched with a ligature. The OVRCRC believed that the killer had been building up to the sexual assault of Krystal Baker as the Huntsville victim had been found nude. On earlier occasions he may not have managed to become sexually aroused, finding himself impotent or disturbed before he could attempt the act.

It is thought that Trellis Sykes and Maria Isabel Solis might share a common killer. Sixteen-year-old Trellis Sykes did not show up at Worthing High School in Houston on 13 May 1994. Her loved ones went out to search for her and found her dead body in the undergrowth on a vacant lot on Redbud Street. Maria Isabel Solis was also 16 when she went missing on her way to school in Houston. She lived with her father and grandmother on the south side of the city. Her mother, Blanca Ortiz, still lived in Mexico City. At 8.40 on the morning of 3 March 2003, she left home to go to the George I. Sanchez High School where she was an honours student. She was last seen getting off the city bus near her school. Students and the manager of a nearby motel heard screams. On 13 August 2003, a body was discovered in a wooded area near a closed US 59 turnaround at the Brazos River not far from Sugar Land, Texas, some 20 miles southwest of Houston. However, the remains were only identified as those of Maria by the forensic laboratory on 9 February 2005.

Other murders in the area might be linked. On 10 May 1978, when Robert Pretty arrived home from work at his house in north Houston, he found cold toast and a half-empty glass of milk on the breakfast table. He heard water dripping in the front bathroom and, when he went to investigate, he found his sons, five-year-old Mark and seven-year-old Scott, face down in the bathtub. In the master bathroom he found his 28-year-old wife, Karen, bound hand and foot, underwater in the bath. The medical examiner said that they had died from a combination of strangulation and drowning. Karen had a telephone cord around her neck. The two boys had been strangled manually. Mark had fought back and been beaten by his assailant. The murders seemed motiveless. Nothing had been taken from the house and only one drawer was opened. Nor had the victims been sexually molested. Karen was still wearing her flowery bathrobe and the boys still had their pyjamas on. The only clue was that the family car, a 1978 Mercury Marquis, was found in an unassigned parking spot at an apartment at 198 Goodson Drive. There is a theory was that the murder of Karen and the two children was a case of mistaken identity. A local drug dealer had been arrested on evidence provided by an informant who lived in the neighbourhood.

And so the I–45 murders continue. Twenty-two-year-old Tamara Ellen McCurry disappeared in Galveston on 1 July 1982 after being seen getting into an orange or yellow van. The headless body of a woman was found in a garbage bag in a state park in Galveston in April 1986. The victim remains unidentified.

Shelley Kathleen Sikes, a 19-year-old University of Texas student, was last seen just before midnight 24 May 1986, when she left work at Gaido's beach-front restaurant in Galveston where she was a waitress. She was heading for her home in Texas City, but never made it. Her car was found at around two the next morning, stuck in the mud alongside the I–45 northbound feeder road just south of the Galveston causeway. The driver's window was broken, and blood was spattered on the door and driver's seat. Despite an intensive search, Sikes was never found. She was thought to be another victim of one of the I–45 serial killers. But then in June 1987 the police got a phone call from a local motel. Resident John Robert King was trying to kill himself and confessed to abducting Sikes and burying her body. He said he and a friend, Gerald Peter Zwarst, high on drugs, had run Shelley Sikes' car off the road and abducted her. Safely in custody, both men blamed each other for Sikes' death and admitted burying the body near King's home. However, King reneged on his promise to tell police exactly where the body was buried. Zwarst was offered immunity from a murder charge in 1990 if he would help find Shelley Sikes' body. Under hypnosis he drew a map of a field in San Leon near Galveston Bay, where he said he last saw Shelley Sikes, but her body was not found. Authorities uncovered a white blouse during the search, but lab tests could not prove it belonged to Sikes. However, her family remain convinced the petite, handmade blouse was hers. King and Zwarst were convicted of aggravated kidnapping in 1988 – the most severe charge prosecutors could pursue without a body –

and they were sentenced to life imprisonment. However, the case remains open.

The murder of 15-year-old Laurie Lee Tremblay is another I–45 case that has been resolved recently. She was last seen alive walking from her family's apartment to the bus stop, on 26 September 1986. Her body was later found behind a restaurant in the 10600 block of Westheimer Road, Houston. None of her jewellery or possessions were taken. So the motive was not robbery.

"We knew we had a serial killer working," said Houston police detective Sergeant John Swain said. "I think that the Police Department danced around that. The powers that be didn't want to admit that, didn't want the public to panic."

The case remained unsolved until 2003 when 41-year-old Anthony Allen Shore was arrested for the murder of Maria Del Carmen Estrada, 11 years before. The 21-year-old Hispanic brunette was last seen on 16 April 1992 when she left her apartment at 7200 Shadyvilla to walk to work. Her body was found hours later face down in the drive-through lane of a Dairy Queen restaurant at 6707 Westview, Houston. She was partially nude and had been sexually assaulted and strangled. "When he had finished having his way with her, he left her . . . like a piece of garbage," said Kelly Siegler, the prosecutor at his trial. The police testified that the nylon cord around Maria Estrada's neck was so tight that it was not even visible.

Advances in DNA testing led to a match being made between scrapings taken from under Maria Estrada's fingernails and Shore, who has been a registered sex offender since January 1998 when he was given eight years probation for the sexual assault of two girls in his own family, aged 11 and 13. Consequently, his DNA was on file. Once in custody, Shore sprang a surprise on his captors.

"He told me he would give me something that I didn't know about," said Lieutenant Danny Billingsley of Harris Court Sheriff's Office. "And that is when he gave me the Laurie Trembley case."

Shore also confessed to murdering Dana Sanchez and Diana

Rebollar. Sixteen-year-old Dana Sanchez was a Hispanic brunette like Estrada. She was last seen talking to her boyfriend on a payphone at West Cavalcade and Airline, Houston, on 6 July 1995. She told him that she was going to hitch-hike over to his home, but she never turned up. Her body was found on North View Park on 14 July. She had been beaten, raped and strangled. Diana Rebollar was another brunette, but she was only nine. Her mother had sent her to a nearby convenience store to buy sugar in the 6600 block of North Main. Diana's body was found behind a vacant building at 1440 North Loop West on 7 August 1994. Again she had been beaten, raped and strangled. Shore was also charged with the 1993 sexual assault of a 14-year-old Houston girl who was attacked by a man who broke into her family's home in the 1900 block of Portsmouth after she returned from school to find the suspect in the kitchen. He tied her up and raped her.

"He said in a calm voice, 'I'm just here to rob your house,'" said the victim, now 25. Shore then covered her eyes and mouth with duct tape and bound her hands behind her back. "He used a knife to cut off my panties. As I was screaming, he got upset and told me I was being too loud." Then she felt his hands around her throat. "I kind of came out of my stupor and realized I had to do something. If I don't do something, I'm going to die." She was able to kick him away, but he threatened her before leaving the house

"He said he knows everything about me," she said. "He'd been watching me come home from school. He knew that I played soccer." During the woman's testimony, Shore leaned back in his chair and stared at a pen he was tapping on the defence table.

After Shore was convicted of the murder of Maria Del Carmen Estrada, he instructed his lawyers not to cross-examine witnesses or make any other effort to persuade jurors not to give him a death sentence for the murder of at least four females over a nine-year span.

"He believes it's time for him to sacrifice his life for what he has done," defence attorney Alvin Nunnery told jurors as the penalty phase of the capital murder trial began. Shore, then 42, wiped away a tear as his attorney explained that his client had instructed him to request the death sentence. Nunnery said: "He's accepted the Lord into his life. He understands that while he would ultimately be free from the pain and the penalty of sin – that is, eternal damnation – he has to pay the consequences for what he did."

Shore's sister Regina Shore Belt testified for him at the penalty hearings. She said that her brother had always displayed a "high, genius-level" intelligence, particularly as a musician.

"He could pick up an instrument he's never seen before and play it like he's been playing it his whole life," she said. But Belt did not ask the jury for mercy. "I and the rest of my family believe that he should have the death penalty," she told the court.

"Evil lives among us," said the prosecutors. "And sometimes evil, as the evidence will show, comes in the form of someone who looks completely normal." But he was in fact "a monster, absolute horrendous monster, capable of things that made this jury cringe as we showed them this week".

Shore was sentenced to death for the murder of Maria Del Carmen Estrada. Consequently he will not stand trial for the other three murders. He is now on death row in Texas and is free to boast about his musical prowess on the internet while soliciting for pen pals.

Shore is a suspect in other I–45 slayings but apparently has not been linked to any of the other cases. Many things point to him as a good suspect, however. He lived in League City until he was 13. He attended Clear Creek High School. Police questioned him in connection with the Calder Road Killings. Also, his past jobs as a telephone service man and a tow truck driver took him far and wide in the Houston area, giving him ample freedom and opportunity to stalk or kill. Shore also abducted Dana Sanchez and Diana Rebollar at or near convenience stores, an oddly common abduction method in the I–45 killings.

One case in particular intrigues investigators. It involves a set of bones found just blocks from where Shore was living when he was arrested. The medical examiner's office was able to determine that they belonged to a young female, but little more. The victim was only wearing a T-shirt. A looped cord was found nearby. Shore used a ligature to strangle.

"We don't have the person identified and until then there is not a lot that can be done," said Lieutenant Billingsley. "There is not a lot in that regard except being able to tie it to some missing person's report."

There are plenty of other related I–45 cases that remain unsolved. In March 1997 a 13-year-old girl was abducted at gunpoint as she was walking home from a shopping centre. She leaped out of her abductor's truck in 200 block of East Fairmont in La Porte, Texas, on Galveston Bay. A police officer driving saw the girl falling out of the pick-up. It made off, but the officer identified it as a green late-model Ford Ranger and the suspect was a man aged between 35 and 45, and between 6 feet and 6 feet 2 inches tall, with greying black hair and beard. Neither the truck nor the man were found.

Some other I–45 murders have been solved. In late January 1999, drifter William Ray Mathews walked into the office of Country Time Mobile homes in Shenandoah, Texas, some 30 miles north of Houston on the I–45. He was carrying a briefcase and sat down and wrote sales assistant Tracy Vickery a note. It said he had a gun and, if she did not do what he said, he would kill her. He forced Vickery into his truck, then he drove off down I–45. But she leapt from his speeding truck. He tried to pull her back in by her hair but he could not hold her. She got away and ran to the Gulf Coast Trades Center to save herself.

Just weeks earlier, on 17 January, 18-year-old blonde Wanda May Pitts had disappeared from the Lodge Motel on the other side of the I–45. She had worked there for about two months and did not have a car. She was on duty in the lobby when Mathews abducted her. He took her to one of the motel rooms and sexually assaulted her, later boasting that she had been a virgin. Within hours of abducting Wanda Pitts he strangled her. After he was arrested for the attempted abduction of Tracey Vickery, Mathews said that he could not remember where he had put Wanda Pitts' body, but about a year later her remains were found off an abandoned gated driveway.

A plea bargain prevented him from being charged with Pitts' murder, but he was convicted of attempting to abduct Tracy Vickery.

In the 21st century the I–45 killings continued. On 12 July 2001, 57-year-old Tot Tran Harriman, a brown-eyed Oriental with black hair streaked with grey, left her son's home League City at around 5 a.m. to drive to Corpus Christi, Texas. She has not been seen since. Weighing 130 pounds and 4 foot 11 inches tall, she was driving a 1996 maroon Lincoln Continental with personalized Florida licence plate on the back, saying "TOTSY". As Florida only requires a rear plate, she had a Navy Seal emblem where the front plate would normally be. Circumstances of her disappearance led police to suspect foul play.

At around 10.15 p.m. on 10 March 2002, 13-year-old Laura Ayala went to a convenience store in a Conoco gas station behind the apartment complex where she lived in southeast Houston to pick up a Sunday newspaper to complete a school project. When she did not return after several minutes, her mother went to the gas station to look for her. The clerk at the store told her that Laura had been there and left after buying the newspaper, alone. Laura's family began a search and found the newspaper and Laura's sandals lying on the ground on her route home. They called the Houston Police Department.

"The girl was gone for about five minutes," said Houston Police Department Sergeant Mike Peters.

The police made an extensive search on foot and horseback throughout the Houston area. They questioned relatives, neighbours, friends, acquaintances and all registered sex offenders. Volunteer groups circulated fliers. The FBI joined the search. An Amber Alert was issued. Laura's photograph was shown on the national television show *America's Most Wanted*. She had braces on her teeth and was last seen wearing jeans and a blue and white checked dress.

Investigators then learned that a girl answering Laura's description left Houston on a bus belonging to the El Expresso Bus Company bus between 10.30 and 11 p.m., three days after Laura

Ayala disappeared. The bus company's records showed that a ticket had been bought in the name Laura A. She was accompanied by a woman named Virginia Ramirez and a man named Julio Barrios. A second bus line may have taken the three passengers on to Reynosa, in Mexico.

In February 2003, the police linked Laura Ayala's abduction to Walter Sorto, Edgardo Cubas and 15-year-old Eduardo Navarro, who had gone on a crime spree of robberies, murders and rapes in the Houston area where Laura lived. Sorto has since been convicted in the murders of 24-year-old Roxana Capulin and 39-year-old Teresa Rangel, who were abducted from the restaurant where they worked on 1 June 2002. DNA in drops of blood found in an SUV belonging to Cubas' father matched Laura's, but they will not discuss their involvement and have not been charged in the case.

Despite this, family and friends still believe Laura is alive and the police have her case listed as an endangered abduction and are continuing with the search. There is a $20,000 reward offered for information leading to the arrest and conviction of the people who kidnapped Laura Ayala.

On the evening of 12 July 2002, 23-year-old blonde Sara Trusty, who used to work at the Gulf Greyhound Park, left her home of Avenue E in Algoa, Texas, six miles from the I–45, to go bicycle riding. She was last seen alive at around 11 p.m. near the Baptist church on Orange Avenue in Algoa. The following morning, the bike was found in the foyer of the church but there was no sign of her. On 28 July 2002, her body was discovered in a dike in Texas City, the other side of the I–45. She had been dead for over a week.

Some escape. On 29 July 2004 an unidentified teenage girl from northwest Houston was stranded with a flat tyre on the West Loop of the southwest Houston freeway near Interstate 10. A man with a tow-truck driver stopped to help. He changed the tyre, but then tried to sexually assault her. The girl managed to escape by stabbing the man in the shoulder and abdomen with a pocket knife. She described her attacker as tall, bald and clean-shaven with a tattoo of a spider web on his left shoulder. His vehicle was a faded black, older model Chevrolet pick-up with "Super Tow" in white letters on the side.

Others are not so fortunate. Soon after 11 a.m. on 23 February 2006 a sister and brother were walking their dog on the beach near the Flagship Hotel in the 2400 block of Seawall Boulevard close to where I–45 ends on Galveston Island. A woman began shouting at them about something floating in the surf which, at first, they thought was a mannequin. On closer investigation, they found a woman's body clad in black sweatpants, a red, hooded sweatshirt and light-blue Asics running shoes with white ankle socks. She still had her sunglasses on. Her body had only been in the water for a short time as it was still warm and rigor mortis had not set in. A post mortem showed that she had died from a single gunshot to the chest. She carried no ID, but her body bore a distinguishing mark in the form of a tattooed ring of flowers around her navel. She was identified as 30-year-old Natasha Nicole Solidum, an elementary school teacher in the Alief Independent School District.

There are striking similarities between many of the I–45 murders. Culprits already arrested may be responsible for more of the killings than they have been charged with. However, it seems clear that others have been at work. It is unlikely that any of the cases from the 1970s will be solved. Notorious serial killer Henry Lee Lucas, who claimed to have committed over a thousand murders, roamed the Gulf Coast when some of the early I–45 murders took place, but he has not been linked definitively to any of the unsolved cases. Lucas said he picked up most of his victims along the interstates by offering them a ride, a drink or dinner.

The police say they are following a suspect who remains at large on the I–45 corridor, but who never has been publicly identified.

"We know a guy, we know him very well, a guy who has killed before and who had some kind of contact with five of the girls, but all the evidence is circumstantial," said Lieutenant Gary D. Ratliff of the League City police.

The unnamed suspect suffered physical injuries in an automobile accident a few years ago and seems to have remained dormant since then, Ratliff said.

And a task force has been studying the murder of prostitutes in the Houston district of Montrose. In all there are about 200 unsolved murders of women and girls in Houston and the surrounding areas since 1971.

The Texarkana Phantom

An unidentified serial killer stalked Texarkana between 23 February and 4 May 1946. He was variously known as "The Phantom", the "Texarkana Phantom" and the "Moonlight Murderer", as he often struck when the moon was full.

The first attack took place near the intersection of Richmond and Robison Roads, near the site of the current site of the parking lot of the Central Mall. Back in 1946, this was still open country where young couples would park to kiss, cuddle, pet and, possibly, make out.

On the evening of 22 February 1946, 24-year-old Jimmy Hollis and his girlfriend 19-year-old Mary Jeanne Larey double-dated with Jimmy's brother and his girlfriend. They went to a movie together. Then Jimmy and Mary Jeanne dropped his brother and girlfriend off, and, on the way to Mary Larey's house, they stopped off at a secluded lane just off Richmond Road.

It was nearly 11.45 p.m. and Jimmy had promised his father that he would have the Plymouth home by midnight. But then, with Mary Jeanne beside him in her Lana Turner sweater, time did not seem so important any more.

They had been there about ten minutes when a man walked up and pointed a flashlight at the couple. They had half expected to be interrupted by a cop. This was in an age when premarital sex still attracted public approbation. But as their eyes adjusted to the light they could see that this man was not wearing a policeman's uniform. Instead he wore a white mask over his head with holes cut out for his eyes and mouth.

He came up on the driver's side of the car and tapped on the window.

"Come out of the car now!" he said.

The couple recoiled, but Jimmy could see he was carrying a gun.

"I don't want to kill you, fellow," the masked man said, "so do what I say."

Jimmy and Mary Jeanne got out of the car on the driver's side. The man then said to Jimmy: "Take off your britches."

Jimmy protested, but Mary Jeanne told Jimmy to take them off so they wouldn't be hurt. As he took off his trousers, the man hit him over the head twice with the butt of his pistol with such force that Jimmy's skull was fractured in two places.

The man then told Mary Jeanne to run and while she fled down the road she heard him kicking and stomping Jimmy. Then the masked man ran after her and knocked her to the ground. Mary Jeanne said later that he did not rape but did sexually abuse her, apparently with the barrel of the gun.

Her ordeal was curtailed by the lights of an approaching car. The masked man punched Mary Jeanne in the face and upper body several times, then disappeared into the darkness.

Mary Jeanne's head wounds were stitched up at the local hospital, but Hollis' injuries left him hospitalized for several months. They did not know it at the time, but they were lucky to be alive. They had seen the attacker and survived. But the description they could give of the masked man was vague. All they knew was that he was about six feet tall. His face was obscured by a rough-looking hood of white material that appeared to be homemade, with holes punched for the eyes and mouth. This was not enough for the police to go on. For now, they supposed – and hoped – the attack on Jimmy Hollis and Mary Jeanne Larey was an isolated incident.

The attack had a lasting effect on the lives of Jimmy and Mary Jeanne. They split. Her ordeal left her unsettled. She suffered many sleepless nights and eventually she left to live with relatives in Oklahoma. She did not return. Even so, she would always remember the attacker's voice.

"I would know it anywhere," she said years later. "It rings always in my ears."

The attack began a long nightmare for Texarkana, an otherwise optimistic town that took as its motto: "Twice as nice." This was because it is comprised of two separate municipalities, Texarkana, Texas, and Texarkana, Arkansas. The city is divided by the state line that runs down State Line Avenue. The two halves of the city have their own city council and their own police and fire departments and city council. The two municipalities fall in two separate counties – Bowie County in Texas to the west and Miller County in Arkansas to the east – so the surrounding areas are patrolled by two separate county sheriffs' offices.

Despite this, the city and its people work together as one entity. It was a centre for woodworking, furniture production, tyre making and engineering. It also boasted a university and an Army depot. Every October the city holds a Fair and Rodeo and it attracts visitors from Oklahoma and Louisiana, which are both only 30 miles away.

In February 1946, like the rest of America, the 44,000-strong population of Texarkana was just beginning to return to normal after World War II. Many of its young men were returning from action overseas. They were settling back into civilian life, looking for work. But there were also many grieving families who would not see their sons again.

Lyn Blackmon of the *Texarkana Gazette* painted a picture of the town back then: "In good weather, families in nice residential sections sat on their front porches after supper, sipping iced tea. They swung on porch swings, rocked in rockers and spoke to neighbours walking home from a movie or from church . . . Few people locked their doors or their windows. The only shades pulled down were in bathrooms or bedrooms."

But then people began bolting doors that had never been bolted before.

Despite its white-picket-fence image, the city did have its seamy side. With so many GIs passing through, there were bars and nightclubs with girlie shows. There were drunken brawls that had to be broken up by the police and even murders were not uncommon. However, the attack on two clean-cut kids like Jimmy Hollis and Mary Jeanne Larey was an unprecedented event. The story made the papers, but most readers assumed that the attack must be the work of a transient. Even the police thought the mysterious hooded man had jumped a freight car and was long gone. However, they were about to be proved most tragically wrong.

Early on the morning of 24 March, a driver on Highway 67 out in Bowie County noticed a 1941 Oldsmobile was parked about 100 yards off the highway in a copse next to South Robison Road. A man appeared to be asleep at the wheel. This was an odd place for someone to pull off the road for a sleep as there were a number of cut-price motels in the area. The driver went to investigate. Peering into the car, he saw two dead bodies. Both had been shot in the head.

Officers from Bowie County Sheriffs Office were summoned. They found 29-year-old Richard L. Griffin at the wheel. He was a US Navy Seabee – a member of the construction battalion – who had been discharged in November 1945. Lying face down on the backseat was his 17-year-old girlfriend, Polly Ann Moore, who worked at the Red River Arsenal on the outskirts of town. She had graduated from high school earlier that year and was living with a cousin on Magnolia Street. The couple had last been seen alive at about 10 p.m. the previous evening after dining with Eleanor Griffin, Richard's sister, at a West Seventh Street café.

Both had been killed by bullets from a .32 calibre pistol, possibly a Colt revolver. While Richard Griffin had been killed where he sat, bloodstains and drag marks indicated that Polly Moore had been killed outside. She had been sexually abused. There were few fingerprints or footprints. A heavy downpour during the night had washed away most of the evidence.

Within three days after the murder Bowie County sheriff's office questioned between 50 and 60 people and tracked down 100 false leads. Eventually they posted a $500 reward for information. None came.

As the investigation stalled, they joined forces with the sheriff's offices of adjacent Cass County and Miller County, the Texas

Department of Public Safety and Texarkana city police departments from both sides of the state line. Eventually the FBI were called in, but they too were stumped.

On the night of 13 April, the Rhythmaires were playing at the VFW Hall on Fourth and Oak Streets. The band had originally been formed by saxophonist Jerry Atkins to entertain the GIs. But they had lost none of their popularity since the war was over and Texarkana teenagers flocked their Saturday night dances.

With the men away at the war, Atkins had recruited female musicians for his band. One of them was 15-year-old Betty Jo Booker, who played the saxophone. As she was underage and the band often played venues that served liquor, Betty's mother – like the mothers of the other girls in the band – insisted that bandleader Jerry Atkins drive the girls to and from the gigs. He had an impeccable reputation. But that night, when the dance ended at around 1 a.m., Betty told her boss that she would not be needing a ride home. Paul Martin, a former school friend, had come by. Paul and Betty Jo had both been at school on the Arkansas side of town. Later Betty Jo had moved to the Texas side where she was a Junior at Texas High School, while Paul moved away to Kilgore, Texas and was a Senior at Kilgore High School. He had come to town that Saturday night to visit her and volunteered to give her a lift to the slumber party she was going to held by her girl friends. Atkins checked out Martin. He seemed to be a clean-cut, sober-looking 17-year-old. Atkins gave his permission for her to go with him and told her to have a nice time.

The following morning Paul Martin's coupe was found abandoned at the entrance of Spring Lake Park, miles from the slumber party Betty Jo had been invited to. Paul's body was found near what is now Cork Lane, north of Interstate 30, a mile from his car. Betty Jo's body was found one and a half miles from the car on Morris Lane by a patch of woods near Fernwood. Both had died from multiple gunshot wounds. She had also been raped.

Forensic examination confirmed that the bullets that had killed Betty Jo Booker and Paul Martin were .32 calibre and matched those that had killed Polly Ann Moore and Richard Griffin three weeks before. Curiously Betty Jo's saxophone was missing.

The police put two and two together and realized Betty Jo Booker and Paul Martin, and Polly Ann Moore and Richard Griffin had probably been attacked by the same hooded assailant who had attacked Mary Jeanne Larey and Jimmy Hollis in February. Up until this point the authorities had been reticent about mentioning the sexual aspects of the attacks. Now they announced that the female victims had been raped. This did not take them any further forward, but might prove an additional incentive of young couples to stay away from secluded areas.

The *Texarkana Gazette* began calling the elusive perpetrator "The Phantom". This was odd because The Phantom was a costumed crime fighter who had appeared in as a newspaper cartoon strip since 1936. His one similarity with the Texarkana Moonlight Murder was that, like all caped crusaders, he wore a mask. However, giving him such a ghoulish name only helped intensify public hysteria.

After the murder of Betty Jo Booker and Paul Martin, the famous Texas Ranger, Captain Manuel Gonzaullas was called in to help with the investigation. Tall and lean, he was known as "Lone Wolf" because he tracked down and faced down criminals by himself. The first thing he did was to issue a bulletin that read:

WANTED FOR MURDER

Person or persons unknown, for the murder of Betty Jo Booker and Paul Martin, on or about April 13, 1946, in Bowie County, Texas. Subject or subjects may have in their possession or may try to dispose of a gold-plated Bundy E-flat Alto saxophone, serial #52535, which was missing from the car in which the victims were last seen . . . This saxophone had just been rebuilt, replated and repadded, and was in an almost new black leather case with blue plush lining.

It is requested that a check be made of music stores and pawnshops. Any information as to the location of the saxophone or description and whereabouts of the person connected with it should be forwarded immediately to the Sheriff, Bowie County, Texarkana, Texas, and the Texas Department of Public Safety, Austin, Texas.

This line of enquiry led nowhere as Betty Jo's saxophone was found several months later in a marshy field in Spring Lake Park, where it had plainly lain since discarded on the night of the murder.

Detectives questioned friends of Betty Jo Hooker and Paul Martin. What puzzled them was how Martin's car wound up so far from their destination. Friends swore that he and Betty Jo were just friends, not sweethearts, so why had they parked up on that secluded road? The best theory they came up with was that they had given someone a lift who had then pulled a gun on them. Perhaps it had been someone from the dance. Jerry Atkins noted that the place where Polly Ann Moore and Richard Griffins had been found on Highway 67 was not far from a place called Club Dallas. Perhaps someone hung out at dances looking for their victims. And there was another puzzle: why were the bodies so far from the car – and so far from each other?

Atkins and three other members of the Rhythmaires were pallbearers at Betty Jo Hooker's funeral. And in her honour, they disbanded the band. They never played again.

After this second double murder, Texarkana was in a state of fear. Few people ventured out at night, and no one ventured out alone. Out-of-town cars were followed. People strung out pots and pans in their backyards so they would be alerted if the Phantom was on the prowl. Hardware shops sold out of locks and guns. And even in the fierce heat of summer, windows remained closed and locked.

Some favoured more direct action. Teenagers, incensed by the murder of two fellow high school students, formed vigilante bands which sometimes unintentionally disrupted police stake-outs. Armed couples would park on lonely roads in the hope of baiting a Phantom attack. With the two Texarkana police departments, the sheriffs' offices of Bowie, Miller and Cass counties, the FBI, the Texas Rangers and the Texas Department of Public Safety all on the job, Texarkana became the most closely guarded city in the United States. Meanwhile local businesses, civic societies, clubs and private individuals contributed the sum of

$4,280 as a reward for the capture of the person behind, as they put it, "the foulest murder ever committed in Texarkana".

Over 300 suspects were brought in for questioning. They were people who had criminal records, loners and odd-balls, people simply considered a little strange by their neighbours or those caught roaming dark spots at night. They were interrogated thoroughly but, in every case, released without charge.

With the police making little progress, rumours abounded – to the point where Bowie County Sheriff's Office and Captain Gonzaullas had to issue a press release, which read:

> The Texarkana newspapers have cooperated with us all through this investigation and we intend to cooperate with them in furnishing them the information they desire when the time comes for divulging that information. The newspapers are not printing rumors and have assured us they will not. Any information the public hears about the case will not be official unless it comes from us through the newspapers. We will continue to work day and night on the investigation. We will appreciate information from citizens and all such information will be treated confidentially.

The news of the killings spread across the country and internationally. Newspapers and radio stations covered the story and the *New York Times*, the *Washington Post*, *The Houston Chronicle*, the *Dallas News* and even *The Times* of London, along with Associated Press, United Press and the International News agencies, all sent reporters.

With little to report but local colour, the journalists focussed their attention on Captain "Lone Wolf" Gonzaullas. In his khaki suit and a white 10-gallon hat – and packing two pearl-handled revolvers on his hips – he became the living embodiment of the Old West. He did not deny the oft-repeated tale that he was the Texas Ranger who sat in the cashier's office in the Crazy Water Hotel in Mineral Wells and gunned down two ex-convicts who sought to rob the place. A good-looking man, he was particularly pestered by the female reporters. And on radio station KCMC, he told listeners: "Check the locks and bolts of your doors and get a double-barrelled shotgun to blow away any intruder who tries to get in."

Unfortunately he was too busy giving interviews to investigate the case and the jealousy of other officers over all the attention he was getting did not foster good co-operation among the law enforcers. In any case, they were unprepared for what happened next.

At around 9 p.m. on the night of Friday 3 May, 38-year-old Virgil Starks was listening to the radio in his farmhouse on Highway 67 in Miller County, 12 miles from Texarkana. He had just opened the newspaper and, after a hard week's work on the farm, he was easing his aching back with an electric heating pad. The dinner had been eaten and the dishes cleared away, and Virgil's wife, 35-year-old Kate Starks, had changed into her nightgown and was lying on her bed reading the *Post* magazine. Her sister lived across the road and some 50 yards down the way was another farmhouse, belonging to the Prater family.

This restful scene was shattered by a shot, following quickly by another one. Both hit Virgil Starks in the back of the head, killing him instantly. Mrs Starks leapt out of bed and ran down the hallway. She saw her husband covered in blood. She thought immediately – the Phantom.

She dashed for the phone and called the operator. But when the operator came on the line, Mrs Starks could not answer. She had been hit in the face by a bullet. As she turned, another bullet hit her, ripping her lower jaw from the upper, smashing her teeth and sending blood gushing to the floor.

Ducking further shots, she fell to the floor and crawled towards the kitchen. But, as she reached the pantry, she noticed that someone was trying to force entry through the back door. She could see the man's silhouette through the curtains of the door's window.

Kate Starks stumbled back through the house and made it out of the front door, just as she heard the back door give way. In her blood-soaked nightgown she made it across the prairie highway to her sister's house. Finding no one at home, she made her way to the Praters' farmhouse down the road. They called for help and she was rushed to the Michael Meagher Hospital – now St Michael's – in Texarkana. Miraculously, she survived. The first bullet had penetrated her right cheek and exited behind her left ear. The second had smashed her jaw then lodged in the muscles under her tongue. Emergency surgery removed it. Her condition remained critical for several days, then she pulled through. But she remained scarred – physically and psychologically – for life.

When the police arrived at the farmhouse, they found two small bullet holes in the window of the front porch window. They were small calibre and had not smashed the glass. Entering the house, guns drawn, they found Virgil Starks' body lying on the floor while the cushions of his easy chair smouldered from the unattended heating pad. There were bloody handprints on the walls and furniture. It seems that the intruder had dabbed his hands in the pools of Virgil Stark's blood. Now the police had fingerprints, lots of them. There were more on a flashlight he had dropped.

Muddy footprints led in from the kitchen door to the Starks' bedroom, where the killer must have gone searching for Kate. Then they led back to the living room and out of the front door. The trail then led across the highway. It seems that he had pursued his quarry. Later bloodhounds traced his scent along the highway for some 200 yards before they lost it. At this point, the killer had probably got into his car and driven off. Road-blocks were set up at both ends of Highway 67, but the killer got away.

Although the newspapers headlined this as another Phantom murder, detectives were not so sure. This time, the killer had not used a .32 handgun but a .22 rifle – an automatic as the killer had loosed off two rounds in rapid succession. Not only was the weapon different, but this time the killer had not struck a young couple in a secluded lover's lane. Before, the killer had been careful not to leave any clues. This time he deliberately daubed the crime scene with fingerprints – and he left his flashlight. Some believed that the killer was not the Phantom at all, but the jealous lover of either Kate or Virgil.

But to Texarkanians the murder had to be the work of the Phantom. It seemed logical that the work of a maniac should become more and more savage with each attack. The change of weapon and MO was immaterial.

The pressure was now on and the police badly needed to make an arrest. But the fingerprints did not help. After being checked by the Arkansas State Police, they were sent to the FBI in Washington, D.C. Still no match was found. Kate Stark was little help either. Questioned weeks after her recovery, she could not give a description of her husband's killer. She had, she said, seen only his silhouette against the curtains.

Two days after the attack on the Starks, the body of a man named Earl McSpadden had been found on rail tracks north of Texarkana. Some reporters speculated that he was the Phantom and that he had committed suicide. However, the coroner's report revealed that McSpadden had been stabbed to death before his body was put on the tracks – which only led to speculation that McSpadden was another victim of the Phantom.

A week later, a sheriff in Atoka County called the Texas Rangers that he was holding a 33-year-old itinerant in Paris, Texas after he had threatened a rancher's wife when she refused to feed him when he knocked on her door. The man was from Lewisville, Arkansas, 30 miles east of Texarkana. The Rangers, the Arkansas State Police and the FBI all questioned the suspect, but he had a solid alibi and his fingerprints did not match.

The authorities then threw their net wider. They contacted every law enforcement agency in the US, asking them for details of any case where the victims of a murder or rape had been parked in some secluded spot. The list they got back included two soldiers at Fort Dix, New Jersey, who were also suspects in the "Black Dahlia" case, a 32-year-old mechanic from Fort Worth, a graduate student from the University of Texas who was dismissed from the US Navy for exhibiting homosexual tendencies and an inmate at San Quentin who had been jailed for the kidnap and rape of a 22-year-old nurse in California – though he had been in jail at the time of the Phantom attacks. Then there was a 42-year-old suspect from College Station, Texas, who owned a .22 calibre rifle and enjoyed sneaking up on courting couples parked in lovers' lanes. He was thought to be in Texarkana at the time, visiting his sister. And there was a section hand on the Missouri Pacific Railroad who had written to the Governor of Texas admitting to the killings. But he also claimed to have killed Satan and challenged FBI Director J. Edgar Hoover and President Harry Truman to a duel.

Closer to home there was a feed store owner in Texarkana, a 45-year-old farm hand, a Texarkana gas station attendant who had been accused of rape and a local Internal Revenue Service agent who had, no doubt, been fingered by a disgruntled taxpayer. They were all released when, once again, their fingerprints did not match those left in the Starks' home.

The only suspect named by the Texas Rangers was 29-year-old Youell Swinney. Max Tackett, the Chief of Police of the Arkansas State Patrol, noticed that a car had been reported stolen just before each attack and, in July 1946 he arrested Swinney at a bus station when he returned to Texarkana after attempting to sell a stolen car in Atlanta, Texas.

According to Tackett and his assistant Tillman Johnson, Swinney said: "Hell, I know what you want me for. You want me for more than stealing a car!"

Swinney had a long record of car theft, counterfeiting, burglary and assault, and in the hotel room he shared with his wife they found a shirt with the name "Stark" stencilled in it. In the police station, Swinney refused to answer questions, but his wife, who had a short rap sheet herself, sang like a bird. She said that they had recently married 70 miles away in Shreveport, Louisiana, and came to Texarkana not long before the murders began. Then, much to everyone's surprise, rather than deny all knowledge of the killings, she said she had been with her husband when he had committed them. She even filled in details that were not widely known and, according to some sources, told her interrogators about a book found at the scene of the murder of Betty Jo Booker and Paul Martin that only Bowie County Sheriff Bill Presley knew about.

The problem was that, each time she told the story, she changed the details. For example, in her first statement about the Booker-Martin killings she said that she and her husband had gone to Spring Lake Park in a 1941 green Plymouth they had stolen to drink a bottle of beer. At one point, Swinney had got out of the car to urinate. After he disappeared, she heard two shots ring out from beyond a clump of trees. When he returned later, his trousers were wet and muddy, and he refused to tell her where he had been. But, later, she said they had gone to the park for the sole purpose of robbing someone and, when they spotted a couple in a parked car, he pulled up alongside it and ordered them to get out. Then, to her horror, her husband had shot Paul Martin, killing him instantly. Swinney had then shoved Betty Jo Booker into the Plymouth and had driven off with her, leaving his wife to wait in Martin's car. After an hour, he returned alone. Later, after persistent questioning by his wife, he confessed that, overcome with lust, he had raped and killed Betty Jo.

Not only was Mrs Swinney's testimony inconsistent, she also had a criminal record, making her, in the eyes of the law, an unreliable witness. What is more, she refused to testify against her husband, which was a wife's right. Nevertheless the police were convinced they had the right man.

Swinney was taken to Little Rock for further questioning under sodium pentothal – the "truth drug" – but they gave him too much and he fell asleep. With no shots left, the authorities had to be content with charging Swinney with car theft. It was his third felony conviction and, under the Habitual Criminal Act, he was sentenced to life imprisonment in Texas State penitentiary in Huntsville.

In 1970, Youell Swinney filed a request for a writ of *habeas corpus*, on the grounds that he was not represented by an attorney at his trial in February 1947. At a hearing in Bowie County an FBI agent testified that the trial judge Robert Vance had advised the defendant to hire a lawyer, but Swinney had chosen to defend himself. However, according to the *Texarkana Daily News*: "Swinney testified . . . that he was not advised by Judge Vance of his right to an attorney, nor was he told of the possible punishment he could receive if convicted of the auto theft charge." Eventually, the Court of Appeals overturned Swinney's conviction and he was freed in 1974.

Youell Swinney died of natural causes in 1993 and no one will ever know if he was the Phantom. Texas Rangers Captain "Lone Wolf" Gonzaullas did not think so. He continued to follow up leads and track down suspects well in to the 1950s. To this day, the case remains unsolved.

It is not even clear if the killings stopped after Swinney was jailed. Certainly there were no more Phantom murders in Texarkana, but the killer may simply have moved on. In October 1946, while Swinney was in jail awaiting trial, a murder took place a thousand miles away in Fort Lauderdale, Florida, that had the MO of the Phantom. Lawrence O. Hogan from Miami Beach and his young girlfriend Elaine Eldridge from Massachusetts were parked in a secluded spot near the ocean when they were shot dead. Again the murder weapon was a .32 calibre pistol, though it seems to have been a foreign make, not a Colt. There were no fingerprints, no clues and the killer simply vanished like a phantom. The killer is still at large.

The Toledo Clubber

The "Toledo Clubber", aka the "Toledo Slugger", terrorized the Ohio city in 1925 and 1926. In 12 attacks, at least five died

Curiously, the Clubber seems to have started out as an arsonist. This is not as unusual as it may seem, as Henry Lee Lucas's sidekick Otis Toole, as well as being a sex killer and cannibal, was also a pyromaniac who reached orgasm at the sight of a burning building.

In 1925, several timber yards in Toledo were torched within a few hours. When guards were posted at other yards to protect them, the arsonist started bombing tenements and private homes. Then, when explosives wrecked the mailbox of a Catholic priest, the FBI were called in.

The bombings suddenly ended, but then a series of attacks on women began. Using a heavy object, the attacker would hit his victims from behind. Then, when they were insensible, he continued to smash their faces in. Sensing the growing panic in the city, the newspapers quickly concluded that the perpetrator must be the same fiend who had set fire to lumber yards and blown up homes.

The first victim was Mrs Frank Hall. She had been sitting outside her home on 10 November 1925 when she was attacked. She was one of the lucky ones who survived. Next Emma Hatfield encountered the Clubber when she was walking down a dark street. Lydia Baumgartner fell victim the same way. Sadly, both would later die from their injuries. Beforehand they both managed to give a report to the police but they were of little help. There followed a series of brutal rapes, which invariably ended with the victim being clubbed unconscious. Three or four women died and at least five others were grievously wounded.

With seven attacks in seven days, the people of Toledo were terrified. The American Legion put a thousand men on the streets and escorts were provided to women who were now afraid to walk alone at night.

A total of $12,000 was raised as a reward for information leading to the maniac's capture. Hundreds of informants called in, but none of their tips ended in an arrest or even the identification of a serious suspect. This may not have been helped by the city authorities, who put out a profile of the Clubber that claimed he was a man of super-human strength, beastlike in appearance with fiery eyes. Naturally, no one of this description was ever found.

Suddenly, the attacks stopped. But then they began again in the autumn of 1926, with two more slayings in a single day. In the early hours of 26 October, 26-year-old schoolteacher Lily Croy was raped and bludgeoned to death within sight of her classroom. That afternoon 47-year-old Mary Allen was found dead in her home. At first the police said that she died from gunshot wounds. Later they admitted that Lily Croy and Mary Allen had been done to death with the same blunt instrument. This all too clearly recalled the Clubber.

A bigger reward was raised and the Toledo police swept the

streets of "odd-balls" and anyone who could be locked up in a mental institution. While there were no more attacks on women, on 23 November 1926 there were more arson attacks. At one single timber yard, $200,000-worth of damage was caused. A nearby ice company suffered another $10,000 in damages. The fire went on to engulf two other businesses, an apartment building, a railroad freight car and the city street department's stable.

Then the crime-wave ceased once more, leaving the police no closer to the perpetrator. They had never found or even identified him. Indeed, to this day, it remains unclear whether the rapist and killer was the same man as the arsonist and bomber.

The Twin Cities' Killer

Between 1986 and 1994 the corpses of up to 34 women littered the streets of the Twin Cities of Minneapolis and St Paul. Most of them were prostitutes in their twenties and thirties. Several were mutilated, dismembered and sometimes even decapitated. No one has been arrested or charged.

The police were not keen to ascribe the murders to one serial killer, with the attendant media hoo-ha. But if it is not the work of one serial killer then two or more are at large, or there are a number of men who have all killed just once. It is hard to say which is worse.

Virginia's Colonial Parkway Killer

Between 1986 and 1989, a serial killer stalked the Colonial Parkway, a scenic route that runs from Jamestown, through Williamsburg to Yorktown. The perpetrator specialized in abducting couples.

The first two victims were 27-year-old Cathleen Marian Thomas and 21-year-old Rebecca Ann Dowski, a lesbian couple who used to like to park at a secluded spot on the Parkway to make love in privacy. Cathleen Thomas was from Lowell, Massachu-

setts and was one of the 100 women of the class of 1981 at the US
Naval Academy at Annapolis – the first co-educational graduat-
ing class at any federal military academy. She then became a
stockbroker in Norfolk, Virginia. Her lover, Rebecca Ann Dowski, was from Poughkeepsie, New York. She worked as a senior
business management major at the College of William and Mary.

On 12 October 1986, a jogger found their car, a Honda Civic,
beside the York River, seven miles east of Williamsburg. The
vehicle had been pushed down an embankment near an area of
the Parkway popular with gay couples. The women's bodies were
discovered in the back seat of the car. A post mortem found rope
burns on their wrists and necks, signs of strangulation and their
throats had been slashed. Their purses and money were found
inside the car, and there was no sign of a struggle. Both women
were found fully clothed and there was no indication of sexual
assault. Their bodies had been doused with a flammable liquid,
and several matches were found. Detectives believe that the killer
had tried to set the vehicle on fire. Failing, the culprit then pushed
the car over the embankment, hoping it would career off the bluff
into the York River.

Twenty-year-old David Lee Knobling of Hampton, Virginia
and 14-year-old Robin M. Edwards of Newport News were last
seen alive on Saturday, 19 September 1987. They had met at an
arcade. The two of them left to cruise York County in Knobling's
black Ford pick-up truck with David's brother and another
friend. The three boys dropped Ms Edwards home before 11
p.m. and went back to the Knoblings' home. But David Knobling
left the house again soon afterward. It seems he must have gone
back to pick up Ms Edwards.

The two were not reported missing until Monday morning
because it was not unusual for David Knobling to spend a night
or two away from home. Robin Edwards' parents thought she
might have run away, so they were waiting for the social services
office in Newport News to open on the morning of the 21st to
report their daughter's disappearance.

David Knobling's pickup was found on 21 September near the
Ragged Island Wildlife Refuge at the foot of the James River

Bridge. There were no signs of a struggle. The keys were in the ignition, the radio was on and Knobling's wallet was on the dashboard. The driver's door was open and the driver's side window was wound halfway down.

"It was raining out that night," said David's mother Kathy Knobling. "So why would David have had the window down, unless someone with a badge approached him and asked for ID?"

Two pairs of underwear and Robin Edwards' shoes were found in the vehicle.

A few days later, their two partially clothed bodies washed ashore almost two miles downriver on the south bank of the James River in Isle of Wight County, near Smithfield, Virginia. Robin Edwards' bra was around her neck under her blouse and the belt on her jeans were undone. It is not known whether he had been molested by the killer or disturbed in her lovemaking with David Knobling. Knobling still had 13 quarters in the pockets of his jeans. The police believe that the two were marched more than 1½ miles through the woods and down a wooden pier, where they were killed and dumped in the river.

Although Smithfield was on the other side of the James River from the Colonial Parkway, the murder of David Knobling and Robin Edwards was linked to that of Cathleen Thomas and Ann Dowski because the Ragged Island Wildlife Refuge was a well known gay cruising area – it became so popular in the early 1990s that it was closed to the public.

On 9 April 1988, Richard Keith Call (known as Keith) from Gloucester County, Virginia and 18-year-old Cassandra Lee Hailey were reported missing. They were students at Christopher Newport College in Newport News and had been out on their first date together.

At about 9 a.m. the next day, Call's 1982 red Toyota Celica was found abandoned on the Colonial Parkway in Yorktown, Virginia by a ranger. The driver's door was open. The keys were in the ignition and the front seat was folded forward. Keith's watch was on the dashboard and Cassandra's purse was on the passenger seat. All their clothes, including their underwear was on the back seat.

Keith's brother, Chris, had been driving along the Parkway at about 4.30 a.m. when he noticed a parked car with a door or trunk open. But he was not certain if the car he saw was his brother's. An employee at the Eastern State Hospital also saw a car with an open driver's door at about 5.30 a.m. Neither body has ever been found, but both are presumed dead as their disappearance fitted a chilling pattern.

On the morning of 5 September 1989, 18-year-old Annamaria Phelps left her Virginia Beach home with 21-year-old Daniel Lauer, the brother of her fiancé Clinton, both residents of Amelia County. They were last seen alive between noon and 1 p.m. at the rest stop for westbound Interstate 64 traffic in New Kent County. At 5.30 p.m., Daniel Lauer's gold 1973 Chevrolet Nova was found at the rest area between Williamsburg and Richmond. The keys were in the ignition and the gas tank was three-quarters full. Annamaria Phelps' purse was in the car, along with clothes that belonged to Daniel Lauer. There were no obvious signs of a struggle inside the car.

The following month, their remains were found by a hunter, covered with a blanket, in the woods less than a mile away. The state medical examiner determined that Annamaria Phelps had been stabbed to death. Phelps, too, had suffered stab wounds but, in his case, cause of death had not been officially determined. However, both were clearly the victims of homicide.

The FBI said that the crimes were related, but no one has ever been identified as the Colonial Park Killer. Investigators have speculated that the killer might be a law enforcement officer, possibly a policeman or a security guard, who had caught the couples in a compromising position in their cars and used the authority of their uniform to get them to get out without putting up a fight. Another theory is that the suspect is a rogue CIA agent from their major training facility known as "the Farm" at Camp Peary in York County.

Washington, D.C.'s Petworth Prostitute Killer

In 1998, the police in Washington, D.C. arrested a suspect in the deaths of two of six women whose bodies were found in the city's Petworth neighbourhood over a 13-month period. Darryl D. Turner, aged 34, was charged with two counts of first-degree murder for the deaths of 39-year-old Jacqueline Teresa Birch and 34-year-old Dana Hill. Both women were known to have worked as prostitutes.

Jacqueline Birch's body was found on 18 November 1997 inside a building about three miles north of the Capitol Building, next door to where Turner lived. Dana Hill lived in the same block as Turner. Her body was found on 1 December 1997 behind an abandoned fast food restaurant about 1½ miles from the Capitol. Both women died from manual strangulation.

Five women who lived in the neighbourhood or visited frequently had turned up dead since November 1996. Three of them were found inside a pair of gutted buildings. The torso of a sixth woman who was thought to have frequented the neighbourhood was found in an alley nearby.

The Princeton Place Task Force that arrested Turner was put together in November 1997, after the community began weekly meetings and *The Washington Post* speculated that a serial killer was at work. The task force included agents from the FBI and the DEA.

On 5 January 2001, Turner was charged with a third murder – that of 32-year-old Toni Ann Burdine. A known drug-user and prostitute, she was found in an open field in the north-eastern section of the city where Turner lived, on 4 May 1995. After Turner's arrest, the police had reopened the Burdine case and the authorities were able to match DNA in the semen taken from her body to Turner's. Turner pleaded not guilty to all three murders.

But killings of other women in the neighbourhood who worked as prostitutes remain unsolved. The cases still open are those of 28-year-old Lateashia Blocker, whose body was found in 1995 in the same empty house as Jacqueline Birch was later discovered; 42-year-old Emile Dennis, whose body was found in a crawl space beneath the townhouse where Turner lived with his wife in December 1997; 41-year-old Jessica Cole, whose mutilated remains were discovered in October 1996; and Priscilla Mosley, aged 49.

As well as the DNA match to the semen found on Toni Burdine's body, Turner's former girlfriend provided damning testimony. In 1997, Turner was charged with choking and raping her. She testified that Turner told her that he preferred violent sex, including strangulation, because he had "trouble achieving sexual enjoyment any other way". And, during the attack, Turner said he was "tired of paying you [women] for sex".

Darryl D. Turner was convicted for first-degree murder. He is now on death row and is soliciting for pen pals via the internet. But as the other murders remain unsolved, there is always the possibility that there is another killer or killers out there.

Washington, D.C.'s Suitland Slayings

In 1986 and 1987, a serial killer was stalking the black community of Washington, D.C. He had murdered eight young black females, before disappearing. He has never been identified or caught.

On 13 December 1986, the body of 20-year-old Dorothy Miller was found in the woods near the Bradbury Recreation Center in Suitland, a suburb just outside the district of Columbia in Maryland. Although she had seemingly died of a drug overdose she was thought to be the killer's first victim because four more bodies were found in the same woods the following month. And, like the others, Dorothy Miller had been violently sodomized.

On 11 January 1987, the kids using the recreation centre noticed a woman's clothes hanging on nearby trees. When they went to investigate, they found the body of 25-year-old Pamela Malcolm, who had been missing from her home in Suitland since 22 October. There was no doubt that she was a murder victim because she had been stabbed to death.

The day after Malcolm's corpse had been recovered, a team of 50 police were combing through the wood for clues when they found two more bodies to the north of the headquarters of the US Census Bureau. They belonged to 22-year-old Cynthia Westbury, who had been missing since mid-November, and 26-year-old Juanita Walls. Both been sodomized and stabbed to death, and both had gone missing from D.C.

The very next day the body of 22-year-old Angela Wilkerson, another D.C. resident, was found near Suitland. Four of the victims had lived within a mile of each other in Southeast Washington. The D.C. residents were all unemployed and at least two of them frequented the same restaurant on Good Hope Road.

There followed three more murders that did not conform to exactly the same pattern, but were thought to have been perpetrated by the same killer.

On 15 January, the naked body of 20-year-old Janice Morton was found in an alley in Northeast Washington. She had been beaten and strangled. On 5 April, the naked body of an unidentified woman was found in a secluded driveway near Euclid and 13th Street, in Northwest Washington.

A 31-year-old suspect, Alton Alonzo Best, was indicted for Morton's murder on 7 April. He confessed to the crime on 9 June. The police maintained that Best knew two of the victims found in Suitland, making him a prime suspect in their killings. However, his arrest did not stop the attacks. On 10 April, with Best behind bars, an unidentified van driver attempted to abduct a 25-year-old woman, just one block from the home of Suitland victim Pamela Malcolm. Five days later, Donna Nichols was beaten to death in a Washington alleyway. On 24 June, Cheryl Henderson, aged 21, was found in a wooded area of Southeast Washington, not more than two miles from Suitland. Her throat was slashed from ear to ear. Then on 21 September another unidentified African-American female was found dead at a Southeast Washington apartment complex. The cause of death was not released and the police refuse to discuss any connection her death might have to the other unsolved cases.

Best has never been charged with any of the other killings and the killer or killers are still at large. The culprit's preference for killing African-American women has led to speculation that the "Freeway Phantom" may have resurfaced, after 15 years of inactivity, but homicide detectives have revealed no evidence of a connection to the earlier unsolved crimes.

Washington, D.C.'s Freeway Phantom

The Freeway Phantom's first victim was 13-year-old Carole Denise Spinks, who was abducted on 25 April 1971. She lived in a quiet block of Wahler Place in Southeast Washington. That Sunday evening it was warm and her older sister sent her to the 7-Eleven half-a-mile away on Wheeler Road, just across the Maryland line in Prince George's County, to buy bread, TV dinners and sodas. She paid for the items, left the store and disappeared. Her body was recovered six days later, a mile and a half from home, lying on the grass embankment of the northbound Interstate 295, one of several freeways passing through Washington east of the Anacostia River, 500 yards south of Suitland Parkway. She had been strangled and, probably, raped.

Ten weeks later 16-year-old Darlenia Denise Johnson disappeared. At 10.30 a.m., on 8 July, she left her apartment to go to her summer job at a recreation centre. Eleven days later her body was found on the side of the I–295, within 15 feet of the spot where Carol Spinks was had been found on 1 May. Her remains were so badly decomposed that the coroner could not determine the cause of death, though it was thought that she had been strangled. Both bodies had been tossed down the hill from above.

Meanwhile, a third victim, 14-year-old Angela Denise Barnes, had been abducted from Southeast Washington on 13 July, shot dead and dumped the same day just over the state line near Waldorf, Maryland. As the method of murder was different, one cannot be sure that Angela Barnes was the victim of the Freeway Phantom, though much of the rest of the MO is the same.

On 27 July, ten-year-old Brenda Crockett was sent to the store by her mother. There was no reason to fear for her safety. The

Crocketts lived in a quiet neighbourhood of terraced houses at 12th and W streets in Northwest Washington, about a block from Cardozo High School.

Her sister Bertha, then seven, recalled that Brenda was very responsible for her age, but when she did not return within an hour, the family grew anxious. While Bertha waited at home, other family members searched the neighbourhood.

"Even at that young age," said Bertha, "I knew something was wrong."

Three hours after Brenda had left, the phone rang in the living room. Bertha answered. It was Brenda on the line. She was crying.

"Momma is going looking for you," Bertha told her sister.

"A white man picked me up," said Brenda, "and I'm heading home in a cab."

She added that she thought she was in Virginia.

Then Brenda quickly said, "Bye" before hanging up. The police believe that Brenda had been forced to make the call and provide a misleading description of her abductor and the location.

Minutes later, the phone rang again. This time, Bertha's mother's boyfriend answered. Brenda told him what she had told her sister, and said that she was alone in a house with a man.

"Tell him to come to the phone and tell me where you're at," said the boyfriend, "and I'll come and get you."

"Did my mother see me?" Brenda asked.

"How could she see you when you're in Virginia?" the boyfriend replied. "Tell the man to come to the phone."

The boyfriend then heard heavy footsteps in the background.

"I'll see you," said Brenda, and the line went dead.

A few hours later, Brenda's body was found by a hitchhiker on US Highway 50 near I–295 in Prince George's Country, in a place where she could not be missed. A knotted scarf was tied around her neck. She had been raped and strangled.

The killer took a two-month summer break in August and September. Then on 1 October, 12-year-old Nenomoshia "Neno" Yates was snatched off Benning Road in Northeast Washington while walking home from a Safeway store at about 7 p.m. Her body was discovered within a few hours, on the shoulder of Pennsylvania Avenue, just over the state line in Prince George's County, Maryland. She, too, had been raped and strangled.

It was then that the moniker "Freeway Phantom" appeared in a headline on the story describing Nenomoshia's death in the now-defunct Washington tabloid, the *Daily News*.

At 18, Brenda Denise Woodward was the Freeway Phantom's oldest victim. On the night of Monday 15 November, she left night school at Cardozo High with a male friend and went to eat at Ben's Chili Bowl on U Street in Northwest D.C. By 10.25 p.m., they were on a bus heading to Northeast Washington. At Eighth and H Streets NE, she got off the bus to catch another to her home on Maryland Avenue NE. She seems to have been abducted from the bus stop.

About six hours later, a police officer spotted Brenda Woodward's body on the grass by an access ramp to Route 202 from the Baltimore-Washington Parkway near Prince George's County Hospital. Her coat had been draped over her chest. She had been stabbed and strangled.

The police found a mocking note in her coat pocket. Its contents are still unpublished, but it was signed: "The Freeway Phantom." Plainly the perpetrator enjoyed reading about his activities in the press. However FBI experts concluded that Woodward had written the note herself, possibly under the coercion of the killer. Nevertheless it was in a steady hand and betrayed no hint of fear or tension.

It was clear to the police that a serial killer was at work. All the victims were young black females. All of them had been abducted from the same geographical area and their bodies dumped near the same location. Most had been raped and strangled. Curiously, four of them had the middle name Denise. But this brought them no nearer to an arrest.

In the tense political atmosphere of the early 1970s – after the city had been torn part by race riots in 1968 following the assassination of Martin Luther King – the fact that all the victims were black led to a furore. More than 70 percent of the D.C.'s 757,000 residents were black, and there was widespread distrust of the police department, which was more than 60 percent white.

"You better bet that if these had been white girls, the police would have solved the cases," says Evander Spinks, a sister of the Phantom's first victim. "They didn't care about us. All the cases involving white girls still get publicity. But ours have been forgotten."

Black Washington was up in arms and, because of the phone calls in the Crocketts' case, they wanted to prove that a white man was to blame, but angry political rhetoric did nothing to advance the murder investigation. Meanwhile the Freeway Phantom lay low.

It was ten months before he claimed his final victim. On 5 September 1972, 17-year-old Diane Williams, a senior at Ballou High School, cooked dinner for her family, then went to visit her boyfriend's house. She was last seen boarding a bus on her way home. A few hours later, her body was found on the side of I–295 just south of the District line, just five miles from the point where Carole Spinks was discovered in May 1971. Again, police noted striking similarities with the other cases – and again, found no evidence that would identify a suspect.

In late March, the Maryland State Police arrested two black suspects – 30-year-old Edward Leon Sellman and 26-year-old Tommie Bernard Simmons. They were charged with the murder of Angela Barnes. Both suspects were ex-Washington policemen, though both had dropped out early in 1971, before completing their mandatory probation periods. They were also charged with the abduction and rape of a Maryland waitress in February 1971. Convicted of murder in 1974, both defendants were sentenced to life.

In the other case, the police had received thousand of tips, but did not have the manpower to handle them as the FBI had been recalled from the case to investigate the Watergate break-in and the subsequent scandal that forced President Nixon from office. Nevertheless D.C. detectives combed the rosters of the area's mental health facilities, examined the employment roles at city recreation centres and did background checks on substitute teachers who might have known the girls. In all, they developed more than 100 potential suspects, including dozens of convicted sex offenders, a real estate developer and a US Air Force colonel stationed at Bolling Air Force Base, across the I–295 from St Elizabeth's Hospital. None panned out.

Meanwhile, a federal grand jury examining the Phantom murders focused its spotlight on "a loosely-knit group of persons" suspected of luring girls and young women into cars – sometimes rented for the hunt – then raping their victims for sport. In 1974, the FBI returned to the case and began investigating the gang known as the Green Vega Rapists, some of whom claimed to have participated in the Phantom killings.

Suspects John N. Davis, aged 28, and Morris Warren, 27, were already serving life for previous rapes when a series of new indictments were handed down in December 1974. Turning state's evidence, Warren received a grant of limited immunity in return for testimony against Davis and another defendant, 27-year-old Melvyn Sylvester Gray. However, Davis recanted, no charges were filed and the investigation went no further. As a government spokesman explained, "The ends of justice can be served just as well if a person is convicted and sentenced to life for kidnapping, than if he is jailed for the same term for murder."

In court filings and in comments to reporters, authorities indicated that they felt that the Green Vega Rapists were responsible for the killings. However investigators now are not so sure, especially in the light of the Suitland murders 13 years later. Once again, the victims were young, female and black, and abducted and discarded in a manner reminiscent of the Freeway Phantom's style and in places not far from his patch. However, authorities refused to speculate upon a link between the crimes, and so both cases are considered "open", with the killers still at large.

In the late 1970s, D.C. homicide Detective Lloyd Davis developed a new Phantom suspect. One day in 1977 Davis had questioned Robert Askins, who had been charged with raping a 24-year-old woman in his house. At that time, the Phantom case was still active and homicide detectives routinely questioned rape suspects as part of the investigation.

Davis learned that 58-year-old Askins had been charged with homicide three times. He had spent time in St Elizabeth's Hospital and had later been convicted of killing a prostitute with cyanide in 1938. His sentence had been overturned on a legal technicality concerning the statute of limitations and he was freed in 1958.

When police searched Askins' house in the 1700 block of M Street in Northwest Washington after his arrest in 1977, Davis found the appellate court papers in a desk drawer. His eyes were immediately drawn to the word "tantamount" that the judges used in a footnote. That same word appeared in the note found in Phantom victim Brenda Woodward's coat pocket, where it seemed strangely out of place. Later, Davis discovered that Askins often used this old-fashioned word at the National Science Foundation, where he worked as a computer technician.

Davis worked the case for nearly three years. He retrieved evidence from the early cases from storage and shipped it to the FBI labs for the latest forensic analysis. Experts found the same green synthetic carpet fibre on all but one of the victims' clothing, for the first time linking five of the six Phantom's murders. Davis then got a search warrant and began digging up Askins' back yard. Despite Davis' best effort, he never recovered any physical evidence linking Askins to the crimes and Askins was never charged with the Phantom murders. However he was sentenced to life for kidnapping and raping two women in Washington, D.C. in the mid-1970s.

Davis retired in 1981, but he was unable to let go of the case. In 2005, he wrote to Askins in a North Carolina federal penitentiary, asking him to confess. Askins promptly wrote back, denying any role in the killings. The *Washington Post* also wrote to Askins. Again he denied being the Freeway Phantom, saying he did not have "the depravity of mind required to commit any of the crimes". But Davis does not believe him.

"I know he did it," Davis says. "I just know it."

D.C. homicide Detective Romaine Jenkins reviewed the Freeway Phantom cases in the late 1980s. Years after she retired, the Phantom's victims still haunt her.

"I always think of these young ladies," she says. "How did he keep these girls? How did he do it without anyone knowing? How did he select them?"

Another officer who took an interest in the Freeway Phantom was Sergeant Rick Fulginiti, a long-time Prince George's County detective. He was working in the cold-case department when he received a tip about a potential suspect.

Fulginiti learned that authorities had located a semen sample taken from a victim during the post mortem that had been kept at the Maryland medical examiner's. So he flew to Utah to get DNA samples from his suspect's relatives and from an old envelope, but when the samples were tested in 2002 technicians were unable to extract any comparable DNA from the sample.

In 2006, D.C. police Detective James Trainum got the task of reviewing the bulging Freeway Phantom files. He employed the geographic profiling technique of ex-Canadian cop Kim Rossmo and the computer system that Rossmo developed to plot the crimes on a map and work out the suspect's "anchor point" – his home, workplace or other significant location.

Together Trainum and Rossmo spent weeks scouring the reports and visiting crime scenes. From the abduction points and the locations where the bodies had been dumped, they worked out that the Phantom's anchor point was in Congress Heights, just south of St Elizabeth's Hospital. Trainum now plans to take an old phone book and reverse directory and plot names onto the geographic profile map. Police also plan to blanket the area with fliers announcing a $150,000 reward for witnesses who call Trainum at 202–727–5037 or 202–727–9099 with information.

Trainum has also contacted the relatives of the victims to tell them that he is, once again, looking into the Phantom killings. One of the people he contacted was Carolyn Morris, Carol Spinks' identical twin, who says the Freeway Phantom wrecked her life. She was overprotective of her four children and was unable to relax if they were out of eyeshot. She could not hold down a job and fell into alcoholism and drug addiction. It was only when they were grown that she found the courage to tell them what had happened 35 years before to the aunt they never knew.

The lives of other relatives of the victims have also been changed irrevocably. One victim's aunt wrote a self-published book, called *The Mystery of the Freeway Phantom*, and a victim's sister spent hours on street corners, wearing revealing clothing in the hopes of attracting the Freeway Phantom.

Patricia Williams, younger sister of Diane Williams, the Freeway Phantom's last known victim, joined the D.C. police in 1982. It had not been her ambition to be a police officer, but after the death of her sister, with whom she once shared a bed, she felt compelled to sign up. She still keeps a push-pin map showing the locations of random attacks on juveniles by adults in her office.

"I'm sure, subconsciously, that I know that if I wasn't able to help Diane, then I can help other children," she told *Washington Post* reporter Del Quentin Wilber.

She rarely goes days without thinking about catching the killer, to find out why he picked her sister and put a human face on the killer.

"I think that would help my healing process," she says.

Like Carolyn Morris and other relatives of Freeway Phantom victims, Patricia Williams has vivid nightmares about her dead sister. In Williams' dreams, she always asks her sister the same question, one that she also would love to ask the Freeway Phantom: "Where have you been all these years?"

Washington State Serial Killers

The Pacific Northwest has had more than its fair share of serial killers. Ted Bundy began his career in Washington State and Green River Killer Gary Ridgway operated there. The murder of 29 women and the disappearance of 12 others in the counties of King, Pierce and Snohomish in Washington State since 1985 are thought to be the work of another killer who is still at large. However, the perpetrator does share some of the Green River Killer's profile. He mainly abducts prostitutes, kills them and dumps their bodies in rural areas.

There are other serial killers at large in the area. One killer's grisly signature is his dismemberment of the bodies. He seems to be responsible for three murders where the victims' bodies were cut up and scattered in remote areas in Snohomish County. One victim was a Bulgarian involved in organized crime whose body was found in 1987, but was not identified for ten years. Another was a Korean immigrant from Bothell on the outskirts of Seattle who had a record for prostitution. Her body was found in 1991 with the remains of a man who has never been identified.

There was another cluster of killings around the area of the town of Index in the Cascades. The bodies of two Seattle women were dumped there in 1988. Both victims were known prostitutes and drug users. They had been stabbed. Three other women – two found dead nearby and a 14-year-old runaway last seen with one of the dead women – may also be victims of the same killer.

Another unknown killer is thought to be responsible for five murders and disappearances in the area of Clarkston and Lewiston on the Idaho border between 1979 and 1982. Some of the victims were dismembered and dumped in a river. Victims include three young women, a girl and a man. Two of their bodies have never been found. Although investigators had a suspect, they have never made an arrest.

A child killer was also at large in Washington State in the 1980s. On 7 September 1983, seven-year-old Lea Kimball vanished after leaving her school bus in rural King County, Washington. Two years later, 12-year-old Brenda Gere disappeared in similar circumstances in Clearview, in neighbouring Snohomish County. However, Brenda Gere apparently arrived home before she was abducted. Her school books were found in the house, but her fate remains a mystery. No trace of her has ever been found. However, Lea Kimball's case officially became a homicide on 7 March 1986, when her skeletal remains were found near Ellensburg, in the southeast of the state. No suspect has been named in Brenda Gere's abduction or in the death of Lea Kimball, but the police are convinced that there is a connection between the two cases.

Random slayings continue in Washington State. On 11 July 2006, 56-year-old Mary Cooper, a Seattle Public Schools librarian, and her 27-year-old daughter Susanna Stodden went hiking a wooded trail in the Mount Baker-Snoqualmie National Forest, near Seattle. They were last seen at around 10 a.m. near Mount Pilchuck in Snohomish County. A hiker found their bodies along the trail to Pinnacle Lake, 20 miles east of Granite Falls at around 2.30 p.m. They had been shot. Police quickly ruled out a murder-suicide. Robbery does not seem to be a motive as Mary and Susanna's wallets, keys and IDs were found in their backpacks. Both women had a passion for the outdoors.

Two weeks later, Snohomish County Sheriff's office said they had "persons of interest", though they have not identified any suspects and they do not have anyone in custody.

There is a heavy methamphetamine problem in the nearby town, there was speculation that the perpetrator could have been a "meth-head". There was a similar case in Portland, Oregon in 4 July 2005, where two hikers were found shot to death on a trail. Again the killer or killers have not been caught. And there is a similar unsolved murder in California, leading investigators to believe that there is a serial killer at work.

Part II

Killers Stalk the Globe

Where America leads, the rest of the world surely follows. The Earth, now, is overflowing with killers at large. Britain, which has always prided itself on the quality of its crime, if not its quantity, is still full of unapprehended murderers. In the 1960s, London produced Jack the Stripper, a rival to Jack the Ripper, who killed six women, but was never caught.

In England and Wales, the 43 police authorities launched Operation Enigma, looking into over 200 unsolved murder cases involving young women. In Glasgow, the police are searching for a current killer who has been butchering prostitutes, while a cold-case unit is still trying to identify Bible John, a killer from the late 1960s who has yet to be caught. Even sleepy old Ireland has a serial killer on the loose.

But then nowhere is safe these days. Canada has pig-farmer Robert Pickton. He denies all charges against him, and he has only been charged with a fraction of the murders he is suspected of, and even those are a fraction of the outstanding murders in Vancouver, let alone the whole of British Columbia. There are certainly more killers at large. Particularly vulnerable are "First Nations" – that is, Inuit and Native American – women. There are allegations of racism – first by the killers who do not value Inuit and Indian lives, then by the authorities who do not investigate the cases with quite the alacrity they exhibit when the victim is white. This mirrors the situation in the United States, where it is possible to murder African-American prostitutes – particularly those lured into the sex industry by drug addiction – seemingly with impunity. Many are not even identified.

Killing has become an international enterprise. One murderer seems to have been at large in the US, then moved his activities on to Portugal and at least four other European countries. This has a long history. Suspects in the Jack the Ripper case went on to kill in the US and Australia. Indeed, one even seems to have commuted back and forth across the North Atlantic.

It is not just free societies that are prone to having killers on the loose. Countries that have suffered political oppression seem to have spawned a particularly vicious variety. Russia has its own serial killers, with several at large. And in South Africa there seems to have been an epidemic. Again the police force, perhaps still infused with the old ethos of apartheid, has a poor record when it comes to dealing with killers who seek out black women as their victims.

In Latin American counties, particularly those that have suffered divisive civil wars, it is almost open season in women. In Guatemala, for example, almost every murder case goes unsolved. The police neither have the resources nor the incentive to investigate. In fact, some of the killers at large seem to be in the police force itself.

But worse is Ciudad Juarez in Mexico. The pandemic of murders there has come to the attention of the English-speaking world because Juarez is just over the border from El Paso, so the killings are reported the papers in Texas. In Juarez so many vulnerable young women have been raped and killed in the most horrible ways that the term "femicide" has been coined. The allegation is that Latin machismo culture and general border-town lawless had combined to create a murderous war on women. In the eyes of women's rights activists, all men in Juarez are potentially killers at large.

Argentina's Highway Maniac

Since 1996 a serial killer has been at large in Buenos Aires State, Argentina. Known as the "Highway Maniac", he has killed at least five times. The victims – largely prostitutes – all had their throats slit or were strangled. Their naked bodies were found along the main road around the eastern city of Mar del Plata, on the Atlantic coast some 240 miles from the capital. One victim had the word *"puta"* – prostitute – carved on her body. Some had their genitals mutilated. Police had several suspects, but not enough evidence to lead to an arrest. Another seven prostitutes have disappeared and it is feared that they are also victims of the killer.

The first victim was 27-year-old Uruguayan Adriana Jacqueline Fernandez. She was strangled with a cable and her naked body was found in a culvert alongside Highway 226 on 1 July 1996. She worked as an artisan in Mar del Plata and was the only victim who was not thought to be a prostitute.

The next victim was 35-year-old Maria Esther Amaro. She too had been strangled and her naked body was found alongside Highway 55 on 29 November 1996. Marks on her wrists indicated that she had been manacled and those on her knees showed that she had been forced to kneel. She had worked as a prostitute in the La Perla district of Mar del Plata and, after she was dead, the killer had carved the word *"puta"* in her flesh.

In mid-January 1997, 26-year-old Vivian Guadalupe Spindola disappeared from La Perla. On 20 January, two legs and an arm, severed at the wrist, was found near Los Acantilados, eight miles south of Los Acantilados. Two days later and ten miles further down Highway 88 a lorry driver found a torso. A tattoo in the pubic region identified the corpse as that of Vivian.

The mutilated body of 27-year-old Mariela Elisabeth Giménez was also found along Highway 88, around 30 miles from Mar del Plata. She had last been seen boarding a bus on 4 May. Her thighs had been cut open and her left arm was missing. A post mortem revealed that these mutilations had been made after she was dead, but other wounds indicated that she had been tortured before she had been killed.

The bodies of these first four victims had been carefully posed, but after that the killer changed his modus operandi. From then on, he sought to conceal the bodies. On 20 October 1998, two kids found a bag under a black coat on a vacant lot on the outskirts of Mar del Plata. In it were the thighs of a woman, neatly severed at the knee and hip. Two ligatures – one of nylon, the other cotton – were found nearby. The following day, three bags of bloody clothes were found less than 50 yards away. It was quickly established that these belonged to 26-year-old Maria of Carmen Leguizamón, who worked as a prostitute in the port area of the city. She was a native of Rosario, 175 miles north of Buenos Aires and 400 miles from Mar del Plata, where her parents thought she was a waitress. Chief investigator Jorge Luis Acosta thought the killer had changed his MO because he had almost got caught.

Around that time, a number of other prostitutes had simply gone missing. Mother of four Ana Maria Nores, aged 26, was two months pregnant when she disappeared on 19 July 1997. After she disappeared, someone called the police and told them to look along Highway 88, but nothing was found. Another anonymous call to the local newspaper, the *Clarin*, said that Ana Nores "would not be the last one".

She had told colleagues in the La Perla district where she worked that she feared that she would be the next victim of what the *Clarin* had dubbed the "Highway Maniac". And three days after she vanished, working girls from the district marched on the local police station, demanding better protection.

Checking their records, the police discovered that another prostitute was also missing from the area. On 23 February, 36-year-old Patricia Prieto – aka Dark Patricia and *La Dominguera* – had left her five-year-old daughter at home and never returned. But she was only reported missing in July when the child's father asked for custody.

On 20 October, 26-year-old Silvana Paola Caraballo was reported missing by the superintendent of her apartment block after he discovered her six-year-old daughter alone and crying because her mother had not returned from work. Silvana Caraballo was working as a prostitute in La Perla to support her family and put herself through an architectural course.

On 14 January 1998, 25-year-old Verónica Andrea Chávez's mother reported her missing when her daughter did not return from work. Verónica Chávez had no arrest history for prostitution and her mother said she worked as a cleaner for a law firm and a hat-check girl at a club. The police discovered that she did not work in either place and, although friends denied that she worked as a prostitute, she was friends with a number of the girls from La Perla.

On 1 March 1999, 30-year-old Claudia Jaqueline Romero vanished from her usual patch. Her husband said that she had had problems with some of the other girls, but would not have run away voluntarily as she loved her family. She left a three-year-old daughter and was three months pregnant when she disappeared. Soon after, 39-year-old Mirta Adela Bordón also vanished.

On 11 September, 26-year-old Sandra Carina Villanueva, a prostitute with a history of arrests, disappeared from the centre of Mar del Plata. Then on 30 October, 33-year-old mother-of-four Mercedes Almaraz went missing from La Perla. That Saturday night she left home in the barrio Las Américas on the outskirts of the city at midnight, wearing a denim miniskirt, violet top and sandals. She was last seen on the corner of España and 11 de Setiembre in La Perla in daylight. She often left her four boys, aged between one and five, in the care of a babysitter for days on end as she also worked as a mule for a drug-smuggler.

The city prosecutor Fabian Fernandez Garello blamed his own policemen for not catching the killer. Prostitution is one of the sources of greater police corruption, he said. He also denounced District Attorney Marcelo Garcia Berro, who became a "person of interest" in the case when his name was found in Veronica Chavez's phone book. She had also been seen getting into his car the night before she disappeared. Berro admitted knowing her but could not explain why she had called him over 20 times on his mobile phone and in the office over the preceding days.

Veronica had dealings with three other policemen, two of whom were involved in the investigation of the cases of Ana Nores and Silvana Carabello. Nores' mother claimed that the police wanted her daughter to act as bait to catch the killer. The families of the two women also alleged that the police used their daughters to sell drugs. There is also speculation that the killer is a policeman who extorts protection money from the prostitutes.

In March 1999, the governor of Mar del Plata offered a $50,000 reward for information leading to the arrest of the Highway Maniac. Soon after, an anonymous informant accused the son of a wealthy family who had been locked away in an insane asylum 30 years before after he had killed three prostitutes in Buenos Aires, dressed in women's clothing. Although diagnosed as a dangerous schizophrenic, the man had been released shortly before the first murder and the doctor who had signed his release was sacked.

Australia's Claremont Killer

In September 2006, the task force investigating the abduction and murder of three young women ten years earlier in Claremont, a well-to-do suburb between Perth and Fremantle, Western Australia, had its manpower trebled after an international panel of experts lead by South Australian Detective Superintendent Paul Schramm, veteran of over a hundred murder enquiries, declared that the case could yet be solved.

"We believe that by careful, incremental gathering of further information there are still opportunities for this to be successfully resolved," he said.

At one time the biggest serial-killer investigation in Australia, the Claremont task force had dwindled from a peak of about 120 officers to a handful of detectives and, in the months before the panel was set up, Police Commissioner Barry Matthews indicated that the task force would have to be disbanded.

All three women disappeared in similar circumstances from night spots in Claremont, around six miles from the centre of Perth, leading police to believe that a serial killer may be responsible. The first victim was 18-year-old secretary Sarah Ellen Spiers. On Australia Day – 26 January – 1996 she went with friends to the Club Bayview on St Quentin Avenue in Claremont. At around 2 a.m. the following morning she left, saying she was going to get a taxi home. Last seen in a phone booth, she then vanished. Her disappearance was completely out of character and attracted massive publicity in Perth.

A taxi driver named Steven Ross came forward with information. He said he remembered picking her up twice. On the night before she disappeared, he had driven her from Wellington Street, Mosman Park, to the Club Bayview. Later, he had driven her from Claremont to South Perth and remembered, from her call, that she had lived in Mill Point Road.

Ross told the police they should be looking for a fellow passenger, a man who had shared the taxi with Ms Spiers. The man did not appear to know her. Another woman, also a stranger, had doubled up in the cab that night. After he dropped the second woman in Dalkeith, he had taken the man and Ms Spiers to the Windsor Hotel, in South Perth. The man had pushed Ms Spiers out of the cab then paid the fare.

"I think he came back to Claremont the next night, found her and killed her," Mr Ross said.

However, the woman from Dalkeith never came forward. Police raided the taxi driver's home in August 2004, armed with a search warrant that listed personal items belonging to the missing women. They probed the garden and searched both dwellings, but found nothing. Sarah Spiers is still missing.

On 9 June, 23-year-old child-care worker Jane Louise Rimmer disappeared from a night spot called the Continental Hotel on Bayview Terrace, just 150 yards from the club where Sarah Spiers went missing. She had been drinking. Friends said that she declined a companion's offer to share a taxi home when the pub closed at midnight. Her body was found by a mother and children in bush land in the south of Perth eight weeks later.

Early in the morning of Saturday 15 March 1997, 27-year-old lawyer Ciara Eilish Glennon also disappeared from the Continental Hotel. She had only returned to work that Monday after travelling abroad for a year. That Friday, there had been drinks in the office and one of the partners in the law firm had offered her a lift to Claremont, which was just about ten minutes from her home. She arrived at the Continental Hotel at about 10.45 p.m.

She stayed there with friends for a short time, but she said she wanted to have an early night and left on her own to catch a cab home. She was never seen alive again. Her body was found on 3 April, off a track in scrub 28 miles north of Perth. Her silver Claddagh brooch was missing. With this murder police admitted that they were searching for a serial killer and Western Australia's Premier Richard Court offered a reward of A$250,000. The Continental Hotel changed its name to The Red Rock and is now known as The Claremont Hotel.

For operational reasons, the police kept the details of the case to themselves. However, they were very forthcoming about their chief suspect, a man named Lance Williams who has not been charged or found guilty of anything. Williams was a civil servant in his forties and lived with his elderly parents in the neighbouring suburb of Cottesloe. Police stopped him on the streets of Claremont at 3 a.m. on 8 April 1998. They had been conducting an intense surveillance operation over some months and said that they had observed him in his car regularly following women as they left nightclubs.

That night, detectives questioned Lance for several hours, then released him. Afterwards, police had his parents' home and a vacant beachfront unit he owns searched, twice. His car was subjected to a thorough forensic examination and the police tried to entrap him in a sting operation using an undercover female officer. She asked him for a lift to Mosman Park, only for uniform officers to surround his vehicle. Nevertheless, Williams co-operated with the police. He supplied DNA samples. At his own request he underwent a lie detector test and, later, he consented to a day-and-a-half of psychological analysis.

Williams denied anything to do with the killings. He said that he only picked up the plain-clothed woman police officer as a good Samaritan and the only evidence the police can come up with against him is circumstantial.

The police openly followed his every move 24 hours a day for over a year. Until October 1999, they sat outside his house in an unmarked car, followed him to work and home again. This became such a cosy arrangement that Lance would phone the police to let them know when he was doing something outside his normal routine, such as attending to a leaving party for a work-mate.

While Williams was under surveillance, and since then, no other woman has gone missing in Claremont. However, four other women have disappeared without trace in Western Australia, but police insist that these cases are not related. One other case does seem to be related though.

According to ABC Radio journalist Liam Bartlett, Sarah Spiers was not the killer's first victim. He claimed that police had told the father of a fourth missing woman, 22-year-old Julie Cutler, that his daughter was probably the first victim of the Claremont killer. Ms Cutler was a university student from Fremantle, who vanished after leaving a staff function at the Parmelia Hilton Hotel in Perth at 12.30 a.m. on 20 June 1988. Her car was found two days later in the surf near the breakwater at Cottesloe Beach. Her body has never been found. She was last seen wearing a black evening dress with a high collar and gold buttons on the shoulder, and black patent shoes.

There may have been other attacks by the same man. In October 1994, a man hiding in the back of a taxi grabbed a 31-year-old woman when she got in near Club Bayview. She leapt out, breaking an ankle. The following New Year, a man dragged a woman from her car after she left Club Bayview. He attempted to sexually assault her but she fought him off. Then in February 1995, a 17-year-old girl was abducted in the early hours of the morning while walking home from the Club Bayview along Gugeri Street, near Claremont subway. She was trussed up with electrical cord, raped and left for dead in Karrakatta Cemetery nearby

At 2 a.m. on 3 May 1996 – after Sarah Spiers' abduction and before Jane Rimmer's murder – a 21-year-old woman was indecently assaulted in the lane behind Club Bayview. The assailant ripped her skirt off and banged her head against a wall six times before she fled. And on 8 November 2000 – after Ciara Glennon's death made the search for a serial killer official – 20-year-old Sarah McMahon disappeared after leaving her workplace on Stirling Highway at 5 p.m. Her car was found abandoned at Swan Districts Hospital in Middle Swan, a small town just inland of Perth. In all the disappearances of 16 women have fallen within the scope of the Claremont investigation.

The police are also investigating the possibility that Bradley John Murdoch, the convicted killer of British backpacker Peter Falconio in 2001, may have been involved, although Murdoch was in jail from November 1995 until February 1997. Murdoch has also been questioned over the disappearance of 17-year-old Hayley Dodd, who was last seen in 1999 north of Perth, and an unidentified woman missing since 1996 from Broome, Murdoch's home town a thousand miles to the north of Perth.

There has also been some scrutiny of Peter Weygers, who was the mayor during the time of the disappearances. His 12-year tenure of office ended in 1997. Weygers had bought a house from taxi-driver Steven Ross, but had allowed him to continue living there in a mobile home in the back yard. Weygers had also been seen driving the Ford station wagon that Ross had used as a taxi when he had picked up Sarah Spiers in 1996.

Weygers was a controversial political figure and leading libertarian who once agreed to launch a book written as a guide for Australian males who wanted to get themselves a virgin Filipina bride. The launch was abandoned amid public outcry. He created more controversy in April 2004 by defending the three-time convicted serial rapist Gary Narkle, describing him as an artist and claiming Narkle had more to fear from his victims than they had to fear from him.

As a politician Weygers made a career this way by thrusting himself into the public spotlight, a trait which would appear to be at odds with the behaviour of a serial killer. He owned 19 investment properties around Perth, mostly inherited from his mother, with whom he lived until her death. He has since married Vicki, a Filipina. Nevertheless in September 2004, the police staged a very public search of his home and, despite his objections, forced him to give a DNA sample.

"This is a gross invasion of privacy. This is a gross invasion of rights. I have no idea what their excuse is for this absolutely disgraceful conduct," he told a journalist, claiming the police scrutiny was part of a State Government plot to discredit him.

In office, Weygers had questioned the mass DNA testing of taxi drivers by investigators in the Claremont case and, later, took up the issue of the human rights of Lance Williams, then still under day-and-night surveillance.

Steven Ross then further muddied the waters by handing out an unsigned 44-point statement to the media. He claimed police had tried to coerce him into making false admissions about Weygers the day before the raid on the civil libertarian's home, including suggesting that Ross delivered girls to the former mayor. Weygers had a reputation, when mayor, for making flirtatious or suggestive remarks to female reporters.

"The police made derogatory remarks about Peter Weygers and implied that I was involved in a homosexual relationship with him," Ross wrote. "I denied that I was in a homosexual relationship with Peter Weygers and that he was not my boyfriend. The police alleged that Peter Weygers exerted an abnormal influence over me, which I denied. The police alleged that Peter Weygers gave me orders that I carried out, which I denied. The police then stated words to the effect that Peter Weygers 'wanted' young girls."

The inability to apprehend the Claremont Killer is seen as a major embarrassment to the Western Australia Police and the "Macro Task Force" set up to investigate the murders has been disbanded and reformed several times. Public confidence has not been helped when several senior officers were implicated in corruption allegations by the Western Australia Police Royal Commission.

In October 2006, it was announced that Mark Dixie, a man on trial in the United Kingdom over the murder in 2005 of the 18-year-old model Sally Anne Bowman, is a prime suspect in the killings, and the Macro Task Force has requested DNA samples from Dixie to test against evidence taken during the enquiry.

Belgium's Butcher of Mons

On 20 May 1998, Belgian police in the city of Ranst, outside Antwerp found the skeletal remains of what was thought to be seven bodies in a container, along with five human heads. They feared that this might be the reappearance of the "The Butcher of Mons", a unidentified killer who had dumped 30 bags containing body parts of at least three women, possibly six, in places around the city of Mons, 60 miles away, in 1997.

The killer left police scientists a gruesome anatomical jigsaw puzzle. Some of the remains were so badly decomposed it was an almost impossible task to discover how many victims there were. The authorities were under intense pressure to solve the murders from Belgian Justice Minister Stephane de Clerck after the outcry that followed the bodies of four young girls discovered 20 miles away, victims of paedophile Marc Dutroux.

The killer, who plainly savoured their discomfort, played a grisly game with his pursuers, dumping the bags filled with body parts in places with chillingly evocative names. The first bags, containing 12 neatly-severed parts of an indeterminate number of arms and legs, were found on 22 March 1997 on the banks of the Fleuve Trouille – the River Jitters – a canal bordering Mons and neighbouring Cuesmes.

Two days later, a limbless upper torso was found on the banks of a tributary of the Fleuve Haine – River Hate – next to a road called Chemin de l'Inquietude – the Path of Worry. The limbs had been severed in the same way as those of another torso found floating in the Haine the previous July. The police have established that it was the work of the same killer.

The *gendarmerie* began an intensive search of Mons, using helicopter, sniffer dogs and infra-red equipment. Then on 12 April another two bags were found in a lay-by on the Rue du Depot – Deposit Road. A week later another was found on the Rue St Symphorien – Symphorien was a Christian martyr who was beheaded in AD 200 – at a place called La Poudrière – the Powderkeg – near Havré.

The killer left numerous clues which allowed a team of specialist psychiatrists to compile a profile. He is thought to be an intelligent, methodical, calculating and obsessive man, who takes pleasure in the ritualistic dismemberment of his victims and the careful distribution of their remains. Detectives believe that there might be a perverse religious motive for the killings. Mons is an ancient religious town with connections to a number of saints associated with decapitation.

A stone head of St John the Baptist can be found over the door of the oldest inn in Mons, which dates back to 1776. The inn was built by a monk, a member of the Catholic Brotherhood of St John the Beheaded. The order was established in the Middle Ages to escort condemned men to the scaffold. It still exists today. The head looks out over the Rue de la Clef – Road of the Key – a fact that investigators feel could be significant, given the clues the killer is volunteering. It may also be significant that relics of the decapitated St Symphorien are kept in a nearby church.

Two of the three victims whose names are known disappeared on a Sunday, and the third may also have done so, though no one seems to have noticed that she was missing.

"We have not ruled out that he is a member of a satanic sect," said Didier Van Reusel of the public prosecutor's department. "The treatment of the bodies is very methodical, which is often the case with Satanists involved in ritualistic killings."

A song about the Butcher of Mons called "Bowels of Murder" appears on *Lovecraftian Dark*, the second album of the heavy-metal band Dawn of Relic.

It was initially thought that the killer was a surgeon or a butcher, due to the precision of the dissection. But further investigation revealed that the killer had not dismembered the bodies by hand. He ran his victims through an automatic sawing machine with several circular blades at 12-inch intervals – the kind of machine normally used for slicing chopping logs into planks. The severed limbs were exactly one foot long.

"There are not that many places you can carry out that operation, with the blood and the smell," said Van Reusel. "And there are not that many people who own a machine like that."

The killer appears to have chosen his victims from a group of transients, who congregate around Mons station and the string of cheap bars opposite. One of the victims was 43-year-old transexual Martine Bohn, a retired prostitute who had worked out of the bars. Having lost contact with her family years before, she disappeared on Sunday 21 July 1996 and it was her torso found floating in the Haine. Her breasts had been sliced off. It is thought that the killer may have been angry at discovering she was not a real woman.

A second victim was 33-year-old Jacqueline Leclercq, a mother-of-four who had separated from her husband. After losing custody of her children, she drifted into the station scene. She had disappeared on Sunday 23 January 1997.

A third victim was 21-year-old Nathalie Godart, who lived in a bedsit in Mons. Her young son had been taken into care. No one had reported her missing. The staff at the Intercity, the Metropole and the Café de la Gare, the bars opposite the station, knew her well.

"She was promiscuous, but not a prostitute," said one bar owner.

The police are aware that the killer is playing a complex game with them. Tests indicate some of the first bags found on the bank of the Trouille had lain there undiscovered for months. They were only discovered only when the last bag dumped there hung conspicuously on a tree, drawing attention to it. The remains they contained were between one week and two years old which indicated that the killer had access to an industrial refrigeration unit.

The killer plainly enjoyed the publicity their discovery brought and he became more audacious. Succeeding bags were placed in highly visible places, with evocative names, at a time when the police search was already fully underway.

Psychiatrists believe the perpetrator relishes not just the killing but also the handling of the corpse. Each of the body parts found had been wrapped individually in its own white plastic bag which is then knotted tightly at the top. These white bags are then placed in the larger grey bags. Each grey bin liner has been tied tightly in the same fashion, and the top of the knot then snipped off with scissors – "very neatly, very precisely, the work of an obsessive," said Van Reusel.

One man was questioned, but was released. He has since left Mons, and is no longer a suspect. All the authorities could do was await the next piece of the puzzle and keep Rue des Sinistres, or Sentier des Morts under surveillance.

The Butcher of Belize

In May 2006, Channel Five, a local television network in Belize, offered a $100,000 reward for information leading to the arrest and conviction of a paedophile serial killer who abused and killed at least five schoolgirls during a 16-month binge.

The first victim was 13-year-old Sherilee Nicholas, who disappeared in September 1998. A month later authorities found a body partially submerged in a ditch of water beside a feeder road near Mile 13 on the Western Highway. The body suffered more than 40 knife wounds and showed signs of rape. Investigators believe the girl tried to fight off her attacker. The child's mother identified the body, but no clues could be found to identify the killer.

Soon after, 9-year-old Jay Blades disappeared. Then, in the northern town of Corozal, 13-year-old Rebecca Gilharry was found raped and strangled. Another child's body was found in northern Belize and another girl was raped, beaten with a rock and left to die in the southern town of Dangriga. She lived to tell her tale to the police.

Fears grew in Belize City when 12-year-old Jackie Fern Malic vanished on 22 March 1999. Jackie's sister told police that a family friend, 40-year-old mechanic Mike Williams, had offered to take the two girls for a ride before school, but they turned him down. Police questioned Williams and released him, only to arrest him later. Two days after she had disappeared, Jackie Malic's body was found on a side road, a few miles away from where Sherilee Nicholas's body was found. She had multiple stab wounds to the face, buttock, knee and upper left arm, and one of her arms had been severed. The coroner drew attention to the many similarities between the two deaths.

On the day of Jackie's funeral, children lined the streets with signs demanding that the killer be caught. A Children's Summit was convened and, in a phone-in programme on the radio, a little boy asked Prime Minister Said Musa: "Why are there special police to protect the tourists, but not the children?"

A week later, the curfew was imposed. No one under 17 was allowed out between 8 p.m. and 6 a.m. Wardens were stationed at all schools to monitor children and watch for suspicious characters. Parents began walking their children to school. This was quite a readjustment for the citizens of Belize. With a population of just 200,000, the quiet central American country had long been relatively free of sex crimes and murder. But with Williams now in jail charged in Jackie Malic's death everyone thought the nightmare was over.

In June, a child's skull and a few bone fragments were found along the Western Highway, near where the other victims had been located. It was assumed that Jay Blades been found at last. But next to the body was Sherilee Nicholas's school bags. Fearing an error in identification, authorities exhumed Sherilee's body against her mother's wishes.

Meanwhile, in June, 10-year-old Karen Cruz disappeared from her home in Orange Walk, just north of Belize City, while her mother was on the front veranda. Her body was found the next day near her home. Newspapers reported suspicions regarding her uncle 38-year-old Antonio Baeza, who lived next door, and suggested he had been stalking the child. Baeza was arrested and charged with murder. But still the killings did not stop.

At the end of the month, nine-year-old Erica Wills went missing. Her body was found three weeks later. She too had been butchered. Found behind a quarry near Gracie Rock, a village 20 miles west of Belize City, her bones had been picked clean by vultures, but her mother recognized her daughter's hair band and her Tweety Bird ring, and was able to identify the body. A thousand people turned out in Belize City late Monday for a candlelight vigil in memory of the victims and Williams was then released.

Then on 15 February 14-year-old Noemi Hernandez disappeared after her grandmother sent her to collect rent money from a tenant. Nine days later her mutilated remains were fished out of the water near the mouth of the Belize River by a Belize Defence Force Maritime Wing patrol boat. She was found headless and her entire left arm was missing. Like the other victims, she had been sexually assaulted and stabbed repeatedly. The similarities between the murders were very striking and lead police to believe it may have been the work of a serial killer, now dubbed Jack the Butcher. As this is the first case of serial killing to hit Belize, the police lacked the experience to deal with the situation and called on Scotland Yard and the FBI for help. It was hoped that Channel 5's reward might help bring the culprit to justice.

The Boy Killers of Brazil

A Brazilian man accused of killing 42 boys in a series of macabre Satanic murders was sentenced to 20 years and eight months in jail on 25 October 2006 for one of the killings. Forty-one-year-old Francisco das Chagas Rodrigues de Brito was found guilty of killing 15-year-old Jonathan Silva Vieira who disappeared in northern Brazil in December 2003. The bicycle mechanic still faces numerous other charges of murder killings and sexual abuse. The police in the Amazonian states of Maranhao and Para maintain that Chagas has confessed.

However, human rights groups following the case were reluctant to accept the police's version of events and expressed reservations over the tactics used to secure Chagas' confession. They also questioned previous police work and the future of three people already jailed or awaiting trial for carrying out some of the killings.

"We've been questioning the police's work on this for 13 years, so we are naturally still a little suspicious," said Nelma Pereira da Silva, head of a local children's rights group who took the case to the Organization of American States in Washington. "We need to wait and see if this is for real."

The police believe that Chagas performed black magic rituals before killing some of the boys. He sexually abused his victims and, in some cases cut off their genitals, before decapitating them and burying the bodies.

During the trial, Jonathan's mother, Rita de Silva, told the court her son had said he was going to pick fruit with Chagas on the day he went missing.

"The monster tried to help out the mothers of the children he killed because he was looking for victims," she said.

She said she had shown Chagas a photograph of her son after he disappeared, and the killer laughed and told her he had not seen him.

"It seemed like he was laughing at my suffering," she said.

The trial was held in the auditorium of a club in Sao Jose de Ribamar, 1,400 miles north-east of Rio de Janeiro, because the courtroom was not big enough to hold the hundreds of victims' relatives.

Prosecutors say they charged Chagas with Jonathan Silva Vieira's murder first because it was the case in which they had the most evidence.

Chagas was arrested in April 2004 after neighbours complained of a stench coming from his ramshackle house on the outskirts of the Maranhao state capital of Sao Luis. Officers secured a search warrant and dug up a dirt floor to find two skeletons. One was identified as a four-year-old boy named Daniel and the other of a child Chagas said was called Diego. Daniel's father recognized scraps of clothing as a T-shirt he was wearing when he disappeared in February 2003.

According to police, Chagas quickly confessed to the killings and those of at least 18 other young boys. The methods he used were similar to those used in the spate of murders that ravaged Maranhao and the neighbouring state of Para between 1989 and 2003. The police said that Chagas lived in both states at the times the killings took place.

The series of killings shocked even Brazil, where violence is common and the murder rate is one of the world's highest. Reports that Chagas sexually assaulted the boys and then castrated them added to the outrage, as did allegations that some of the earlier killings that took place in Para between 1989 and 1993 were related to a satanic cult. Such things are not uncommon in Brazil.

On 27 November 1998, Brazilian police arrested six members of the United Pentecostal Church of Brazil, who had beaten and kicked to death six people, including three children, purportedly so that the perpetrators would be taken to heaven "after wiping out the enemies of God". The cult practiced their bizarre rituals on a remote rubber plantation where men, women and children were subjected to vicious ritual beatings. Among those arrested was Francisco Bezerra de Moraes, aka Toto, who was believed to be the leader of the 30-member sect.

The killings began two weeks before the arrests when Bezerra announced during a sermon that he could hear "voices from Jesus Christ" telling him that the former pastor of the group and all his followers must be punished. Bezerra, his wife and two other men then began beating, whipping and kicking other worshippers. For the next several days "disciplinary" torture continued in nearby shacks.

"Each day began with a ceremony venerating of Toto's wife," said a survivor. "Then came the torture."

Torture were accompanied by prayers and chants of "Out, Satan!" Among the dead were two brothers aged three and four, who were allegedly killed by their father, and another 13-year-old boy. The mother of the dead brothers was also murdered. The former pastor of the sect escaped and raised the alarm. When police arrived, they discovered the bodies of the dead out in the open, decomposing, torn apart and being eaten by animals.

Then in August 2003, five men went on trial in the Brazilian city of Belem accused of sexually mutilating and murdering young boys in Altamira, a town in the Amazon. They were said to be members of a satanic cult who murdered and mutilated for ten years before being caught. One of the five, Valentina Andrade, was the leader of an occult sect based in Argentina and two were doctors.

Chagas originally told police he did not remember attacking the boys or castrating his victims because his memory was erased at the moment of the killing. Nevertheless, he pleaded guilty to the murder charge. In mitigation he and other witnesses, including his sister, testified that he had been abused as a child by his grandmother and a man named Carlito. Chagas told the court that when he murdered Jonathan Silva Viera, he felt a pent-up rage stemming from those childhood experiences.

"I was seeing Carlito in front of me," he said.

The killings were so brutal and the inaction of the local police so shocking that the Organization of American States launched a campaign to pressure local authorities into more rigorously investigating the cases. Several foreign and Brazilian human rights groups also petitioned the federal government to intervene in the investigation.

As result, the police in the northern state of Maranhao announced that Francisco das Chagas confessed to the mass killing of 18 boys around Sao Luis from 1991 to 2003. They believe the bicycle mechanic may have killed three others during the same period. Police in neighbouring Para state want to question him concerning the whereabouts of 10 youngsters who were either killed or disappeared there.

In spite of the concerns from human rights groups, the state's attorney general said the detailed evidence provided by Chagas showed "strong signs" he was responsible, based on his own confessions. But there are concerns. The Organization of American States criticized the state government for failing to cooperate with their inquiry. Children's rights activitist Pereira da Silva said her organization would focus its attentions on identifying the officers responsible for the imprisonment of Roberio Ribeiro Cruz, who was sentenced to 19 years after supposedly admitting to killing an 11-year old in 1998, and the arrest of two others who are awaiting trial for the slaying of another child in 1996.

According to the police Chagas has now confessed to the killings of 30 boys in Maranhao state and 12 others in Para state between 1991 and 2003, but then retracted his confession again. If convicted of all murders, Chagas would be Brazil's most prolific serial killer. However, most people involved in the case have their doubts that he is guilty of all the murders he is charged with and are concerned that other child killers are at large.

Brazil's Killer Beach

Brazilian police said they are hunting another serial killer who has tied up, raped and repeatedly stabbed four women before dumping their bodies in a field close to a motorway. Sergeant Marcelo de Jesus Bispo said officers found the four corpses in Itabuna in the northeastern state of Bahia, 282 miles south of the beach resort of Salvador.

Then in 2005, the police in Maranhao began combing the state's beaches for more clues to the identity and whereabouts of a middle-aged man suspected of killing two women, from Spain and Germany. A Brazilian woman was also missing, believed she could be a victim of the same killer.

"Everything indicates we are dealing with a serial killer," Maranhao's public secretary, Raimundo Cutrim, said. "The women were travelling alone, were beaten to death and were found buried."

Police said the tourists had all been seen with a man answering the same description.

The body of 27-year-old Nuria Fernandez from Spain was found on an island off the coastal city of Sao Luis on 25 March 2005. Eight days before, the body of 46-year-old German Marianne Kern was found at a nearby beach. The Brazilian Valeria Augusto Veloso disappeared from the same place at around the same time.

On 26 March, police arrested a man who allegedly used Kern's credit card after her body was found. He said he got the card from a man whose description fitted that of the suspected killer.

Canada's Beast of British Columbia

In a series of letters to 27-year-old Thomas Loudamy of Fremont, California, accused murder Robert Pickton asserted his innocence and praised the British Columbian judge for dropping 21 of the 27 murder charges against him. He has pleaded not guilty to the remaining six and has expressed his concern about the expense of the investigation which he claims is an attempt to make him a fall guy for all the missing women in British Columbia. There are at the very least 65 women missing from Vancouver's Downside Eastside alone, the area where Pickton is said to have selected his victims.

The ten blocks of Vancouver's Downtown Eastside comprise not just the poorest area in British Columbia, but the poorest in the whole of Canada. They call the neighbourhood "Low Track". At its centre is the intersection of Main and Hastings, called "Pain and Wastings" by locals. Its shabby hotels, rundown bars and dilapidated pawn shops are home to 5,000 to 10,000 at any one time. Crack cocaine and heroin are supplied by Asian gangs and bikers who are frequently involved in turf wars. Most of the women addicts support their habits by prostitution, giving Low Track the highest HIV infection rate in North America.

Low Track became famous for its "kiddy stroll", which featured prostitutes as young as 11. Some underage girls work the streets; others are kept by pimps in special "trick pads". New "twinkies" – runaways lured by the bright lights – arrive every day. Over 80 percent of the prostitutes in Low Track were born and brought outside Vancouver. A survey in 1995 showed that 73 percent of the girls had started in the sex trade as children. The same percentage were mothers with an average of three children each. Some 90 percent had had their children taken into care. Most did not know where their children were. In 1998, on average, there was one death a day from drug overdoses among these women.

But there were other dangers. In 1983, women began to go missing from Low Track. The police did not notice the trend for nearly 14 years. That was hardly surprising as most of the inhabitants were transients, and runaways change their names and addresses regularly. Some simply moved on. But by 1997, the police began to fear that more than two dozen had been murdered. It was then that they began to compile a list.

The first of the 61 names to be put on the list was that of 23-year-old Rebecca Guno, a prostitute and drug addict last seen alive on 22 June 1983. She was reported missing three days later. Such rapid reporting is unusual. Forty-three-year-old Sherry Rail – the next on the list – was not reported missing until three years after she disappeared in January 1984.

Elaine Auerbach, aged 33, told friends she was moving to Seattle in March 1986 but she never turned up and she was reported missing in mid-April. Teressa Ann Williams, the first First-Nations woman on the list, was 15 when she was last seen alive in July 1988, but was not reported missing until March 1999. Thirty-year-old Ingrid Soet, a schizophrenic on medication, disappeared on 28 August 1989 and was reported missing on 1 October 1990. The first black woman on the list was Kathleen Dale Wattley. She was 32 years old when she vanished on 18 June 1992 and was reported missing 11 days later.

There was then a three-year hiatus. But in March 1995 47-year-old Catherine Gonzales, a drug user and sex-trade worker, disappeared. She was reported missing 9 February 1996. In April 1995, 32-year-old Catherine Maureen Knight went missing. Her disappearance was reported to the police on 11 November. Dorothy Spence, a 33-year-old First-Nations woman, vanished on 6 August 1995. Her disappearance was reported earlier on 30 October. Then 22-year-old Diana Melnick disappeared two days after Christmas and was reported missing two days later.

There was another hiatus until 3 October 1996 when 22-year-old drug user and prostitute Tanya Holyk disappeared. Her family knew something was wrong when she didn't come home to see her son, who was about to turn one, after a night out with friends. Pickton has since been charged with her murder. She was reported missing on 3 November. Olivia Gale Williams, aged 21, disappeared on 6 December 1996 and was not reported missing until 4 July the following year.

Twenty-year-old Stephanie Lane left her two-year-old son with her mother along with an uncashed welfare cheque, though she continued to call on birthdays and holidays. Then on 11 March 1997, she was released from hospital after an episode of drug psychosis. She was last seen alive at the Patricia Hotel on Hastings Street later that day. She has not been heard of since.

Twenty-two-year old Helen Mae Hallmark was last seen alive on 17 June 1997 and reported missing on 23 September 1998. Her sister wrote a poem to her memory.

Janet Henry, who also went missing in June 1997, came from the KwaKwaQueWak Nation in Kingcome Inlet in British Columbia, the youngest in a family of thirteen. She had a happy childhood until her mother fell ill and her father died. The children were sent to residential schools and foster homes, losing all ties to their native culture. Her sister Lavina was raped and murdered when she was 19. Another sibling killed himself.

A bright young woman, Janet graduated from high school, became a trained hairdresser, married and had a daughter, who she was devoted to. But when the marriage broke up in the late 1980s, her husband was given custody of their daughter. Janet was devastated and her life went into free-fall. She moved to Vancouver's Downtown Eastside and begun attending parties where she exchanged sex for drugs.

She had already had one brush with a serial killer. In the early 1980s, she met Clifford Olson, who drugged and raped her, but her life was spared. Olson pleaded guilty to 11 murders in 1982. All too aware of the dangers of her profession, Janet would phone her brothers and sisters frequently to let them know she was okay. She was reported missing on 28 June 1997, two days after her last contact with her siblings.

Marnie Lee Frey, 27, was last seen alive in August 1997, though she was not reported missing until 4 September 1998. She had a baby at 18 and asked her parents to adopt the child.

"She said, 'Mom, this is the only thing I can do for her. I love her dearly, but I know I can't look after her as a mom,'" her mother recalled.

Her parents pretended that the child, Brittney, was Marnie's younger sister but were forced to tell her the truth in the light of the publicity surrounding the case.

Jacqueline Murdock, aged 26, was last seen alive on 14 August but was not reported missing until 30 October 1998. Thirty-three-year-old Cindy Louise Beck disappeared in September 1997 and was reported missing on 30 April 1998. Andrea Fay Borhaven, aged 25, had no fixed address until she vanished sometime during 1997, it is thought. Her disappearance was only reported to the police on 18 May 1999. Thirty-eight-year-old Kerry Lynn Koski disappeared in January 1998 and was reported missing on the 29th of the month.

Four more women would disappear before Vancouver police were prompted to take an interest in the case. Twenty-three-year-old Jacqueline McDonnell disappeared in mid-January 1998 and was reported missing on 22 February 1999 and 46-year-old Inga Monique Hall was last seen alive in February 1998 and reported missing on 3 March.

Twenty-nine-year-old mother-of-two Sarah Jane deVries was last seen on the corner of Princess and Hastings in the early morning of 14 April 1998 and reported missing by friends later the same day.

"This started when she was 12," said her mother Pat. "She has HIV, she has hepatitis C. What I do for her now is look after her kids the best I can."

When Sarah went missing, her children were seven and two.

"It's very hard to tell a seven-year-old that somebody is missing," said Pat. "It's something you can't come to terms with, you can't work through, because there's never an end to it."

Nobody has seen or heard from her since. This was unprecedented as she always called on her mother's birthday, Mother's Day and her own birthday.

Ex-boyfriend Wayne Leng said Sarah underwent "a lot of turmoil" in her 29 years, particularly as she was a child of mixed parentage adopted by an all-white family on the West Side. As Sarah herself observed in a diary she left behind: "I think my hate is going to be my destination, my executioner."

Leng put up posters around the Vancouver's Downtown Eastside carrying Sarah's picture and details of a $1000 reward. But three phone calls he got on his pager around midnight one Saturday night left him chilled.

"Sarah's dead," said a man's slightly slurred voice, with music pounding in the background. "So there will be more girls like her dead. There will be more prostitutes killed. There will be one every Friday night. At the busiest time."

The second message featured the same voice and had the same music playing in the background.

"You'll never find Sarah again," the man said. "So just stop looking for her, all right? She doesn't want to be seen and heard from again, all right? So, 'bye. She's dead."

The final message said: "This is in regard to Sarah. I just want to let you know that you'll never find her again alive because a friend of mine killed her and I was there."

Leng said the mystery caller knew things about Sarah deVries not known by many others.

Sheila Catherine Egan was 20 when she vanished in July 1998. Her disappearance was reported on 5 August. She had been a prostitute since the age of 15.

In September 1998, a First Nations' group sent the authorities a list of women they said had been murdered in Downtown East-side and demanded a thorough investigation. The police responded by saying that some of those listed had moved away and were still alive. Others had died from drug overdoses or disease. However, the complaint prompted Detective Dave Dickson to take a second look at the list of all the Low Track women who had simply disappeared without a trace. By now it had enough names on it to persuade Dickson's superiors to allow him to set up a cold-case task force.

Throwing its net wide, the task-force started with 40 cases from all parts of Vancouver dating back to 1971. But in an effort to find a pattern, the roster was narrowed to 16 prostitutes from Low Track who had disappeared since 1995. By the time the task force made its first arrest the number had climbed to at least 54 women, who had vanished between 1983 and 2001. By then the task force had swelled to 85.

In the last three months of 1998, while the task force was compiling old cases, four more Low Track prostitutes vanished. Thirty-one-year-old Julie Louise Young was last seen alive in October 1998 and finally reported missing on 1 June 1999. Drug-addict Angela Rebecca Jardine was 28 when she went missing, but she was mentally handicapped and had the mind of a 10-year-old child. She had been working Low Track's streets since she was 20. Last seen between 3.30 and 4 p.m. on 20 November 1998 at a rally of around 700 people in Oppenheimer Park in Vancouver's Downtown Eastside, she was reported missing on 6 December. Twenty-nine-year-old Michelle Gurney, a Native American, disappeared in December 1998 and was reported missing on the 22nd. Twenty-year-old Marcella Helen Creison got out of jail on 27 December 1998. She was last seen at 1 or 2 o'clock in the morning around the corner from the Drake Hotel and never returned to the apartment where her mother and boyfriend were waiting with unopened Christmas presents. She was reported missing on 11 January 1999.

The task force's investigations were given added impetus in March 1999 when Jamie Lee Hamilton, a transsexual and former prostitute who went on to become the director of a drop-in centre for sex-trade workers, called a news conference complaining of the police's lax attitude towards missing prostitutes.

First the task force had to decide if there was a serial killer at large in Vancouver. Inspector Kim Rossmo was convinced there was. The founder of the "geographic profiling" later used in the "Freeway Phantom" case, he was then working for the Vancouver Police Department. He mapped unsolved crimes in an attempt to highlight any pattern or criminal signature overlooked by detectives working on individual cases. Geographic profiles work on the premise that most serial criminals operate close to home. By analyzing the spatial patterns of the attacks, it is said to be possible to trace one serial killer to within two-fifths of a mile of his home. The idea came from studying the way African lions hunt, which almost perfectly matches the predations of a serial killer. Lions look for an animal that exhibits some indication of weakness – the old, the very young, the infirm, the vulnerable – then they go to a watering hole and wait, because they know their potential victim will be drawn there.

"We see that all the time with criminal offenders," says Rossmo, now a Research Professor in the Department of Criminal Justice at Texas State University. "They go to target-rich environments to do their hunting. Spatial patterns are produced by serial killers as they search and attack. The system analyzes the geography of these, the victim encounter, the attack, the murder and body dumpsites."

In May 1999 Rossmo spotted an unusual concentration of disappearances in Downtown Eastside. However, his superiors dismissed his conclusions, insisting that some of the missing women had left Vancouver voluntarily. Rossmo resigned, but he went on to establish geographic profiling as a respected technique used worldwide to track serial killers.

The task force were further hampered by the fact that Canada's "Violent Crime Linkage System" did not track missing persons unless there was some evidence of foul play – and none had been found in the cases of the missing women so far. And the data was incomplete. In some cases, the police did not even have a date when the woman had gone missing, and prostitutes and pimps were reluctant to co-operate with officers who would ordinarily put them in jail. However, in June 1999, investigators met with relatives of several missing women. They reviewed police and coroners' databases throughout Canada and the United States, and checked drug rehabilitation facilities, hospitals, mental institutions, AIDS hospices, witness-protection programmes and cemetery records, looking for evidence that women on the list might still be alive or had perished from natural causes.

Disturbing news came from Agassiz, 60 miles to the east of Vancouver, where the bodies of four prostitutes had been dumped in 1995 and 1996. None of them were on the Low Track list. And in Edmonton, capital of the adjoining province of Alberta, the police believe a serial killer might be connected to the bodies of 12 prostitutes found around that city since 1986.

Some women who made the list were then discovered alive. Twenty-two-year-old Patricia Gay Perkins left Low Track and her one-year-old son in an effort to make a new life for herself. No one was concerned and it was 18 years before she was reported missing in 1996. She then appeared on the published list of the Vancouver's missing prostitutes. On 17 December 1999, she phoned from Ontario to tell the police she was alive and drug-free.

Fifty-year-old Rose Ann Jensen was found in December 1999. She disappeared in October 1991. Reported as missing soon after, she made the list in 1998. The following year, police discovered that she was alive and living in Toronto when they were scanning a national health-care database.

Linda Jean Coombes was reported missing twice – once in August 1994 and again in April 1999. However, she had died of a heroin overdose on 15 February 1994. Her body arrived in Vancouver's morgue without identification. She was so wasted that her own mother did not even recognize a photograph of her. But she was eventually identified in September 1999 by DNA and removed from the list.

Karen Anne Smith was reported missing on 27 April 1999, but was removed from the list when it was discovered that she had in fact died of heart failure in hospital in Edmonton on 13 February 1999. Twenty-four-year-old Anne Wolsey was reported missing by her mother on 1 January 1997. In March 2002, her father called from Montreal to tell police his daughter was alive and well.

Although five names were removed from the list of missing women, more were added and it became clear to the task force that some of the women must have been the victims of foul play. The police then began to look for suspects among men with a history of violence against prostitutes. Suspicion fell on 36-year-old Michael Leopold, who had been arrested in 1996 for assaulting a Low Track streetwalker. He had beaten her and tried to force a rubber ball down her throat, though was scared off when a passer-by heard the girl's screams. Although he told a court-appointed psychiatrist about his fantasies of raping and murdering prostitutes, more went missing while he was being held. He was eventually absolved of any involvement in the disappearances, but was sentenced to 14 years in prison for aggravated assault.

Another suspect was 43-year-old Barry Thomas Neidermier, a native of Alberta. He had been convicted of pimping a 14-year-old girl in 1990, which seems to have left him with a grudge against prostitutes. In April 2000, he was arrested for violent attacks on seven Downtown Eastside prostitutes. The charges against him include abduction, unlawful imprisonment, assault, sexual assault, theft and administering a noxious substance. While none of Neidermier's victims appeared on the missing list, he was considered "a person of interest".

Then there was the unidentified rapist who attacked a 38-year-old woman outside her Low Track hotel in August 2001. During the attack, the assailant boasted that he had raped and killed other women in the Downtown Eastside. And there were others. The Downtown Eastside Youth Activities Society compiled a daily "bad date" file, recording reports by local prostitutes of "Johns" who attacked or threatened them.

Towards the end of 1998, 37-year-old Bill Hiscox told the police of the goings on at the pig farm in Port Coquitlam just outside Vancouver owned by David Francis and Robert William "Willie" Pickton. The brothers also owned a salvage firm in Surrey, southeast of Vancouver. Hiscox got the job through a relative who had been a girlfriend of Robert Pickton in 1997. He had to go out to the pig farm to pick up his pay-cheques and described it as "a creepy-looking place".

After reading newspaper reports on Vancouver's missing women, Hiscox grew suspicious of the Pickton brothers, particularly as Robert Pickton was "a pretty quiet guy" who drove a converted bus with deeply tinted windows. The brothers also ran a registered charity called the Piggy Palace Good Times Society. A non-profit society, its official mandate was to "organize, coordinate, manage and operate special events, functions, dances, shows and exhibitions on behalf of service organizations, sports organizations and other worthy groups". In fact, the Piggy Palace – a converted building at the hog farm – was a drinking club for local bikers which featured "entertainment" provided by Low Track prostitutes.

Police were already aware of the Pickton brothers. David Pickton had been convicted of sexual assault in 1992, fined $1,000 and given 30 days' probation. Pickton attacked the victim in his trailer at the pig farm, but she managed to escape. Soon after Piggy Palace opened, the Port Coquitlam authorities sued the Pickton brothers and their sister, Linda Louise Wright, for violating local zoning laws. Their farm was designated for agricultural use, but they had converted a farm building "for the purpose of holding dances, concerts and other recreations" that drew as many as 1,800 persons. After a New Year's Eve party on 31 December 1998, the Picktons were served with an injunction banning future parties and the Piggy Palace Good Times Society was stripped of its non-profit status.

Robert "Willie" Pickton was charged with attempted murder on 23 March 1997 after Wendy Lynn Eistetter, a drug addict and prostitute with a wild and reckless past, was rescued from the roadside by a couple driving past the pig farm at 1.45 a.m. She was partially clothed, had been stabbed several times and was covered in blood.

Earlier in the evening, Pickton had picked her up and driven her to the pig farm, According to a police report, Pickton then "did attempt to commit the murder of Wendy Lynn Eistetter, by stabbing her repeatedly with . . . a brown-handled kitchen knife". She has been handcuffed at the time, but had managed to grab the knife, stab Pickton and escape. He later showed up at Eagle Ridge Hospital, where he was treated for one stab wound.

A provincial court judge released Pickton on a $2,000 cash bond with the undertaking that he stay at the farm and not have any contact with Ms Eistetter.

"You are to abstain completely from the use of alcohol and non-prescription drugs," the judge ordered.

"I don't take them," Pickton replied.

A trial date was set, but the charges were stayed before the matter went to court because the attorney-general's office decided "there was no likelihood of conviction". Despite the grievous wounds Wendy Eistetter suffered, she was a prostitute and, therefore, an "unreliable witness".

Though Pickton had walked free, the stabbing had convinced Hiscox that Pickton was responsible for "all the girls that are going missing . . . [Pickton] frequents the downtown area all the time, for girls". Hiscox told the police: "All the purses and IDs are out there in his trailer."

However, when the police searched the pig farm – three times according to press reports – they found nothing. While the Pickton brothers would remain "persons of interest", their farm was not put under surveillance. Meanwhile the list of missing women grew longer. By the year 2000, it had expanded to more than three times the number of missing women first listed in 1998. This was not just because women had continued to vanish from Low Track. Other women who had disappeared earlier were now coming to the attention of the authorities.

Forty-two-year old Laura Mah was last seen on 1 August 1985, but was not reported missing until 3 August 1999. Nancy Clark – aka Nancy Greek – was 23 when she was last seen on the evening of 22 August 1991 in Victoria, the capital of British Columbia on Vancouver Island across the strait from the city of Vancouver itself. Concerns about Clark's well-being were raised one day after her disappearance because she had failed to return home to look after her two daughters – aged eight years and eight months – which was out of character.

"It was the birthday of her child that day and, for a sex street worker, she was a bit of a home-body," said Victoria Policeman Don Bland. "That's what was suspicious at the start, because she would never have done that."

However, Officer Bland expressed her doubts that Nancy Clark should be on the Low Track list as she had no connection with Vancouver and only worked the streets of the capital.

Elsie Sebastian, another Native American, was 40 when she went missing on 16 October 1992. Leigh Miner, a 34-year-old heroin addict and prostitute, phoned her sister to ask for money on 17 December 1993. That was the last time anyone heard of her. She was reported missing on 24 February 1994. Seventeen-year-old Angela Mary Arsenault was last seen on 19 August 1994 and reported missing ten days later. Thirty-six-year-old Frances Ann Young was missing on 9 April 1996. Last seen leaving her home three days before to go for a walk, she was suffering from depression at the time of her disappearance.

Fifty-two-year-old Maria Laura Laliberte – alias Kim Keller – was last seen in Low Track on New Year's Day, but was only reported missing on 8 March 2002. Forty-two-year-old Cindy Feliks was last seen on 26 November 1997 and reported missing 8 January 2001, while Sherry Leigh Irving was last seen in April 1997 and reported missing the following year.

Ruby Anne Hardy, mother of three, disappeared at the age of 33 some time in 1998, but was not reported missing until 27 March 2002. Native Americans Georgina Faith Papin and Jennifer Lynn Furminger vanished in 1999 along with Wendy Crawford, but did not make the list until March 2000. Thirty-year-old Brenda Ann Wolfe, who went missing on 1 February 1999, made the list a month later. Tiffany Louise Drew was 27 when she disappeared on 31 December 1999, but she was not reported missing until 8 February 2002.

Publicity surrounding the list encouraged the reporting of missing persons. Forty-two-year-old Dawn Teresa Crey was last seen on Main and Hastings on 1 November 2000 and was reported missing on 11 December. Debra Lynn Jones, aged 43, disappeared on 21 December 2000 and was reported missing four days later on Christmas Day. Twenty-five-year-old Patricia Rose Johnson went missing from Main and Hastings on 3 March 2001 but took three months to make the list. Heather Kathleen Bottomley, aged 24, made the list the same day she was last seen – 17 April 2001 – even though the police described her as a "violent suicide risk". However, Tricia Johnson's death had attracted more attention. Shortly before she disappeared she had been befriended by portrait photographer Lincoln Clarkes who was recording the lives of the drug-addicted prostitutes of Low Track for his books *Heroines*. She took time off from her revolving-door hustle for heroin and sex to talk to him about her world – how she had broken her boyfriend's heart, abandoning him and their two young children to embrace heroin and crack cocaine instead of the family.

Throughout the project Clarkes stayed close to Johnson, who was his original "heroine". They became friends. During that time she tried to quit drugs for the sake of her kids. But her father's suicide sent her into a tailspin. She had quit rehab and had been repeatedly arrested for breaking and entering.

The last time Clarkes heard from Patricia was a message she left on his home answering machine in February 2001.

"Hey, it's Tricia, Lincoln," she said in a sing-song voice. "Trying to get a hold of you, trying to find what's up! I wish I had a number you can call me back at, but I don't. So all I can do is keep trying."

Soon after she stopped cashing her welfare checks, stopped phoning her family and even stopped contact with her two children. Her mother, Marion Bryce, spoke of the terrible warning she had given her daughter who had already survived five years on the streets.

"She was here on New Year's Day," she told reporters, "and I told her, 'Patty, you're not even going to see 25 if you keep on – you'll be missing like those women down there.'"

Bryce later contacted Clarkes, who gave her a photo of Patricia in shoulder-length hair, wearing a leather jacket, her lips puffy, burned by a crack pipe. Later, to attract attention to the plight of the missing women, Clarkes brought her another portrait, accompanied by a film crew.

Days after this blaze of publicity, Patricia Rose Johnson was listed as Missing Woman No. 44. After five years working the streets of Low Track, her last known possessions were recorded as "a book (title not given), a comb, condoms, water, a spoon, cigarettes, a lighter, belt, watch, rings and a chain".

Weeks after Johnson disappeared, the Royal Canadian Mounted Police joined the case and promptly assembled a team of federal investigators that would grow to 30 members. But that did nothing to stem the growth of the list.

Thirty-three-year-old Yvonne Marie Boen was listed only five days after she disappeared on 16 March 2001. Her mother, Lynn Metin, began to worry when her daughter, who had three sons, failed to show up in March 2001 for a visit with her middle son Troy, whom Metin was raising.

"She was supposed to be here that Sunday to pick him up and she didn't show up," Metin told the *Vancouver Sun* in 2004. "She never contacted me. That just wasn't her. Every holiday, Troy's birthday, my birthday – it just wasn't like her not to phone."

Heather Gabriel Chinnock, aged 29, vanished the following month, followed by Andrea Josebury, aged 22, on 6 June. Her grandfather Jack Cummer said Andrea was straightening out her life and was providing a good home to her infant daughter in an East Vancouver apartment some time before she disappeared.

"She was working very hard, she needed a lot of things, but she was doing it all herself," Cummer told the *Sun*. "Andrea was worn to a frazzle, but the baby was well cared for."

However, he said, social services received a complaint about the well-being of the girl and seized her, which sent his granddaughter back into the downward spiral of drugs and prostitution.

"The thing is that she lost her whole reason to live," Cummer said.

The child was adopted and the Cummers are not able to see her. Andrea, he said, either did not realize or would not accept the finality of the adoption, and would tell her grandparents that she was going to try to get her daughter back.

"She decided that she was going to straighten up and her prime objective was to get the baby back. I didn't have the heart to tell her that she was never going to do that," he said.

Twenty-nine-year-old Sereena Abotsway, went missing on 1 August. Adopted at the age of four, she had always been trouble.

"She was sweet and bubbly but she was very disturbed," said her adoptive mother Anna Draayers. "She gave her teachers a headache and we tried to teach her at home but there was not much you could do. At that time we did not have a name for the condition, but it is now known as foetal alcohol syndrome."

The Draayers never lost contact with the child.

"She was our girl, and we loved her a lot," they said. "She phoned daily for 13 years since she left our home at age 17."

And hope was at hand.

"She had come home in July," said Mrs Draayers, "and she agreed to come home and celebrate her 30th birthday on 20 August, but she never showed up."

Diane Rosemary Rock, aged 34, was last seen on 19 October 2001 by the owner of the motel where she was living and was reported missing on 13 December. Diane, her husband and three children moved to British Columbia in 1992 for a fresh start in life. But in their new home, Rock's personal problems resurfaced and she was back using drugs again. After a while her marriage fell apart and she was on her own. The last member of the family to see her was her teenage daughter. That was in June 2001 when they met her to celebrate the teenager's birthday.

Mona Lee Wilson, aged 26, disappeared on 23 November 2001 and made the list a week later. She was the last to vanish. Her common-law husband Steve Ricks told reporters he had last seen her get into a car with two men.

"She told me many times she'd like to die," Ricks said. "She was sick of this hell, all the hooking and drugs."

Disappearances had been going on for over two decades now, but even more disturbingly they were getting increasingly more frequent. Detectives looked back at the earlier cases to see if other known criminals could have been responsible.

The elusive "Green River Killer" had been killing runaways and prostitutes over the border in Washington State for much of the period. On 30 November 2001, 52-year-old Gary Leon Ridgway was charged with murdering four of the Green River victims. Two years later he pleaded guilty to 49 murders. There were reports that Ridgway had visited Vancouver, but the police could make no connection between him and the missing women.

Dayton Leroy Rogers was abducting, torturing and killing prostitutes in Oregon in 1987. He was arrested on 7 August 1987, after murdering a prostitute in a parking lot in front of witnesses. Only then did it become clear that he was responsible for the murder of seven women whose bodies had been found in a wooded area near Molalla, 20 miles outside the city. Some had had their feet cut off, possibly while they were still alive. But Rogers was soon cleared on any involvement in the earlier Vancouver abductions.

George Waterfield Russell Jnr – aka "The Charmer", "The Bellevue Killer" and, coincidently, "The East Side Killer" – was also considered. He had killed three women in Bellevue, Washington in 1990. But he was discounted because he killed his victims in their own homes and then displayed them in elaborate poses, after he had raped and mutilated their corpses.

Other serial killers were suspected. In 1995, Keith Hunter Jesperson, a British Columbian, had been arrested in Washington State, for the murder of his girlfriend 41-year-old Julie Winningham. He had strangled her and dumped her body at the roadside. A long-haul truck driver, he then said he had murdered women widely across North America, dumping their bodies like "piles of garbage" along the roadside. At one point he boasted about 160 murders, though he has been convicted for just eight. But, again, the police could not find a link between the man the newspapers dubbed the "Happy Face Killer" and the missing women from Low Track.

Seemingly mild-mannered US Navy veteran and father of two John Eric Armstrong was arrested in April 2000 for the murder of a number of Detroit prostitutes and promptly confessed to killing 30 women around the world during his time in the Navy. However, his ship the USS *Nimitz* did not put into port near Vancouver when any of the women went missing.

Middle-aged father of five, Robert Yates was convicted of killing 15 women in Washington State in October 2000, but is thought to have killed at least 18, most of whom were drug addicts and prostitutes. The earliest killings he admitted to were those of two women in Walla Walla in 1975 and a woman in Skagit County in 1988, both close to the border. However, evidence could not place him in Vancouver at the time of any of the disappearances.

Vancouver had its own home-grown suspect in the person of Ronald Richard McCauley, a twice-convicted rapist. Sentenced to 17 years imprisonment in 1982, he was paroled in September 1994. In September 1995, he was arrested again after he picked up a prostitute at Vancouver's Astoria Hotel in July and drove her to Hemlock Valley, where she was beaten, raped and dumped from his truck. The woman reported the incident to police and McCauley was convicted of rape and attempted murder in 1996.

McCauley came to the attention of the police again when the bodies of prostitutes Tracy Olajide, Tammy Lee Pipe and Victoria Younker were found that year near Agassiz and Mission near Hemlock Valley. He was also a suspect in the murder of Mary Lidguerre whose body was found in north Vancouver two years later, and the disappearance of Catherine Maureen Knight, Catherine Louise Gonzalez and Dorothy Anne Spence who went missing in 1995. Despite circumstantial evidence against him, he was never charged. Eventually he was cleared of the three Hemlock Valley murders by DNA evidence in 2001. But after telling a parole hearing that, had he not been arrested, he "would have become a serial killer such as Clifford Olson" he was declared a dangerous offender and jailed indefinitely.

On 7 February 2002, Robert Pickton was arrested for the possession of illegal firearms. Meanwhile the task force began scouring the pig farm once again. Pickton was released on bail, but arrested again on 22 February – this time on two counts of first-degree murder. The victims were identified as Sereena Abotsway and Mona Wilson. On 8 March, it was revealed that DNA recovered from the farm had been conclusively identified as Sereena's. Both had gone missing since Bill Hiscox had first reported his suspicions to the police

A month later, Pickton was charged with three more counts of murder – those of Jacqueline McDonnell, Heather Bottomley and Diane Rock. He was charged with the murder of Angela Josebury, six days later. Then on 22 May, a seventh first-degree murder charge was filed against Pickton when the remains of Brenda Wolfe were found on his farm. Again, all these women had gone missing after Hiscox first fingered Pickton.

This begged the question: if Pickton was the Low Track slayer, why had the searches of the farm in 1997 and 1998 not unearthed any evidence? And how could he have continued to abduct and murder victims afterwards, when he should have been under surveillance by the police?

The authorities were adamant that the evidence had been hard to come by as Pickton went to great lengths to dispose of the bodies. They were said to have been left out in the open to decompose or be eaten by insects. Otherwise they were fed to the pigs on the farm. Forensic anthropologists spent two years and $70 million shifting through the soil on the farm in an attempt to find traces of remains. Then in March 2004, the authorities said that the victims' flesh may have been ground up and mixed with pork from the farm. This pork was never sold commercially, but was handed out to friends and fed to visitors to the farm – perhaps even visiting prostitutes themselves.

Meanwhile Pickton maintains his innocence of all charges. But even if he is guilty as charged, what happened to the other women who went missing from Vancouver's Downtown Eastside? Their number is disputed. The task force maintain there are another 47 unaccounted for. However, when Pickton was arrested, the Prostitution Alternatives Counselling Education said that 110 streetwalkers from British Columbia's Lower Mainland had been slain or kidnapped over the past two decades. The Royal Canadian Mounted Police have 144 cases of prostitutes murdered or missing with foul play suspected across the province. So it is likely that there is another – or possibly several – killers at large in British Columbia.

Canada's "Highway of Tears"

A serial killer, or killers, seem to be at work along Highway 16 in northern British Columbia. The stretch that runs the 450 miles from Prince Rupert to Prince George has become known at the "Highway of Tears". It is regularly flanked by posters showing pictures of teenage girls and young women under the word "Missing".

It is a lonely stretch of road, especially in winter – though it can be staggeringly beautiful when the sun comes out and rays of light coming through the clouds play on the frozen lakes, creeks and vistas of mountains that disappear in the clouds. Sometimes at sunrise and sunset, the snow on the mountain peaks glows neon pink.

On some parts of the road there is nothing but wilderness for miles, interrupted by the occasional ranch house with smoke trailing from the chimney. There are signs warning: "Caution: Moose Next 20 km."

Travelling through the towns along the way – Vanderhoof, Fraser Lake, Burns Lake, Houston, Telkwa and Smithers – the car radio announces meetings of the local knitting circle and the snowmobile club. Young residents have few choices but to hitch-hike when they travel from town to town.

There are many side roads off the highway, leading to remote logging sites, lakes and other rural recreational spots. It is the kind of sparsely-populated rural countryside that attracts tourists and sports fishermen from Europe and the US – including late-night talk show host David Letterman – and, it seems, murderers.

The disturbing pattern of disappearances was first noticed in 1995, but they seem to have started much earlier. The victims were young girls, mostly Aboriginal in origin, and aged 15 to their early 20s. They vanished after being seen hitch-hiking along the highway.

Fifteen-year-old Monica Ignas appears to be the first victim. She went missing near Terrace on 13 December 1974. Her partially clothed body was found in a gravel pit on 6 April 1975, about four miles from Terrace. She had been strangled.

One area resident, Janet Hultkrans, recalls that Ignas used to hitch-hike from Terrace to her home just past Thornhill, on the outskirts of town.

"Maybe she was the first [to disappear]," she says. "She wasn't much older than my kids and I had picked her up once and driven her to school, so she is forever in my memory. She was a nice girl and doesn't deserve to be forgotten."

In the early hours of 27 August 1989 a 24-year-old "First-Nations" woman named Alberta Gail Williams disappeared from Prince Rupert. The police were notified and the family under took a frantic search.

"I just knew something was wrong," said Alberta's sister Kathy Williams.

"My father said, 'It makes me so sad to see my kids out there looking through bushes,'" Claudia Williams, another sister, recalled. "He said, 'If she's not alive I want to know what happened.'"

Nearly a month later, on 25 September, some hikers came across a body near the Tyee Overpass on Highway 16, about 23 miles east of Prince Rupert. It was identified as that of Alberta Williams. The body was flown to Vancouver for a post mortem and the coroners there confirmed that she had been murdered, though the police never released details of how she had been killed.

Earlier in that summer, Alberta and Claudia had come to Prince Rupert to take a summer job at a local fish company. They had family in town. The season had drawn to a close and 26 August was their last payday. They intended to move to Vancouver. But first they went out to celebrate in Popeye's Pub – now known as the Rupert Pub – with sister Kathy, cousins Carole and Phoebe Russell, along with Phoebe's boyfriend Gordon McLean. At around 2.30 a.m., Alberta left first, followed by the rest of the revellers.

"When I got outside, she turned towards the old Greyhound building and I lost her," said Claudia.

What happened next remains unclear. The local paper reported that Alberta attended "a local bar and then a house party". The Williams family heard something similar.

"I heard she was at a party and some people saw her," said Alberta's uncle Wally Samuel. But the people with her did not come forward.

The local newspaper also reported that Alberta Williams was seen with an unidentified man later that night.

"She loved people," said Claudia. "Out of all my sisters she's the best. I really think she'd be around today if she wasn't the friendly person she was."

"Murder investigations such as this remain active until they are solved," said Constable Jagdev Uppal of the Royal Canadian Mounted Police some 15 years after the event. "The investigation into Alberta's death, particularly at the time of the event, was extensive and includes over 200 tips. Due to the seriousness of the matter, and to protect the integrity of the investigation, details regarding the evidence are not being released."

A new series of killings began with 16-year-old Ramona Wilson, who was last seen hitch-hiking along Highway 16 to visit a friend in Smithers, 130 miles east of Prince Rupert, on 11 June 1994. Her remains were found near Smithers airport in April 1995.

Ramona's best friend Kristal said: "Ramona was such a dear friend and a young woman with more drive than anyone else I knew at age 15. She had hopes and dreams for her life . . . I still wonder what the purpose of her murder was, but I know that I have to look to the future as opposed to sitting back and wondering why things happen."

Kristal was also one of the last people to see 16-year-old Delphine Nikal, who went missing while hitch-hiking east along Highway 16 from Smithers to her home in Telkwa on 13 June 1995. She has yet to be found. Delphine's cousin Cecilia Anne Nikal had been missing since 1989 and another cousin Roberta Cecilia Nikal had been murdered.

Before Delphine Nikal disappeared, 15-year-old Roxanne Thiara went missing from Prince George in November 1994. Her body was found dumped near Burns Lake on 9 December 1994. Another murder occurred that same day.

Sixteen-year-old Alishia Demarah Germaine – also known as Leah Germaine or Leah Cunningham – had attended a pre-Christmas dinner hosted by the RCMP at the Native Friendship Centre on George Street, leaving at around 8.00 p.m. She was then seen at the Holiday Inn, on George Street, and at J. C. Funland.

At 11.45 p.m. that night, the police were called to Haldi Road School on Leslie Road. Three people who had taken a short cut through the schoolyard had come across the body of a young woman. It was Leah Germaine, dead from multiple stab wounds. The teenage had been a drug-user and supported her habit by working the city streets as a prostitute, though it seems she had plans to straighten out her life and finish her education. She never got the chance.

A composite drawing of the man Leah was seen with that night was produced. The police found the man, but this led them no closer to finding Germaine's killer. The police were also on the look-out for the owner of a dark blue pick up truck with a home-made canopy on the back that was parked on Fifth Avenue downtown, near the Post Office the night Germaine was killed. Some of Germaine's personal effects were found nearby – though the owner was considered a potential witness rather than a suspect.

Early on in the investigation, there were some suspicions that Germaine's murder and those of Roxanne Thiara, Ramona Wilson and Delphine Nikal were connected. All the victims were between the ages of 15 and 20. Thinking that a serial killer might be at work, a team of investigators, including two FBI trained behavioural profilers, came to the area for a week in 1995. They dismissed the theory even though some made connections to an earlier murder of a First-Nations woman.

On 24 July 1990, the body of 21-year-old Cindy Angus Burk was found near a highway in Kiskatinaw Provincial Park outside Dawson Creek, 160 miles northeast of Prince George. She had been raised primarily in Regina, Saskatchewan and later moved to Carmacks, Yukon Territory. Cindy was new to northern British Columbia in the summer of 1990. She was last seen around mid-July in Prophet River, north of Fort St John and at that time was thought to be heading to Saskatchewan. At the time of the discovery of Cindy's body an extensive search of the area was conducted, numerous people were interviewed and forensics were gathered and analyzed. Despite exhaustive efforts no one was arrested. But the file remained open and over 16 years later, on 16 November 2006, a 60-year-old man was arrested in Fort St John and charged with second-degree homicide in con-nection with Cindy's death.

Despite the detectives' scepticism, the disappearances continued. On 7 October 1995, 19-year-old Lana Derrick, a forestry student at Northwest Community College in Terrace, disappeared. She was last seen at a service station in Thornhill while home from school at the weekend. She has never been heard from since.

Things went quiet on Highway 16 for the next seven years. Then on 21 June 2002 a Caucasian woman went missing while hitch-hiking down Highway 16. Nicole Hoar was a 25-year-old young tree planter from Red Deer last seen hitching her way from Prince George to her sister's home in Smithers. She was hoping to attend the Midsummer Music Festival, but never arrived.

Her family and friends got the story of her disappearance out to all the major news organizations. They organized a massive poster campaign and a reward was offered. The RCMP searched the area using helicopters and other aircraft. Two hundred volunteers including more than 60 members of trained search and rescue teams combed the highway. Despite everything, no sign of Nicole Hoar was ever found.

A campaign called "Take Back the Highway" was started. On 17 September 2005, there were marches, speeches and prayers to commemorate the dead in communities between Prince Rupert and Prince George. But four days later 22-year-old Tamara Chipman went missing somewhere between Prince Rupert and Terrace. She was last seen hitch-hiking eastbound on Highway 16 near Prince Rupert's industrial park around 4.30 p.m. on 21 September 2005. She had been in Prince Rupert partying with friends for the previous three days.

She wasn't reported missing by her family until 10 November as they thought she might have been visiting relatives in the Lower Mainland. It was also thought that she might have been hiding out from the law. She was facing three separate assault charges at the time, including one alleging forcible entry and assault with a weapon. Before she was reported missing, three warrants were issued for her arrest for failing to show up in court. She was also trained in judo, 5 feet 10 inches tall and weighing 130 pounds, and it was not thought that an assailant could easily have over-powered her.

"She was pretty spunky," her father said. "She took judo lessons for years, so she knew how to look after herself pretty good."

Tamara Chipman was said to be very close to her father and stepmother, though she sometimes did not contact her family for a couple of days and it was not unusual for her to be gone for weeks. But after 21 September 2005, her rent was not paid and no use was made of her bank account.

She did not have a job and liked spending time on her former boyfriend's boat, liked water-skiing and looking after her two-year-old son Jaden, who she left in the care of his father, 42-year-old Rob Parker, when she took off. Parker, Chipman's ex-boyfriend, said he was one of the last people to talk to her in Terrace on 17 or 18 September. She called him despite there being a no-contact court order in place.

"That's the last time I ever heard her voice," he said.

Parker said he had heard about her being seen hitch-hiking from Prince Rupert back to Terrace.

"I don't believe she ever got here," he said and believes that she got lost like other women along Highway 16. He agreed to take a lie-detector test.

Ten RCMP officers were assigned to the investigation and Tamara's family undertook an extensive search of the highway. Her father walked long stretches of the road looking in every culvert. Officers also contacted the major crimes unit in Prince George which continues to investigate the disappearance of numerous women along Highway 16 over the last decade.

Meanwhile, 24-year-old Crystal Lee Okimaw disappeared from a women's shelter in Prince George on 16 January 2006. Foul play was suspected.

The remains of 14-year-old Aielah Saric-Auger were found by a passing motorist on the side of Highway 16 near Tabor Mountain 10 miles east of Prince George on 10 February 2006. She was last seen by her family on 2 February. At the time, family members said she stayed overnight with a friend, but there were report of a sighting of her getting into a black van the following day. Two retired RCMP officers who had worked on the earlier investigation told the *Prince George Citizen* that Aielah had been the victim of a serial killer who was also responsible for the deaths of Ramona Wilson, Roxanne Thiara, Alishia Germaine and, possibly, Delphine Nikal.

Retired RCMP officer Fred Maile, who helped crack the Clifford Olson serial killer case in British Columbia by getting

Olson to confess to 11 murders, told the *Vancouver Sun*: "I am 100-per-cent certain that there's a serial killer there. I went up there twice to look at the cases of Delphine Nikal and Ramona Wilson. We felt the same individual had grabbed them."

He had been asked by the Calgary-based Missing Children Society to investigate these two Highway 16 cases and found too many similarities.

"They were both native, both about the same age and they were hitch-hiking in opposite directions," Maile recalls. "The whole situation smacks of someone driving that highway and living there."

The unusual thing about serial killers, he said, is that they can sometimes go years between murders.

"They look for an opportunity," he said. "There's usually not two or three individuals in the same area that do this."

He also points out that a serial killer can appear normal and go undetected.

"They don't stand out as monsters. They blend in with the rest of us. Look at the Green River killer."

Arlene Roberts, a volunteer fire-fighter who lives on Highway 16 just west of Terrace, agrees that there is a killer who preys on young women at work. She often sees people hitch-hiking along the highway.

"It's male and female, young and old," she says. "But it's only the young women who are going missing."

Highway 16 also runs east to Edmonton, where the police have the unsolved murders of 12 prostitutes on their hands. In that case, RCMP have offered a reward of $100,000 and released a profile that suggests the killer or killers drive a truck or SUV which is cleaned at unusual hours. It is thought that the killer may be a hunter, fisherman or camper, who is comfortable driving on unmetalled roads, and is probably connected to towns south of Edmonton.

Some 175 miles south of Edmonton is Calgary where, in a 19-month period in the early 1990s, five women – four of whom were prostitutes – disappeared. Their bodies later appeared, dumped around the outskirts of the city.

The first woman to disappear was 16-year-old street urchin Jennifer Janz, who disappeared in July 1991. Her badly beaten body was discovered in a shallow grave on 13 August 1991 in the Valley Ridge district of northwest Calgary. Reported missing on 30 August 1991, the body of 17-year-old Jennifer Joyes was found in a shallow grave on 6 October 1991, just a mile south of where Janz had been buried. Both had reportedly been attempting to escape life on the streets. Keely Pincott, who disappeared three months later, was found nearby.

Tracey Maunder went missing in October 1992 and 20-year-old Rebecca Boutelier disappeared in February 1993. She was found stabbed to death on 11 March. Their bodies were found in fields east of the city rather than to the west like those of Jennifer Janz, Jennifer Joyes and Keely Pincott.

Then the killings stopped. Police believe that the perpetrator might have been jailed for another murder. During the same time period these five women were murdered city officials also have unsolved murder files on six other women.

Later Barry Thomas Neidermier became a suspect in the murders of Jennifer Janz and Rebecca Boutelier. A convicted pimp, he had become a "person of interest" in the case of Vancouver's Downtown Eastside's missing prostitutes after being arrested in Lethbridge, Alberta, a hundred miles south of Calgary. Forty-three-year-old Barry Thomas Niedermier was charged with brutal sexual assaults from 1995 to 1997 against seven prostitutes working in downtown Vancouver, where he had been living. He was also questioned by police in Edmonton and Calgary in their own missing prostitute cases, including those who had gone missing in the late 1970s and 1980s. In 1990 Neidermier had been sentenced to 14 months imprisonment for pimping a 14-year-old girl whom he brought from Calgary to Vancouver.

As if RCMP did not have enough unsolved cases on their hands, according to Amnesty International Canada, Tamara Chipman's disappearance bought the number of missing or murdered women along the highway to 33 – all but one were Aboriginal. This was based on information gathered for a report Amnesty released in October 2004 called *Stolen Sisters: Discri-*

mination and Violence Against Indigenous Women in Canada. This cited a 1996 federal government statistic that native women between 25 and 44 are five times more likely to die as the result of violence than other women in the same age group.

The report also included a figure gathered by the Native Women's Association of Canada, which estimates that more than 500 native women may have been murdered or gone missing over a 20-year period prior to 2004.

The Amnesty International report also cited nine cases of violence against native women, including the murder of Helen Betty Osborne, a 19-year-old Cree student from northern Manitoba who dreamed of becoming a teacher but was abducted from the street of The Pas, Manitoba by four men, raped and killed on the night of 12 November 1971. Her naked body was found later by the police.

It took more than 15 years to bring one of the four men to justice. The Aboriginal Justice Implementation Commission conducted an investigation into the length of time involved in resolving the case and concluded that the most significant factor was racism. The Commission found that police had long been aware of white men sexually preying on native women and girls in the town of The Pas but "did not feel that the practice necessitated any particular vigilance."

A formal apology from the Manitoba government was issued by Manitoba's Minister of Justice in 2000 and a scholarship was created in Osborne's name for aboriginal women.

But at least the case of Helen Osborne was resolved. Many more have not been – like that of 16-year-old Deena Lynn Braem of Quesnel, BC. She was last seen alive at around 4 a.m. on 25 September 1999, just two days before her 17th birthday. She was later reported as missing and the police immediately suspected foul play.

On 10 December 1999, human remains were found near Pinnacles Park, just west of Quesnel. A post mortem identified the body as that of Deena Braem. She had been murdered.

On Friday, 24 September, she had attended Correlieu Secondary in Quesnel, where she was just beginning her final year. She lived in Bouchie Lake, some six miles to the west of Quesnel, but her parents had given her permission to stay the weekend with a friend in the city to celebrate her birthday. Together they went to an outdoor party in the Quesnel area. It was well part midnight when they left. Deena had been drinking alcohol, but according to friends was not drunk. They got a lift back to Quesnel and were dropped off at a residence on English Avenue at around 2.30. But then, at Deena's urging, they went out again.

Deena had decided she wanted to go home to her Mom and Dad instead of staying in town with friends. The two girls walked the short distance to the intersection of North Fraser Drive and Edkins Street, then up North Fraser Drive to Fuller, while they tried to hitch a ride. It was cold and Deena's girlfriend went home, leaving Deena to hitchhike alone. Witnesses saw two males in their teens or early twenties in North Fraser Drive around that time and the case remains unsolved. But then in Quesnel there are a remarkable number of unsolved cases.

On 26 November 2004, the family of Barbara Anne Lanes, aged 57, reported her missing. She had not been seen for a week. The sightings were investigated but none were confirmed, and police have no clues about where she is or how she disappeared. Laurie Joseph Blanchard was last seen in Quesnel on 2 July 1972, when he was preparing to move to New Brunswick. His body was found on 13 August 1972. He had been murdered. Mary Agnes Thomas disappeared under suspicious circumstances near Quesnel on or about 10 September 1971. Her body has never been recovered. Herman Alec disappeared under suspicious circumstances near the Nazko Indian Reserve on 14 October 1977. His body has never been found. Santokh Kaur Johal disappeared under suspicious circumstances near Quesnel on or about 1 April 1978. Her body has never been recovered. Janice Ellisabeth Hackh disappeared under suspicious circumstances near Quesnel on or about 24 August 1979. Her body has never been found. Wayne Albert Taylor disappeared under suspicious circumstances near Quesnel in or around January 1976. His body has never been recovered. Mary Jane Jimmie was found murdered on the banks of the nearby Fraser River on or about 26 June

1987. Duncan Harris was found on a sidewalk in Quesnel on 6 July 1988, apparently the victim of an assault. He later died in hospital from these injuries. William Henry Terrico was found murdered in his home on 12 December 1989. Brian Mirl Chaffee was reported missing on 22 September 1990. He was last seen at his home on 18 September 1990. His body was found on 24 September 1990. Dale Melvin Johnson disappeared under suspicious circumstances on August 15, 1996. His body has never been recovered. Not bad for a city of around 10,000 people.

Thirty-one-year-old Melanie Dawn Brown, another First-Nations woman, was found deceased in a basement suite located in the 400 block of Olgivie Street in Prince George at around 4 p.m. on 8 December 2004. A post mortem confirmed that she had been murdered. Police have not released the exact cause of death. She is considered a candidate for a Highway 16 killing.

Nineteen-year-old Corrine Cunningham of the Katzie Reserve near Pitt Meadows, outside Vancouver, disappeared at 3 p.m. on 24 November 2005 after she left "New Transitions" in the Pitt Meadows Industrial Park. She had the mental capacity of a 12-year-old and a tendency to befriend older men. Her new black BMX bicycle was also missing.

Seventy-one-year-old Helena Jack, a member of the Cheslatta Carrier Nation, was murdered on 29 July 2004 in the garage beside her cabin in Burns Lake, which is in the 600-block of Highway 16. Police believe a man named Vincent Sam followed her into the garage on the night of the assault. Sam was arrested in August 2004, shortly after Burns Lake Fire and Rescue discovered the severely beaten body of Helena Jack in a burnt-out garage beside a cabin on the 600-block of highway 16. Evidence found in the garage directed the police search to a local motel room. They believe their suspect tried to wash his body of evidence linking him to the crime, before returning to his residence later that night. But investigators found DNA in the motel room that matched DNA found at the crime scene. It belonged to Vincent Sam. Sam was charged with Helena Jack's murder on 4 September 2004. He was convicted of first-degree murder and sentenced to life in prison.

Belinda Ann Cameron – aka Belinda Ann Engen – disappeared in early May 2005, from Esquimalt near Victoria. She was a schizophrenic and needed daily medication to keep the condition in check. She was also a drug user thought to be involved in the sex trade. Foul play is suspected. She could have been the victim of Robert Pickton, like Victoria resident Nancy Creek, if he had not already been in custody.

Another possible victim of a second Low Track slayer is 24-year-old Doras Gail Shorson, who was last seen on 2 April 2005 when she left the family home on Larner Road, Surrey. She was a drug-user who worked in the sex trade in Surrey or Vancouver. And 14-year-old Lorna Ulmer-Billy was last seen home in the 15100 block of 86 Avenue in Surrey, BC, at around 9 p.m. on 7 January 2005 when her stepfather looked in to check she was still asleep. It was thought that she left home early the next morning to meet some friends. However, she has run away before to Squamish and Vancouver.

Twenty-year-old Rene Gunning has been missing since 19 February 2005 when she left Edmonton for her home in Fort St John in the company of another female from Dawson Creek. The pair were thought to be hitch-hiking.

Seventeen-year-old Lisa Paul disappeared from her home on 4 August 2005. Lisa was known to frequent the Downtown Eastside of Vancouver. Twenty-nine-year-old Charlene Kerr was found dead in a pool of blood in the Gastown Hotel in 1990. She was a prostitute and drug user.

Fourteen-year-old Tawyna Megan Lisk called a friend on 18 July 2004 and said that she was going to Calgary, Alberta. It is thought she planned to hitch-hike.

Sarah Strachan, aged 16, was last seen on 7 February 2004 from Coquitlam, just a few miles from Pickton's pig farm. Also missing is her Caucasian friend Leah Nestegarde, aged 14.

Then there is the case of 39-year-old Ada Brown of Prince George who died three weeks after suffering a serious head injury during a beating. Her family said that she sought medical attention on three different occasions following the beating and was turned away.

"When she died, and we went to the funeral home, my sister and I didn't recognize her," said sister Terri Brown. "It was obvious she had been badly beaten – several times – yet the authorities had ruled she died of 'natural causes'."

Chelsea Acorn, aged 14, disappeared from Abbottsford, BC, late in the afternoon of 10 June 2005. It is believed that Chelsea has run away and could be in the Surrey area 25 miles away.

This is just a small sample of the mayhem in British Columbia. But the "Highway of Tears" seems to stretch right across Canada. There are countless unsolved cases out there and numerous killers at large. One even exploits Native Americans' low tolerance for alcohol, takes First-Nations women to his hotel room and pours vodka down their throats until they die. He is still at large.

Costa Rica's Psychopath

A serial killer known as *El Psicópata* – "The Psychopath" – has been stalking Costa Rica. Between 1986 and 1996 he has killed at least 19 people, though the police say that number could exceed 31, but then there are other killers at large in the small Central America state.

The Psychopath preys on young couples in the secluded wooded area to the south of the capital San José. He always attacks at night. It is thought that he is a hunter who plans his attacks, waiting and watching until a couple arrive. He usually waits until the couples start making love before shooting them with a 45-calibre weapon, thought to be an M3 machine gun, then mutilates the breasts and sexual organs of his female victims with a US Army knife. It is believed that he follows his potential victims for several days before killing them, leaving no tracks.

Most of the killings have been committed in a wooded area south of the Florencio Freeway that runs from San José out to Cartago. The area stretching south to Desamparados is now called the "triangle of death" by the locals. The killings often occur near a brook or river, also giving the perpetrator the nickname "The Psychopath of the Rivers".

To start with, the killer also exhibited a unique pattern to his murders. After the murder of two couples, he then murdered a single women. But, in that case, he did not mutilate the bodies, though it was thought that he carried out acts of necrophilia. His attacks occurred every other month, on a full moon. However, the pattern has now become less clear. The authorities now think that killer began with a murder known as Alajuelita Massacre – the murder of seven women and girls on 6 June 1986 in the town of Alajuelita, which lies within the triangle of death. His last known attack was on 26 October 1996 when he found Ileana Alvarez and Mauricio Cordero parked in their Nissan Sentra. He forced them to get out of the car and walk 500 yards before he shot them. However, the police now think he may also be responsible for the disappearance of 12 other young people in 1996.

Several psychological profiles of the killer have been drawn up. One sees him as a "Rambo" type – a deranged former military or police official. Another theory is that he was a Nicaraguan guerrilla, or a Costa Rican who had gone to fight in the civil war there. Other theories say he could be the son of a wealthy politician or a landowner. Police believe the killer is probably in his thirties or forties, and could be highly intelligent.

On 26 June 1998, the Judicial Investigative Organization of Costa Rica announced they had arrested a serial killer who operated in the triangle of death. The killer was a 52-year-old construction worker, the father of 11 children whose favourite hobby is hunting. He sexually abuses his victims, then kills them with hunting rifles, and buries them under concrete. However, there seems to be no connection between this new unnamed killer and the Psychopath.

There is also another serial killer at large in Costa Rica known as *El Descuartizador* – "The Quarterer". He specializes in killing drug addicts – usually defenceless youths and women. He then cuts up their bodies and then scatters the pieces. It is not known how many he has killed as his victims are usually estranged from their families and on the fringes of society.

At one time these various killings were thought to be the work of one man – the San José Ripper. He first struck on 20 April

1989, when the bodies of Edwin Mata Madrigal and Marta Navarro Carpio were found in a river. Then at 11.15 a.m. on 13 November 1989 human remains were discovered in a drain in San José. Police dogs located the body parts of two corpses, though their heads and hands were not found and only one of their feet was recovered. The victims, a man and a woman, were thought to be aged between 18 and 25.

Pieces of another two corpses of a similar age were collected between December 2000 and February 2001. This time the women had a bite mark made by the teeth of a man on her right breast, while the man had a piece of wood shoved up his anus. The corpses were badly mutilated and, again, the heads, hands and feet were missing.

Again they were in various waterways and had been tattooed. Both these cases exhibited the MOs of both the Psychopath and the Quarterer. The police believe that the San José Ripper may be toying with them.

England – Jack the Ripper

Jack the Ripper has never been caught, or even, convincingly identified – so, technically, he is still at large. Whoever he was, he killed five women for certain in a ten-week period from 31 August to 9 November 1888, though he may have been responsible for the deaths of four more. All five had their throats slashed and were disembowelled and mutilated. The killer paid special attention to the destruction of the breasts and female sexual organs. Interestingly, if you plot the five murders on a map, they mark out the points of a pentagram, the five-pointed occult star.

The murders all took place in the Whitechapel area of London's East End, which was well known for vice at the time. In 1888, there were 62 brothels and 233 boarding houses catering to prostitutes and their clients in the narrow lanes there. Pox-ridden, middle-aged, alcoholic prostitutes hung around in alleyways and doorways, offering their sexual favours standing up. Usually they would simply bend down and hoist up their skirts so their client could enter them from the rear. This made it particularly easy for Jack the Ripper to pull a knife and despatch his victim before she realized what was happening.

Forty-five-year-old Emma Elizabeth Smith was possibly the first victim of the Ripper. On the night of 3 April 1888, she solicited a well-dressed gentleman. Later that night, she collapsed in the arms of a constable, saying that she had been attacked by four men. They had cut off her ear and shoved a foreign object up her vagina. She died a few hours later.

Then on 7 August 1888, Martha Tabram was stabbed to death. There were 39 frenzied wounds on her body, mainly around the breasts and sexual organs. Both Smith and Tabram, like the Ripper's later victims, had their backs turned when they were attacked.

The first of the women known for certain to have been killed by the Ripper was 42-year-old Polly Nichols. Her body was found in Buck's Row at 3.15 a.m. on 31 August 1888. She did not cry out. The attack took place under the window of a sleeping woman who did not wake. The body revealed that she fought for her life, but was overcome by her attacker. Her throat had been slashed twice, so deeply that she had almost been decapitated. There were deep wounds around her vagina, but no organs had been removed. Pathologists examining the corpse concluded that the killer had some medical knowledge. Polly had almost certainly turned her back on her killer for an assignation there on the street. While she was turned away from him, he pulled out a knife, put it to her throat and pushed her forward on to it as he slashed her. This explained the depth of the wound and would have meant that all the blood would have sprayed forward and not over the assailant, leaving him clean to make his escape unnoticed.

The police realized that they had a maniac on their hands. Detectives were sent out into the East End, searching for men who mistreated prostitutes. The name "Leather Apron" came up several times in the investigation. A shoemaker called Pizer was picked up. He used a leather apron and sharp knives in his trade, but his family swore that he was at home on the three occasions women had been attacked.

On 8 September 1888, 47-year-old Annie Chapman was bragging in the pubs of Whitechapel that the killer would meet his match if he ever came near her. She was wrong. Later, she was seen talking to a "gentleman" in the street. They seemed to strike up a bargain and went off arm-in-arm. Half-an-hour later, she was found dead in an alleyway. Her head was only connected to her body by a strand of flesh. Her intestines were found thrown over her right shoulder, the flesh from her lower abdomen over her left. Her kidneys and ovaries had been removed. The killer had taken them with him. He had also left a piece of leather near the corpse. The police realized that this was all too convenient. The killer was obviously an avid reader of the newspapers and had read of the arrest of Pizer. He also left a blood-soaked envelope with the crest of the Sussex Regiment on it. It had been reported that Martha Tabram had been seen in the company of a soldier shortly before her death and the newspapers said that her wounds could have been caused by a bayonet or army knife.

Three weeks after the death of Annie Chapman, the Central News Agency received a letter that gloated over the murder and the false clues. It regretted that the letter was not written in the victim's blood, but it had gone "thick like glue" and promised to send the ear of the next victim. The letter was signed "Jack the Ripper". On 30 September 1888, the Central News Agency received another letter from the Ripper, apologizing that he had not enclosed an ear – but promised that he was going to do a "double".

At 1 a.m. that night, 45-year-old "Long Liz" Stride, a Swedish prostitute whose real name was Elizabeth Gustaafsdotter, was found in a pool of blood with her throat slashed. The delivery man who discovered her body heard the attacker escaping over the cobblestones. Around the same time, 43-year-old prostitute Catherine Eddowes was being thrown out of Bishopsgate Police Station where she had been held for creating a drunken disturbance. As she walked towards Houndsditch she met Jack the Ripper. He cut her throat, slashed her face and cut at her ear, though it was left still attached. He removed her intestines and threw them over her shoulder. The left kidney was missing altogether.

The murder of two women in one night sent London into a panic. Queen Victoria demanded action, but the police seemed powerless. East-End resident George Lusk set up the Whitechapel Vigilance Committee to patrol the streets. Two weeks later, Mr Lusk received a small package through the post. It contained half of Catherine Eddowes' kidney. The other half had been fried and eaten, according to the accompanying note which was again signed "Jack the Ripper". Queen Victoria concluded that the Ripper must be a foreigner. No Englishman would behave in such a beastly way, she said. A cabinet meeting was called to discuss the matter. They ordered checks on all the ships tied up in the London docks. This proved to be a huge waste of police man-power.

The last victim that was certainly the Ripper's was unlike the others. She was young, just 24, and attractive. Her name was Mary Kelly and she only turned to prostitution occasionally to pay the rent. She was killed indoors and she also cried out.

On the night of 9 November 1888, she was seen on the street soliciting a "well-dressed gentleman". Sometime between 3.30 and 4 a.m., the woman sleeping in the room above Kelly's heard Kelly scream: "Oh, murder." In the morning, the rent man found her mutilated corpse.

Being indoors and undisturbed, the Ripper had been able to spend more than an hour on his grisly task. Mary Kelly's clothes were found neatly folded on a chair so it is thought that she took her "gentleman" back to her room and undressed herself ready for sex. It was then that he pulled out his knife. This time she had been facing him, saw the murder weapon and cried out. He slashed her throat, almost decapitating her, but blood splashed on his clothes, which were found burnt in the stove. Then he set about her corpse. Both breasts were cut off and placed on the table, along with her nose and flesh from her thighs and legs. Her left arm was severed and was left hanging by the flesh. Her forehead and legs had been stripped of flesh and her abdomen had been slashed open. She was three months pregnant at the time of the attack. Her intestines and liver had, once again, been removed and her hand was shoved into the gaping hole left. There was blood around the window where the Ripper was thought to have escaped, naked except for a long cloak and boots.

Other murders followed that may have been the work of the Ripper. The headless corpse of Elizabeth Jackson, a prostitute working in the Chelsea area, was found floating in the Thames in June 1889. In July that year, Alice McKenzie, a prostitute in Whitechapel, was found with her throat cut from ear to ear and her sexual organs cut out. And street-walker Frances Cole, also known as "Carroty Nell" because of her flaming red hair, was found in Whitechapel with her throat cut and slashed around her abdomen. A policeman saw a man stooped over the body, but he ran away before the constable could get a good look at him.

The description of the Ripper that has seized the public imagination comes from a friend of Mary Kelly's who saw her with a man that night. He was five feet six inches tall, about 35, well-dressed with a gold watch chain dangling from his waistcoat pocket. Kelly was seen in conversation with him.

"You will be all right for what I have told you," he said.

"All right my dear," she replied, taking him by the arm. "Come along, you will be comfortable."

A few hours later a chestnut vendor saw a man matching that description, wearing a long cloak and silk hat with a thin moustache turned up at the end and carrying a black bag.

"Have you heard there has been another murder?" he said.

"I have," the chestnut seller replied.

"I know more of it than you do," said the man as he walked away.

There are a huge number of theories as to the identity of the Ripper. The police had 176 suspects at the time. The most popular is the mad Russian physician Dr Alexander Pedachenko who worked under an assumed name in an east London clinic that treated several of the victims. A document naming him as the Ripper was said to have been found in the basement of Rasputin's house in St Petersburg after the mad monk's assassination in

1916. However, some have pointed out that Rasputin's house did not have a basement.

A Dr Stanley is another popular suspect. He is said to have contracted syphilis from a Whitechapel prostitute and thus took vengeance on them all. He fled to Buenos Aires where he died in 1929, after confessing all to a student.

V. Kosminski, a Polish Jew who lived in Whitechapel, threatened to slice up prostitutes. He went insane and died in an asylum. East European Jewish immigrants, who were unpopular in London at the time, were regularly blamed for the Ripper killings. It was said that the murders were ritual Jewish slaughters performed by a *shochet*, a butcher who kills animals according to Talmudic law. This theory was given some little credence by the confused message "The juwes are not the men that will be blamed for nothing" that was scrawled on a wall in Whitechapel after the murder of Catherine Eddowes. "Juwes", the Masonic spelling of "Jews", also gave rise to the theory that the murders had been some Masonic rite. The police commissioner Sir Charles Warren was himself a high-ranking Mason. He had the graffiti removed to prevent inflaming anti-Jewish feelings in the area, he said. Sir Charles Warren resigned after the murder of Mary Kelly, admitting his utter failure to solve the case.

Another Polish immigrant, Severin Klosowich – alias George Chapman – was also suspected. He was a barber's surgeon in Whitechapel and kept sharp knives for bloodletting and for the removal of warts and moles. He poisoned three of his mistresses and went to the gallows in 1903.

Thomas Cutbush was arrested after the murder of Frances Cole for stabbing women in the buttocks. He died in an insane asylum.

The insomniac G. Wentworth Bell Smith who lived at 27 Sun Street, off Finsbury Square, was a suspect. He railed against prostitutes, saying, "They should all be drowned."

Frederick Bailey Deeming confessed to the Ripper's murders. He had killed his wife and children in England, then fled to Australia where he killed a second wife. He was about to kill a third when he was arrested. It is thought that his confession was an attempt to delay, if not evade, the gallows in Australia.

Dr Thomas Neill Cream poisoned prostitutes in London and went on to murder more in the United States. He is said to have told his hangman "I am Jack . . ." as the trapdoor was opened.

The police's prime suspect was Montague John Druitt, an Oxford graduate from a once-wealthy family. After failing as a barrister, Druitt became a school teacher, but he was a homosexual and was dismissed for molesting a boy. He moved to Whitechapel where he was seen wandering the streets. In December 1888, his body was fished out of the Thames. There were stones in his pockets and it is thought he had drowned himself.

Salvation Army founder William Booth's secretary was also a suspect after saying "Carroty Nell will be the next to go" a few days before the slaying of Frances Cole. Alcoholic railway worker Thomas Salder was arrested after the murder of Alice McKenzie. He also knew Frances Cole, but was released due to lack of evidence.

Sir Arthur Conan Doyle, creator of Sherlock Holmes, believed that the Ripper was a woman. His theory was that "Jill the Ripper" was a midwife who had gone mad after being sent to prison for performing illegal abortions.

The spiritualist William Lees staged a séance for Queen Victoria to try and discover who the Ripper was. The results frightened him so much he fled to the Continent. The Ripper, he believed, was none other than the Queen's personal physician Sir William Gull. Gull's papers were examined by Dr Thomas Stowell. They named the Duke of Clarence, Prince Albert Victor, commonly known as Prince Eddy, the grandson of Queen Victoria who died of syphilis before he could ascend to the throne, as the Ripper, Stowell says. Another suspect is James Kenneth Stephen, a homosexual lover of Prince Eddy. The two of them were frequent visitors to a homosexual club in Whitechapel.

The painter Frank Miles, a friend of Oscar Wilde's, has also been named as the Ripper.

But Ripperology constantly moves on. In 1976, Stephen Knight published *Jack the Ripper: The Final Solution* airing the theory that the Ripper murders were not the work of a single mad man, but rather an establishment conspiracy to cover up a morganatic marriage entered into by the demented heir to the throne Prince Eddy.

In 1973, when Knight was working on a documentary about the Ripper murders for the BBC, a contact at Scotland Yard advised him to speak to a man named Sickert who knew about the secret marriage between Eddy and a poor Catholic girl, later divulging Sickert's address and phone number.

The man was Joseph Sickert, son of the famous painter Walter Sickert. Joseph briefly outlined a tale in which Prince Eddy, while slumming as a commoner under the aegis of the artist, met a girl named Annie Crook in a tobacconist's shop in Cleveland Street. Annie soon fell pregnant and she, Eddy and their daughter Alice were living quite happily in Cleveland Street until the Queen found out. She was furious. Not only was Annie a commoner, she was also a Catholic. Under the Act of Settlement of 1701, it was illegal for the monarch or the heir to the throne to marry a Catholic. And under the Royal Marriage Act 1772, royal children were prohibited from marriage without the specific consent of the monarch. Royalty was unpopular at the time and any scandal might risk revolution.

Queen Victoria handed the matter over to her prime minister Lord Salisbury, who organized a raid on the couple's Cleveland Street apartment. With the aide of the Queen's physician Sir William Gull, Annie was committed to a lunatic asylum where attempts were made to erase her memory, eventually driving her insane.

But Alice had escaped. When the raid had taken place, the child had been in the care of Mary Kelly, an orphan rescued from the poor house by Walter Sickert who was employed as Alice's nanny. Forced back on her own devices, Mary left the child with nuns and returned the East End, where she fell into a life of drink and prostitution. However, in her cups, she often told her story and some of her fellow women of the night – notably Polly Nichols, Liz Stride and Annie Chapman – encouraged to her to pressure the government for hush money.

Learning of the threat, Salisbury called on Gull once more and coachman John Netley, who had often ferried Eddy on his forays into the East End, to get rid of the troublesome women. They performed the Ripper murders and built up the image of Jack with letters and the symbols of Freemasonry. Assistant Commissioner of the Metropolitan Police Sir Robert Anderson was employed as look-out, Joseph Sickert said. As Chief of the Criminal Investigation Department, he was also in the perfect position to cover up the crime and hamper any investigation.

The women who knew the secret were duly despatched, along with Eddowes, whose murder, Sickert said, had been a mistake. She often went by the name of Mary Kelly and the conspirators thought that she was the woman they were looking for. When they discovered their mistake became known, they found the real Mary Kelly and killed her in a manner so gruesome that it would scare anyone else who had got a whiff of the scandal into silence. They had even organized a scapegoat in the person of poor barrister, Montague Druitt, who was chosen to take the blame and was, Sickert hinted, murdered for it.

The daughter Alice grew up quietly in the convent and, by an odd twist of fate, later married Walter Sickert and gave birth to their son, Joseph. Sir William Gull died shortly after the murders, but there were rumours that he had been committed to an insane asylum. Annie Crook died insane in a workhouse in 1920. Netley was chased by an angry mob after he unsuccessfully tried to run over Alice with his cab shortly after the murders. He was believed to have been drowned in the Thames.

Joseph said that his father Walter Sickert was tormented with guilt over the murders and, as a form of expiation, painted clues into several of his most famous paintings. Checking out the story, Knight found that a woman named Annie Crook lived at 22 Cleveland Street at that time and that she did give birth to an illegitimate daughter. This was also handy for the homosexual brothel at 19 Cleveland Street, centre of the Cleveland Street Scandal of 1889, in which the notorious bi-sexual Prince Eddy was thought to be implicated.

However, before Stephen Knight had finished writing *Jack the Ripper: The Final Solution*, he had fallen out with Joseph Sickert. This is partially because he rejected Sickert's story that Sir Robert

Anderson was the third man in the killings. Instead Knight insisted that Joseph Sickert's own father, Walter Sickert, was the third man. Joseph Sickert was not unnaturally offended by this suggestion, withdrew his co-operation and held back part of the story. From what Joseph Sickert told him, Knight concluded that Sir William Gull was the evil genius behind the Ripper murders. Sickert later claimed he kept back the name of the ringleader because he did not want to bring shame on the culprit's family. But as Knight's story came into general currency Sickert found that his omission had rebounded on him. The shame was now being heaped on his family. He was particularly upset when the 1985 TV film *Murder by Decree* portrayed Prince Eddy as the heartless seducer of the naïve Annie Crook, who he intended to dump. Sickert was offended by this, believing that his grand-parents had shared a great love. They had suffered enough in their lifetime, he thought. It did not seem fair to him that they should be slandered after their deaths and he resolved to reveal the vital details he had withheld.

In doing so he confirmed everything that he had told Stephen Knight, though he continued to insist that Sir Robert Anderson, not Walter Sickert, had been the third man. But there were more men in the gang – maybe as many as 12. These included Lord Euston and Lord Arthur Somerset, two of those who took the fall in the Cleveland Street Scandal.

The reason Stephen Knight concluded that Walter Sickert, not Sir Robert Anderson, was the third man was because Sickert knew too much simply to have been a bystander. When he had told his son what he knew of the Ripper murders, he divulged details that only someone who had been there when the murders happened would have known. But Joseph Sickert had withheld the source of his father's information. Walter Sickert had been told the inside story of the Ripper murders by Inspector Frederick George Abberline, the policeman in charge of the investigation. Abberline, in turn, had been told the story by one of the men involved – the heir to the throne Prince Eddy's tutor J. K. Stephen, one of the favoured suspects of the lone-madman theory of the murders. Stephen, Sickert said, was one of the Ripper gang and part of the conspiracy. Abberline had written down what Stephen had told him in three diaries which he had given to Walter Sickert, who passed them on to his son. Both father and son regularly referred to the diaries to keep the details of the Ripper murders fresh in their minds.

One of the reasons that Knight discounted Anderson as a member of the Ripper gang was that he had been out of the country at the time of the double murder of Elizabeth Stride and Catherine Eddowes. But Sickert maintained that Anderson's role, as a detective, was able to collect and collate information on the whereabouts of Mary Kelly and the other blackmailers. The fact that Catherine Eddowes was not one of the blackmailers and was killed by mistake, because she had been unfortunate enough to use the pseudonym Mary Kelly, seems to confirm that whoever was in charge of tracking the women down had slipped up or was not available at the time.

Sickert continued to maintain that Sir William Gull and John Netley were the men who actually performed the murders and mutilations. However, he later revealed that Gull had not begun his murderous campaign on his own initiative. He was acting on the orders of more prominent men. His orders came from his Masonic superiors in the Royal Alpha Lodge No 16. The chief conspirator, Sickert maintained, was none other than Lord Randolph Churchill, father of wartime leader Winston Churchill. Although the Freemasons deny Lord Randolph Churchill was ever a member, Sickert maintained that he was *Magister Magistrorum* – the master of masters. There are other indications that he was a mason, but had joined under the alias Spencer. Like his son, he often used the double-barrelled surname Spencer Churchill.

Lord Randolph Churchill had a twisted reason to hate women. By 1888 he was already suffering from bouts of madness, caused by the tertiary syphilis that would kill him. He blamed his condition and the loss of his meteoric political career on the woman who had given him the disease. It seems that Sir William Gull, an expert on syphilis, was treating him. By 1886, because of his condition, Lord Randolph Churchill ceased having sex with his wife, the beautiful American Jenny Jerome. She began to take lovers. This left Lord Randolph Churchill alone and bitter. His condition left him reliant on drugs. Like his son, he was a big drinker. He was also audacious and brooked no opposition. He even defied the Prince of Wales, threatening to publish incriminating letters which would lose him the throne if the Prince did not back down in an affair involving Churchill's brother Lord Blandford. The Prince of Wales did as Churchill demanded but refused to speak to him again for eight years. Lord Randolph Churchill believed that he had been robbed of the chance to be prime minister and did anything he could to exercise power behind the scenes. He saw himself as a second Machiavelli and was known to be unscrupulous. He was certainly a man who could have cooked up the Ripper conspiracy and would have had the expertise to pull it off.

Winston Churchill was a tireless defender of his father, whitewashing him in his biography *Lord Randolph Churchill*. As Home Secretary in 1910, Winston Churchill was in a perfect position to remove any evidence linking his father to the Ripper murders from the police files. When they were opened in 1988, the Ripper files were found to be far from complete. Soon after, Winston Churchill quit the Freemasons. There were other connections between Churchill and the conspiracy. Walter Sickert gave Winston Churchill painting lessons and Churchill had been induced into the masons by Lord Euston.

Joseph Sickert maintained that J. K. Stephen was related to Annie Crook and may have introduced Eddy to her. Sickert also believed that Lord Randolph Churchill got carried away with the power the Ripper conspiracy gave him. After killing Mary Kelly and the other blackmailers, he intended to finish the job by killing Annie Crook, her daughter Alice and Prince Eddy himself. It was then that Stephen broke with the other conspirators and, breaking his Masonic oath, talked to Inspector Abberline. Like so many others involved in the conspiracy, Stephen died in a lunatic asylum. He starved himself to death after being told of Eddy's death in 1892. Four days later, Abberline retired from the police force.

As *Jack the Ripper: The Final Solution* points out, the conspiracy among the highest echelons of the police force and the establishment was so powerful that even though Abberline knew the truth there was nothing he could do about it. The Ripper case had to remain officially unsolved or it would have opened the very can of worms the conspirators had sought to conceal.

Joseph Sickert told the rest of what he knew to Melvyn Fairclough, who recounted it in his book *The Ripper and the Royals* published in 1991. The book confirms the thesis of Stephen Knight's book and adds a myriad of detail. However, Fairclough's book over-eggs the pudding, tying the Ripper conspiracy to an assassination attempt on Queen Victoria and the abdication crisis of 1936. Distraught at being forcibly parted from his wife, Prince Eddy intended to exact his revenge by killing his own grandmother. And, apparently, Prince Eddy did not die in 1892. Being thought unsuitable to ascend to the throne, he was proclaimed dead then hidden away in Glamis Castle – ancestral home of the Bowes-Lyons – until he died in 1933. In recompense, the master of Glamis, the Earl of Strathmore, was to see his daughter, a commoner, sit on the throne of England. Elizabeth Bowes-Lyon – who later became Queen Elizabeth, then the longstanding Queen Mother – was romantically attached to the Prince of Wales who became Edward VIII before marrying his brother the Duke of York who became George VI. Apparently Edward – or David as he was known before ascending to the throne – had discovered the secret of Glamis and had decided to abdicate in protest at the treatment of Eddy, who was rightfully king, before he even met Mrs Simpson. Hence Ms Bowes-Lyon's change of partner. For my money, this is one conspiracy theory too far.

But there are still more theories. In 1987, Martin Fido fingered "David Cohen" – the name given to an unknown Jewish madman incarcerated in Colney Hatch lunatic asylum in December 1888. He died there in October the following year. The last murder known for sure to have been the Ripper's occurred on 9 November 1888. Fido believes that "Cohen" was identified by Joseph Lawende, a witness who had seen a man talking to the Ripper's fourth victim Catherine Eddowes shortly before she was murdered. But Lawende refused to testify against a fellow Jew, knowing that he faced the hangman's rope, so the police detained "Cohen" under the Lunacy Act instead to keep him off the streets. Fido also believes that the police were convinced of his guilt but rivalries between the Metropolitan and City Police have obscured his real identity. It is a nice theory but hardly satisfying as nothing more is known about "Cohen" – other than he was a foreign-born Jew, a tailor living in a homeless shelter in Whitechapel aged 23 in 1888, who was extremely violent and had to be kept in a straitjacket. However, his wild assaults on other patients, his shouting and dancing, his noisy acts of vandalism, his inability to take care of himself and his need for restraint all seem at odds with the Ripper who slipped unnoticed in and out of the shadows, cutting up his victims with the practised skill of a surgeon.

In 1991, Northamptonshire police officer Paul Harrison concluded that Joseph Barnett, the common-law husband of the Ripper's last known victim Mary Kelly, was Jack. Harrison contends that Barnett was a sensitive man who thought he could save Mary from the streets. Instead she dragged him down into the gutter with her. An earlier, unrelated murder of a prostitute had persuaded her to suspend her activities as a streetwalker. When she started again, he was driven half-mad with jealousy. He tracked down other prostitutes she knew and killed them in the most gruesome way possible, hoping to scare her back off the streets. When this failed, he murdered and mutilated her. Having rid himself of the source of his psychological problems, Harrison maintains, Barnett had no reason to kill again. But Harrison draws a comparison between Barnett and the serial killers Peter Sutcliffe, the Yorkshire Ripper, and Dennis Nilsen. Neither Sutcliffe nor Nilsen stopped killing until they were caught, but Barnett went on to live a long and untroubled life as a coster-monger. As far as I am aware, there is little outlet for the Ripper's raging bloodlust in the retail fruit trade.

In 1992, David Abrahamsen, a fellow of the American College of Psychoanalysts, brought his psychological insight to bear on theory that Prince Eddy and his Cambridge tutor J. K. Stephen were the murderers. From the psychological point of view,

Stephen Knight had already explained how Prince Eddy and J. K. Stephen fitted into the Ripper plot.

Ripperology was revivalized in 1993 with the publication of *The Diary of Jack the Ripper*. This concluded that the author of the diary, said to be a 49-year-old Liverpudlian cotton-merchant James Maybrick, a substance abuser with a history of domestic violence, was Jack the Ripper. For several years Ripperologists debated whether the diaries were fake. However, in his 1997 book *Jack the Ripper: The Final Chapter*, Paul Feldman, who believes the diaries are genuine, tied Maybrick into Stephen Knight's conspiracy theory.

In 1994, Melvin Harris resurrected the story that the journalist and devil-worshipper Roslyn D'Onston – or Dr Roslyn D'O Stephenson – was the Ripper. D'Onston himself wrote to the police in 1888 accusing Dr Morgan Davies, a surgeon at the London Hospital in Whitechapel. A failed doctor and a drug addict, D'Onston was said to have killed the women to give his journalistic career a fillip. It was said that his stories in the newspapers carried details about the murders that were never released by the police. In 1890, he became involved with Mabel Collins, the editor of *Lucifer*, the magazine of the Theosophical Society. He later went into business with Baroness Vittoria Cremers, who revealed in the 1920s that she had found neckties caked with dried blood in D'Onston's room. She said he had told her that they belonged to Jack the Ripper. They eventually found their way into the possession of the Satanist Aleister Crowley, who claimed that D'Onston was indeed the Ripper and that his ritual murders were done for magical purposes in an attempt to become invisible. Crowley himself claimed in court to have killed many times for the purposes of black magic. He was never prosecuted. The case against Onston was effectively dealt with and dismissed by Stephen Knight, but still it persists.

In 1995, Stewart Evans and Paul Gainey dismissed the Ripper diary and came up with a new suspect – Francis J. Trumblety, a Canadian woman-hater and fraudster who was arrested in America in connection with the assassination of President Lincoln. After his release, he moved to England. In 1888, the year of the

Ripper murders, he was in London, lodging in Whitechapel, Evans and Gainey maintain. On 2 December 1888, he was arrested for unnamed sexual offences. Released on bail, he headed for Le Havre where he took a ship back to New York. The New York police were alerted and kept an eye on him. Detectives were also despatched from England. But Trumblety gave them all the slip and went on to continue his murderous campaign in Jamaica and Nicaragua. He returned to New York in 1891, where he killed again. All this was covered up, Evans and Gainey say, because the Metropolitan Police were embarrassed that they had had the Ripper and released him. Trumblety, they maintain, "killed for no apparent motive other than enjoyment". In which case, after a couple of years of murderous pleasure, he must have stinted himself for the last 12 years of his life. He died in Rochester, New York, in 1903, without, apparently, sating his bloodlust again.

In 1996, former private eye Bruce Paley again accused Joseph Barnett, Mary Kelly's common-law husband, of the crime. Paley claims Barnett fits the FBI's psychological profile of a modern serial killer. Most are white males in their twenties or early thirties. Barnett was 30 at the time of the murders. They come from dysfunctional families, though it would be hard to find a family that was not dysfunctional in the Whitechapel area in the late 19th century. According to top FBI psychological profiler Robert K. Ressler, serial killers come from families where the mother is cold and unloving, while the father is usually absent. Barnett was six when his father died and his mother had disappeared by the time he was 13. Paley says that she possibly abandoned her family. This fits with Ressler's theory that the most important single factor in creating a serial killer is a sense of loneliness and isolation consolidated between the age of eight and 12.

Serial killers often suffer from a physical defect. Barnett had a speech impediment. Serial killers tend to be intelligent men, stuck in jobs below their capabilities. Barnett was a fish porter, though he was well spoken and had had some schooling. A serial killer's first crime tends to be precipitated by a period of stress. Barnett had lost his job shortly before the killings started, forcing Mary to return to prostitution. This gave Barnett a motive for killing her, and it could have given him a reason for venting his wrath on other prostitutes. As a fish porter, he would have been a familiar figure on the streets of the East End in the early morning and, through Mary, he would probably have been known to all the victims. Being a fish porter also meant he was skilled with a knife, boning and gutting fish.

However, according to the FBI, serial killers tend to have been emotionally or sexually abused as a child and come from a family where drugs or alcohol were abused. It is not known if this was the case with Barnett. They also continue to kill until they are caught. But for following 38 years, Barnett led a blameless life. Although he certainly continued having relationships with women – electoral rolls show that he lived with a common-law wife for at least seven years – he never felt that murderous rage well up inside him again. And, it seems, in all that time he never ever felt the urge to tell anyone of his crimes or record the fact that he was the world's most notorious killer for posterity.

In 1997, James Tulley used the same psychological profiling methods to identify the Ripper. But he absolved Barnett and picked one James Kelly instead. In 1883, Kelly had stabbed and killed his wife. He admitted the crime and was sentenced to death, but was reprieved and sent to Broadmoor. In January 1888, he escaped and hid out in the East End of London, before fleeing to France at the end of the year. He returned to England in 1892 to sail to the US. In 1896, he gave himself up at the British Consulate in New Orleans. Instead of having him arrested, the vice-consul arranged for him to work his own passage back to Liverpool. Arriving in England, he absconded again, this time heading for Canada. In 1901, he surrendered himself at the British Consulate in Vancouver, but again he gave the authorities the slip. For the next 26 years he travelled back and forth across the Atlantic, spending more and more time in England. Eventually in 1927, he turned up at the gates of Broadmoor, where he surrendered himself once more. He died in the asylum two years later. Tulley says the authorities kept quiet about Kelly because they had let the Ripper escape in the first place. The fact that they made no effort to apprehend him in North America or when he was back in Britain, Tulley says, was part of the cover-up. Once again, there is no indication that Kelly killed again in the 39 years he was at liberty after the Ripper murders, even though he was a dangerous fugitive from justice. It seems you can kill five prostitutes in a couple of months, then give it up just like that, cold turkey.

In 1998, South Wales magistrate Bob Hinton again used those self-same psychological profiling methods. But he came up with George Hutchinson, a witness who gave a detailed description of a man he said he saw with the Ripper's last victim Mary Kelly the night she died. Again Hutchinson was a white male, at 28 in the right age group, and as a barman and labourer in the right sort of menial job. With those criteria, the East End of London in the 1880s must have been brimming over with the serial killers. Hutchinson certainly knew Kelly and admitted giving her money – presumably for services rendered. His own testimony put him at the scene of the crime. Hinton also says that senior policemen discounted Hutchinson as a witness – a point that Stephen Knight covered in his book 22 years earlier. Hinton systematically trashed Hutchinson's evidence and believes that he stopped killing because Mary Kelly "the object of his obsession [was] obliterated". Hinton was not sure when Hutchinson died, but says he must have been either the George Hutchinson who died in Newark in 1929, the George Hutchinson who died in Bradford in 1934 or the George Hutchinson who died in Darlington in 1936. So again Hutchinson lived at least another 41 years without feeling the urge to kill again, or tell anyone that he was Jack the Ripper.

In 1999, Stephen Wright, reviewing all the literature from an American angle, concluded like others that the Ripper's diary was a hoax. He dismissed all the other theories, then claimed to be the first to finger George Hutchinson as the Ripper. Maybe Hinton's book had not crossed the Atlantic when Wright was at work, but Wright makes no more convincing a case than Hinton does. The most recent theory is that Walter, the pseudonymous author of the Victorian pornographic classic *My Secret Life*, was the

Ripper. The clues, apparently, are all in the book. Walter is now thought to be Henry Spencer Ashbee, who left his huge collection of erotica to the British Museum.

In 2002, Patricia Cornwell published *Portrait of a Killer: Jack the Ripper – Case Closed*. In it she dusted off the Stephen Knight theory, but concluded that Walter Sickert was the sole killer. The clues were all in his paintings. Although she spent a reputed $6 million on research, the book was widely discounted. She had hoped to prove her case with DNA taken from one of his paintings, which she cut up, but has failed to do so.

However, new books are being written about Jack the Ripper all the time. Each develops a theory more off the wall than the last. It is a wonder that no one has yet suggested that Jack the Ripper was an alien who abducted East End prostitutes to perform bizarre anatomical experiments on them. Perhaps it is coming.

England – Jack the Stripper

As in the case of Jack the Ripper, the file on Jack the Stripper has never been closed. He killed six women in 1964 and left their naked bodies in the River Thames or along its banks.

The first body was found under a pontoon at Hammersmith on 2 February 1964. The victim had been strangled and the remnants of her underwear had been shoved down her throat. She was small, five foot two, and apart from her stockings she was naked.

The body was identified as that of Hannah Tailford. She was 30 years old and lived with her boyfriend in West Norwood. She had a three-year-old daughter, an 18-month-old son and was pregnant at the time of death.

By day, she worked as a waitress or a cleaner. At night she supplemented her meagre wages by working as a prostitute on the streets of Bayswater. Her record showed four convictions for soliciting.

She had disappeared from her flat ten days before her body was found, though a man and his wife said they saw her on Charing

Cross Road, just two days before. She was depressed and suicidal. They tried to cheer her up.

Forensic experts concluded that she had been dead for just 24 hours when she was found, and they believed that she may have been drowned in a bath or pond before she was dumped in the river. Tide tables showed that she must have entered the Thames at Duke's Meadow in Chiswick, a popular spot for courting couples as well as for prostitutes and their clients.

By interviewing over 700 people in London's underworld of vice, the police discovered that Hannah had been a star turn at sex parties and that she often attended kinky orgies in Mayfair and Kensington. A foreign diplomat known for his perverted tastes had been one of her clients, but he had been out of the country at the time of her disappearance.

This left the police with little to go on. They believed that Hannah had been attacked and sexually assaulted. Her knickers had been shoved in her mouth to stop her screaming as she was killed. But they could not even prove that she had been murdered and the inquest recorded an open verdict.

Hannah Tailford's passing would have been mourned by those who knew her – and dismissed as one of the professional risks of being a prostitute by those who did not – and then forgotten about if a death with eerie similarities had not occurred two months later. On 8 April 1964, the body of 26-year-old Irene Lockwood was found among the tangled weeds and branches on the river bank at Duke's Meadow. She was naked.

The pretty young redhead also worked the streets of Bayswater and Notting Hill. She, too, was small like Hannah and had attended kinky parties. She also performed in blue movies. Both girls solicited cab drivers late at night. And both were pregnant when they died.

In both cases, it was impossible to determine how they had died. Marks on the back of Irene's head showed that she could have been attacked from behind and the police believed that she had been killed elsewhere, then brought to Duke's Field.

The police also suspected that both girls were mixed up in a blackmail racket. In Hannah's flat, they found an address book and photographic equipment. Irene's flatmate Vicki Pender, who had been found battered to death a year earlier, had once been beaten up after trying to blackmail a client who had been photographed with her without his knowledge or consent.

But the most striking similarity between the two killings was that the victims were found naked. There was no sign of their clothes, which were never found.

On 24 April, another naked female body was found – this time in an alley off Swyncombe Avenue in Brentford. The victim, 22-year-old Helen Barthelemy, had been strangled, probably from behind.

Three of her front teeth had been extracted after death. It was also established that her body had been stripped of its clothing after her death and fresh tyre marks in the alley way indicated that she had been killed elsewhere and dumped there.

Helen was also a prostitute. Educated in a convent, she had become a stripper in Blackpool. In Liverpool, she had served a prison sentence for luring a man into an ambush where he had been robbed. When she was released she came to London and went on the game. She was known to cater for any sort of perversions, though she would often entertain local black men for free because they were more sympathetic than her kinky clientele. One Jamaican man admitted being with her on the night she disappeared, but he had a strong alibi and was quickly ruled out as a suspect.

With three similar killings, the papers caught on to the story. The victims' nudity was obviously the most sensational aspect and the Sundays quickly dubbed the mysterious murderer "Jack the Stripper".

Looking back in their records, Scotland Yard found another case that fitted Jack the Stripper's modus operandi. On 8 November 1963, three months before Hannah Tailford's murder, the body of 22-year-old Gwynneth Rees had been found buried in a shallow grave in an ash tip near Chiswick Bridge. She was naked except for one stocking. At first, the police thought that she had been the victim of an abortion racket. Then it was discovered that she had been the target of a sexual attack. The body had lain there since May or June and it was thought that she may have been sunbathing when she was attacked. Now, though, it looked like she was another victim of Jack the Stripper.

Kenneth Archibald, a 54-year-old caretaker, walked into Notting Hill police station and confessed to the murder of Irene Lockwood. He was already a suspect. His card had been found in Irene's flat. He said that he had met her in a pub on the night of the murder. On open land near Barnes Bridge they had quarrelled over money. He had lost his temper and put his hands around her throat so she could not scream. He had strangled her accidentally. When she was dead, he had taken her clothes off and rolled her into the river. Then he took her clothes home and burned them.

Archibald, however, said he knew nothing about the murders of Hannah Tailford, Helen Barthelemy or Gwynneth Rees. He was charged with the murder of Irene Lockwood. But when he appeared in the Old Bailey, he retracted his confession. As there was no other evidence against him the jury acquitted him.

The forensic scientists paid special attention to Helen Barthelemy's body. It had not been buried like Gwynneth Rees's, nor had it been in contact with water. However, it was filthy, as if it had been stored somewhere dirty before it had been dumped.

A minute examination of her skin showed that she was covered from head to toe in tiny flecks of paint. Home Office scientists concluded that her naked body had been kept somewhere near a spray-painting shop.

It was clear that the man who had killed Helen Barthelemy and the other victims sought the company of prostitutes in the Bayswater area. The police organized an amnesty for girls working the streets in that area and appealed for anyone to come forward who had worried about odd or eccentric clients, especially those who made them strip naked. The girls' response was overwhelming.

Policewomen went out on the streets, posing as prostitutes. They carried tape recorders in their handbags. The experiences they recorded were often unpleasant, but they failed to move the enquiry forward.

On 14 July 1964, another body was found. At around 5.30 a.m., a man driving to work down Acton Lane had to brake hard to miss a van speeding out of a cul-de-sac. The police were called. At the end of the cul de sac, outside a garage, they found the naked body of Mary Flemming.

Again the murdered girl was a prostitute who worked in the Bayswater area. Her body had been kept for approximately three days after her death. Once more, her clothes had been removed after death and there were tiny flecks of paint all over her naked body.

Mary had been warned of the dangers of continuing to work the streets where Jack the Stripper was on the prowl. She took to carrying a knife in her handbag. It did her no good. Like the other victims, she had been attacked from behind. And no trace of her handbag, the knife or her clothes were ever found.

Pressure on Scotland Yard, by this time, was intense. Over 8,000 people had been interviewed, 4,000 statements had been taken, but the police were still no nearer to finding the culprit. Plain-clothes policemen blanketed the area the murdered girls had worked. But on 25 November 1964, the body of 21-year-old Margaret McGowan was found on some rough ground in Kensington. The hallmarks were unmistakable. McGowan was a prostitute and an associate of society pimp Dr Stephen Ward, who stood trial during the Profumo scandal. She had been strangled and her body was left naked. Her body had lain on the open ground for at least a week, but had been stored somewhere else before being dumped there. Again her skin was covered in tiny flecks of paint.

The evening she went missing, McGowan and a friend had talked about the murders in the Warwick Castle on Portobello Road. The two of them had gone their separate ways, McGowan with a client. McGowan's friend gave a good enough description of McGowan's client for the police to issue an identikit picture of the man. But no one answering the description was found. The police also noticed that McGowan's jewellery was missing, but a check on all the pawn shops also drew a blank.

Christmas and New Year passed uneventfully, then on 16 February 1965, the naked body of 28-year-old Bridie O'Hara was found in the bracken behind a depot in Acton. Like the other victims, she was short, five foot two, and worked as a prostitute. Her clothes had disappeared along with her engagement and wedding rings. They were never found. Again, her body was covered with tiny flecks of paint. But this time there was a new clue. One of her hands was mummified. That meant it had been kept near a source of heat that had dried the flesh out.

Scotland Yard threw all their resources into the case. Every premises in an area of 4 square miles was to be searched and samples of any paint found compared to the flecks on the victim's bodies. The police also worked out that all the victims had been picked up between 11 p.m. and 1 a.m., and dumped between 5 a.m. and 6 a.m. This meant that Jack the Stripper was a night worker, probably a nightwatchman who guarded premises near a spray shop.

They also worked out that he was a man of about 40 with a high libido and curious sexual tastes. The police dismissed an earlier theory that the culprit was on a crusade against prostitution. They now believed that the culprit could not satisfy his bizarre requirements at home, turning to prostitutes who would do anything for money in order to indulge his craving. Detectives now realized that, during orgasm, the man went into a frenzy which resulted in the girls' deaths. He could not help himself and had learned to accept that murder was the price he had to pay for sexual satisfaction.

All this was little enough to go on. But the police held regular press conferences saying that a list of suspects had been drawn up. They were working their way through them and the killer would soon be behind bars. In fact, the police had no list and were not nearly as confident as they pretended, but they felt that it was best to keep up pressure on the culprit.

The murders fell into a ten-week cycle and the police were determined to prevent the next one. They threw a police cordon around a 20-square mile area of central London and every vehicle entering or leaving it at night was recorded. Anyone moving in or out of the zone more than three times was tracked down.

The police would visit their home under the pretext of investigating a traffic accident – to spare the embarrassment of those who were where they were not supposed to be. The suspect was then interviewed out of the earshot of his family.

Weeks of searching paid off. A perfect match was made between paint found under a covered transformer at the rear of a spray-painting shop in the Heron Factory Estate in Acton and the paint flecks on the victims' bodies. The transformer itself generated enough heat to mummify flesh left near it.

Every car entering or leaving the estate was logged and all 7,000 people living in the vicinity were interviewed. At a specially convened press conference, the police announced that the number of suspects was being whittled down to three, then two, then one.

Despite the huge amount of man-hours put in, all Scotland Yard's detective work was a waste of time. It was these press conferences that worked.

In March 1965, as the detectives continued their meticulous search, a quiet family man living in south London killed himself. He left a suicide note saying that he could not "stand the strain any longer". At the time the police took little notice.

By June 1965, Jack the Stripper had not struck again. The ten-week cycle had been broken. The police wanted to know why. They began looking back at the suicides that had occurred since the murder of Bridie O'Hara in January.

This particular suicide victim worked at a security firm and his duty roster fitted the culprits. Despite an intensive search of his house and extensive interviews with his family, no evidence was ever found that directly linked him to the murders. Nevertheless, the murders stopped and the police were convinced, from the circumstantial evidence alone, that this man was Jack the Stripper.

By July 1965, the murder inquiry was scaled down. It was wound up the following year. In 1970, Scotland Yard confirmed that the South London suicide was Jack the Stripper. But they have never named him and, officially, the file on the Jack the Stripper case is still open.

England and Wales – Operation Enigma

In Britain the Police Standards Unit set up Operation Enigma to re-examine unsolved cases involving the murder of prostitutes and other vulnerable women. The files on numerous cases have been reopened and police will be harnessing the skills of criminologists at home and abroad, including the psychological profilers of the FBI.

One series of killings went back to January 1987 when the half-naked body of Marine Monti, a 27-year-old prostitute and heroin addict, was found on waste ground near Wormwood Scrubs prison in west London. She had been beaten and strangled. Next the partially clothed body of 22-year-old prostitute Janine Downes was found in a hedge alongside the road leading from Telford to Wolverhampton in February 1991. She had also been beaten and strangled. The other seven victims over the next seven years followed a similar pattern. They too had been strangled or beaten to death. Nearly all were prostitutes and their bodies found partially clothed or naked on open ground. Cleverly, each had been dumped in a different police district, minimizing the chance that the authorities would tie them together.

According to FBI profiler Richard Ault a single killer is likely to be at work. The perpetrator is the type that the FBI categorizes as an "organized killer". He would be someone of above-average intelligence, socially competent, often living with a woman and driving a well-maintained car but, after some stressful event, he kills.

"Such an individual is likely to be personable and not stand out," he says. "He is able to blend in because he can approach and solicit victims."

However, although the Assistant Chief Constable of Essex Police James Dickinson, who is co-ordinating Enigma, acknowledges some common traits in the nine murders, he points out that the investigating teams do not feel think there were sufficient grounds to link the nine inquiries formally. But nobody has been brought to justice for the murders of Gail Whitehouse from Wolverhampton in October 1900; Lynne Treuholme, who was found dead in Chester massage parlour in June 1991; Natalie Pearman from Norwich on November 1992; Carol Clarke, who was abducted from Bristol and found in Sharpness Canal, Gloucestershire in March 1993; Dawn Shields from Sheffield, who was found buried in Peak District in May 1994 and many, many more.

Ghana's Assassin of Accra

A serial killer or group of serial killers have been at work in Ghana who may have political connections. In 1999 alone, some 21 women were slaughtered in cold blood in and around the capital Accra. By July 2000, the number had climbed to 25 and, when two murders occurred within a week, thousands of women took to the street in protest. Dressed in black with red armbands, they demanded the resignation of the Minister of the Interior and the Inspector-General of Police.

Angela Dwamena-Aboagye, executive director of the Ark Foundation, an organization that aims to empower women, led the protest after the body of an unidentified young woman wearing a blood-stained skirt and torn underwear was found at Asylum Down, a neighbourhood close to the centre of the city. A condom was found close by.

The previous week the body of a middle-aged woman was found in the same condition in another part of the city. Until then, most of the killing had taken place in Mataheko, a lower middle-class residential area to the southwest of the city. Until then Accra, with a population of just two million, had been considered safe.

The Ghana branch of the Federation of International Women Lawyers (Fida) wrote to the then President Jerry Rawlings and to parliament, asking them to treat the situation as "a national crisis".

"We wish to state without hesitation that we're deeply aggrieved, highly disappointed and extremely agitated by this unnecessary and unjustified shedding of innocent blood," said Elizabeth Owiredu-Gyampoh, President of Fida.

The women protesters said that the situation would have been treated a lot more seriously if the victims had been men.

"As it is, it's the lives of ordinary people that are being lost so the big men don't care," said Angela Dwamena-Aboagye.

The police were also being accused of lacking professionalism. Sylvia Legge, who made the initial report of the most recent killing at a nearby police station, says she was not treated seriously by the police.

"I made the report at 06:30, but the police officer in charge eventually saw me after 10:00, almost four hours later," she told a local radio station.

But the police claimed that they are starved of resources. The equipment they have for testing blood samples pre-dates World War II.

In July 2000, Charles Ebo Quansah was arrested in the Accra suburb of Adenta for the murder of his girlfriend Joyce Boateng, but he was also charged with the murder of 24-year-old hairdresser Akua Serwaa who was found dead near the Kumasi Sports Stadium in the Ashanti region, 125 miles inland from Accra. He had previous served jail terms for rape.

In custody, he reportedly confessed to the murder of nine other women around Accra and Kumasi, though he was charged with only one. He was found guilty on the basis of a lie-detector test and sentenced to death. However, when he appealed to the High Court, the Commission of Police failed to respond to a subpoena to produce the polygraph machine and, later, denied that the police department had one – though there were hints that a lie-detector test had been administered by "white men" from the FBI. There was also evidence that Quansah had been tortured. Previously, when a list of suspects in the case had been read out in parliament, Quansah's name was not on it.

Meanwhile the killings continued. In December 2000, a corpse was found in a bush in an uninhabited area off a major road in the south-east of the city bringing the total to 31. The dead woman was in her mid-thirties or early forties. She was lying face-up, naked except for a brassiere. A pair of leggings were lying near by. Police said there were abrasions on her hands, but otherwise there were no signs of struggle. It was thought that she may have been killed elsewhere and her dead body dumped where she was found. Police allowed scores of people to walk past the body, in the hope that someone would identify her. But no one knew her.

On Monday men and women alike called into radio phone-in programmes, alarmed at the sheer frequency of the murders.

"I'm not going to sell *kenkey* [a popular cooked milled-corn dish] late at night any more, I don't feel safe; I'm going to close early and go home," said Abena Nyarkoa, a food seller in Madina, a suburb where two women had been found dead that month.

The murders became a political issue and Interior Minister Nii Okaidja Adamafio and his deputy Kweku Bonful were voted out of office. In a TV broadcast, presidential candidate John Kufuor made finding the killer a plank in his 2000 election campaign. Jerry Rawlings had already stepped down and Kufuor won the presidency. However, in 2003, Rawlings alleged that 15 ministers in President John Kufuor's cabinet had a direct hand in the women's murders that had now climbed to 34 – though the killings had taken place while Rawlings himself was head of state.

Police questioned Rawlings about his claims at his residence in Accra, but the former president refused to name names. He said he will only reveal the names of the ministers involved if the government would invite an independent investigator to administer a lie-detector test on him and those implicated in order minimize the telling of lies in the case.

Ghana's Inspector General of Police, Nana Owusu-Nsiah, said he was "profoundly disappointed with the utterances and conduct of the former president". He said that police had conducted thorough investigations over nine years, which eventually led to the arrest and capture of a serial killer, who pleaded guilty to murdering eight of the women. He pointed out, once again, that the Ghana Police Service did not have a lie-detector.

At the time former President Jerry Rawlings made the allegations against leading members of President Kufuor's ruling New Patriotic Party, he was due to be called to give evidence before Ghana's National Reconciliation Commission about the alleged torture and murder of members of political opposition during his own period of nearly 20 years in power. Rawlings ruled Ghana for several months after leading a coup in June 1979. He came to power again in a second coup in 1982 and was subsequently elected president in 1992 and 1996. But he chose not to contest the presidential elections of 2000 which brought Kufuor to power.

Charles Ebo Quansah was only ever charged with 11 of the murders and the case against him in nine instances seems flimsy at best. Whether or not they now hold high office, the killers in the other cases are still at large.

Guatemala's Plague of Death

Guatemala is a paradise for serial killers. In a population of just 15 million, two women are murdered there every day. Even more men are murdered, but the gap is closing fast.

In 2005, 665 women were killed – more than 20 percent up on the previous year. No one really knows why because the crimes are rarely investigated. According to the BBC, not one of those 665 murders has been solved.

The newspapers in the capital Guatemala City carry a regular tally of the number of female corpses found dumped in the streets. But these discoveries are so commonplace that a regular murder barely rates a sentence at the bottom of an inside page. A short paragraph may be given over to the story if the woman had been tortured, trussed naked in barbed wire, scalped, decapitated, dismembered, abandoned on wasteland or, as is common, dumped in empty oil drums that serve as giant rubbish bins. Some reports mention in passing that "death to bitches" or some other insult has been carved into the woman's flesh. Rarely, though, is there any mention that the woman or girl – sometimes as young as eight or nine – has been raped. According to director of Guatemala City's central morgue Dr Mario Guerra the majority have.

Little effort is made to identify the victims. They have often been taken far from the place where they were abducted and subjected to unimaginable tortures before being killed. Many are so badly mutilated they are unrecognizable. In Guatemala, there is no fingerprint or DNA database, no crime or victim profiling and no real forensic science. No one investigates and witnesses do not talk. It can take a woman's family months to trace their daughter to the morgue. Some are never claimed. They are simply designated "XX", or "identity unknown" and buried in unmarked communal graves.

Guatemala is a lawless country where people kill with impunity. This began in the 1950s when the United Fruit Company, fearful of losing its holdings under government land reforms, encouraged CIA efforts to foster a military coup, destabilizing the country. Left-wing guerrillas took to the hills. Civil war raged for 36 years. Large areas of the countryside were razed and the rural population, mainly Mayan Indian, were massacred. Villagers were herded into churches, which were set on fire. Whole families were sealed alive in wells. Politicians were assassinated with impunity. Women were routinely raped before being mutilated and killed. The wombs of pregnant women were cut open and foetuses strung from trees. Life became very cheap indeed.

By the time the UN brokered a peace deal in 1996, over 200,000 had been killed, 40,000 "disappeared" and 1.3 million had fled the country or became internal refugees – all this in a country of little over ten million. Today the graves of entire massacred villages are being exhumed, yet no one has ever been held responsible for these crimes.

In 1998 the Catholic Church published a report saying that 93 percent of those who had perished in the preceding decades of genocide had died at the hands of the armed forces and paramilitary death squads. Ronald Reagan described the accusation of genocide as a "bum rap" and the bishop who wrote this report was bludgeoned to death on his doorstep. To placate foreign outrage, three army officers were convicted of his murder.

Once the civil war was over, the paramilitary squads were stood down and those in the army responsible for the sadistic repression were eased out. Three generations of killers now walk the streets of a country awash with guns. There are at least 1.5

million unregistered firearms in Guatemala and an estimated 84 million rounds of ammunition were imported in 2005 alone.

Many former paramilitaries found employment in the police force, corrupting it. Drug traffickers have moved in and organized crime has moved into the highest ranks of the government. In 2003, Amnesty International labelled Guatemala "a corporate Mafia state" controlled by "hidden powers" – an "unholy alliance between traditional sectors of the oligarchy, some new entrepreneurs, the police, military and common criminals".

In 2005, the ombudsman's office issued a report saying it had received information implicating 639 police officers in criminal activities in the past 12 months. The crimes range from extortion and robbery to rape and murder. As most of the population is afraid to report crime committed by the authorities, this figure is almost certain to be a considerable underestimate of police complicity.

"A key element in the history of Guatemala is the use of violence against women to terrorize the population," says director of the Centre for Legal Action on Human Rights Eda Gaviola. "Those who profit from this state of terror are the organized criminals involved in everything from narco-trafficking to the illegal adoption racket, money-laundering and kidnapping. There are clear signs of connections between such activities and the military, police and private security companies, which many ex-army and police officers joined when their forces were cut back."

Guatemala also has a particularly "macho" culture. A man can dodge a charge of rape if he marries his victim – provided she is over the age of 12. A battered wife can only prosecute her husband if her injuries are visible for over ten days. Having sex with a minor is only an offence if the girl can prove she is "honest" and did not act provocatively. And in some communities it is accepted that fathers "introduce" their daughters to sex.

Then there are the *pandilleros* – the gangsters who live in the poorest barrios of Guatemala city. Vicious infighting takes place between rival street gangs – known here as *maras*, after a breed of swarming ants. This makes Guatemala City one of the deadliest cities in the world, with a murder rate five times higher than even Bogotá in war-torn Colombia, per capita.

The country's largest gang, the Mara Salvatrucha, has now spread throughout Central America and northwards. From California, its tentacle have reached out across the United States. In 2005, it was held responsible for two killings in Long Island and is increasingly making its presence felt on the East Coast. In Guatemala, young women are often the victims of inter-gang rivalries. Usually the authorities dismiss the casualties as prostitutes.

But 19-year-old Manuela Sachaz was no prostitute. She was a baby-sitter, who had recently arrived in Guatemala City to look after Anthony Hernandez, the 10-month-old son of working couple Monica and Erwin Hernandez. Together they shared a small apartment on the second floor of a block in the Villa Nueva district of Guatemala City.

On 23 March 2005, the child's mother Monica Hernandez came home from work. She had no key to the apartment and there was no answer from Manuela inside. She went to see her mother Cervelia Roldan to ask her if she had seen Manuela. She had not and together they went back to the apartment together and started calling out Manuela's name, but there was no answer.

A middle-aged police officer lived in a nearby apartment. He came to the front door of his apartment block.

"It was about five in the afternoon," Cervelia Roldan recalled, "but he was wearing just his dressing gown. He seemed very agitated and told us to look for Manuela in the market."

When Erwin Hernandez arrived home and again got no answer, he broke a window and opened the apartment door. Inside he found the body of the baby-sitter and their child. Manuela was lying on the floor in a pool of blood. The baby was sitting in a high chair, his breakfast still on the table in front of him. Both had been beheaded. The nanny had also been raped and mutilated. Her breasts and lips had been cut off, her legs slashed.

Three days later their police neighbour shaved off his beard and moved away.

"Neighbours told me later how he used to pester Manuela," says Cervelia. She claims that, after the double murder, Manuela's bloodstained clothing was found in the policeman's house. The authorities dispute this. They say the blood on the clothing did not match that of the baby or his nanny.

Cervelia says she has seen the policeman in the neighbourhood several times since the killings.

"He laughs in my face," she says. "What I want is justice, but what do we have if we can't rely on the support of the law?"

In mid-December 2001 Maria Isabel Veliz was just a happy teenage girl with a part-time job in a shop. Earlier that year she had celebrated her 15th birthday by attending a church service wearing a white dress with flowers in her hair. She had a deep religious faith.

"Sometimes my daughter would visit me at work and pretend she needed to use my computer for her homework. But what she really wanted was to leave me a note telling me how much she loved me," said her mother Rosa Franco, a secretary who had been studying for a law degree.

"She was proud of what I was trying to do," said Rosa, who was left to raise her daughter and two younger sons alone. In a note written on Valentine's Day that year, Maria told her mother to "always look ahead and up, never down". That has been almost impossible since the day her daughter disappeared.

Rosa remembers every detail of the day her daughter vanished.

"As usual, she did not want breakfast – she wanted to stay thin – though I persuaded her to have a bowl of cornflakes before she left for work," Rosa said. "I had given my daughter permission to work in a shop during the Christmas holidays, as she wanted to buy herself some new clothes. I wasn't well that day and went to sleep early. When I woke up the next day and my daughter wasn't there, I went to the police to report her missing. They said she'd probably run away with a boyfriend."

That night, while watching a round-up of the news, Rosa recognized the clothing Maria Isabel had been wearing when she left for work the day before. The body of her daughter had been found lying face down on wasteland west of Guatemala

City. Her hands and feet had been bound with barbed wire. There was a rope around her neck. Her hair had been cut short and all her nails had been bent back. Her face was disfigured from numerous punches, her body punctured with small holes. She had been raped and stabbed.

When Rosa went to the morgue and discovered the brutal details of her daughter's injuries, she fainted.

"When I collapsed, they told me not to get so worked up," says Rosa, who later suffered a heart attack.

Rosa then began pushing the authorities to find her daughter's killers. She gave them telephone records showing that Maria's mobile phone had been used after her death. And she tracked down witnesses who had seen her daughter being pulled from a car. The police accused Rosa of meddling and denounced her daughter publicly as a prostitute. Such smear tactics are often used to intimidate the families of murder victims.

Undeterred, Rosa continued to demand that the police investigate the death of her daughter. Instead they merely increased the level of intimidation. Rosa's teenage sons are often followed home from school. Cars are parked outside her house day and night, their occupants watching – undeterred even when a journalist visited to check out her story. Human-rights workers told the *Sunday Times* that such surveillance was a sign that the murder had a connection with officialdom and organized crime.

"I'm afraid," Rosa said. "But when I see reports of more and more murders of girls and women, I know what other mothers are going through. I vow I will not give up my fight."

In 2006, BBC correspondent Olenka Frankiel went to Guatemala to investigate the killings there. She found 21-year-old Claudia Madrid lying dead in the gutter. She had been shot while out for a walk with her children.

"Investigators walk past her husband in the morgue as he waits to identify her body," said Frankel. "They will never question him."

The husband was phlegmatic.

"It's the fashion here to murder women," he said. "They never investigate such third class crimes."

Also in the morgue were two refuse sacks containing the body of a woman cut into 19 pieces and found in the street.

"Her decapitated head lies in the road," said Frankiel. "Police remove her limbs from the plastic bags to show the press. If no one comes to identify her she will be classed XX, and buried in an unmarked grave."

Then there was the naked swollen body of another woman found in a dried up river bed.

"Her mouth hangs open," said Frankel. "Her eyes and a gash in her skull have been pecked by vultures. An investigator says: 'She was probably a prostitute.' He points at her hands. 'Red nail varnish,' he says . . . In Guatemala, the victim is always to blame. Another XX."

Olenka Frankiel came across a dental technician whose neighbours ran to tell him they had seen kidnappers force his 20-year-old daughter into a car. He went to the police and begged them to put up road blocks to help save her. They told him nothing could be done for 24 hours. By then she was dead. Her body was found, mutilated and covered in teeth marks. She had been shot numerous times.

"I don't want to live," he told human-rights activist Norma Cruz. "I wish someone would shoot me."

"There is total indifference from the authorities to these crimes," says Cruz.

Months later, the man returned to the home he and his family had abandoned in fear and found the blood- and saliva-stained clothes his daughter was wearing when she was killed. This treatment of vital evidence is commonplace. It is routinely contaminated and returned to the families, or buried with the victim.

The police were no more helpful when Nancy Peralta went missing just a few months after Maria Isabel Veliz. When Nancy's younger sisters Maria Elena and Liliana reported that the 30-year-old accountancy student had not returned home from university in February 2002, the police told them to come back a few days later if she did not show up. The following day, their father read that the body of an unidentified young woman had been found on the outskirts of Guatemala City. He phoned the morgue but was told that it could not be that of his daughter as her physical description did not match. However an item of clothing on the body recovered was the same as one she had been wearing when she left home. When he went to the morgue to check, he found his daughter had not only been killed, but her body had been horrifically mutilated. She had been stabbed 48 times and her head was practically severed.

"When I talk to the police, they refer to my sister jokingly as 'the living dead'," says Nancy's sister Maria Elena, who is now studying law in the hope of bringing her sister's murderer to justice. "They insisted that she was not dead as some other student had assumed her identity to enrol on a new university course. They showed no interest in investigating what had happened."

One complaint of the Peralta family and Rosa Franco is that even the most basic forensic tests that could help identify the murderers were never carried out at the morgue. Morgue chief Dr Guerra complains of the lack of a forensic laboratory on site and the absence of DNA-testing facilities in the country. If they were taken, sample would have to be flown to Mexico or Costa Rica for analysis.

"Until a few years ago, the US helped train our workers in forensic science," said Guerra. "But now that help has stopped."

Police Chief Mendez, who runs a special unit set up in 2005 to look into the murder of women, explained why less than 10 percent of cases are investigated and, of the 527 murders of women in 2004, only one resulted in prosecution.

"Women are coming out of their homes and participating in all aspects of society more," he said. "Many men hate them for this ... This is a country with many *machistas*."

Nearly 40 percent of the women killed are listed as housewives and over 20 percent as students.

Mendez says that the mutilations of women killed are the result of "satanic rituals" used as initiation ceremonies for new gang members. The Ministry of the Interior claims that Manuela Sachaz and Anthony Hernandez could have been murdered because Manuela was a gang member – even though the 19-

year-old had only recently arrived from the countryside and had little, if anything, to do with the *barrios*.

Believing that the Guatemalan authorities are being deliberately obstructive, the Peralta family and Rosa Franco are planning to take their cases to the Inter-American Commission on Human Rights set up in 1959. But most victims' families have neither the know-how or resources to launch such a legal fight. Instead they sit in queues waiting to talk to human-rights workers and beg for news about what is being done to bring those who murdered their loved ones to justice. The answer is usually nothing.

Despite the frequency of the killings, the Guatemalan police rarely admit that they have one or many serial killers on their hands. However, in 2000, they conceded that a man that they dubbed as "Guatemala's Jack the Ripper" was at large on the streets. In three months he strangled five prostitutes and they believed that he may also have killed streetwalkers in El Salvador and even Los Angeles. The killer uses plastic sheeting to strangle his victims and is fond of scrawling angry, moralistic messages on their backs in blood-red marker.

The killer began his work in Guatemala City on 27 January when police discovered the body of an unidentified prostitute who had been strangled in a run-down, pay-by-the-hour hotel downtown. On the victim's back, the killer wrote he "didn't like it, but couldn't help killing" and that his spree of murders had already taken the life of two prostitutes in Los Angeles. Authorities in California said they had no record of similar killings.

The body of Roxana Jamileth Molina was discovered two weeks later in a dingy hotel room on the western edge of Guatemalan capital. She had been strangled. On 6 March, the owner of a hotel nearby led police to the remains of another strangled unidentified prostitute.

Four days later, the killer's fourth victim was found in downtown Guatemala City. On the woman's body, etched on her back in flowery handwriting, was written: "Death to all the dogs. Seven down, three to go." More had plainly died. Then on 29 March, the body of a fifth strangled prostitute was found in Huehuetenango, 80 miles northwest of Guatemala City.

For once, they put officers on the streets at all hours, warning prostitutes and passing out computer-generated composites of the man they suspect was behind the killings. The pictures was compiled from witnesses who said they had seen the suspect enter various hotels with prostitutes who were later found murdered. The killer was depicted as a short, olive-skinned, 35-year-old man with sunken brown eyes and closely cropped black hair. The police said he had a Salvadorean accent and uses the last name Blanco.

"Everyone is scared," said Rosa, a prostitute who charges $5 a trick to support her two children. "They all say, 'I wonder if the next man I go with could be this killer.' What we do is dangerous . . . this killer is hunting us."

Even so, the prostitutes refuse to co-operate with the police. Although prostitution is not illegal in Guatemala, they have as much to fear from the police as their clients.

At one time, Enio Rivera, the director of Guatemala's national police force, claimed that the authorities were so close to an arrest that the suspect left the country.

"We're afraid our suspect has fled to El Salvador," Rivera told reporters in April 2001. "We have been in close contact with authorities there because we are convinced this man will kill again."

He said that police did not know for sure how many women the serial killer had slain but that authorities in neighbouring El Salvador were ready to blame the same suspect for the murder of a prostitute there that March. Rivera also said the killer had used his red marker to mark his victims with the letters MS, the initials of the gang "Mara Salvatrucha".

"If he returns to Guatemala, the prostitutes are the ones in danger," police spokesman Faustino Sanchez said. "If we are going to catch this delinquent, we will have to do it with their help."

It was only after this serial killer got away that murder statistics were compiled by sex and the number of women being killed became apparent. Human-rights workers, who are regularly subjected to death threats and intimidation, say blaming the murder of women on gang violence is a deliberate oversimplification of the problem. Women are not only being "killed like flies" because they are considered of no worth, they say, but also they are being used as pawns in power struggles between competing organized crime networks.

This problem, it seems, has been going on for millennia. In the rainforests to the north of modern-day Guatemala City, in the country's northern rainforest, archaeologists recently entering a long-sealed Mayan crypt found the remains of two women. One was pregnant. They were arranged in a ritual fashion, making it clear that they had been sacrificed as part of a power struggle between rival Mayan cities.

An attempt by the UN to set up a commission with powers to investigate and prosecute the country's "hidden powers", which they hope would serve as a model for other countries recovering from civil was, was dismissed by the Guatemalan authorities as "unconstitutional". A debate began about how the terms of the commission can be amended to make it acceptable. But as the talking continues, so does the killing.

On just one day in June 2006, 12-year-old Hilda Macario was eviscerated with a machete while resisting rape – Hilda survived, but was shunned by her community because of the stigma attached to sexual violence – and 21-year-old Priscilla de Villatoro was stabbed to death by her boyfriend for refusing to have an abortion.

"Women here are dying worse than animals," says Andrea Barrios of the Centre for Legal Action on Human Rights. "When the municipality announced this summer that it was launching a campaign to exterminate stray dogs, the public took to the streets in protest and it was stopped. But there is a great deal of indifference towards the murder of women, because a picture has been painted that those who die somehow deserve what they get."

Hilda Morales, the lawyer heading a network of women's groups formed as the problem has escalated: "Neither the police nor the government are taking this seriously. Yet what we are observing is pure hatred against women in the way they are killed, raped, tortured and mutilated."

The situation is unlikely to change, she says, unless international pressure is brought to bear. Meanwhile the murder figures, not just of women, but also of political dissidents, male and female, continue to soar.

"Despite these cruel figures," says Guatemala's President Oscar Berger, "I am optimistic. We have reformed the police and we have more radio patrols."

No one is holding their breath.

Iran's Spider Killings

A new gang of serial killers are at large in Mashhad, one of Iran's holiest cities. They have been strangling the local prostitutes and drug users and dumping them into local streets and canals. Newspapers have dubbed these slayings "the spider killings" because of the way the women were found wrapped in their black chadors.

The first body was found on a roadside in July 2000. The dead woman was 30-year-old Afsaneh, a convicted drug user and suspected "truck woman" – a prostitute who services truck drivers and delivery men. The following week, two more prostitutes were found strangled with their own headscarves. In both their scarves were tied with two knots on the right side of the neck.

Five months later, three more women were killed. The police then formally acknowledged a link between the killings and set up a special task force. It was thought the killings could be the work of religious vigilantes; the reform-minded parliament in Tehran ordered an inquiry. The authorities were especially sensitive about the killings because they occurred in Mashhad – the name literally means Place of Martyrdom. Iran's second biggest city, it is one of the most sacred sites for Iran's Shiite Muslims, drawing more than 100,000 pilgrims a year to the burial and shrine of the caliph Harun ar-Rashid and Ali ar-Rida, the eighth Shiite imam. But right next to the shrine there is an area inhabited by prostitutes and drug addicts. The drugs come from Afghanistan which is just a two-hour drive away and the general poverty of the city is fuelled by the 200,000 refugees who fled there from Afghanistan.

On 1 April 2001, following the parliamentary inquiry, the local investigative team was replaced with a special squad from Tehran. Within two weeks, three more prostitutes were dead, suggesting that the killings had a political motive.

On 27 July 2001, 39-year-old Saeed Hanei, a married man and father of three, was arrested. He confessed to the murder of 16 of 19 dead prostitutes in Mashhad over the past 12 months. He claimed to have been doing God's work. After he had despatched 12 women, the drought that had been gripping the region lifted. The rains, he said, were a sign that God approved of what he was doing, so he killed four more.

A volunteer in the Iran–Iraq war during the 1980s, Hanei declared that he was not a murderer, but rather that the deaths were a "continuation of the war effort". He was an "anti-street-woman activist" who was only doing God's will by ridding Iran of moral corruption. He believed the spider killings were acts of piety, saying that when the drought ended: "I realized God looked favourably upon me, that He had taken notice of my work."

He said he wanted to "clean his neighbourhood", adding: "I would have killed 150 if I hadn't been arrested."

Hanei would lure prostitutes to his apartment in late afternoon while his wife was out of the house, posing as a customer and often strangling them with their own scarves.

"Fourteen of 16 victims were junkies," Hanei claimed, "and two or three of them had drugs on them."

Indeed, all but one had convictions for drug offences or prostitution. All forms of prostitution have been banned in Iran since the 1979 Islamic revolution, but it has become more common in recent years. Hanei said that he began his murderous campaign after his wife was mistaken for a prostitute by a taxi driver. At first he went out looking for men who were soliciting prostitutes, but got beaten up, so he turned to killing the prostitutes instead.

Hanei's slaughter of street drew support from religious extremists and the conservative press.

"Who is to be judged?" wrote the newspaper *Jomhuri Islami*. "Those who look to eradicate the sickness or those who stand at the root of the corruption?"

Friends at the Mashhad bazaar said: "He did the right thing. He should have continued."

And the hard-line paramilitary group Ansar-e Hizbollah warned that declining morality among women could lead to more such killings.

"It is likely that what happened in Mashhad and Kerman could be repeated in Tehran," it said in its weekly publication.

However, within a few weeks of his arrest Hanei was charged with having "improper relationships" with his victims before strangling them, though Hanaei claimed that intelligence officers subjected him to psychological torture to force him to confess to adultery. As a result Hanei was charged with 13 counts of having sexual relations with married women as well as the 16 murders.

At his trial, Hanei insisted that the women he murdered were a "waste of blood" – a concept in Iran's Islamic code that meant the victims deserved to die. As families of the victims looked on, Hanei said it was his religious duty to cleanse society of corrupt elements.

This was of little comfort to ten-year-old Sahar and eight-year-old Sara, the children of Hanei's 14th victim. They recalled how their mother Firoozeh left home at about 5.30 p.m. one day to buy opium.

"We were all waiting for her but she never came home," said Sahar.

Hanei was sentenced to death, but he was shocked and angry when the moment came for his hanging in April 2003. Unlike at his highly publicized trial, there were no cameras at his public hanging to record how he screamed in protest, baffled that his ideological allies never came to his rescue.

"Even until the last second before his execution, Hanei thought someone in the government would come to save him," said young Iranian film-maker Maziar Bahari, who made the documentary *And Along Came a Spider* about Hanei.

Hanei's most vehement defender is his own 14-year-old son,

Ali, who said his father was "a great man" who was cleansing the Islamic republic of the "corrupt of the Earth".

"If they kill him tomorrow, dozens will replace him," Ali said before the execution. "Since his arrest, 10 or 20 people have asked me to continue what my Dad was doing. I say, 'Let's wait and see.'"

He was right. Police now fear that a gang of "spider killers" is now at work.

Ireland's Dublin Death-Dealer

In October 1998, the Irish Garda set up a six-man squad to track down a suspected serial killer responsible for the deaths of six young women aged between 17 and 26 who disappeared in the historic Leinster region of Ireland to the south of Dublin. Known as Operation Trace, it had come up with no leads by 2001 and was slimmed down to a staff of two.

Information about the six missing women and other cases the team had looked at were put into the Canadian Violent Crime Linkage System and every detail was fed into a serial killer profile system set up in the British National Crime Faculty in Bramshill College, Lancashire, England. The geographic profiling developed by the Canadian Detective Inspector Kim Rossmo was also employed there. But in October 2006 a detective took the files to the FBI academy at Quantico to be analyzed by the bureau's computer program ViCLAS – Violent Crime Linkage Analysis System. The FBI's profilers would also run them though their specialist computer systems.

The bureau was also provided with information on suspects on suspects, such as Robert Howard from County Laois, who raped and killed at least one young woman in London, but had been cleared for the murder of 15-year-old schoolgirl Arlene Arkinson, who went missing after attending a disco at Bundorn in County Donegal with friends in August 1994. She was last seen in a car driven by Howard. She has never been seen again, but the defence argued that the prosecution had to show that she was dead and

painted her as a troubled teenager who talked of running away.
After more than 21 hours of deliberation over six days, the jury
acquitted Howard. The court was never told of his previous
conviction in England and there have been allegations that his
activities were covered up by the security forces.

The Garda say that Operation Trace established that no single
suspect could have been responsible for all six disappearances,
but that in three cases the possibility of a serial killer exists and
they are still appealing for any information from the public.

"They're still out there," said a spokesman. "There are still
people who know and who are covering for the perpetrators."

But definite leads have been rare. In September 2005, the
Garda arrested the chief suspect in the disappearance of Fiona
Sinnott, along with another man and three women. The arrests
were made after fresh information about the possible location of
her body came to light. None of those held was charged but the
Garda excavated a field near Killinick in County Wexford.
Nothing was found.

Fiona Sinnott was from Bridgetown, County Wexford, and has
been missing presumed dead since 9 February 1998. She was last
seen leaving the Butler's pub in Broadway near Rosslare at closing
time with her former boyfriend and the father of her baby
daughter, Sean Carroll. Their daughter, Emma, was 11 months
old at the time.

Carroll has told the Garda that he spent the night at Sinnott's
cottage in Ballycushlane, County Wexford, and that she was there
next morning when he left.

In July 2005 two sites in the Mulrankin area, near her family
home in Bridgetown, were excavated by the Garda after a
clairvoyant contacted the Sinnott family. Again nothing was
found.

"The one thing that marks the killer out is his ability to get rid
of the body – which usually leaves us with no forensics, DNA or
MO," says Brian McCarthy, a veteran private eye who has been
on the trail for nearly ten years, on and off.

McCarthy was hired by the family of missing 26-year-old Irish-
American student Annie McCarrick, who was studying literature

in Dublin. He suspects that the man who was responsible for the disappearance of McCarrick, who went missing after visiting Johnny Fox's pub in Glencullen in the Dublin Hills on 3 March 1993, was also involved the cases of at least two other missing women – Deirdre Jacob and Jo Jo Dullard. All three were of a similar age and were last seen on their own, and they all went missing in an area less than 30 miles in diameter covering counties Kildare, Wicklow and Dublin. But that it as far as the evidence takes him.

Eighteen-year-old Deirdre Jacob was last seen on 28 July 1998, walking to home to Roseberry, Newbridge in County Kildare. She was a trainee schoolteacher and described as a very balanced person – not the type of person who would disappear voluntarily.

Beautician Jo Jo Dullard, aged 21, vanished on 9 November 1995 after making a call from a public phone box in Moone, County Kildare. She had phoned a friend to say she intended to hitch-hike from there to her home in Callan, County Kilkenny after missing the last bus. She hung up, saying a lift had arrived. Around that time a woman answering Jo Jo's description was seen leaning in the back door of a dark-coloured Toyota Carina-type car. The car and its driver have never been traced.

"There is linkage there, but no physical evidence – not even a piece of clothing," says McCarthy.

The serial killer theory was scoffed at when the Garda originally began investigating the disappearance of McCarrick back in March 1993. However, her father John McCarrick was a retired policeman. When he went to a Garda station to report his daughter missing he was shocked. The officer who dealt with him did not have a notepad, so he wrote the details on the back of his hand.

Far from content with this approach, McCarrick pulled strings back in the US. Eventually, the American ambassador Jean Kennedy Smith and Vice-President Al Gore lobbied the Irish government on behalf of the McCarrick family, prompting one of the largest missing persons investigations in Irish history. Meanwhile the McCarricks offered a $150,000 reward for information.

Five years after Annie McCarrick disappeared, Operation Trace was set up at Naas Garda Station. Soon they identified seven other missing people who fitted a similar disturbing pattern. They were young women, all from Leinster, of a similar age, leading busy, seemingly happy lives until they vanished without trace. They were not victims of suicide, accidents or organized crime. But the most troubling feature of all was that, as they were assumed to be dead, no trace of their bodies had ever been found.

"The facts speak for themselves," says retired detective inspector Gerry O'Carroll. "For decades we had virtually no missing women; now we have up to ten in a relatively small area around the east coast, with various common threads. I believe these women were victims of one or two serial killers working together."

O'Carroll has looked at the missing women's cases as part of his investigation of the 1999 slaying of 17-year-old Dun Laoghaire schoolgirl Raonaid Murray. He became convinced that the suspected murders of Annie McCarrick, Deirdre Jacob, Jo Jo Dullard and Fiona Sinnot were linked to those of 26-year-old part-time model Fiona Pender and 17-year-old Ciara Breen.

Fiona Pender, from Tullamore, County Offaly, was seven-and-a-half months pregnant when she disappeared on the evening of 23 August 1996. She was last seen leaving the flat she shared with her boyfriend in Church Street in the town. She had spent the previous day, shopping for baby clothes and was in good spirits, while Ciara Breen disappeared from her home in Batchelors Walk, Dundalk, in the early hours of 13 February 1997, taking no possessions with her.

Like Brian McCarthy, Gerry O'Carroll was intrigued with the fact that no bodies had been found. It then dawned on the detectives that there may have been earlier cases where the perpetrator was not so adept at concealing the evidence. Looking back through the files it appeared that the killer's first victim may have been 23-year-old Phyllis Murphy, who was found raped, strangled and partially hidden in bushes in the Wicklow Mountains in 1980.

The body of 23-year-old Patricia Furlong was dumped in the Dublin Mountains only a few miles from Glencullen in July 1982.

She had been raped and strangled. The late DJ Vinnie Connell was convicted of her murder ten years later, but the verdict was overturned by the Court of Criminal Appeal.

Five years after Patricia Furlong died, 27-year-old mother-of-two Antoinette Smith from Clondalkin on the outskirts of Dublin vanished after attending a David Bowie concert at Slane Castle in Meath. She had returned to Dublin and went to the Harp Bar on O'Connell Bridge before moving onto a discotheque in Parnell Street. Nine months later ramblers discovered her remains in a shallow grave at Glassamucky Breakers, Kilakee in the Dublin Mountains. She, too, had been raped and strangled. Her head was reported to have been covered by a plastic bag.

Three years later, on the same stretch of mountain bog where Antoinette Smith's body was found, a man unearthed a woman's hand in the turf bank he was clearing. It belonged to 30-year-old mother-of-two Patricia Doherty from Tallaght, Dublin. She had last been seen alive six months before on 23 December 1991 when she left her home to do some Christmas shopping.

Patricia Doherty's and Antoinette Smith's remains were found not far from Johnny Fox's pub, where Annie McCarrick disappeared fifteen months later. And Patricia Furlong's body was dumped only a few miles away. Brian McCarthy suspects at least two other missing women, Jo Jo Dullard and Deirdre Jacob may also be buried in the mountains.

His prime suspect is a married man with children who can be placed in or around the scenes where Annie McCarrick, Deirdre Jacob and Jo Jo Dullard went missing. According to McCarthy, the man had a history of sexual violence against women, but his killing spree has temporarily been halted by a spell in jail on another charge.

There are indications that the killer claimed another victim, though she was outside the age range of this other prey. This was Eva Brennan, age 40, from south Dublin, who disappeared after leaving her parents' home in Terenure to return to her flat in Rathgar in July 1993. Perhaps her killer is in jail, but he may soon be at large again.

Italy's Gay Killings

The murder of a man paid by opera singers to clap during their performances rekindled fears that a gay serial killer may be at large in Italy.

Although 57-year-old Salvatore Romano was not known to be gay, detectives believe that his suffocation and bludgeoning with a brandy bottle bore all the hallmarks of a killer who targeted figures connected with high culture. Romano was the last of the *capoclaques*, professional clappers who led the applause from the gods.

Mr Romano was found on Sunday 8 September 2002 in his home, where it is thought that he had dined with his killer or killers. One report said police found three plates and three glasses.

Police were looking for a young man seen running down the stairs with a cigarette in his mouth and for Mr Romano's red scooter, which was used for the escape. A fingerprint on a glass was one of the few clues.

A neighbour said that, at about the same time, she heard someone screaming: "Help me, I'm dying."

Mr Romano was gagged and his feet and hands were tied to his neck – a classic Mafia method of inducing suffocation and now typical of the homosexual murders.

There have been dozens of similar cases in Italy since 1990. There are more than 19 unsolved gay murders in and around the Italian capital. Two occurred in the Pigneto area of the city where Mr Romano lived.

On 5 January 1998, former senior assistant to the pope 67-year-old Enrico Sini Luzi was found in his home near the Vatican wearing only his underwear and socks, with his head beaten in. On his wrists there was adhesive left by sticky tape; a red cashmere scarf was tightened around his neck. His home showed no sign of forcible entry.

Luzi's former position as a "gentleman of His Holiness" is a voluntary one, usually held by members of well-to-do families, which involves assisting visitors in papal ceremonies.

Franco Grillini of the Italian homosexual lobby group Arci-Gay/ArciLesbica told Agence France Presse: "The victim is a

wife's lovers. Mele also mentioned a third lover of his wife, Francesco Vinci, who had been jailed briefly following an accusation of adultery by his own wife. Then it came out that Barbara had been the lover of Francesco Vinci's two brothers Giovanni and Salvatore as well. Mele said that his wife's killer could easily have been one of her numerous lovers. The police now had more suspects than they could easily handle.

But the following day, 23 August 1968, Mele confessed to the murder. But he also incriminated Salvatore Vinci who, he said, had given him the gun. Mele said that, when his wife and son had not returned home by 11.20 p.m., he went looking for them. When he reached the town square of Lastra a Signa, he met Salvatore Vinci, who told him that Barbara had gone to the cinema with Lo Bianco and Natalino. Vinci chided Mele for allowing his wife to cuckold him so publicly. He told him that he had to put a stop to the situation. Vinci had a gun with him, Mele said, and the two of them drove to the Giardino Michelacci movie theatre in Signa on the other side of the Arno.

They found Lo Bianco's Alfa Romeo parked outside and waited for the couple to come out of the cinema. When Lo Bianco and Barbara, with Natalino in her arms, appeared and drove off in Antonio's car, Mele and Vinci followed. They stopped at the cemetery just outside Signa. When they started to make love, Vinci pulled out the gun and handed to him, Mele said.

Mele then walked up to the car and started firing, continuing until the gun was empty. Afterwards they drove to the bridge in Signa and threw the gun in the Arno, then went home.

"I killed my wife and her lover because I was tired of continually being humiliated," Mele concluded. "My wife had been cheating on me for a number of years, but it was only a few months ago that I decided to do away with her."

There were great holes in this confession. The most glaring was that he had failed to mention how Natalino had turned up at the farmhouse. If the boy had been woken by the gunfire, surely he would have recognized his own father. Nevertheless Mele was formally arrested and held pending formal charges.

The police then tried to find the weapon, but when a prosecutor questioned Mele about the gun again, he changed his story. Instead of throwing it in the Arno, Mele said, he had given it back to Salvatore Vinci. Soon after Mele retracted his entire confession and began accusing Vinci's brother Francesco of the double murder. It was Francesco who had owned the weapon, Mele said, and Francesco who had killed Barbara and her lover.

This change of story did not help him in court and, in 1970, Mele was found guilty of the double murder and jailed for 14 years – a lenient sentence was handed down on the grounds of partial insanity. And that was thought to be the end of it. Then there was another double murder.

On the moonless night of 14 September 1974, with Stefano Mele safely in jail, 19-year-old Pasquale Gentilcore and 18-year-old Stefania Pettini parked up in Pasquale's father's Fiat 127 overlooking the River Sieve in Borgo San Lorenzo, just north of Florence and 18 miles from Signa. They were enjoying a romantic moment when someone began firing at them. The next day a passer-by found the car and called the police.

Detectives found the half-naked body of Pasquale Gentilcore in the driver's seat. He was peppered with gunshot wounds. Copper-jacket shell casings surrounded the scene and there was no evidence of a struggle.

Outside the car to the rear was the naked body of Stefania Pettini. She had been stabbed and mutilated. Her corpse was posed with her arms and legs spread-eagled, and a branch protruded from her lacerated vagina. Her handbag was found in a nearby field, its contents scattered.

A post mortem showed that Pasquale had been shot five times, killing him. Stefania had been shot three times, but she had still been alive when the killer carried her from the car and slashed her. She had died of one of 96 stab wounds inflicted on her naked body. The knife had a single-edged blade 1.5 cm wide and between 10 and 12 cm long. The gun was a model 73 or 74,. 22 automatic Beretta, while the bullets were of a distinctive Winchester type made in Australia in the 1950s.

A mentally unstable man named Giuseppe Francini walked

into the police station and confessed to the murders, but he was unable to describe in detail how the killings were carried out. The police also suspected Guido Giovannini, a voyeur reported to have been spying on couples in the area, and 53-year-old self-proclaimed healer Bruno Mocali. But they could find no evidence linking either man to the crime, and they were eventually ruled out. The perpetrator was plainly a sexual deviant maniac, but the police, who had not yet made the link to the 1968 murder and with no clues or leads to pursue, filed the case away as unsolved.

Seven years later, on another warm summer's night, there was another double murder. On 6 June 1981 an unknown gunman fired eight shots into a Fiat Ritmo. Inside were 30-year-old Giovanni Foggi and his lover, 21-year-old Carmela de Nuccio. The following morning, a police sergeant on a country walk with his young son spotted the copper-coloured Ritmo parked at the roadside. The sergeant then noticed a woman's handbag was lying beside the driver's side door with its contents scattered on the ground. Taking a closer look, he noticed that the driver's side window had been smashed. At the wheel was a young man whose throat seemed to have been slashed.

When detectives arrived, they found the body of a female victim in a ditch some 20 yards away from the car. She had been stabbed in the abdomen and her T-shirt and jeans were slashed. Her legs were spread and her genital region cut out and removed. It seems the perpetrator had had plenty of time to perform this crude surgery. There were no witnesses and no tracks.

The post mortem demonstrated that both had died of multiple gunshot wounds while in the car. The young man had then been stabbed once in the chest and twice in the neck. The woman's dead body had then been carried to the ditch. The medical examiner concluded that the girl's genitals had been excised with an extremely sharp instrument, which the killer plainly had some knowledge of using.

Ballistics revealed that the bullets came from a .22-calibre automatic pistol. Again they were the same distinctive Winchester rounds. Veteran detectives quickly made the connection with the

Gentilcore and Pettini case. The bullets from all four bodies matched. Florence, it seemed, had a serial killer on its hands – though still no one had made the connection with the 1968 crime.

The red Ford of peeping Tom Enzo Spalletti had been seen parked nearby. When questioned he gave a confused alibi. Detectives' interest was further piqued by the fact that he mentioned a copper-coloured Ritmo and two dead bodies to his wife at 9.30 a.m. on the morning they had been discovered, telling her that he had read the story in the newspaper – though the papers didn't report the murders until the following day. Spalletti was arrested and jailed pending trial.

Four months later Spalletti had to be freed when another couple were murdered in exactly the same way. As he was behind bars, this was plainly a crime he could not have committed.

On 23 October 1981, 26-year-old Stefano Baldi and his 24-year-old girlfriend Susanna Cambi decided to spend the evening parked in their Volkswagen at a beauty spot near Calenzano, five miles north of Florence. Later that evening, another courting couple found their bodies.

Stefano Baldi was found next to the car. Half-naked, he appeared to have been shot and stabbed many times. Susanna Cambi was lying on the other side of the car. Her wounds were similar to Baldi's – only her genitals had been excised like those of Carmela de Nuccio.

The medical examiner concluded that both victims had been shot through the front windscreen of the car, but were both still alive when they were stabbed. The same .22 Beretta as before had been used. The knife used to stab the victims had a single-edged blade, between 5 and 7 cm long and approximately 3 cm wide.

The instrument used on Susanna Cambi's genitals appeared to be the same as the one used on Carmela De Nuccio, but the murderer seemed to have been rushed. The killer had performed the operation with less precision and a larger area was excised. He had cut through the abdominal wall and punctured the intestine.

The press now dubbed the killer the "Monster of Florence" and two separate couples came forward and reported that they had seen a lone male driver speeding from the crime scene in a red Alfa

GT. However, despite the growing press coverage no further leads were forthcoming.

The following summer another couple were targeted. On 19 June 1982, 20-year-old Antonella Migliorini and her boyfriend, 22-year-old mechanic, Paolo Mainardi, were making love in a parking spot off the Via Nuova Virgilio, near Montespertoli, 12 miles south west of Florence. They were just putting their clothes back on when the killer appeared out of the bushes and started shooting.

Antonella Migliorini died instantly but Paolo Mainardi survived the initial burst of gunfire. Although badly injured, he started the Seat, switched on the headlights and slammed the car into reverse. But he ended up in a ditch. The killer walked over, shot out the headlights and emptied the pistol into the wounded driver. Then he pulled out the ignition keys and threw them into the undergrowth.

When he left, Paolo Mainardi was still alive. Unfortunately he was not found until the next morning and died a few hours later, without regaining consciousness and before he was able to give the police any vital clues. However, Silvia della Monica, the prosecutor assigned to the case, persuaded the newspapers to report that Paolo Mainardi was alive when he reached hospital and that he had given a description of the killer before he died. All of the reporters agreed, and the information appeared in the afternoon paper.

The idea was to rattle the killer. It worked. After the afternoon paper hit the streets, one of the paramedics who had accompanied Paolo Mainardi to the hospital received two telephone calls from a person who first claimed to be with the prosecutor's office. The second time he identified himself as the killer and he wanted to know what Mainardi had said before he died.

A few days later, police Sergeant Francesco Fiore made the connection to the 1968 murder of Barbara Locci and Antonio Lo Bianco, when he had been seconded to Montespertoli from Signa, ten miles away. Francesco began to wonder if there was a connection with the crimes of the Monster. At his insistence, the bullets were compared. They matched. Not only had all the bullets been fired by the same .22 Beretta and were the same distinctive Australian batch, they all came from a single box of 50 shells. It was clear that the Monster of Florence had killed Barbara Locci and Antonio Lo Bianco in 1968 – or, at least, was using the same weapon and bullets.

Plainly Stefano Mele, Locci's jealous husband, could not be the Monster since he had been in jail ever since. But he was not released. The Carabinieri simply assumed that he had an accomplice in the original crime who had continued killing after Mele was imprisoned. They interviewed Mele again, but he continued to claim his complete innocence and refused to co-operate with the investigators. Nevertheless, in August 1982 police arrested Francesco Vinci, who Mele had first accused 14 years before.

On 9 September 1983, Wilhelm Horst Meyer and his friend Uwe Rusch Sens, both 24, were asleep in a Volkswagen camper van some 19 miles south of Florence when the Monster paid them a visit. He fired through the window, killing the German holiday-makers instantly. There were no mutilations to the bodies, so the police did not immediately associate the murders with the Monster. It was only when ballistics found that the bullets were from the same batch as those used in the other killings that the connection was made.

The police wondered whether the killer had changed his pattern. Or perhaps he had simply made a mistake. One of the victims had long blonde hair and could have been mistaken for a girl, especially at night. There were reports that the two men were homosexual lovers, though there is no evidence to that effect. It may also have been, when the killer realized that he did not have a dead girl on his hands, that he abandoned his plans to stab and mutilate the bodies.

However, the murder of Horst Meyer and Uwe Senes brought to light some other common features of the crimes. The killer usually struck on a Friday or Saturday night, when the moon was hidden by the clouds. The victims had all spent their last evenings at a discotheque – except Barbara Locci and Antonio Lo Bianco who had been to the cinema. The killer had also rifled through the woman's belongings. Was he looking for something that might contect him to the victim? Or was he hunting for some macabre souvenir?

Although Francesco Vinci had been in custody at the time of the murder of Horst Meyer and Uwe Senes, his lawyer failed to persuade the judges to release him, even though he clearly could not have committed the latest murders. State Prosecutor Mario Rotella now believed that the crimes were committed by a gang of Sardinian-born peasants, of which Mele and Vinci were members. They arrested Mele's brother Giovanni Mele and a friend Piero Mucciarini. Both remained in custody until a few months after the next murders.

Other bizarre theories were doing the rounds. Religious historian Massimo Introvigne pointed out that Florence, home of Dante's "Inferno", had long been linked to sorcery. Occult sects, he said, were stalking lovers' lanes to commit ritual murders. Detectives had already toyed with the idea that the killer had taken the women's genitals to be used as a trophy by some religious cult.

There was more unsettling news. Shortly after the murder of the two German campers, the paramedic who had accompanied Paolo Mainardi to the hospital in 1982 got another phone call from the killer, demanding to know that Mainardi had said before he died. Disturbingly, the paramedic was in Rimini at the time. How did the killer know he was on holiday and how did he know where to contact him?

At 9.40 p.m. 29 July 1984, 18-year-old sales girl Pia Rontini and 21-year-old university student Claudio Stefanacci were parked in a sky-blue Fiat Panda off a provincial road between Dicomano and Vicchio, just north of Florence. They were just about to make love when the killer began firing at them.

Claudio's body was found on the backseat of his car wearing only underpants and a vest. He had been shot four times and stabbed ten times. Not far from the vehicle, behind some bushes, lay the naked body of Pia. She had been shot twice and stabbed twice in the head. The killer had then dragged her by the ankles some ten yards into the bushes. As before she had been left in a spread-eagled position and her genitals had been excised. This time the killer had also cut off her left breast and slashed her body more than a hundred times. The police then asked, did the removal of the left breast have any occult significance? Or was the killer becoming more sadistic?

Again the knife used was single-edged. Both victims had been shot through the car window. The weapon was the familiar .22 Beretta automatic and the bullets matched those used in the previous crimes. No fingerprints were recovered from the scene and detectives had come to believe that the killer wore surgical gloves during the murders. Sixteen years had passed since the first murder and, despite the arrest of four suspects, the police were no closer to stopping the "Monster of Florence".

The killer struck again over a year later. On 8 September 1985, he murdered a French couple as they camped in the San Casciano area just south of Florence. The murderer slashed open their tent and fired several shots into the bodies of 25-year-old Jean-Michel Kraveichvili and 36-year-old Nadine Mauriot. According to the medical examiner, they had been making love at the time with the man lying on his back and the woman on top of him.

Nadine Mauriot had been shot four times. Three bullets had penetrated her skull; a fourth had passed through her throat. Kraveichvilj had also been hit four times – twice in the upper arm, once in the mouth and once in the right elbow. Even so, he managed to get to his feet and scrambled out of the tent but, after about 30 yards, the killer caught up with him and stabbed him to death. Then he pushed him down a bank into some bushes. The killer then returned to the tent, dragged out Nadine Mauriot's body and began to mutilate it.

According to the medical examiner, the shots were fired at a close range – no more than 20 inches. Once again the woman's genitals and left breast were removed. It was estimated that this would have taken around ten minutes. In that time, he was not disturbed.

Soon after detectives thought they had got lucky. A copper-jacketed Winchester bullet was found on the pavement in front of a hospital nearby. The idea that the killer used surgical gloves and his evident interest in dissection lead the police to question the hospital staff. But no suspect emerged and the trail went cold again.

The following day an envelope arrived at the office of assistant public prosecutor Silvia Della Monica. The address was made up of letters cut from a newspaper or magazine in the style of a ransom note. It contained a single spelling mistake. Inside the envelope was a folded sheet of paper that had been glued along its edges. Inside the paper was a small plastic bag. Inside that was a cube of flesh cut from Nadine Mauriot's missing breast. The killer was now taunting the authorities.

In 1986 the police admitted their strategy of focusing on the Sardinian peasant gang was wrong. They began again from scratch and, over the next eight years, questioned over 100,000 people.

By 1991 several leads seemed to point in the direction of Pietro Pacciani, a 68-year-old semi-literate farm labourer in San Casciano whose hobbies included hunting and taxidermy. In 1951, Pacciani had killed a travelling salesman he had caught sleeping with his fiancée. He had stabbed the man 19 times. He had then stomped the man to death and sodomized his corpse. Released from prison after 13 years, he married, but was jailed again from 1987 to 1991 for wife-beating and the sexual molestation of his two young daughters.

Anecdotal evidence suggested that Pacciani was involved in the Satanic group with Giancarlo Lotti, Giovanni Faggi and Mario Vanni – all well known voyeurs who haunted local lovers' lanes. Pacciani and Vanni were also said to have participated in black masses, using female body parts, at the house in San Casciano. Nurses at a clinic where Pacciani had worked as a gardener claimed he told them a mysterious doctor presided over these occult ceremonies.

Florence's head of detectives, Michele Giuttari, had his doubts. He believed that the semi-literate Pacciani was not organized enough to have planned the crimes and too slipshod to have got away with them. Nevertheless, on 17 January 1993, Pacciani was arrested.

Pietro Pacciani finally went on trial on 1 November 1994 charged with 14 counts of murder – the 1968 murder of Barbara Locci and Antonio Lo Bianco were left off the indictment.

Determined to vindicate themselves, the prosecutors demanded
that the trial be televized. It became compulsive viewing.
Although the evidence was grisly – one police guard collapsed
during a particularly gory session – the case against Pacciani was
largely circumstantial. Throughout he protested his innocence.
Nevertheless, he was convicted of 14 murders and sentenced to
life imprisonment. As he was dragged from court, he screamed: "I
am as innocent as Christ on the cross."

In February 1996 the court of appeal overturned Pacciani's
conviction after the public prosecutor admitted the evidence
against him was unsound. But just hours before Pacciani was
released, his friends 70-year-old Mario Vanni, 54-year-old
Giancarlo Lotti and 77-year-old Giovanni Faggi were arrested
for their involvement in five of the double murders.

Detectives had returned to the theory that the Monster of
Florence was not just one killer but a gang. According to the
police Lotti confessed that he and Pacciani were responsible for
the killings. On 12 December 1996, the Court of Cassation
cancelled Pacciani's acquittal and ordered a new trial.

Pacciani never made it to his retrial for the Monster of Florence
murders. On 23 February 1998, he was found dead, face down on
the floor of his home with his shirt up around his neck and his
trousers down around his ankles. His face was blue and disfigured, and the police thought that the 71-year-old Pacciani had
died of a heart attack. But the post-mortem revealed that a
combination of drugs had caused his death. The investigating
magistrate, Paolo Canessa, believed that Pacciani was silenced in
case he revealed more details about the murderous cult at his
retrial.

On 24 March 1998, Mario Vanni and Giancarlo Lotti were
sentenced for their involvement in five of the double murders.
Vanni got life; Lotti 26 years. Giovanni Faggi was acquitted.

That should have been the end of it. But in 1994 Thomas
Harris, author of *The Silence of the Lambs*, had attended Pacciani's trial and he set his third Hannibal Lecter book *Hannibal* in
Florence. While this was being filmed in the city, it stirred
memories of the Monster of Florence and people began to ask,

if Pacciani had been murdered, surely the Monster of Florence himself, if he was an individual, or another member of one of the gang, if he was not, was still at large. As it is, the case remains officially unsolved.

Mexico's Juarez Ripper

In Ciudad Juarez, Mexico, directly across the border from El Paso, Texas, there is a killing spree that has lasted for more than a decade and shows no sign of abating. In February 2005, Amnesty International put the body count at over 370, with more than 400 potential victims listed as missing. That year alone the death toll topped 28, according to the BBC. Even so, in August 2006, Mexico's Federal Government dropped its investigation.

The first official victim of *El Depredador Psicópata* – or "the Juarez Ripper" – was Alma Chavira Farel, whose body was found on 23 January 1993 in an empty lot in a middle-class neighbour-hood of Campestre Virreyes. She had been raped both vaginally and anally, beaten and strangled. There was a bruise on her chin and she had a black eye. She was wearing a white sweater with a design on it and short blue pants. No mutilations were reported at the time, but later victims were said to have suffered slashing wounds to their breasts similar to those of Chavira. In all like-lihood she was not the killer's first victim at all. Juarez is a city of transients where disappearances exceed recorded homicides each year.

No one is sure how many people live in Ciudad Juarez. Official estimates hover around one million, while there are probably more like two million people there at any one time. Many are street people who don't show up in the official statistics. For others, it is a stopping-off place on their way to the US which lies just across the Rio Grande. It is also home to numerous drug traffickers and other criminals who use it as a temporary base for cross-border operations.

Under the North American Free Trade Agreement, Mexico has set up over 330 *maquiladoras* in Juarez. These are factories that use cheap labour to produce goods to sell over the border. The wages range between US$3 and US$5 a day. Nevertheless thousands of young uneducated female workers from southern Mexico, known collectively as *maquilladoras,* flock to work in these factories. The owners prefer hiring women because they are less trouble. They also put up with the squalid work conditions, sexual harassment and violent shanty towns where they are forced to live. Some 70 percent of the labour force is female.

This piques Mexican men's traditional Latin *machismo.* It also drives men into crime or to find work in the other traditional male preserve – the police force. However, the police earn so little that bribery is an accepted practice and there is enough drug money flowing through the city to ensure that the legal system is thoroughly corrupt. Any offence can be overlooked for the right price. Largely individual murders are overlooked, but it was hard to hide that the overall murder rate for women in Juarez is twice that of Mexico as a whole. The rate for women aged between 15 and 24 in Juarez is five times that of the rate in Tijuana, another border town, and more than ten times that of El Paso on the US side.

In May 1993, a second victim was added to the Juarez Ripper's list when a body was found on the slopes of Cerro Bola, a hill that carried a sign saying: "Read the Bible." She had been raped and strangled. A third corpse appeared in June; she had been stabbed and the body set on fire. On the 11th, another anonymous victim was found partially naked in the playground of Alta Vista High School on the way to a dirt road at the edge of the Rio Grande. She had been tied to a stake, raped, stabbed and had her head beaten in.

By the end of the year, 16 more murders had been added. The last, on 15 December, was "solved", along with three others – though the Juarez police had an unfortunate reputation for torturing confessions out of innocent suspects. In the dozen cases that remain unsolved, five of the victims remain unidentified. At least four were raped. Four had been stabbed to death and four strangled. One had been shot and one beaten to death. In two cases, the body was so badly decomposed that a cause of death could not be established.

The following year the Juarez police had eight unsolved murder cases involving women. In three other cases they named "probable suspects", but none of them were arrested. Three of the victims remain unidentified today. The ages of those identified ranged from 11 to 35. In the cases where the cause of death could be determined, one was beaten to death, one burned alive, two were stabbed and six strangled. At least four of the victims were also raped. State criminologist Oscar Maynez Grijalva was already warning that, in at least some of the cases, a serial killer was at work.

His words would be remembered the following year when a killer began to reveal a signature. Three of the four bodies found in September 1995 had their left nipple bitten off or their right breast severed. By then, at least 19 women had been slain – making 1995 the worst year yet. Eight of the victims are still unidentified. At least four had been raped. Where the cause of death was established, one was shot, one stabbed and six strangled. Again in two cases, "possible suspects" were named and the police claimed to have "solved" one of the murders. In October, they arrested Abdul Latif Sharif, an Egyptian chemist living in one of Juarez's wealthier neighbourhoods.

Sharif was arrested in 1995 after a prostitute accused him of raping her at his home. She claimed that Sharif also threatened to kill her and dump her corpse in Lote Bravo, a desert region south of town where the bodies of other victims were found. But these charges were dropped after the police had discovered that Sharif had dated 18-year-old Elizabeth Castro Garcia, who had been found raped and murdered in August.

In custody Sharif allegedly confessed to five *El Depredador Psicópata* murders. But publicly he has always maintained that he was innocent.

"They are pinning this all on me because I am a foreigner," he claimed. "I'm just a drunk, I'm not a murderer."

Sharif was born in Egypt in 1947. Later, he claimed to have been sexually abused as a child, sodomized by his father and other male relatives. In 1970, he emigrated to America and settled in New York City. He was known for drunken womanizing.

Lovers thought him charming and funny. Years after the event, it was said he had an obsessive interest in young girls.

Sacked for suspected embezzlement in 1978, he moved to New Hope, Pennsylvania. A former friend there named John Pascoe claimed that, on a deer-hunting expedition, Sharif tortured a wounded buck. Pascoe also claimed that girls seen in Sharif's company often disappeared later, though no missing person reports tied to Sharif ever surfaced. The friendship ended in 1980, Pascoe said, after he found possessions of a "missing" girl in Sharif's home and a spade caked in mud on the porch.

By 1981, Sharif had moved to Palm Beach, Florida. A talented chemist and engineer, Sharif was hired by the oil company Cercoa Inc., who gave him his own department. But then on 2 May 1981 he beat and raped a 23-year-old woman neighbour, later claiming that it was consensual sex that got a little rough. Afterwards, he showed remorse, saying: "Oh, I've hurt you. Do you think you need to go to a hospital?"

Cercoa hired a top lawyer for Sharif's defence who plea bargained the rape charge down to sexual battery and five years' probation, though the law called for the deportation of aliens conviction of crimes involving "moral turpitude". On 13 August, the night before he was to plead guilty, he attacked a second woman in her home in West Palm Beach. This time he kicked and threatened to kill her, before asking her to fix him a drink and for another date the following night.

The prosecutor of the first case was not informed of the second and, as soon as Sharif was paroled, he was rearrested, then bailed again. On 11 January 1982, Sharif was sentenced to 45 days in jail for the second attack and Cercoa finally sacked him.

Sharif moved to Gainesville, Florida, where he set up a company and was married briefly. The short-lived marriage ended in divorce when he beat his bride unconscious. On 17 March 1983, he beat and repeatedly raped a 23-year-old college student who answered his ad for a live-in housekeeper, telling her: "I will bury you out back in the woods. I've done it before, and I'll do it again." He was arrested and held without bail pending trial. Sharif escaped from the Alachua County jail, but was soon recaptured. However, other women who had told the police that he was terrorizing them now refused to co-operate further in case he escaped again. On 31 January 1984 Sharif was sentenced to 12 years imprisonment for rape. The prosecutor told local reporters that Sharif would be deported when he was released, though the authorities were seeking to tie him to unsolved murders in Florida and New Jersey. In January 1977, the body of a pretty 30-year-old brunette called Sandra Miller had been found at the side of the road. She had been killed by a single stab wound. Sharif worked at a chemical plant just two miles from the remote farmhouse where Miller lived with her five-year-old daughter and Sharif and Miller used the same bar. He was a prime suspect in the case

However, when Sharif was paroled in October 1989, he was not deported. Instead, he moved to Midland, Texas, when he got a job with Benchmark Research and Technology. His work there was so exceptional that the US Department of Energy singled him out for praise, and he was photographed shaking hands with US Senator Phil Gramm.

Sharif was arrested again 1991, this time for drink driving. It then came to the attention of the authorities and Sharif was liable for deportation. Hearings dragged on for two years. Then Sharif was arrested for holding a woman captive in his home and repeatedly raping her. His lawyers cut a deal. Sharif would leave the country voluntarily if the charges were dropped and, in May 1994, Sharif moved across the border to the exclusive Rincones de San Marcos district of Ciudad Juarez and worked at one of Benchmark's *maquiladora* factories.

On 3 March 1999 Sharif was convicted of the 1994 rape and murder of Elizabeth Castro Garcia, though six other murder charges were dropped. He was sentenced to 30 years in prison. The police named Sharif as the Ciudad Juarez serial killer, but the murders continued – even escalated – after his arrest. Between Sharif's arrest in October 1995 and the first week of April 1996 at least 14 more female victims were slain in Ciudad Juarez. Their ages ranged from ten to 30. In cases where the cause of death was established, one had been shot, one strangled and ten stabbed. At least four had been mutilated after death. Significantly, one – 15-

year-old Adrianna Torres – had her left nipple bitten off and her right breast severed. The scale of the slaughter was staggering. The police admitted that of the 520 people who had disappeared over the past 11 months, most were adolescent females. The populace was terrified.

The police then came up with a bizarre theory to explain why the killing continued while Sharif was in jail. After the raped and mutilated body of 18-year-old Rosario Garcia Leal was found in 8 April 1996, they picked up members of a street gang called *Los Rebeldes* – "The Rebels". One of them, Hector Olivares Villalba, said that the gang's leader Sergio Armendariz Diaz – aka *El Diablo* – had half a dozen Rebels rape and murder Rosairio Garcia Leal on 7 December 1995. Although Olivares' confession was made under torture and he later recanted, the police used it to moved against *Los Rebeldes*, raiding their club and arresting some 200.

Armendariz, Juan *"El Grande"* Contreras Jurado, Fernando Guermes Aguirre, Carlos Barrientos Vidales, Romel Cerniceros Garcia, Erika Fierro, Luis Adrade, Jose Juarez Rosales, Carlos Hernandez Molina and Olivares were all accused of being in the pay of Sharif. The police said that he had hired them to rape and murder at least 17 women in copycat killings to make it look as if the original "Ripper" was still at large. Juan Contreras told police Armendariz had sent him to collect "a package" from Sharif in prison. It contained $4,000 in cash. Then, Contreras said, he had joined Armendariz and other Rebels in the rape and murder of a young woman known only as Lucy. Contreras also later recanted, and the charges were dropped against suspects Ceniceros, Fierro, Guermes, Hernandez and Olivares. However *El Diablo* remained in jail serving a six-year sentence for leading the gang-rape of a 19-year-old fellow inmate in February 1998.

It was said that the Rebels liked torturing their victims on a sacrificial slab before stoving their heads in. Several victims had bite marks on their bodies. Chihuahua's medical examiner claimed that dental casts from Armendariz match bite marks found on the breasts of at least three of the victims. However, the Rebels claimed they were tortured by police and displayed burn marks on their bodies caused by cigarettes and cigars. And in 1999, a Mexican court ruled that there was insufficient evidence to charge Sharif with conspiracy in any of the murders attributed to *Los Rebeldes*.

By then the police theory was already looking distinctly threadbare as the murders continued despite the round-up of the Rebels. Between April and November 1996, at least 16 women were killed. Three were shot, five stabbed and one was found in a drum of acid. In some cases advanced decomposition made it impossible to determine cause of death or whether the victim had been sexually assaulted. Eight could not be identified.

The following year there were another 17 unsolved murders involving females aged from 10 to 30 years. Sexual assault was confirmed in only four cases, but other corpses were found nude and in positions that suggested that there had been a sexual motivation for their killing. Where the cause of death could be established, three were shot, three strangled, five were stabbed and two beaten to death. Seven of the dead were never identified.

The murder rate continued to climb. In 1998 there were 23 unsolved murders following the same general pattern. There was the usual mix of shootings, stranglings, stabbings, beatings and burnings. Six remained unidentified. Not only were the police helpless but complicit. On 21 September 1998, Rocio Barrazza Gallegos was killed in a patrol car in the parking lot of the city's police academy by Pedro Valles, a cop assigned to the Ripper case.

The spate of murders in Ciudad Juarez was now attracting media attention internationally. In May 1998, the Associated Press reported more than 100 women raped and killed in Ciudad Juarez. In June they put the figure at 117, while the women's advocacy group Women for Juarez said it was somewhere between 130 and 150.

On 10 June 1998 Mexico's Attorney General Arturo Chavez told the Reuters news agency that, with Sharif still safely behind bars, "police think another serial killer may be at work due to similarities in three crimes this year". The story was taken up again by AP who reported on 9 December 1998: "At least 17 bodies show enough in common – the way shoelaces were tied together, where they were buried, how they were mutilated – that investigators say at least one serial killer is at work. And 76 other cases bear enough similarities that investigators say one or more copycats may be at work."

However a team of three profilers from the FBI's National Center for the Analysis of Violent Crime in Quantico, Virginia, spent a week reviewing the cases and concluded that "the majority of the cases were single homicides . . . It is premature and irresponsible to state that a serial killer is loose in Juarez."

The first quarter of 1999 began with eight more victims. Then while Sharif went on trial for the rape and murder of Elizabeth Castro Garcia in March 1999, another suspect emerged. Before dawn on 18 March a 14-year-old girl named Nancy arrived at a ranch on the outskirts of Ciudad Juarez. Sobbing and covered with blood, she said she had been raped, strangled and left for dead. Miraculously she survived. The attacker, she said, was the bus driver who had picked her up when she left work at the *maquiladora* at 1 a.m. When he had dropped off all the other passengers, he drove out into the desert and stopped, claiming the bus had mechanical problems. Then he grabbed her by the neck and asked her if she had ever had sex. The last thing she remembered before she lost consciousness was him telling her that he was going to kill her.

The bus driver's name was Jesus Guardado Marquez, aka *El Dracula*. A check of the records revealed that 26-year-old Guardado had a previous conviction for sexual assault. But by the time police went to arrest him, he had fled with his wife. Guardado was arrested a few days later in Durango, some 550 miles to the south. He claimed that he was beaten by the police when he was returned to Ciudad Juarez. However, the police said that Guardado confessed to a number of the murders and named four accomplices who were also *maquiladora* bus drivers – Victor Moreno Rivera (*El Narco*), Bernardo Hernando Fernandez (*El Samber*), Augustin Toribio Castillo (*El Kiani*) and Jose Gaspar Cerballos Chavez (*El Gaspy*). Together they were called *Los*

Choferes – "The Chauffeurs". More sinisterly, they are also known as *Los Toltecas* – "The Toltecs" – who were the blood-thirsty forerunners of the murderous Aztecs. Moreno was the leader of the gang, the police said, and he too was in the pay of Sharif.

They were charged with 20 murders, but protested their innocence. The only evidence against them was their own confession which had been extracted by torture. Sharif denied having any contact with the Chauffeurs and maintained he knew nothing of any conspiracy.

Again, the arrest of *Los Choferes* did nothing to stem the murders. By May 1999 it was reported that "nearly 200 women" had been murdered since 1993 – a substantial leap from October 1998's figure of 117.

Celebrated profiler Robert Ressler, who heads the Virginia-based corporation Forensic Behavioural Sciences, visited Juarez at the invitation of the authorities and concluded that his former employer, the FBI, were wrong. He found that 76 of the murders fitted into a pattern. The victims were all women aged between 17 and 24. Most of them had been raped and strangled, and more than a dozen had been killed on their way to, or on the way home from, work at a *maquiladora*. But he concluded that the killings were not the work of a lone serial killer.

"I think it's probably two or three," he said. One of them, he thought, was an American coming across the border to take advantage of the situation in Juarez. The police had already demonstrated their inability to catch one killer. There were plenty of dark streets and abandoned buildings, and with a transient population of young women there were plenty of victims to choose from.

"It's an ideal situation for an American with money," said Ressler.

The founder of the Citizens' Committee Against Violence Astrid Gonzales Davila said: "The failure to solve these killings is turning the city into a Mecca for homicidal maniacs."

Candice Skrapec, the Canadian-born professor of criminology at California State University in Fresno, also identified 67 cases where she thought serial killers were involved. She told the *Toronto Star* she believed that three or four killers were at large in the 182 post-1993 cases she had studied and "there may be even more murders that could be tied to the three suspected serial killers, and that they were operating in 1992".

Skrapec believed that "Railway Killer" Angel Maturino Resendez, was one of the perpetrators as he had lived in the *barrios* there and much of this family – including his uncle, Rafael Resendez-Ramirez, whose name he used as one of many aliases – still live in Juarez. On 13 July 1999, at the urging of his brother and his sister, Resendez crossed the Ysleta Bridge over the Rio Grande into the United States and surrendered to the Texas Rangers after a six-week televised manhunt that made him the most wanted man in America. The US authorities had held back on charging Resendez, fearing the Mexican government would prevent the suspect's extradition if he was liable to face the death penalty – in Texas he would receive death by lethal injection. But a $125,000-reward had been offered for his capture and his family feared that he might be shot by a bounty hunter. Instead, they brokered his surrender and claimed the reward themselves.

Resendez was charged with nine counts of murder. The first was the murder of a 21-year-old college student who was bludgeoned to death while walking with his girlfriend along a railway line in Kentucky on 29 August 1997. After that eight more bodies were found in victims' homes along a railroad track from Texas to Illinois as he travelled from state to state. His last two victims were a 51-year-old woman and her 79-year-old father who were found dead in their home near the line in Gorham, Illinois, on 15 June 1999.

Although Resendez could be a suspect in at least some of the Juarez killings, it is unlikely that he was responsible for the majority of the unsolved cases. Indeed, they continued after his arrest.

In December 1999, a mass grave was found outside Ciudad Juarez. It contained nine corpses – three belonging to three US citizens. This invited renewed attention across the border with some, again, suspecting the involvement of the Mexican police. The *Dallas Morning News* wrote: "Still a mystery is what happened to nearly 200 people, including 22 US citizens who, in many cases, vanished after being detained by men with Mexican police uniforms or credentials."

These missing persons became known as *Los Desaparecidos* – "The Disappeared". Some were thought to be victims of Juarez's drug wars. But the Association of Relatives and Friends of Disappeared Persons in El Paso believe they may have been kidnapped by the police.

Maquilladoras still went missing and on 6 November 2001 a mass grave containing the skeletal remains of eight women were found in employ plot just 300 yards from the headquarters of the Association of Maquiladoras, the organization that represents most of Juarez's US-owned export assembly plants. Police then announced creation of a new task force to investigate the murders and a $21,500 reward for the capture of those responsible.

Three days after the grave had been opened bus drivers Gustavo Gonzalez Meza, *La Foca*, and Javier Garcia Uribe, *El Cerillo*, both 28, were charged with killing the eight women. The prosecutor claimed they "belonged to a gang whose members are serving time for at least 20 of the rape-murders". The victims were identified as 15-year-old Esmerelda Herrera, 17-year-old Laura Ramos, 17-year-old Mayra Reyes, 19-year-old Maria Acosta, 19-year-old Veronica Martinez, 20-year-old Barbara Martinez (no relation to Veronica), 20-year-old Claudia Gonzales and 20-year-old Guadalupe Luna.

The suspects claimed that their statements were extracted under torture. Their lawyers received death threats. On 5 February 2002, one of them was killed by police after a high-speed chase. The police claimed they "mistook him for a fugitive" and a judge ruled that the shooting was "self-defence". Meanwhile it was revealed that DNA tests had failed to confirm the police's early identifications of the victims. New DNA tests apparently confirmed the identification of Veronica Martinez, though it threw no light on the other seven cases. Then Gonzalez died in jail, ostensibly from complications arising after surgery.

By now 51 suspects were in jail, but still the killing did not stop. Ten days after Garcia and Gonzalez and Garcia were arrested, the body of another young woman, stripped and beaten to death, was found in Ciudad Juarez. *Maquilladoras* protesters were reportedly harassed by police and the Inter-American Commission for Human Rights moved in to investigate. The new Mexican President Vicente Fox sent in "federal crime specialists". Resentful, local prosecutors told the *Dallas Morning News* that "27 of the 76 cases" were resolved, while "the other killings involving women have been isolated incidents".

On 9 March 2002, member of the Texas state legislature joined a protest march through El Paso. Then a federal deputy attorney general in Mexico City claimed that the killings were committed by "juniors" – the son of prosperous Mexican families whose wealth and influence had protected them from arrest. He was quickly found another job. Later that year the FBI returned to lend a hand but have failed to further the investigation.

Juarez's leaders are particularly conscious of the effect the killings are having on the image of the city. When a large wooden cross was erected as a memorial to the murdered women, the mayor received a letter from the chamber of commerce, complaining that this would damage tourism.

The day that letter was received – 23 September 2002 – the bodies of two more women were found in Ciudad Juarez. One victim was strangled and partially undressed; the other, the police said, had died of a drug overdose. Special investigator David Rodriguez was "sceptical" of that claim. Another young woman was found beaten to death two weeks later. Then Martha Sahagun de Fox, Mexico's new first lady, addressed more than a thousand women dressed in black who marched through Mexico City in protest at the deaths.

In January 2003, residents of Lomas de Poleo reported finding three corpses, but the Attorney General Jesus Solis and the police refused to confirm or deny whether they were connected to *maquilladoras* murders. These were not the first corpses found in this desert area near a rundown suburb. Two others had been found nearby in October 2002. One of them identified as 16-year-old Gloria Rivas.

On V-Day, 14 February 2004, in Ciudad Juarez, busloads of female students from around the world calling themselves "vagina warriors" marched into town for special performances of *The Vagina Monologues*, performed by such film stars as Jane Fonda and Sally Field, to highlight and denounce what was now being dubbed "femicide". It did no good.

On 17 February 2003, two teenagers searching the wasteland for cans and bottles found three more bodies. When the police turned in Mimbre Street at 2 p.m., they found the remains of three women dumped there. While the bodies were being removed, an onlooker found a fourth.

At a press conference two days later the police said that they had identified three of the victims – 16-year-old Esmeralda Juarez Alarcon who had vanished on 8 January 2003, 17-year-old Juana Sandoval Reyna who had been missing since 23 September 2002 and 18-year-old Violeta Alvídrez Barrios who had disappeared 4 February 2003. All three had last been seen alive in downtown Juarez. When asked about the fourth victim, the police refused to acknowledge that there was another body and called a halt to the press conference. With no end to the killings in sight, the authorities are in a state of denial.

There is no shortage of suspects. Along with those already in jail, a number are still at large. There is Armando Martinez, alias Alejandro Maynez, who was arrested in 1992 for the murder of a woman in Chihuahua City, some 220 miles to the south of Juarez. He was released "by mistake" and then conveniently vanished along with his police file. Ana Benavides, who was accused of killing and dismembering a couple and their child in Juarez in 1998, claimed that Martinez committed the triple-murder and framed her.

Then there is Pedro Padilla Flores. Convicted in 1986 for the rape and murder of two women and a 13-year-old girl, he confessed to other killings but was not charged. Padilla escaped in 1991 and is still at large.

The police themselves remain under suspicion. At least ten women have accused Juarez police officers of sexual assault and kidnapping over the past five years. No charges have been brought. But an unnamed policeman is sought in connection with the murder of 27-year-old Laura Inere and 29-year-old Elizabeth Gomez in 1995.

In April 1999, Julio Rodriquez Valenzuela, the former police chief of El Sauzal, Chihuahua, was accused of attempting to rape a 16-year-old girl near where two previous murders had been committed. Chihuahua authorities report that he fled "to El Paso or New Mexico". He remains a fugitive.

Also on the run are ex-Mexican federal agents Jorge Garcia Paz and Carlos Cardenas Cruz. They are sought for questioning in the disappearance of 29-year-old Silvia Arce in 1998 and the death of 24-year-old Griselda Mares, who was allegedly killed in error by police in a dispute over stolen guns.

Former Chihuahua state policeman Sergio Hernandez Pereda fled in 1998 shortly after the murder of his wife. He is still at large.

Former Ciudad Juarez policeman Dagoberto Ramirez was fired in 1999 after he was accused of murdering his lover. He claimed that she had committed suicide and was released, but the police officials did not reinstate him.

Melchor Baca, a former federal policeman, has been on the run for eight years. He disappeared after killing a male friend of his wife at the courthouse where they both worked. And then there is Pedro Valles, the cop who was assigned to investigate the Ciudad Juarez murders and killed his girlfriend at the state police academy in 1998. He is still at large.

Then there are the conspiracy theories. Some maintain that the murders are the work of organ harvesters who are collecting spare parts for transplants. Others believe that they are the work of a satanic cult like that run at Matamoros by Adolfo de Jesus Constanzo who died in a shoot-out in 1989. Some of his cannibalistic followers are still thought to be at large.

As drug gangs are at work in the area, it had been mooted that the missing women were addicts or small-time mules, who were executed because they knew too much. In November 2004, the FBI report accused unnamed narcotics traffickers for the torture and death of 17-year-old Lilia Garcia in the February 2001. Her body was found 100 yards from the spot where eight other victims were discovered. Then there are the juniors, or perhaps a cabal of rich and powerful sadists whose wealth puts them above the law.

Meanwhile Abdul Sharif won a judicial review in the Elizabeth Garcia case. The murder conviction was upheld, but his 30-year sentence was reduced to 20. However, the prosecutors say that Sharif may be charged with other murders. But as he has already been in jail for over 11 years, fresh charges are hardly going to stop the killings.

In 2004, a federal special prosecutor was appointed. Her remit extends to investigating the incompetence of the local police. But so far she has drawn a blank. However, a $2.7 million fund to aid the families of the victims has been established. Amnesty International has criticized the Mexican government's efforts to investigate these crimes and the United Nations has condemned Mexico's record on violence against women. But nothing helped. There were more than 28 related murders in 2005.

On 15 August 2006 Edgar Alvarez Cruz was arrested by US Marshals in Denver, Colorado and charged with 14 of the murders. Jos Francisco Granados and Alejandro Delgado Valles, aka *El Calá*, have also been arrested in connection with these 14 murders. Two of the men are said to be drug addicts and the third a psychopath. Even if these men are found guilty as charged, it seems that there are plenty more serial killers at large in and around Ciudad Juarez.

Even if they are caught, many will escape justice as much crucial evidence has been lost, incinerated or even intentionally destroyed, some in exchange for money for suspects seeking to clear their names, according to a recent report from Mexico's National Human Rights Commission. In the winter of 2003, homeless men took refuge from the harsh cold inside the warehouse housing many of the case files. To keep warm, the men used the files as fuel, or so the story goes.

The following year, an official was appalled by the smell that permeated the warehouse. He discovered the source of the stench was clothing, caked with blood, worn by one of the victims, a ten-year-old girl whose corpse had been dumped in the desert. Nauseated by the odour, the official, a crime scene investigator, ordered the clothes washed and deodorized with fabric softener.

"I was aghast," said an investigator for the Human Rights Commission. "We lost crucial hair, fibre, prints, semen and God knows what other vital potential evidence."

Far from an isolated incident, this is part of a pattern of the mishandling of evidence that will make solving the killings even more daunting for a new crop of investigators and will ensure the perpetrators remain at large. In a review of the investigation by the special prosecutor's office, some 177 state officials were found to have been responsible for negligence or omission in the original investigations. However, none of these officials has been brought to justice by the state authorities as the statute of limitations has been applied in their favour. Others have been forced to resign after refusing to fabricate evidence or documenting the use of torture in the investigation.

Portugal's Lisbon Ripper

A Portuguese serial killer is being hunted across Europe. Known as the "Lisbon Ripper", he is being sought by police in Portugal and other four countries where he has killed.

The Ripper first struck in Lisbon city in July 1992. The victim was found with her throat cut. She had been disembowelled. Soon after a second victim was found within 50 yards of where the first had been dumped and in March 1993 a third body was discovered.

The killer then seems to have travelled further afield. Over the next four years, victims appeared in the Netherlands, Belgium, Denmark and the Czech Republic. All were young, drug-addicted prostitutes. In each case, the method of killing was identical. This has convinced the Portuguese police and Interpol that the same man was responsible. Victims have been strangled or had their throat cut. Then they have been disembowelled with a piece of glass. He does not appear to have raped his victims.

Detectives also travelled to New Bedford, Massachusetts, in an attempt to link the Lisbon Ripper murders with a string of similar unsolved slayings there in 1988. The theory is that he was a member of New Bedford's large Portuguese population who left the city and continued his twisted ways back in his native Portugal, then out across Europe. Police believe he may have been a long distance lorry driver. However, no solid link was ever established.

He is believed to be tall, white, and aged between 35 and 40 at the time of the European killings. He has a pathological hatred of women and is thought to be suffering from AIDS, perhaps contracted from a drug-addicted prostitute.

Russia's Rippers

Police in the Altai administrative district of central Siberia have been searching for a serial killer responsible for the murders of at least five teenage female applicants to the Altai Technical University. Ksenia Kirgizova, Anzhela Burdakova, Yulia Tikhtiyekova, Liliana Voznyuk and Olga Shmakova disappeared between 26 June and 15 August 2000 after sitting entrance exams at the university campus in the Siberian city of Barnaul.

Two other women – the mothers of the university applicants – have also gone missing. Some bodies of women killed in the area have been found in ditches, in woods and in the Obj river near Barnaul, a city of 700,000. The police set up check points, questioned thousands and conducted widespread searches, but no trace of the five young women could be found. Then in October 2000, two bodies suspected of being those of students Ksenia Kirgizova and Anzhela Burdakova were found in a forest 25 miles from Barnual. Investigators later positively identified one of the bodies as Kirgizova's.

Investigators believe the killer has been active around Barnaul for several years and has been responsible for an undetermined amount of unsolved murders. Forty-year-old Alexander Anisimov was arrested, but committed suicide in mysterious circumstances after several days in custody.

On 5 February 2001, a man identified only as Alexander, a 30-year-old driver for the Barnaul police department's drunk tank, was arrested after a 22-year-old Barnaul University student told the police she had jumped out his apartment to escape. She said that Alexander had made sexual advances in his apartment the previous evening but she rejected him. In the morning, she managed to escape by jumping off a balcony while Alexander was in the bathroom. A recent police search of the suspect's apartment found about 300 photographs of sexual orgies and a collection of women's underwear. However, despite intense speculation, city prosecutor Nikolai Mylitsin dismissed him as a suspect in the abduction of the five girls.

"When a man is accused of sexual violence we check whether he had anything to do with all unsolved rape and murder cases," he said.

Then on 10 February, the police in Novosibirsk, 120 miles north of Barnaul, arrested three men and one woman on suspicion of kidnapping and murder. An official said the suspects have confessed to abducting and killing a 16-year-old Barnaul resident named Irina Serova. But she was not one of the five girls who went missing while applying to enter Altai State Technical University. The three men, aged 20 to 27, and the 27-year-old woman were charged with kidnapping and forcing girls into prostitution.

Roman Kuminov, a senior investigator overseeing missing person reports in the Altai district, said the gang is thought to have lured girls from across Altai with promises of well-paid jobs before selling them as prostitutes.

If convicted, the suspects face up to 15 years in prison, he said.

Kuminov did not say whether murder charges would be brought against the group, although two bodies believed to be the missing girls' have been found. Kidnappings have become common across Russia and especially in Chechnya, but few suspects are detained.

Russian police in the city of Perm in the Urals had little more luck when hunting a serial killer who claimed seven victims in less than three months in 1996. On 28 August, Perm's police chief Andrei Kamenev said: "His latest victim was a woman who was raped and stabbed in an elevator shaft in the same Perm neighbourhood where six other women have been attacked in recent months."

Police believe that one person is responsible for all the crimes, but the only suspect was not recognized by victims who survived the attacks. This was all the more disappointing as in June the police had arrested a man in Perm who they charged with murdering and disfiguring six women. The murders took place over a single month. In each case, the attacker struck the victim in the head and mutilated her face.

Meanwhile a serial killer was stalking the streets of Moscow. Between dusk on 21 July and dawn on 22 July 2003, four women were murdered in the capital of the Russian Federation. That brought the body count to ten for that month.

The first six victims were strangled. At midday on 1 July, 28-year-old Yulia Bondareva had taken a walk with her boyfriend in the botanical gardens. After the couple parted, Yulia set off towards the underground. An hour later, her body was discovered. She had been gagged with a piece of her own shirt, beaten, raped and throttled.

Before dawn the following day, the police discovered the body of 17-year-old Kseniya Medintsevaya dumped in the courtyard of a kindergarten. Her face was smeared with blood and her dress was ripped open. Again she had been raped, beaten and strangled. She had last been seen alive at 11 p.m. in her apartment the previous night.

On 4 July, the naked body of 28-year-old Irena Gera was found several miles from the centre of Moscow where she lived. She had been raped and strangled with the strap of her handbag.

The next victim was a 25-year-old Ukrainian prostitute named Alexandra. She was found strangled in her apartment on 8 July. One end of a belt was tied around her neck. The other was attached to a door handle.

Near Alexandra's apartment, the police found the partially clothed body of 32-year-old teacher Elena Tolokonnikova on 11 July. Last seen out with friends the night before, she had not returned home.

Then on 15 July, the decomposing body of a woman was found near a pond. The remains were not identified. However there were signs of the handiwork of the same killer. Like the other victims, she was short, slim, with a fair complexion and long, light-coloured hair.

The seventh victim was 17-year-old student Tatyana Nikishina. She was killed on 21 July. Her assailant had tried to rape her. Then he strangled her with her bra and left her body in the northwest of the city. Police did not release the names of the other three victims slain that night. However, the killer seems to have begun to adopted a variety of methods. One was bludgeoned as well as strangled, another purely bludgeoned, hit by a blunt object from behind, and the third was killed having her head smashed against concrete. The youngest victim was 17; the oldest 35.

Moscow police have organized a task force to investigate the murders, but did not, at first, admit a serial killer was at work, due to the various methods of strangulation and bludgeoning he had employed. Some victims were strangled with ligatures, others manually. Some were beaten; some sexually assaulted. Seven of the ten victims were found in the northern section of the city, but the other three were killed several miles away in the northeast. There was no single MO.

At least six were well educated. One, Alexandra the Ukrainian prostitute, was not. She was the only one to be found indoors. She had been soliciting in a nearby market that day and could have picked up what she thought was a client, or she might have been followed home. There were other inconsistencies. Yulia Bondareva, the first known victim, was attacked and killed in a public park in broad daylight, while the others were killed at night. Why had Irena Gera travelled from her home to the city's northern section where she was attacked and murdered? And why did Kseniya Medintsevaya leave her apartment in the middle of the night?

Russian Interior Minister Boris Gryzlov said that the ten women were killed by different assailants, claiming that three men had already been arrested. And a senior police official characterized the bunching of murders as "coincidence".

Then on 23 July, a man stepped from a wooded area and

grabbed a female pedestrian by the throat. He pulled her to the ground and dragged her into the bushes. A woman looking out of the window of an apartment opposite called the police, who caught the man. He was an immediate suspect in Moscow's string of unsolved murders. However, he was soon dismissed as a copycat. On 28 July, while he was in custody, the body of a 42-year-old woman was found in a schoolyard northwest of the city. She had been raped and strangled. As in the case of 17-year-old Kseniya Medintsevaya, she had been dumped outside a kindergarten. A pattern appeared to be emerging.

Investigators found three victims who had survived similar attacks. In each case the assailant had concealed himself in bushes or behind a fence, then sprang out on the unsuspecting victim as she walked past. They also provided detailed descriptions of their assailant. He was a white male with short hair, a thin face, small eyes, bushy eyebrows, a large nose and thick lips. Aged between 35 and 40, he was between five foot seven and five foot nine, and wore jeans and a dark T-shirt.

These details were never released to frightened Muscovites, who drew their own conclusions. Women remained indoors while the men were sent out to do errands. They knew that, if a serial killer was at work, he was killing at a terrifying rate. But he could not be found.

Then in mid-June, the body of a woman was found in Bitsa Park in the south of the city. The following day, her work colleague at a small grocery store in southwestern Moscow Alexander Pichushkin was arrested. A loader there, he confessed to killing the woman and said that he had planned to kill as many as 64 people.

In all Pichushkin has so far confessed to killing 62 people, beginning in 2000, but investigators say they do not have sufficient proof to believe everything he says. However, prosecutors charged him with 49 counts of murder on 14 December 2006. There are questions about his sanity and the killings in the north of the city were far from his usual patch, opening the possibility that a second killer is at large there.

Scotland – Glasgow's Bible John

Bible John was the nickname given to a killer who murdered three women in Glasgow in the 1960s. He has never been caught or identified and as late as December 2004 the Scottish police were still actively investigating the case.

On the evening of 22 February 1968, Patricia Docker decided that she needed a night out. Her husband, a corporal in the RAF, was stationed in England, leaving the 25-year-old nurse and her young son lodged with her parents. It was a Thursday night and they were happy to babysit the toddler.

Patricia got dressed up for the occasion and it seems she went to a number of ballrooms that evening. She was seen at the Majestic, then moved on to Barrowland Ballroom. This was popular with her friends as, on a Thursday night, it catered to those aged 25 and over. It was busy. Patricia did not particularly stand out and it was difficult to identify all her dance partners. However, it seems that someone offered to walk her home. She never got there.

At dawn the following morning, a cabinet maker on his way to work found the naked body of a dead woman in a quiet lane a few yards from the Dockers' house. She had been strangled with her own tights, but none of her other clothing could be found. The police determined that she had been dead for several hours. They came to believe that she had been strangled elsewhere and dumped there. When they heard that Patricia Docker had not returned home, the police came to the obvious conclusion and Patricia's parents had the gruesome task of identifying the body.

In an attempt to find some clue to identify the killer, the police widened their search for Patricia's clothes, handbag and other belongings. Divers even searched the river nearby, but nothing was found. One local resident told the police that she thought she had heard cries for help during the early hours of 23 February, but none of the journalist and photographers who had attended a colleague's party near where the body was found that night remember anything. A photograph of a policewoman dressed in clothes similar to those Patricia was wearing that night was circulated in the area, but no one remembered seeing her after she left the dancehall.

Glasgow had had recent experience of serial killers. Ian Brady, who was convicted of the Moors Murders in 1966, had been born there. Ten years before Patricia Docker was killed, Peter Manuel became one of the last people to be hanged in Scotland. A sociopath and burglar, he had killed at least eight people around the city. So when Patricia's naked body was found dumped in the street, Glaswegians feared the worst. But that did not stop them having fun.

A year and a half later, 32-year-old Jemima McDonald fancied a Saturday night out. On the evening of 16 August 1969, she dropped off her three kids with her sister Margaret for the night. Then Jemima headed for the Barrowland. High bouffant hair-styles were still in fashion in Glasgow in 1969, so she travelled across town with a scarf over her hair. Then, when she arrived at the ballroom, she headed straight for the ladies, where she took out her rollers and finished off her makeup.

On the dance floor Jemima attracted attention. Other dancers noticed that she spent much of the evening dancing with a tall man in his late twenties or early thirties. He wore a blue suit. His red hair was cut short and his appearance was neat. Early the next morning, she was seen leaving the ballroom with him.

The next morning, when Jemima did not come to pick up her kids as expected, Margaret grew worried. Later she overheard street children talking about something grisly they had discovered in a derelict building nearby. Fearing the worst, Margaret got the kids to direct her to the building. There she found her sister's dead body.

Jemima was fully clothed, but there were similarities to the Patricia Docker case. Both women had been strangled with their own pantyhose. Both had been found near their home. Jemima's handbag was missing. Later the police found another similarity between the two cases. Both had been having their period when they were killed.

A search of the area rendered no new clues and an attempt to question those who had been at the Barrowland that night also proved fruitless. Many of them were married and were out with people who were not their spouse, so were less than forthcoming.

An appeal from the stage also drew a blank. A policewoman dressed in Jemima's clothes retraced her final steps. But eventually the police released a sketch of the tall man Jemina had been seen leaving the Barrowland with. Jemima's family offered a reward of £100, a first in the history of Scottish murder investigations. But this, too, proved futile.

Despite all the publicity the murders were getting, it did not put people off going to the Barrowland. Twenty-nine-year-old Helen Puttock was hell bent on going there on the night of 30 October 1969. Her husband, who was going to stay at home with their two young boys, begged his wife to be careful. But Helen was not worried. She would not be alone. She was going with her sister Jean and said she was sure they would be safe together.

Helen spent most of her evening dancing with a tall young man with red hair. When they left the Barrowland, the three of them took a cab home together. During the journey, the man said that his name was John, he played golf badly, but a cousin had recently hit a hole-in-one. Jean also remembered he mentioned that he had a sister. He said they had been raised in a strict religious household and he was still able to quote long passages of the Bible – hence his pseudonym.

According to one account, John seemed upset by Jean's presence. He wanted be alone with Helen. He also condemned the evil women who went to dancehalls like the Barrowland. Ignoring Jean for much of the ride, he did not even say goodbye when they dropped her off.

The next morning Helen's fully clothed body was found in the street by a man walking his dog. Again she had been strangled with her own nylons and her handbag was missing. She, too, was menstruating when she was murdered. As if to draw attention to the fact, the killer had removed her sanitary towel and tucked it under her armpit. And this time he had left two clues that might help identify him – a semen stain on her dress and a bite mark on her wrist.

Thanks to Jean, the police now had an accurate description. The suspect was around six feet tall, of medium build. He had blue-grey eyes and light reddish hair, which he kept cut short. His watch had a military-style band and the teeth marks on the body confirmed that two teeth in the upper-right part of his mouth overlapped.

A new artist's impression of the suspect was circulated – this one in colour. It culled over 4,000 calls from people who thought they had seen or knew the man in the picture. Jean was called to the police station over 250 times to see suspects, but none of them turned out to be the man she and her sister had shared a taxi with. Men who bore a resemblance to the killer and had been eliminated from the enquiry were issued cards by the police, showing they had been questioned and cleared. One of them was used in a reconstruction of Helen's last evening, with a police-woman playing Helen, that was aired on the BBC. Helen's husband made an appeal to his wife's killer to turn himself in and offered his life savings as a reward for information leading to his arrest.

Over 50,000 statements were taken and over 100 policemen worked on the case, with younger officers in plain clothes mingling with the dancers in the Barrowland. Taxi drivers and bus crews received particular attention. One man said he had seen a young male with scratches on his face on the bus on 31 October. He had got off at a stop on Gray Street. Police combed the area, but found nothing.

The suspect's military wristwatch band and his short hair lead the police to believe that he might be a member of the armed forces – or even a policeman. Dentists were questioned about patients with overlapping teeth and golf clubs were asked about anyone who had recently scored a hole-in-one. A Dutch psychic called in by a local newspaper drew a map, but a search of the area drew a blank.

Although psychological profiling had yet to be developed, in the mid-1970s, a Glasgow psychiatrist concluded that, although Bible John was sociable, he was prudish. He would read widely on subjects ranging from sorcery to the Nazis, and went to the cinema by himself. This did not help.

Although only three murders have been officially ascribed to Bible John, he may have committed others. In 1977 another young woman who spent her last night in a Glasgow dancehall was found strangled and without her handbag. This sparked a renewed round of interest in Bible John.

In 1983, a wealthy Glasgow man hired a private detective to find a childhood friend who he thought resembled Bible John. The man was found living in the Netherlands, but was cleared.

Another man who had been cleared was identified only as John M. He had been a suspect in the investigation in the 1960s. He bore a close resemblance to the sketch that was circulated, but Jean had failed to identify him. Nevertheless, he continued to be a prime suspect until, in 1981, he committed suicide.

In the 1960s, DNA fingerprinting was as yet undreamt of. But in 1996, DNA from the semen left on Helen Puttock's clothes was compared to a sample taken from one of John M.'s siblings. The match was inconclusive. Nevertheless the police requested the exhumation of John M.'s body from a graveyard in Stonehouse, Lanarkshire.

The resulting publicity led to the harassment of John M.'s family. But when the test were completed it was found that the DNA did not match. Nor did his teeth match the bite-mark on her wrist. Jean said that she always knew that John M. was not the killer and she had repeatedly told Strathclyde Police they had the wrong man. John M. was reburied and his family finally left to grieve in peace.

But the investigation was still not over. In October 2000, Professor Ian Stephen, a leading criminal psychologist who is said to have inspired TV's *Cracker*, passed the name of a new suspect on to the Lothian and Borders Police, asking them to forward it to Strathclyde. He said he obtained the new lead from an expatriate Scot living in the US who suspected a member of his extended family was Bible John. The suspect was the son of a policeman. He was married in the Glasgow area and lived in Lanarkshire with his wife and two children until he moved to England in 1970.

According to the file Professor Stephen passed to the police, the suspect's behaviour changed dramatically in the late 1960s when he increasingly went out alone at night and sometimes failed to return until the following day.

Professor Stephen told the BBC: "I would like to think that his name has already been considered and ruled out but I am not hopeful. The police were looking for a stereotype, a known sex offender at the time. The profile appears to fit that of Bible John. While the information is circumstantial I think the police have got to have a serious look at it."

The Strathclyde Police said they would look at the new information.

In December 2004, DNA taken from a Glasgow crime scene two years earlier was an 80 percent match to the semen found on Helen's clothing. Samples are still being collected from a number of suspects in their 50s and 60s and, in May 2005, a spokesman for the police said: "Science will solve these killings. We have no doubt of that."

That October Strathclyde Police set up a new Unresolved Case Unit to re-examine the evidence in the Bible John Killings. They are using new processes to identify traces of evidence that previously could not be found.

"Now with the advent of DNA profiling, someone who's just held something for a brief period, or held someone, you're going to transfer your DNA," said Dr Adrian Linacre, a lecturer in forensic science at Strathclyde University.

Throughout it all, the Barrowland Ballroom had soldiered on and now proudly proclaims that it is "the best rock venue in Scotland".

Scotland – Glasgow's Sex-Worker Slayings

The night of Friday 27 February 1998 was one of the coldest nights of the winter in Glasgow. While it was freezing outside, it was warm inside Base 75, the prostitutes' drop-in centre in Robertson Street. Other women remembered 27-year-old Margo Lafferty being there that night. She was trying on a new suit she'd bought. It was pale blue with a mini-skirt and a lacy top. The consensus was that suited her, though one of the girls said that Margo had put on weight. She was broadly liked. Some remember her as a kind girl, one who would lend another girl money if she needed to buy a pair of tights from the all-night garage down by the river, though others say she was violent.

Base 75 closed at 11.30 p.m. and Margo went to work. Early on Saturday morning she was in one of the lanes that run off the main streets in the shopping and business area. There were security lights on the buildings, but prostitutes entertained their clients in the dark doorways there. That night, though, a monster was on the loose. In the morning Margo was found dead in a disused builders' yard on West Street, then utilized as a car park. Her body was curled up in the foetal position, her blood soaking into the mud. She had suffered repeated blows to the head, which was then beaten against a wall. Then she had been strangled. She was naked. This was a telling detail. Margo was not a girl who undressed for her johns.

In her stomach were the remains of her last hurried meal – cheap white bread, the orange segment she had gulped down, a cherry from a can of fruit cocktail. There was mud all over her skin as the killer had dragged her naked body through the puddles in the carpark. This was particularly distressing for her mother, who remembered Margo as a scrupulously clean girl.

"When people hear the word 'prostitute' they think, 'dirty midden'," she said. "But Margo used to do my head in with her showers and baths. She'd have three or four a day. She was so very, very clean. When she had her own wee house you could have eaten a meal off the floor. She was very particular about herself and her environment."

Margo had six brothers, though her younger brother Billy had been killed in a road accident at the age of 18. He had been left brain-dead in a coma when they had to switch off the ventilator. Her father had died when she was just a toddler. After a night of drinking, he had choked to death in his sleep. His death left the family struggling and her mother would go without food so the children could eat. But they were a happy family and the house was always full of the children's friends – there would be as many as 14 for Sunday lunch.

The others remember Margo Lafferty as a carefree child, full of laughter and charming enough to wheedle sweets from the man on the ice-cream van when she had no money. As a young girl she had been soft-hearted, always ready to help a pal in trouble. Once she brought home a schoolfriend who'd lost her mother. The girl stayed with the family for six years and whenever Margo got something the other girl got the same.

Margo's older brother Monty, who assumed the role of father figure, treated his little sister like a princess, always buying her frilly things. But she was a tomboy, who would wear her trousers right up to the school gate before changing into the uniform skirt she hated. She could play football better than most boys and captained a local team.

"She was never 'feared of anybody or anything in her life," her mother said. "She was the only one that would face up to Monty. The rest of them would never answer him back, but Margo would stand and confront him."

Curiously for a girl of her calling, she was not interested in boys. Local lads were crazy about her, but when they came on to her she would reject them.

"I can't be bothered with it, Ma," she would tell her mother. "They're too serious."

The family lived in Barlanark, then a run-down estate riddled with drugs. Margo started sniffing glue, then moved on to harder things.

"She was a daring lassie," said her mother. "She wasn't scared to try anything once. If only she'd realized where it was going to end up."

As addiction took hold, her life became increasingly chaotic. She would spend the night out with one "friend" after another, selling her body to buy drugs. One minute she would be the life and soul of the party, the next she would crashed out on the sofa.

One day, her mother came home to find Margo lying on her bedroom floor in a coma. Her face and lips were blue, and there was a syringe sticking out of her groin. Her mother pulled the needle out and slapped Margo's face to get her breathing. It took a quarter of an hour to bring her round. When her mother explained what had happened, Margo called her a liar. Her mother said: "I'm sorry, Margo. I can't take any more of this."

"Fine, Ma," Margo replied and left.

"I didn't put her out of the house," said her mother. "The lassie knew herself she couldn't go on like that. It had got to the stage where you were 'feared to leave her in the house. You didn't know what was going to be missing when you got back. I told her I would keep her, but I wasn't knocking my pan in to keep her drug dealers."

She knew that Margo could look after herself. Although only five foot, she was tough, aggressive and knew how to use her fists. Many of the other girls on the streets would turn to her when they needed physical protection.

"I've seen her taking the jacket off her back and giving it to an old woman in the street, but she had a bad temper," said her mother. "You needed to watch her because she'd hit you as soon as look at you. She was very brave physically. Not that she went out looking for bother, but she wouldn't run away from it either. That was why I told the police that Margo fought, that whoever had murdered Margo had been well and truly scarred. She would fight for every minute of her life and every second."

Indeed she fought ferociously with her killer, gouging the flesh of his face.

Margo was the seventh prostitute to be murdered on the streets of Glasgow in six years. Another would follow. But hers was the only case where the police secured a conviction. Men accused in two other cases were acquitted. Suspects in another were released. And in four cases no arrests have been made. But, as we have seen, prostitute murders are notoriously difficult for the police. Between 35 and 40 remain unsolved in England and Wales each year.

In Glasgow all the murdered women were drug addicts who had turned to prostitution to support their habit. Such women are often estranged from society and there is little pressure on the police to discover who was responsible for their fate. And by the nature of their calling, few admit knowing them.

The killings began in 1991 when 23-year-old Diane McInally was found dead in Pollok Park, near the Burrell Collection, Glasgow's famous art gallery. On 15 October, her body, clad only in a black mini-dress and stockings, was dumped under a bush. She came from the Gorbals, where drugs were bought and sold openly on the streets. It was thought that she was killed because she owed drugs money. Two men were arrested for her murder, but later released due to lack of evidence.

In April 1993, 26-year-old mother-of-two Karen McGregor was found dead in the Scottish Exhibition and Conference Centre. She had been battered around the face and head with a solid object, strangled and sexually assaulted with a foreign object.

The police had an obvious suspect. Her husband, Charles McGregor, was arrested and charged with the murder. Two witnesses said that they had seen him beat his wife to death with a hammer, but retracted their statements in court. Another witness said they had seen Karen's battered and bruised body, but grew fearful and ran off before observing the situation further. A woman testified that she had seen McGregor in the cemetery, crouching over his wife's grave and saying: "I'm sorry, Karen. I'm sorry. I didn't mean it." And a fellow prostitute gave evidence that Karen was fed up giving all the money she had earned to her husband to feed his drug habit.

However, when McGregor appeared in court, he did not look like a junkie. He wore a smart suit and overcoat, and had his hair neatly cut – looking every inch the thrusting young businessman. The jury were impressed and returned a verdict of "not proven" – a third option allowed by Scottish courts. He later died of a drug overdose.

On a warm summer evening in June 1995 the body of Leona McGovern was found in a Glasgow car park. She had been stabbed seven times with a screwdriver, then strangled. The petite 22-year-old, barely five feet tall, had been sleeping rough. Two weeks before her death, her boyfriend died of an overdose.

"He meant a lot to her," said Detective Chief Inspector Nanette Pollock, who was leading the investigation. "When he died she really lost it."

Then Leona had found her best friend dead in bed.

On the night she died she owed her dealer money and asked her brother to lend her £35, but he could not give it to her. About 7 p.m., a security guard said he saw a man stabbing something on the ground. At the time he thought it was a bag of garbage as he could not imagine witnessing a murder take place in the street in broad daylight – even in Glasgow.

A man was arrested and charged with Leona's murder – but, again, the jury returned a not-proven verdict. He claimed the murderer was another man who had been seen with Leona in the last two weeks of her life. He was not her boyfriend, just another homeless person she hung around with. Inspector Pollock thought their relationship entirely innocent.

"Homeless people tend to stick together," she said. "They're in the same situation. She'd lost a lot in her life."

The body of 34-year-old mother-of-two Marjorie Roberts was pulled out of the River Clyde in August 1995, four days after she drowned. Citywatch cameras taped her walking by the river with a man. A month later the same man was arrested after trying to push another prostitute into the river. She managed to struggle free and ran to a taxi driver for help. However, she did not want to press charges. As a prostitute and drug user, she did not want the glare of publicity.

"She was a drug addict," said Marjorie's younger sister Betty. "They don't care about their own life."

There were no witnesses and no marks on Marjorie's body – nothing to indicate that she did not slip and fall into the water accidentally, perhaps, at night when it was pitch black, or even jump in and drown.

"She had Valium in her body," said Betty. "When she went into that Clyde she had no strength to fight."

It was Marjorie's boyfriend who introduced her to drugs. At first, she took temgesics – a barbiturate used to treat withdrawal symptoms. Then people in the projects where she lived began selling heroin. Marjorie's boyfriend left her and the children and she started letting prostitutes use the house to take drugs. By the time he came back Marjorie herself was on the game.

"He just went, 'Well, hen. As long as you're using plenty of protection.' He didn't care," said Betty. " 'She was dead shy and quiet. She never had any confidence. That's how we couldn't believe she could go and do that."

As her habit grew, her life slipped downhill. In her last few months, she slimmed down until she looked like a skeleton. She would sit motionless with her face covered for hours on end. Eventually, her doctor prescribed Valium.

Like Karen McGregor and Marjorie Roberts, 26-year-old Jaqueline Gallagher had only been on the game for five or six months when she died. Jacqui's own mother did not even know her daughter was a prostitute.

"I know those girls," she said. "See the way they're dressed? When I saw Jacqueline she was never like that. She was always prim and proper. People used to say, my God, she's beautiful. If she was a wee bit taller she could be a model."

Like Leona McGovern and Margo Lafferty, Jacqueline Gallagher was only five feet tall. She had met her boyfriend when she was just a teenager. He was ten years older and already on drugs – but then, so were most of her friends. According to Gordon, they were very much in love.

"On our 10th anniversary she was running about and singing, 'Our House in the Middle of the Street'," he recalled. "She was happy. I came in with a big, massive card and I got her a gold necklace. She loved gold. I put bits of gold in her coffin, things that we'd given each other."

Their idyllic life together was marred only by drugs and the periods he spent in prison for shoplifting. While he was inside, she wrote hundreds of love letters to him that he kept in a plastic shopping bag. One read: "Gordon, I know myself it's not going to be long till you're walking through the door, and baby I will be there for you. I always will be, Gordon, no matter what. You know that yourself, baby."

However, on his last stint in prison Jacqui did not visit him as she had before.

"She knew I hated this," said Fraser Gordon.

He knew the risk she was running, earning money as a prostitute.

"I told her, I worry about you from the moment you walk out that door to the moment you walk back in," he said. "It's frightening. You don't know how much strain you're putting on me."

On the night she died in 1997, Jacqueline was picked up by car from the kerbside in Glasgow. Later her half-naked body was found on a grass verge near a bus stop in Bowling, a village four miles outside the city. She was hidden in shrubbery and wrapped in a home-made curtain. The fabric was pink and grey, and the lining white with blue polka dots. The police never managed to discover where it came from – even after it was shown on the nationwide TV programme *Crimewatch*.

The police had a suspect – 43-year-old George Johnstone of Erskine, who was one of her clients. But he was cleared and the real killer is still at large.

"Somebody knows who killed my daughter," said her mother. "I didn't know she was a prostitute but it doesn't matter what she was doing. She was a lovely girl and didn't deserve to be killed."

Gordon Fraser was devastated by Jacqui's death. Six months later, he was found on the roof of his house, throwing down slates and threatening to kill himself by setting himself on fire.

Twenty-one-year-old single mother Tracy Wylde was the only victim to be murdered indoors. Like Marjorie Roberts and Jacqui Gallagher, she was new to the game and only went out on the street a couple of nights a week.

She lived in a top floor flat, which she kept impeccably. People were always trooping up and down the stairs to her flat, leading neighbours to wonder if she was a drug dealer. According to her friends she was not, just a timid girl who could not say no – though others say she was warm and funny, with enough confidence to talk to everybody.

"I was shocked when I heard about the prostitution," said a neighbour who lived downstairs. "I said to her about the risks she was taking, but she said she'd rather go out and earn money like that than steal it off anyone else. She knew what that was like."

But her work as a prostitute allowed to keep her three-year-old daughter Megan, who was always conspicuously well dressed.

Tracy had had a troubled upbringing. She had been raised by her grandparents and called her grandfather "Dad". He came up to her flat nearly every day and even dropped her off in the city centre sometimes when she was working on the streets.

"I feel sad for her," said her downstairs neighbour. "It couldn't have been an easy life for her."

Tracy was killed in the early hours of 24 November in her home. Strangely no one heard anything that night. Her block had poor soundproofing and residents could overhear neighbours' conversations and footfalls. But not even her downstairs neighbour, a young mother who was kept up by her 11-week-old baby, heard a thing.

After Margo Lafferty died on 28 February 1998, the police discovered that she had gone with two violent criminals that night. On the dark piece of waste ground where she was found dead, they picked up two condoms. One contained the semen of Brian Donnelly, who had previously tried to set fire to the house of his former girlfriend and their son, and he had also mugged an old woman. The other contained the semen of Scarborough construction worker David Payne, a convicted sex offender who had been jailed for holding up a woman at knife point and indecently assaulting her.

That night Donnelly had been out celebrating his 19th birthday but went into a rage after being rejected by a couple of female work colleague. Instead he decided to go with a prostitute and was captured on CCTV with Margo before the pair went to the disused builders' yard in West Regent Street for sex. The jury was also shown CCTV footage showing a man, who the Crown said was Donnelly, walking away wearing a leather jacket Margo had borrowed.

The following day, work colleagues noticed the gouges on Donnelly's face. He told one he had been involved in a tussle with a woman whose boyfriend had tried to jump a taxi queue before him. But he told another colleague he had been scratched by a cat. His workmates did not believe him and gave his name to detectives investigating Margo Lafferty's murder.

During the trial, Donnelly alleged that the murder was committed by David Payne, who had been working in Glasgow at the time. However, Payne was seen with Margo on CCTV before she was seen with Donnelly. Despite his previous conviction for a violent sex crime, Payne denied being the murderer.

At his trial in 1998, the prosecutor Calum MacNeill told Donnelly: "We will never know why you killed her, whether it was a disagreement over payment, or your anger which lacks self control, or out of shame or disgust or contempt that you had for the heroin addict prostitute you had just used. You punched and kicked her and she fought back, scratching you. You were incensed, you 6 feet 3 inches and her only 5 feet tall. You were fuelled with anger and got out of control and banged her head off the wall before strangling her and finally dragging her body along the yard."

He was found guilty on a majority verdict, but in 2001 the Court of Criminal Appeal in Edinburgh overturned the conviction on the grounds that the trial judge, Lord Dawson, had misdirected the jury over the CCTV footage.

Lord Dawson had told the jury that they were entitled to consider any evidence that Donnelly had any of the dead woman's property on him or in his possession, saying specifically: "You'll remember in that connection the video tape evidence where you saw a young man wearing a dark jacket."

Gordon Jackson, QC for Donnelly, told the appeal judges there had been no suggestion during the trial that the man caught on camera wearing a dark jacket was either young or was Donnelly.

Lord Allanbridge, who heard the appeal with Lord Cameron and Lord Caplan, said: "We consider that the trial judge did misdirect the jury in inviting them to consider 'the video tape evidence where they saw a young man wearing a dark jacket'. This was an open invitation to the jury to consider the 3.14 a.m. video recording and to recollect their viewing of it, so that they themselves might speculate about the disputed identity of a male person shown on the recording. Such a procedure is incompetent.

"If the jury concluded that the recording showed the appellant wearing the deceased's jacket after her death, this could have been a very persuasive factor in their deliberations on the murder charge. We are accordingly satisfied that the misdirection of the trial judge in this case has led to a miscarriage of justice."

They quashed the conviction, but granted the Crown leave for a retrial. At a second trial in 2001, it took the jury under an hour and a half to bring in a unanimous verdict of murder.

After the trial, Margo's mother said: "I always knew Donnelly was the monster who murdered my daughter . . . He wasn't any innocent young boy. I hoped someone would kill him when he went into prison after the first trial. I was wishing retribution would be served in another way. There's no closure in this for me. Not as long as he breathes. I believe in the Old Testament, in an eye for an eye and a tooth for a tooth . . . She might have been a prostitute but she was still a lovely lassie with a heart of gold."

And Mrs Lafferty still has to live with the consequences.

"You're sitting in work and people are talking, new staff maybe, not the ones that were there at the time. And they always bring Margo's name up if anything happens. They'll maybe come across a wee caption in the paper and they go, 'Look at that. These lassies deserve it.' I just get up and walk away. Or occasionally I'll say, 'Look at it this way. They're out there, taking the chance of being jailed, and there's others sitting next to you that are giving it away for nothing.' Margo could have been out mugging old folk or breaking into houses. But she didn't do that. She went out and did a job of work."

Margo's brothers did not know what she did for a living and had to read about it in the newspapers as well as living with the grief of losing their sister. Mrs Lafferty was afraid they would get themselves in trouble if they came to the court and the jury voted for acquittal, but the verdict was heard in total silence.

When Margo died it was three months before the family could bury her. And they were not allowed to cremate her, in case the body had to be exhumed later to look for further evidence, though Margo herself would have preferred to be cremated.

"She was afraid of creepy crawlies, couldn't bear the thought of worms going through her body," said her mother, but she now thinks the bureaucrats did her a favour. "Now I know I can go up to her grave and just stand there and talk to her. I know she's never going to stand in front of me or cuddle me, which she always used to do. But at least I know where she is."

Margo's mother also has a grandchild to bring up who reminds her of her lost daughter.

"She's so full of confidence. So was Margo, full of her own importance," she says. "I hope she keeps that."

Meanwhile, the murder of Margo Lafferty led to the girls in Glasgow's red light district being given lessons in self-defence by specially trained police officers. They were issued with personal attack alarms and leaflets offering practical safety advice. The leaflets provide advice on what clothes to wear, where to sit in a client's car, how to deal with a violent client and how to protect their money.

But that did not help 27-year-old Emma Caldwell, who went missing on 4 April 2005. Her badly decomposed remains were found on 8 May in thick undergrowth near Biggar, South Lanarkshire, over 30 miles away. It was found by a member of the public walking their dog in woods at Kilnpotlees, Roberton, at about 1 p.m., near two service stations on the M74 motorway link to the south at Happendon and Abington.

Emma Caldwell grew up in Erskine, Renfrewshire. Her mother said: "She was just a happy, happy child – we had a happy life. She was a lovely child, full of fun. A magical child who loved horses. There used to be a thing in the family – we'd say, 'What would you like, Emma?' She'd say, 'A horsy, a horsy'. We'd say, 'When would you like the horsy?' She'd say, 'Right now, right now I'd like the horsy'."

Indeed she had worked as a horse-riding instructor before her sister, Karen, died from cancer in 1998. Then her whole world seemed to collapse. She left home, because she was a heroin addict and became a prostitute to support her habit. At the time she went missing she was living a women's hostel in the Govanhill area. It was been reported that Emma may have been forced to walk to the woods before being murdered, but the police said she almost certainly died very soon after the last sighting of her in Govanhill.

Officers studied CCTV footage and warned men who did not come forward that they would be visited by detectives. In any effort to jog the public's memory, the police projected a 60-foot image of Emma on to the side of a semi-derelict tower block in the Gorbals district of Glasgow.

The BBC's Crimewatch programme aired CCTV footage showing the last recorded moments of Emma's life. It showed her leaving Inglefield Street women's hostel for the last time, then talking briefly to two people outside before heading for the city centre. The driver of a BMW passed her, stopped and did a three-point turn in Inglefield Street. She was last seen at around 11 p.m. on 4 April, walking down Butterbiggins Road towards Victoria Road.

Later the police came across footage of a woman getting into a silver Skoda Felecia car outside the Riverboat Casino on the Broomielaw, Glasgow's historic quayside. Detectives have traced every owner of a silver Skoda Felecia car in Scotland, but have been unable to track down the driver. This line of enquiry might even be a blind alley.

Detective Superintendent Willie Johnston of the Strathclyde Police said: "I am unable to say with any authority that the person who entered the car was Emma. However, I do know that she could have been in Broomielaw at that time."

The charity Crimestoppers offered a reward of £10,000 to anyone who could help track down her killer. But a year after she went missing 50 officers were still working on the case. The police then released recordings of 999 calls she made the weeks before she disappeared, expressing her concern about children playing on a railway line.

The officer leading the inquiry said the calls showed the kind nature of the "caring" young woman and he hoped they would help to jog people's memories.

"I want to demonstrate to the public, who may still have reservations about coming forward, that despite her lifestyle, Emma was a loving, caring individual who was genuinely concerned for the children on the railway line," he said. "It may also prompt people who recognize her voice and know something that could be relevant to this investigation to come forward. I make no apologies for constantly reminding members of the public of this crime and will continue to do so until the person or persons responsible have been brought to justice."

The murdered Glasgow vice girls may not be the victims of a serial killer. It seems likely that a different killer is responsible for each murder. But that makes life no safer for Glasgow's prostitutes, as long as the killers are at large.

On 8 September 2006, 29-year-old Gillian Gilchrist, from Ibrox, was thrown from a car by a man who had picked her up in the red light district of Glasgow. She lost part of an arm.

She had been picked up by a man in a dark coloured car in Holm Street at Wellington Street, in the heart of the red light district. He drove to Arkleston Road near to Arkleston Cemetery, on the outskirts of the suburb of Paisley, where he threw her from the car at around 1.50 a.m. From there she stumbled 100 yards across a field and onto the westbound M8 motorway, where she was found by a man in a taxi who did not want to be named.

"Suddenly the taxi brakes and there was this woman in the road," he said. "She was covered in blood. I ran to help her and called 999 and tried to get her off the motorway, it was then I noticed she had no arm. It was the most horrific thing I have ever seen, I put my jacket around her and gave her first aid."

Her arm was severed four inches above the wrist and doctors were unable to reconnect it.

Her sister Debbie, told the Scottish *Sun*: "I don't understand why someone would want to do that to a lassie. In a way Gillian is lucky because she could well be dead."

"We have tried so hard to get her off the streets," said her stepmother Anne Gilchrist. "I just pray this is the wake-up call she needs – we will all be there to help her."

The Glasgow edition of the *Daily Record* offered a £10,000 reward for information leading to the conviction of the attacker. The police are treating the attack as attempted murder and searching for a man in his forties with a full head of hair, driving a dark-coloured saloon.

South Africa's Serial Killers

Since the end of apartheid there has been an explosion of serial killers in South Africa. Take the case of Lazarus Mazingane, who was given 17 life sentences for murder and rape, and over 700 years for other offences in Johannesburg High Court on 3 December 2002.

Dubbed the "Nasrec Strangler", he preyed on women commuting between Soweto and Johannesburg. Many of the bodies were found near the Nasrec Exhibition Centre. His victims are black females, mostly between the ages of 20 and 35, who are lured from minibus taxis.

Judge Joop Labuschagne said Mazingane was a "cruel and inhuman person" who showed no remorse, and should be permanently removed from society to which he was a menace.

"He stalked defenceless women whom he robbed and raped before he killed them," said the judge.

Mazingane was working as a taxi driver at the time and many of the victims were attacked along his route or when seeking transport. His first victims were throttled – not fatally – then raped. But as his vicious career progressed, he murdered by strangulation.

"All these women were young and in the prime of life," said Judge Labuschagne. "I listened to the evidence of mothers ... and loved ones who told me of their tragic losses. Nothing I do or say today can compensate them, but perhaps they can find some compensation in the conviction of the accused and these sentences I am imposing."

The court also noted that some of the victims were men such as Gert Aspeling, who was shot dead when he refused to hand over his car keys after stopping to change a wheel. Mazingane then drove off with the dead man's paralyzed wife in the car and dumped her in the veldt without her wheelchair.

The judge remarked that the chances of rehabilitation were "very poor if not non-existent", noting that Mazingane had already been convicted of attacking his own wife.

In all, Mazingane was convicted of 74 charges, and was sentenced to life imprisonment on each of the 16 murder counts and life imprisonment for the most recent rape, which fell under the new legislation. He was sentenced to 18 years on each of the remaining 21 charges of rape. On the 20 counts of aggravated robbery he had been convicted of, he was sentenced to 25 years for the most recent one, and 15 years for each of the remaining 19. And he was sentenced to another 10 years on each of five counts of attempted murder. One victim had been shot three times but survived.

He received eight years for each of three counts of kidnapping, plus two years for assault, three years on each of the two charges of illegal possession of a firearm, and three years on each of the four charges of illegal possession of ammunition.

Twenty-eight-year-old Mazingane was already serving 35 years for a crime committed late in 1998 – the kidnapping, rape and robbery of an attorney's wife and an attack on a motorist who stopped to help. He was in jail for that offence when he came to the attention of Superintendent Piet Byleveldt, who was investigating the unsolved Nasrec killings. However, the charges eventually laid against Mazingane were only the tip of the iceberg. At the time Police Director Henriette Bester detailed the extent of the Nasrec offences: "There are 53 cases, of which 51 of the victims were killed. Of the 51 murder victims, 32 were female, all of whom were raped. Seventeen of the victims were children between the ages of five and eight, of whom 11 were girls."

Mazingane was convicted of only 16 of the slayings. He may have committed more that he was not charged with, but the chances are that there is at least one other killer – maybe more – still at large.

Then there is the mysterious case of David Selepe and the murder of more black women in Cleveland, an industrial suburb of Johannesburg. On 3 September 1994, just four months after South Africa's first multi-racial election, a woman's body was found on in the bushes near the Jupiter train station next to the township of Heriotdale. Four days later, a second body was found next to the M2 freeway, on the other side of Heriotdale. Later that same day, the third body was found near a mine dump nearby. All three were partially naked and had been raped and strangled. There was nothing on the bodies or around them to aid in their identification. However, their clothes indicated that, before the attacks they had been neatly dressed. They were certainly not prostitutes – the usual prey of serial killers.

Once stories of a serial killer began to circulate in the press, the Brixton Murder and Robbery Unit discovered that they had two similar cases, whose bodies had been found in the same area on 16 and 31 July. The first – that of a schoolgirl – had a curious message written on it. The murder had written in black ink on the inside of her left thigh: "We must stay here for as long as you don't understand." On her right thigh, he wrote: "She a beach and I am not fighting with you please."

Brixton Murder and Robbery Unit took over the investigation from the local Heriotdale force. So when, on 19 September, a sixth woman's body was found near a mine dump in Heriotdale, they went to investigate. Again the victim had been strangled. Her dress had been pushed up over her hips and her jumper had been pulled over her head.

What puzzled detectives was that none of the women they had found matched missing person reports. Although they were apparently respectable women, none of them had been reported missing. So identikits of the women were prepared to release to the press and television.

All six bodies had been found within a radius of just over three miles so, on 21 September, the police began to search Heriotdale and the surrounding area of Cleveland in earnest. They employed a police helicopter, two dogs and some 140 officers. They found the remains of two more bodies in an advanced state of decomposition. Their clothing had been pushed up under their armpits and they appeared to have been strangled with either their own belt or undergarments.

The police now had a total of eight dead women on their hands. All of them were aged between 18 and 30, black and well-dressed. Medical examiners established that at least two of them had been raped. And, disturbingly, there may be many more victims. The area was littered with numerous pieces of female underwear.

Also on the 21st, the body of the women found two months before was identified by her husband. Her name was Hermina Papenfus. Aged 25, she was a nurse at the Sandringham Clinic.

The search of the Cleveland area continued and, on 23 September, the police found a rock splattered with blood, a pair of women's sandals and a bloodstained shirt in the bushes some 50 feet from a footpath that ran between the factories. The police believed that these belonged to the fifth or sixth victim. A search of the wider area discovered no more corpses.

On 26 September, the body of the woman found on 3 September near the Jupiter station was identified by her father. She was 23-year-old Ntombi Maria Makhasi, a resident of Orlando West in Soweto. A student of fashion design at the Elna Design School in Johannesburg, her teachers described her as friendly and responsible. She disappeared on 2 September after telling a classmate that she would not be at school that day because she was going to the province of KwaZulu-Natal a couple of hundred miles to the southeast to visit her mother who was ill. Her father told the detectives that she used buses and South Africa's numerous taxis and minibuses for transport. Hermina Papenfus also used the taxis.

Dr Micki Pistorius, South Africa's first psychological profiler, joined the investigation on 28 September. The similarities between the cases were manifest, she said. All the victims were black, young, attractive – women who took a pride in their appearance and were not destitute. The killer's modus operandi was consistent. He had taken the women to an industrial area, raped them and strangled them with a piece of their own clothing – usually a belt, bra or pantyhose. Then he left the body totally or partially naked.

Pistorius concluded that the killer was a black man in his late twenties or early thirties. Based on the women's appearance, he was charming, well-dressed and well off with an expensive car – it was unlikely that women like these would go with someone who did not have a winning personality and portray himself as a man of means. Investigators thought that he might have derived some of his income from fraud or theft. He was certainly self-employed – at that time, few black men with a regular job would have the means or the free time to go around picking up women. Pistorius also surmised that he was married.

The message left on the body of the first victim indicated that he had a profound hatred of women. He called his first victim, a schoolgirl, a "beach" – presumably meaning "bitch". The written message also suggested that he had difficulty expressing his feelings. He could not tell the woman what he felt when she was alive, so he wrote it on her body when she was dead.

Pistorius told the *Beeld* that the killer "feels dead inside. He probably thinks about death all the time. He fantasizes about every murder and tries to commit the perfect murder, because he has a drive to kill, but he doesn't understand it. To kill is the only way he can release his feelings and his identity." Asked whether he would stop killing, she said: "He can't."

Another thing Pistorius noted was that Ntombi Makhasi's body was found on 3 September in the exactly same place as Hermina Papenfus' body had been found on 31 July. Then on 19 September, a third body was found there. Pistorius suggested that the police keep the area under surveillance. But the killer was one step ahead. His profile concluded that he was an arrogant and intelligent man who read the newspapers. He knew what was going on and switched his dumping ground.

On 8 October, another woman's body was found near Geldenhuis train station, which is one stop from the Cleveland station, on the opposite side of Heriotdale from Jupiter station where Ntombi Makhasi had been found on 3 September. The new victim had clothing stuffed in her mouth and had been strangled with her pantyhose. There were some indications she had been raped, but the body had been lying in the veldt for several days and was badly decomposed.

It was plain that this was the work of the same killer, even though he had dumped the body in a new location. The police then looked back in their files and discovered that two other women's bodies had been dumped near Geldenhuis station, one on 6 August, the other on 3 September. The modus operandi in the 6 August case was almost identical. The victim was found with her jumper pulled over her head. She had been strangled with her own blouse which was still tied around her throat and her panties and pantyhose had been stuffed into her mouth.

On 13 October, the police offered a reward of 200,000 Rand (£14,000) for information leading to the arrest and conviction of the killer. Four days later, a man identified his daughter from a picture in the newspaper. She was 26-year-old Amanda Kebofile

Thethe who was last seen leaving her parents' home at 9 a.m. on 2 August. She was going to pay a bill in Johannesburg, then go on to Soshanguve, north of Pretoria, some 50 miles away, where she worked as a teacher. As her body had been found on 6 August, she had already been buried in an unmarked grave.

Although the police had repeatedly appealed to the public to report missing persons, Amanda Thethe's aunt Nomvula Mokonyane spoke out about what had happened when the family had tried to report her niece's disappearance to the police. A week after Amanda disappeared, they had gone to the police station at John Vorster Plain, Johannesburg, to report her missing, only to be informed that they could not do so due to "lack of stationery" and they were told to go to another station. So they went to the station in Krugersdorp, near where they lived. A week later, when they inquired if any progress had been made, they were told that the file had been mislaid. Plainly, little had changed in the police force since the old apartheid days. However, Mokonyane did praise Brixton Murder and Robbery for their handling of the case since Amanda had been identified.

On 20 October, another victim was identified by her parents. Her name was Malesu Betty Phalahadi. The 25-year-old had last been seen alive on 2 September and was thought to have been travelling by train to visit a friend in Mabopane, near Soshanguve, where Amanda Thethe worked as a teacher. But 2 September was the same day Ntombi Makhasi disappeared. Both Malesu Phalahadi's and Ntombi Makhasi's bodies were found the next day – Malesu's near Geldenhuis station; Ntombi's near Jupiter station.

Curiously, Malesu's parents had only been alerted to the fact that their daughter might have been the victim of a serial killer when a woman phoned Malesu's mother Grace Lehlake on 19 October and asked if she knew where her daughter was. As Grace did not, she asked the woman the same question. She replied that Grace should call the police and hung up. Who this woman was remained an intriguing mystery. Was she the friend that Malesu was supposed to be visiting? If so, why did she hide her identity and why did she not contact the police directly? Or was it someone who knew the killer? If so, why wait two-and-a-half months before calling?

But there was another distressing discovery to be made in the case of Malesu Phalahadi. Her fiancé was a local policeman, who found out his lover was dead when he recognized her clothes among the evidence being examined at the Brixton Murder and Robbery Unit.

Both Ntombi Makhasi and Malesu Phalahadi had been intending to head northwards through Pretoria when they had gone missing, so detectives began to throw their net a little wider. They then discovered that there had been two similar cases in Pretoria West, some 30 miles to the north. A woman's body had found by a cattleman in a patch of open field on 19 August. The same man found a second body about 330 yards from the first on 7 October. Both women were black and neatly dressed. They had been strangled with their stockings and left partially clothed. Once again they had no possessions that could aid identification. One of them was later exhumed in the hope of finding evidence that would tie their cases to the Cleveland murders. Pretoria and Johannesburg are more than 30 miles apart. This reinforced the idea that the killer had a car.

Then two more victims were identified. One was 28-year-old Dikeledi Daphney Papo, whose body had been found in the search of Heriotdale on 21 September. It could not be established when she had gone missing or what she had been doing beforehand. The other was 25-year-old Dorah Moleka Mokoena. She had been found in Heriotdale on 19 September. Interestingly, she worked as a cashier at the Danville toll booth to the west of Pretoria and she had left home on the morning of 9 September to take a taxi to work, but had never arrived.

Three days after Dorah Mokoena disappeared, a man had phoned her boss, saying that Dorah had been in an accident and would not be returning to work. He asked for her salary to be paid into her account, as she was in a critical condition and needed money. Her boss then asked the man who he was. He fell silent for a minute, then said his name was "Martin".

Then the body found on the M2 freeway in Heriotdale on 7 September was identified. This was 24-year-old Refilwe Amanda

Mokale who went missing on 5 September. Her body was found two days later next to the M2 freeway in Heriotdale. She had been studying fashion design at Intec College in Pretoria. The day she disappeared, she was seen on Church Plain in Pretoria, talking to a man who, she said, offered her a job selling mobile phones. She had an appointment to meet him again the following day. The eyewitnesses said that he was a black man between 25 and 30 years old, who spoke Zulu. Other women who had been offered jobs by the man came forward. An identikit was drawn up and published on 10 November.

Meanwhile, the identification of the two victims found in Pretoria West lent more clues. One of the women was 30-year-old Peggy Bodile. She had an appointment with an unknown man on 4 October at the Paul Kruger statue on Church Plain in Pretoria, echoing the case of Refilwe Mokale. Her body was discovered three days later.

The other was 32-year-old Joyce Thakane Mashabela. She left home to visit her sister by taxi on 9 August. Her body was found on 19 August. But on 14 August, a man calling himself "Moses Sima" phoned Joyce's employer, claiming he had found her identity papers while walking through a patch of veldt on his way to work. He handed them over to the family the next day, insisting that he had found only the papers and knew nothing more. But that begged the question: how did he know where Joyce worked or what the number was?

On 10 November the police identified the body of the girl found on 16 July, which they believe was the killer's first victim. This was 18-year-old Maria Monene Monama, who was still at school. She was last seen on the morning of 14 July when she left home on her way to Pretoria. Although her body was found two days later, her parents did not discover what had happened to her for four months.

Then the last body, that of 24-year-old Margaret Ntombeni Ledwaba, was identified.

By 18 November, the police were closing in on a suspect. He was a 31-year-old black man, living in a house in Boksburg, east of Johannesburg and some $12\frac{1}{2}$ miles from Cleveland. Although he was married, he did not live with his wife and he was often seen in the company of other women.

A suave and a flashy dresser, he drove a Mercedes-Benz, fitting the profile. He was also self-employed, owning and running a women-only computer school called the Vision English Girls College from offices he rented in Pretoria. And, like many independent businessmen in South Africa, he owned a number of taxis. But things had been going badly. The college's four employees had not been paid their salaries. He owed 50,000 Rand (£3,500) in rent and utility bills. The Mercedes was not registered in his name, but that of a black woman. Although he was paying the instalments on the car, he was 20,000 Rand (£1,400) behind on the payments. He had come to the attention of the police when a woman had contacted them, complaining that the suspect had offered her a job, but had then tried to rape her.

The suspect's name was David Abraham Selepe. The problem was that he had fled his creditors two weeks before, supposedly going overseas on business. He had not gone that far. On 15 December, he was arrested trying to sell the Mercedes in the port of Maputo, the capital of Mozambique, 280 miles to the east. Detectives found newspaper clippings of the Cleveland killings in the boot. There were also footprints on the lid, suggesting that someone had been locked inside.

Returned to South Africa, he was questioned for the next four days. Apparently, he waived his right to legal representation. The police said that he confessed to the murder of 15 women in the Cleveland area – four more than they were investigating. They did not get around to questioning him about the women found in Pretoria West. While he was happy to make a verbal confession, the police said, he refused to sign a written confession.

The police also say that Selepe agreed to take them to the places where he had left the bodies. On 17 December, he took them to three places where bodies had been found. He then showed detectives the four previously unknown sites where he had said he had dumped bodies.

The following day, Selepe agreed to go to the place where Amanda Thethe's body had been found on 6 August. Three officers investigating the case – Joseph du Toit, Timothy Mngomozulu and Felix Tiedt – accompanied him. From Geldenhuis station, they had to cross rough terrain so Selepe's ankle chains were removed. The police said they did this to prevent Selepe from being injured – and later accuse them of brutality.

After Selepe had pointed out the place where Amanda Thethe's body had been found, he told them that he had hidden her underwear in a plastic bag which had been shoved underneath some bushes nearby. His handcuffs were removed so that he could search for the bag. When he found the bag, Detective Tiedt bent down to recover it. He was then hit across the back with a stout branch, knocking him down. Detective Mngomozulu yelled, "Stop! Stop!" Then a gunshot rang out. Selepe fell to the ground. Bleeding profusely from a head wound, he was rushed to Johannesburg Hospital, where he died that evening.

The police claimed that this was a tragic accident that marred an otherwise brilliantly successful investigation. Since Brixton Murder and Robbery had taken over the investigation, only two months had passed before they identified the suspect and in another month they had arrested him, even though he had fled the country.

But there was a furore in the press. The *Beeld* said that three police officers should surely have been able to subdue a man only wielding a branch. And if they had to shoot to prevent him escaping, why had they not shot him in the legs? Other newspapers speculated that the police might have had ulterior motives and the *Sowetan* said that "an innocent man may have paid for the crimes of a monster who is still alive".

On 20 December, the police were forced to issue a statement saying that Selepe had not admitted "in so many words" that he was the Cleveland strangler. However, he had "said things which strengthened our suspicion". This cast doubt on Selepe's so-called verbal confession. One of the Brixton police's media officers, Lieutenant-Colonel Eugene Opperman, first told reporters that Selepe had been handcuffed at the time of the attack, and later changed the story. He was suspended in an effort to salvage the police's image, which was further damaged when it came out that the police had failed to notify Selepe's widow of her husband's death. Linda Selepe had found out about it from neighbours who read about it in the papers. Although the couple had been estranged for more than a year, she said: "They killed the truth when they killed my husband. Had they brought him to court then, the South African public would have known the truth that David was not a killer."

Minister of Safety and Security Sydney Mufamadi tried to retrieve the situation. He held a press conference, stating that Selepe's death did not mean the case was now closed. Then he spent four hours with the relatives of the Cleveland victims, assuring them that both the murder of their loved ones and Selepe's death would be thoroughly investigated.

During Selepe's "confession", detectives said that there were two men – accomplices – named "Tito" and "Mandl" they should talk to. This became the investigators' top priority. They located a man they thought to be Tito. He was questioned at length and volunteered to provide blood and hair samples for forensic examination, but he was cleared of any connection to the murders. The man identified as Mandl had been in jail awaiting trial when the murders took place. Even so he was questioned, then dismissed from the enquiry.

Even though this line of enquiry drew a blank, the police continued to insist that David Selepe could be tied to at least six of the Cleveland victims. Blood said to be Selepe's was found on one of the victims' panties. And human blood, supposedly from one of the victims, was found in Selepe's car. But the police would furnish no further details. They said that more evidence linked Selepe to four more victims, but, again, would not say what it was. This was dismissed as a feeble attempt to save face.

On 7 February 1995, the investigating officer in David Selepe's death Colonel Adrian Eager delivered the post-mortem report to the Attorney General, after it had mysteriously gone missing for a week. The Attorney General stated that the investigation into the death of David Selepe had been thorough and that no one would be held accountable. An inquest in nearby Germiston into David Selepe's death found, unsurprisingly, that no one could be held criminally responsible for his death. Sergeant Mngomozulu, the coroner said, had acted in self-defence.

However, public confidence was shaken when Colonel Eager testified that he was not even sure that "David Selepe" was the dead man's real name. When the suspect had been convicted of fraud on 2 May 1985, he had been caught carrying false identity papers in the name of David Selepe and, as they did not know his real name, he had been charged and sentenced under that name. The records of the Department of Internal Affairs revealed that Selepe had first obtained legal identity papers under that name in May 1992. Between then and 21 June 1994, five sets of papers had been issued to him.

Despite public misgivings about the Selepe affair, it was generally thought that the Cleveland killings were over. However, on 13 February 1995, the body of a young black woman was discovered in the veldt near Village Deep, some six miles from Cleveland. She had been strangled with her own underwear and her clothes had been pushed up to above her waist. The police claimed it was a copycat.

At the end of February, four women told the police that a black man had approached them the previous October and November offering them jobs. The man was attractive with large eyes. He had expensive clothes and spoke Sotho rather than Zulu. He also claimed to be a vegetarian and drank milk. When the Cleveland murders came up in conversation, he made off, although he did not match the description of David Selepe.

The brother of the woman found on 13 February identified her as 22-year-old Nelsiwe Langa. She had last been seen two weeks before her remains were found. Despite the obvious similarities with the Cleveland murders, the police maintain that a different man was responsible. However, other bodies found near Atteridgeville, outside Pretoria showed an almost identical modus operandi to the Cleveland cases.

The township of Atteridgeville has hosted an extraordinary concentration of serial killers. In 1956 the "Atteridgeville Mutilator" killed six boys over five months, mutilating their bodies. He was never caught or identified. In the 1960s Elias Xitavhudzi, known as "Pangaman", murdered 16 white women and dumped their bodies around Atteridgeville, before being caught and executed. His sobriquet comes from the *panga* – an African version of the machete used for cutting sugar cane in KwaZulu-Natal – which he used to despatch his victims. Then in the 1970s, there was "Ironman" who robbed his victims late at night before bludgeoning them to death with an iron bar. Ironman took the lives of at least seven victims in this manner before disappearing. He has never been identified.

A half-naked woman's body was found on 4 January 1995 in a field outside Atteridgeville. It was severely decomposed and she was never identified. On 9 February a second body was found. This woman was completely naked, though her clothes had been piled on her chest and held in place by rocks. Identified from her fingerprints, she was 27-year-old Beauty Nuku Soko, who had disappeared on her way to visit her sister in Klipgat, 20 miles to the north. Four days later Nelsiwe Langa was found.

On 6 March, workmen digging a ditch in Atteridgeville found a woman's breasts poking out of the soil. They unearthed the body of 25-year-old Sara Matlakala Mokono, who was last seen three days before, on her way to see a potential employer.

On 12 April, another body was discovered in the veldt near the Skurweberg shooting range in Atteridgeville. She was partially naked. Her hands had been tied behind her back with a bra and she had been strangled with a ligature. Most of her clothes were found scattered around the area, but her panties were missing. She was later identified as 25-year-old Letta Nomthandazo Ndlangamandla, a black woman whose profile exactly fitted the victims of David Selepe. The police warned the media that another serial killer might be at large, possibly a copycat of the Cleveland killer.

Soon another disturbing discovery was made. Not 22 yards from the place Letta Ndlangamandla had been found, the police discovered the body of a child. It was Letta's two-year-old son Sibusiso. Earlier in the month, when Letta went to meet a man in Pretoria North who had offered her work, she had no one to leave Sibusiso with, so she took the child with her. They had been dead too long to determine whether the mother or child had died first.

Although Sibusiso showed signs of an injury to his head it was not possible to determine if this was the cause of death. This left open the chilling possibility that Sibusiso had died of exposure, alone in a field near his mother's corpse, too young to summon help.

On 13 May, the body of 29-year-old Esther Moshibudi Mainetja was discovered in a corn field near Hercules, seven miles away in Pretoria West. Last seen the evening before when she left a café to go home, she had been strangled with her own clothing and the lower part of her body was left uncovered.

Over the next month, five women went missing. Then on 13 June the body of 25-year-old Francina Nomsa Sithebe was found. At first sight, she appeared to be sitting against a tree on June 13. She was still wearing her dress. But her panties and handbag strap had been fashioned into a halter that secured her neck to the tree.

The body count continued to rise. On 16 June, the naked body of 19-year-old Elizabeth Granny Mathetsa was found in the industrial district of Rosslyn, ten miles north of Atteridgeville. She had disappeared three weeks before.

Then on 22 June, the body of 30-year-old Ernestina Mohadi Mosebo was found in Rosherville, just outside Johannesburg. The killer had moved to the Cleveland strangler's stamping ground. Like the Cleveland killer's victims, Ernestina Mosebo had been raped and strangled. Her papers were found nearby, aiding her identification.

On June 24, the remains of Nikiwe Diko were found back in Atteridgeville. Her body had been torn apart by wild dogs. Her head was found over 40 yards from her trunk. Her hands had been tied together with her panties and she had been strangled with her pantyhose. They had been tied around her neck and wound so tightly with a stick that shards of bone punctured the nylon. Her killer had also shoved a stick up her vagina. Her husband identified her by the wedding ring that remained on her finger. He had last seen her on 7 April, when she had gone to meet someone about a job.

The Atteridge murders were now about to make another curious intersection with the David Selepe case. On 17 July 1995, Absalom Sangweni, who lived in a caravan in Beyers Park, outside David Selepe's home town of Boksburg, watched as a man and a woman walked into the veldt some way away from his trailer. He called out to them as a fenced section would stop them going far. The man merely shouted back that he knew the area.

Some time later, the man reappeared. This time he was alone. He appeared furtive and ran off. Absalom went into the field to investigate and found the woman. She was lying still on the ground and had plainly been viciously assaulted. He rushed to fetch help. When Sergeant Gideon O'Neil arrived, he found the body still warm, but there was no pulse. Another policeman arrived with a first aid kit, but they could not revive her. The woman had been strangled with the belt of her own dress. There were few clues to the identity of the murderer and Absalom had been too far away to give a useful description of the man. The victim was later identified as 25-year-old mother-of-four Josephine Mantsali Mlangeni. Like the others, she had gone to meet someone about a job.

Although this murder had taken place 30 miles away in the townships of Johannesburg, it fell under the auspices of a special investigating team now set up by the Pretoria Murder and Robbery Unit under Captain Vinol Viljoen. Again profiler Micki Pistorius was brought in. When they combed through the files, they found a confusing picture. The killer showed no clear modus operandi. Some of the victims had their hands tied; others did not. And of those who had been tied, some had their hands behind; others in front. There was even a question whether they had all been murdered by the same man. Soon there was more material to work on.

On 18 July, 21-year-old Granny Dimakatso Ramela was found in Pretoria West, lying face down with a garrotte around her neck. Unusually, she was fully clothed. She had been missing for nine weeks.

On 26 July, the body of 28-year-old Mildred Ntiya Lepule was found in a canal near the Bon Accord Dam at Onderstepoort, just outside Pretoria to the north. Her panties had been drawn over her face and she had been strangled with her tights. She was last seen alive the previous day by her husband, who had taken her to Pretoria to meet a man about a job.

By this time Dr Micki had set up a board in the operations room and arranged the victims in order and spotted a pattern. Rather than killer's modus operandi being haphazard, it was clear that he had been refining his technique. To start with, the victims had been throttled manually. Then the killer began to strangle them using a ligature, often a bra or some other piece of clothing. Lately he had garrotted them, using a stick to tighten a piece of their clothing around their necks. He was finding out which way worked best.

Early on, the victims had not been not tied up. Next, their hands had been tied in front with a part of their own clothing. Then, their hands were tied behind their backs.

Unfortunately Dr Pistorius would have ample opportunity to discover whether the killer's sadistic techniques would develop further. On 8 August 1995, the body of 25-year-old Elsie Khoti Masango was found at Onderstepoort. Missing for three and a half weeks, she was identified from the contents of her handbag. Another body was found nearby the following day. The woman had been burnt beyond recognition and she was never identified. It does not seem that the incineration was deliberate and was probably the result of a veldt fire. It was not known how long the body had been there.

The killer then returned to Boksburg. On 23 August, the body of 30-year-old Oscarina Vuyokazi Jakalase, who had gone missing on 8 August, was found there. But there were more victims scattered around Onderstepoort. On 28 August, a woman's body was found at the Bon Accord Dam. Two days later, a second body was found nearby, which seemed to have been there for some months. Neither could be identified.

The police were now crawling all over Onderstepoort, so the killer left his next victim in the Cleveland area. Another unidentified body was found there on 12 September.

Then on the evening of 16 September, a police reservist taking his dog to hunt rabbits in the veldt stumbled across a body at the Van Dyk Mine near Boksburg. Over the next two days, nine more bodies were found within a radius of some 900 feet. In her book, Catch Me a Killer, Dr Pistorius describes this as "one of the most horrific crime scenes I had ever seen".

"Decomposed bodies were strewn over the veldt," she says, "some only metres away from others. Maggots were feasting and the stench penetrated our nostrils and clung to our clothing."

Despite the advanced state of decomposition, it was clear that the most recent victims had been murdered where they lay and Pistorius pictured the killer leading his latest victims into the field amongst the rotting corpses, where he raped and killed them. The poor women would have been paralyzed with fear. Indeed a stain on one victim's jeans showed she had wet herself in terror.

More than 30 members of the East Rand Murder and Robbery Unit combed the area, along with forensic experts. Dogs and a helicopter were brought in. The head of the South African Police, National Commissioner John George Fivaz, surveyed the area from the air. The police even brought in Dr Mervyn Mansell, an entomologist at the Agricultural Research Council in Pretoria, who had developed a way to use maggots to estimate the time of death.

Then President Nelson Mandela came out to view the site and meet the detectives and forensic experts. With that amount of media attention, it was clear that the strangler would find a new killing ground.

It was soon clear that the Boksburg killer was the same man who had been at work in Atteridgeville and Onderstepoort, so Captain Frans van Niekerk of the East Rand Murder and Robbery Unit, the investigating officer at the scene in Boksburg, contacted Captain Viljoen in Pretoria to share information.

The multiple-murder scene itself yielded a number of clues. First, it was little more than three miles from Boksburg Prison where violent offenders were kept. There was a railway line nearby, as in the Cleveland murders. And between ant heaps across the nearby veldt, the police found knives, mirrors, underwear, feathers, black and red candles, and other objects related to traditional healing *call muti*. Particularly powerful in *muti* is the use of human body parts, especially the internal organs, the tongue, eyes and genitals hacked from a live victim. Over the years there have been numerous "*muti*-murders" in South Africa. Usually the victim is throttled until they are unconscious, the body part removed, then the victim is left to bleed to death.

. But these were not *muti* murders. Dr Pistorius saw the hand of the Atteridgeville killer on every victim. Worse, his method of killing had developed again. The four last victims found at Boksburg were tied so that, as they struggled, they would strangle themselves.

Those found at the Van Dyk Mine included 26-year-old Makoba Tryphina Mogotsi, who went missing on 15 August, and Nelisiwe Nontobeko Zulu, also 26, who disappeared on 4 September on her way to look for a job. Forty-three-year-old Amelia Dikamakatso Rapodile was identified by the contents of her handbag, which was found on the murder site. She worked at Johannesburg International Airport and last seen alive on 7 September when she left work to see a man who had promised her a better job. Her cash card had been used at ATMs in Germiston three times later on the night she disappeared. Her hands were tied behind her back and then to her neck with her pantyhose. There was 31-year-old Monica Gabisile Vilakazi, who left her four-year-old son with her grandmother on 12 September when she went to look for work. Last seen by her parents in Germiston, 21-year-old Hazel Nozipho Madikizela was also found with her hands tied to her neck with her underwear. Forty-five-year-old Tsidi Malekoae Matela was only identified over a year later, in November 1996. She was originally from neighbouring Lesotho. The other four women remained unidentified.

A reward of 500,000 Rand (£35,500) was offered, but Commissioner Fivaz insisted that, although the Van Dyk Mine murders may be tied to those at Atteridgeville, they had no connection to the Cleveland murders – those had been committed by David Selepe.

Micki Pistorius called retired FBI profiler Robert Ressler, whom she had met at a conference on serial killers in Scotland, and he flew to South Africa on 23 September. Two days later, while a prayer service was being organized on the Van Dyk Mine site, they were already plying files. It became clear that the 10 women found at the Van Dyk Mine, the two others in Boksburg, the six found around Onderstepoort, the eight women and one boy found at Atteridgeville and the one found in Cleveland since the death of David Selepe were related. However, they believed that more than one killer was involved and that they may have worked together on at least some of the murders.

As before, the victims found at the Van Dyk Mine were middle-class black women, largely in their twenties and thirties, who took pride in their appearance. They seem to have been ensnared in almost every case by the offer of a job. The killing fields were carefully chosen. The killer or killers were very familiar with them. Although they were remote enough that the perpetrator was unlikely to be interrupted, they were easily reached by road and rail. The offender was organized and intelligent, leaving few clues at the murder site. He was also growing in confidence. The bodies of the first victims at Atteridgeville were widely scattered. Those at Onderstepoort were closer together, while the Van Dyk Mine victims were practically on top of one another and he made no attempt to hide them.

In his books *I Have Lived in the Monster: Inside the Minds of the World's Most Notorious Serial Killers*, Robert Ressler said that the killer would have "a high sex drive and reads pornography. His fantasies, to which he masturbates, are aggressive, and he believes women are merely objects to be abused. He enjoys charming and controlling women. When he approaches a victim, it is done in a very calculating way, and he is very conscious that he is eventually going to kill the victim, and savours the thought while he softens her up."

The general theory was that the killer had been hurt and rejected by a woman. He was raping and killing her over and over again in the guise of his victims, which was why they were all so similar.

Dr Pistorius, in her book *Strangers on the Street*, outlined the profile. The killer, she said, was a black male in his late twenties or early thirties. He was self-employed with access to money, possibly obtained by theft or fraud, and would drive an expensive car. He would wear ostentatious clothing and jewellery. Intellectually sharp, he would also be streetwise. Ostensibly a charming ladies' man, he would be competent socially while, underneath it all, he would detest women. No loner, he was probably married, separated or divorced. He would enjoy socializing and would visit places where alcohol is sold. He was following reports of the story in the press and may even have told someone that he is the killer in a roundabout fashion. He would have a very high sex drive and use pornography. After the murders, he would masturbate over the crimes and collect mementoes, which he would dispose of. And he would have been exposed to sexual violence, probably when he was young.

The problem with this profile was that it also fitted the Cleveland killer. That would not normally have mattered, as serial killers often have similar characteristics. But in this case the modus operandi were almost identical and the killers were working in the same area. Once again, it cast doubt on the guilt of David Selepe. This concerned Commissioner Fivaz, who asked Robert Ressler to re-examine the case against David Selepe. With Dr Pistorius, Ressler combed through the files and they concluded that Selepe was involved in the Cleveland killings.

But, by now, the police had a suspect. They learnt from Amelia Rapodile's colleagues at Johannsburg International Airport that her appointment on 7 September was with a man named Moses Sithole. Sithole had said he ran an organization called Youth Against Human Abuse. They found an application form for a job there that Amelia had completed. There was a phone number on it. It belonged to Kwazi Sithole who lived in Wattville, three miles southeast of Boksburg. She was Moses Sithole's sister, but he did not live with her and she did not know where he was.

Detectives' suspicions were confirmed when Tryphina Mogotsi was identified soon after. Tryphina had been a laundry worker at an organization helping street children in Benoni, three miles east of Boksburg, called Kids' Haven. A man who said he was from Youth Against Human Abuse had visited Kids' Haven and spoken to Tryphina Mogotsi about a job with his organization. They made an appointment to discuss the post. Moses Sithole had made other visits to Kids' Haven. He once delivered two destitute teenage girls to the home, accompanied by a photographer from Johannesburg newspaper, *The Star*. A second occasion he came with the newspaper article and said he wanted to organize a fund raiser. Soon after, Tryphina Mogotsi disappeared.

Despite the publicity surrounding the discovery of the bodies near the Van Dyk Mine, the killings did not stop. Just a week later, Agnes Sibongile Mbuli, aged 20, was on her way to meet a friend when she went missing. On 3 October, her dead body turned up at Kleinfontein train station near Benoni. That day, a man who gave his name as Joseph Magwena called the office of *The Star* and spoke to reporter Tamsen de Beer who answered the phone. The man said his name was "Joseph Magwena" and claimed that he was the "Gauteng serial killer" – Gauteng means "place of gold" and is the name of the province containing both Johannesburg and Pretoria.

"I am the man that is so highly wanted," he said, and told her that he wanted to turn himself in. The reporter contacted the police, who recorded three more calls from the man that month. In each conversation, he gave some detailed information about the murders that could not be gleaned from the media.

He said he had started killing because a woman had falsely accused him of rape. In jail, he suffered abuse by fellow prisoners. Now he was getting his revenge.

"I force a woman to go where I want and when I go there I tell them: 'Do you know what? I was hurt, so I'm doing it now. Then I kill them'," he said. He admitted using the victims' clothing, particularly underwear, to strangle them because there would be no fingerprints. And he confirmed what Dr Pistorius had suspected – that the women killed near the Van Dyk Mine had seen the other victims before they died.

He accepted responsibility for the murders in Atteridgeville, Pretoria and Boksburg, but he said he had nothing to do with the Cleveland killings. He also vehemently denied killing Letta Ndlangamandla – and in particular her two-year-old son as he loved children. He convinced the police that he really was the killer when, on 9 October, he directed them to the body of an unidentified woman near Jupiter train station. Then on 11 October, he directed them to the body of Beauty Ntombi Ndabeni in Germiston, the day after she disappeared. This time he had used a comb to tighten her pantyhose around her neck.

In co-operation with the police, Tamsen de Beer arranged a meeting with the caller at a station, but he gave the police the slip. So on 13 October they released a picture of Moses Sithole to the media, and appealed for help.

But the killer would not, or could not, stop. The following day, the body of an unidentified woman was found at the Village Main Reef Mine near Johannesburg. Her neck had been tied to a tree by her shoelaces.

A few days later, Sithole contacted his sister's husband, Maxwell, who worked at the Mintex factory in Benoni, saying that he needed a gun. Maxwell arranged to meet him at the factory. The police seized the opportunity and installed Inspector Francis Mulovhedzi as a security guard, but without telling his new work colleagues.

At 9 p.m. on 18 October 1995, Sithole arrived at the factory and asked for Maxwell. Mulovhedzi was told to go and fetch Maxwell as he was the new guy. But he was reluctant to go as he wanted to stay with Sithole. This made the suspect suspicious and he ran off. Inspector Mulovhedzi gave chase and cornered him in an alley. But it took gunshot wounds to the legs and stomach, before he could arrest him. Sithole was rushed to the Glynwood Hospital in Benoni, with the police terrified that, in a repeat of the David Selepe case, he would die before he could be convicted.

Operated on the following day, Sithole survived. Two days later he was taken to the Military Hospital in Pretoria, where security was much tighter – even though Sithole was in no condition to escape. He was not even well enough to appear in the magistrates' court in Brakpan, five miles south of Benoni, on 23 October, where he was charged with 29 murders.

He was born in 1964 in Vosloorus, a black township ten mile south of Germiston. The deprivation he experienced as a black man in apartheid South Africa was exacerbated by the death of his father. His mother, Sophie, was unable to support their five children and abandoned them at a local police station, telling them that they were not to tell the policemen that she was their mother. He was sent to an orphanage over 300 miles away in the homeland of KwaZulu, Natal. There he suffered systematic abuse. After three years, the teenage Sithole ran away, first seeking refuge first with his older brother Patrick, before going to work in the gold mines of Johannesburg.

A handsome and charming man, Sithole was sexually precocious from an early age, but his relationships were short-lived. There is speculation that his mother's abandonment of her children might have sparked his aggressive attitudes towards woman. However, he told some of his rape victims who survived of bad experiences he had had at the hands of a girlfriend.

It is not recorded when Sithole raped his first victim, but his first known incidence was in September 1987. The victim was 29-year-old Patricia Khumalo, who appeared as a witness at his murder trial. Three other surviving rape victims came forward at that time. They included Buyiswa Doris Swakamisa, who was attacked in February 1989. She reported the assault to the police, Sithole was convicted and sent to Boksburg Prison for six years. Even though he maintained his innocence, he was released after four years for good behaviour. It is thought that his imprisonment taught him a brutal and perverse lesson – in future he would leave no victim alive to testify against him.

While Sithole was in jail, he met a woman named Martha who was visiting one of her relatives, another inmate. They began writing to each other and, when he was released in 1993, he moved in with her in Soshanguve. But when Martha fell pregnant, she returned to her parents in Atteridgeville. Sithole followed some months later. On 5 December 1994, Martha gave birth to a baby girl they named Bridget. In February 1995, after his killing spree had started, Sithole paid *lobola* – the traditional bride-price – for Martha. But soon they separated, leaving Sithole apparently to sleep at railway stations.

Nevertheless, Martha had visited her husband three times after he was arrested. But then on 28 October, it revealed that Sithole was HIV-positive. He had probably contracted the disease from one of his victims. After that, Martha would have nothing further to do with him. The police were lambasted for not telling Martha of his condition.

Meanwhile, the detectives began the laborious and unpleasant business of questioning Sithole in his hospital bed. Both Captains

Frans van Niekerk and Vinol Viljoen visited Sithole in the Military Hospital, but Sithole was unforthcoming. It was only when a female detective was brought in that he began describing his crimes, masturbating while he did so.

According to *The Star*, Sithole told detective: "I can point out the place in Atteridgeville, as well as in Hercules. That's where I started. Nearer to Johannesburg I did not kill people, because that's where I stayed. I did not even count . . . Atteridgeville I killed many – about 10. I caught them with my hands around the neck and strangled them. I thought of something to tie them up . . . I used stockings. I placed it around their necks."

He chose the locations before the victims and claimed he raped only the pretty ones. He also said that he killed only during daytime, though he did not like the sight of blood.

According to the *Beeld*, he also said: "I heard fuck-all if they spoke to me and thought about other things." And he forced the women to look down while he raped and killed them and he would masturbate while he watched them die.

There were certainly glaring disparities between Sithole and the profile of the killer Ressler and Pistorius had come up with. Sleeping on railway stations, he did not have an expensive car like David Selepe. And he denied working with an accomplice as they had speculated, though he claimed that some of the killings he had been accused of had been committed by copycats.

In court, all the confessions he was supposed to have made were disputed. Sithole's lawyer said that he had been provided with a list of victims' names and other details, then been forced to confess his "guilt" in interviews that were recorded. This is hardly an unusual courtroom ploy but, in this case, the police were their own worst enemies. According to the detectives, Sithole had waived his right to legal representation during the questioning. When public defender Tony Richard arrived at the hospital he was told this, but he insisted on speaking to Sithole himself, who told him that his wife was getting a lawyer for him. Nevertheless the police continued to question Sithole without a lawyer being present. The police then brought in a magistrate to record Sithole's confession. However, Magistrate Greyvenstein noted that Sithole was in pain and, when she asked him why he had no lawyer, he said he had been not been able to get one because the police had not allowed him to see anyone. Consequently Greyvenstein refused to take his confession. At the trial Sithole claimed that the police were infuriated by this and told him that he would "see shit" if he did not give his confession to a second magistrate – which he duly did.

On 3 November, Sithole was moved to a solitary cell in Boksburg Prison. When he was taken out to identify the crime scenes, he complained of pain due to his injuries. He took the detectives to a number of locations where bodies had been left. And on 6 November, he took them to the Gosforth Park mine slag heaps west of Germiston, where they found the body of another unidentified – and, as yet, undiscovered – woman who would go to an unmarked grave.

On 13 November 1995, Sithole appeared on crutches in Brakpan Magistrates' Court which was guarded by heavily armed police officers and sealed off with razor wire to protect him from relatives and other outraged members of the public. For further security he was shuffled through at 7.30 in the morning. On 5 December, he was transferred to the Krugersdorp Prison, so a psychiatric report could be prepared at the nearby Sterkfontein Psychiatric Hospital. It was determined that he was fit to stand trial.

In September, Sithole was provided with a new attorney named Eben Jordaan, a private practitioner whose discounted fees would be picked up by the state. Then it was finally announced that Moses Sithole would stand trial for 40 counts of rape, 6 counts of robbery and 38 counts of murder. As part of that total another murder had been added to the charge sheet. The new victim was 22-year-old Rose Rebothile Mogotsi. She had last been seen on 15 September when she went to look for work. Her body was found in Boksburg three days later.

Controversially, four of the murders were slayings Cleveland killer David Selepe had been charged with. The victims were 18-year-old Maria Monene Monama, 24-year-old Refilwe Amanda Mokale, 32-year-old Joyce Thakane Mashabela and 26-year-old Amanda Kebofile Thethe – whose murder scene Selepe had been visiting when he had been shot. The newspapers, who had never accepted the police account of Selepe's death, went wild.

Asked any of these four were included in the six victims police claimed were positively linked to Selepe at the turn of 1994, they refused to comment "as the Sithole case is considered to be *sub judice*," according to the *Cape Times*. The names of the six supposedly connected to Selepe have never been released.

Sithole's trial eventually began on 21 October 1996. He was now being called the "ABC Killer" – A for Atteridge, B for Boksburg and C for Cleveland – and pleaded not guilty to all of the charges with a grin on his face.

The first three charges to be heard concerned rapes that occurred in 1987 and 1988. Although the names of rape victims who survived to testify are usually suppressed, these brave women identified themselves in court in the hope that their attacker would be locked away forever.

Twenty-nine-year-old Patricia Khumalo was the first to testify. In September 1987, she was looking for work and her sister introduced her to a man named "Martin" who they both identified as Moses Sithole in court. Martin said he had work for Patricia and on the 14th she got on the train with him in Boksburg. Alighting at Geldenhuis station, Martin said that he knew a short cut through the veldt. There he attacked her.

"He grabbed me by the clothes in front of my chest," she said. "I was frightened. He ordered me to lie on the ground and raped me." He raped her more than once. "I pleaded and cried and asked him not to kill me. He said he wouldn't, because I have the kind of eyes that makes him feel sorry." It was the day before her daughter's birthday.

Her attacker had tied her hands with her bra and pulled her dress over her head, then ordered her to stay there while he made his escape. Patricia Khumalo cried as she related this ordeal. In the dock, Sithole smiled.

Sithole's attorney Eben Jordaan asked Patricia Khumalo whether her attacker had not rather been David Selepe. She said no. She had recognized the picture of Sithole in the newspapers after he had been arrested and she recognized him here in court.

In September 1988, Thembi Ngwenya was working in a clothes shop when she met a man who offered her a job that paid better. But before she handed in her notice, she thought of her friend 26-year-old Dorcas Kedibone Khobane, who was unemployed, and she put them in touch. On 28 September, Dorcas Khobane accompanied the man, who identified himself as "Samson", to Cleveland. Again they stopped at Geldenhuis station and took a shortcut through the veldt. There he hit her and pulled a knife.

"He threatened to kill me with it and to cut me into pieces unless I did as he asked," Dorcas said the court. "He pushed me on the ground and took my panties off. He dropped his pants to his knees and he raped me."

Then he engaged her in conversation.

"He told me he had a girlfriend in Vosloorus named Sibongile. He said he wanted me to go look for him at her home because she had stolen some things from him, but did not say what. He then asked if we could sleep together again."

When Dorcas Khobane refused, he raped her again. Even then he was in no hurry to leave, but someone was coming and he fled. In court, Dorcas Khobane identified Moses Sithole as Samson, the man who raped her.

Again, in the dock, Sithole seemed amused, but he buried his head in his hands when Sibongile Nkosi took the stand. She was 17 years old in 1988 when she got involved with the 24-year-old Sithole, who then called himself Martin. Sibongile told the court that she had been afraid of him then and was still afraid now. He had often hit her and had threatened to kill her family if she left him. She said he beat her in private, then when someone visited he would put on a show of affection. Eben Jordaan suggested that his client would deny that he ever laid a finger on her. Sibongile Nkosi asked if she should strip naked so that the court could see the scars.

Sibongile's younger sister Lindiwe Nkosi then testified that, in October 1988, "Martin" had invited her to visit her sister in Soweto. She was 15 at the time. On the way, they got off the train at Geldenhuis station. Luring her into the veldt he asked Lindiwe if she wanted to have sex with him. When she said no, he pulled out a bottle of petrol and said he would kill her and burn her body if she did not have sex with him. Then he beat her, raped her and throttled her until she lost consciousness. When she came round, he said he would kill her and her niece if she told anyone what had happened.

Although the rape of Buyiswa Doris Swakamisa had been dealt with in 1989, she appeared in the 1996 trial to testify about his modus operandi. Her presence in court reinforced the point that Sithole's subsequent victims seem to have been selected for their resemblence to Buyiswa Swakamisa and explained why there had been no crimes between 1989 and 1993, when Sithole had been in prison for her rape.

Buyiswa Swakamisa testified that she had met a man calling himself "Lloyd Thomas" in February 1989. He offered her a computer job and said he would take her to his business. Walking through the veldt near Cleveland, he produced a *panga* from a rolled-up newspaper he was carrying under his arm and said he was going to have sex with her. Then in a dramatic gesture he "threw the *panga* to one side and said if I did not want to have intercourse with him, I could run away, but had to make sure that he did not catch up with me or he would kill me. I just stood there. He came towards me and slapped me and ordered me to take off my clothes. When I did not he slapped me twice with his open hand."

In the event, he could not get an erection. So he forced her to kiss his neck and stick her fingers in his ears. And when he was ready, he raped her. Afterwards he was in the mood for conversation again. This time he said that "he hated women because he once had a child with a girlfriend in Alexandra and that his girlfriend had poisoned the child". Then he tied her up, took her money and left. Once freed she went to the police, but nothing happened until, months later, she saw him in the street. She called the police and he was arrested. Only then did he give his name as Moses Sithole.

This was apartheid South Africa and Buyiswa Swakamisa was forced to travel to the police station in the police vehicle with her rapist. He cursed her and himself for not having killed her.

The most controversial charges levelled again Sithole were the murder of Amanda Thethe and the theft of her cash card. David Selepe been charged with her murder and pointing out where it had happened when he was killed. Amanda's cash card had then been used to withdraw money from a cashpoint three times after she was dead. The man using it had been photographed by a security camera. Earlier the police had identified the man in this photograph as David Selepe. Now they charged Sithole with the robbery as well as her murder.

Four weeks into the trial Siphiwe Ngwenya took the stand. She had worked at Kids' Haven with Tryphina Mogotsi and identi-fied the man on the security camera photo as the man who had offered Tryphina a job when she went missing. This was Moses Sithole who, for once, was not using an alias.

Even more damning was the testimony of Kwazi Sithole, Moses' sister. She also identified the man in the photograph as her brother. What's more, she said that women often phoned her house about jobs her brother had offered them.

It then came to light that Sithole had known Amanda Thethe. When he had visited her father's home some months before she went missing, she introduced him as her boyfriend "Selbie". In early August, the prosecution contended, her boyfriend had raped her, stuffed her underwear into her mouth, tied her blouse around her neck and strangled her. Amanda's aunt saw "Selbie" again. He attended her niece's funeral. This is not uncommon among serial killers, who like to relive the moment of killing.

Amanda Thethe was not the only women Sithole had a re-lationship with before he killed her. Dan Mokwena, a work colleague of 19-year-old Elizabeth Mathetsa, had been sitting outside their workplace with her in early 1995 when a man walked up. Elizabeth introduced him as her boyfriend "Sello". Dan Mokwena said that he saw Sello again a week before Elizabeth Mathetsa went missing on 25 May 1995. She was found dead in Rosslyn on 16 June. In court Dan identified the man he knew as "Sello" as the prisoner in the dock, Moses Sithole.

The aliases continued to multiply. Mary Mogotlhoa knew Sithole as "Charles". They had had a brief relationship shortly before his arrest. It lasted only two weeks, but he had given her a watch, which Tryphina Mogotsi's mother identified as her daughter's. Mary Mogotlhoa also said that, after they had broken up, Sithole had gone to the police, told them that she had stolen 500 Rand (£35) and accused her of raping him.

Otherwise he repeatedly used the offer of a job as a bait. In March 1995, Wilhelmina Ramphisa met a man calling himself "David Ngobeni" who offered her a job. She completed in an application form he gave her, but he failed to turn up to their next appointment. Months later, she saw her potential employer again – on the TV news. It was Moses Sithole and she had had a lucky escape.

A lorry driver named Piet Tsotsetsi testified that he received a number of calls on the phone in his lorry from women about jobs they said he had offered them. He was completely mystified by this. However, at the time, Sithole was working at the same company washing the vehicles. After he was arrested, the calls stopped. Elsie Masango's sister testified that a man calling himself "Piet Tsotsetsi" had offered Elsie a job shortly before she disappeared.

Other witnesses testified, many of them parents who had to identify their raped and tormented daughters. No matter how harrowing the testimony, Sithole sat and smiled.

The only time he cried was when his wife Martha entered the court to testify against him with their one-year-old daughter Bridget asleep in her arms, but afterwards refused to let him see the child. This sudden upsurge of tears allowed those whose testimony he had sat through with a look of mild amusement on his face to laugh at him.

There was a brief respite when, on 12 November, the trial was suspended after Sithole had fallen down and re-opened his leg wound. When he returned from hospital, the grandmother of Monica Vilakazi testified that a man identifying himself as Moses Sithole had phoned her home on 11 September 1995, the day before her granddaughter went missing. He said they had met the previous month and had now found Monica a job in Germiston. The following day she left her grandmother's house to become one of the women found at the Van Dyk Mine. Three days after Monica went missing, there was another phone call. This time the caller said his name was Jabulane, but Monica's grandmother recognized his voice as Sithole's. Before Monica's funeral, the man phoned again this time identifying himself as "Mandla". Sithole was in custody at the time and Mandla insisted that he would be acquitted. And he taunted the old woman, saying that Monica got what she deserved.

The curious thing here was that "Mandla" was the name of one of the men David Selepe had claimed as an accomplice. This name had not been mentioned in the newspapers at that time. Perhaps the police had not interrogated the right "Mandla" after David Selepe's death.

Peter Magubane, the photographer from *The Star* who had accompanied Sithole and the two street kids to Kids' Haven, said that he had introduced himself as "Patrick" – his brother's name. It was there Sithole met Tryphina Mogotsi.

Voice identification specialist Dr Leendert Jansen was called as an expert witness to identify the voice on the recordings the police had made of the telephone conversations between *Star* reporter Tamsen de Beer and "Joseph Magwena".

"I have no doubt that the unknown voice is in reality the voice of Moses Sithole," he said.

American voice analysis expert Loni Smrkovski was flown to South Africa to confirm Dr Jansen's findings.

Then Inspector Mulovhedzi testified about Sithole's arrest. According to Mulovhedzi, he identified himself as a police officer and told Sithole to stop. He then fired two warning shots. Then, Mulovhedzi said, Sithole came at him with an axe.

"He turned back and had an object in his hand and came towards me," he said. "My life was in danger and I fired a shot at his legs . . . He kept on fighting. He hit me on my right hand and I fired some more shots. He fell to the ground."

During cross-examination Eben Jordaan suggested that there was no axe. Sithole had merely bumped into the officer and, when he turned to say sorry, Mulovhedzi drew his gun and started shooting.

As the trial went on, the police continued to solicit the public's help to identify eight more of the victims. Then on 3 December, in the sixth week of the trial, the prosecution introduced surprise new evidence. It was a video made in Boksburg Prison not long after Sithole's arrest, showing him speaking about the women he had murdered.

It had been made fellow inmates Jacques Rogge and Mark Halligan and masterminded by Charles Schoeman. They were ex-police officers who had been jailed for a three million Rand (£210,000) diamond heist in Amanzimtoti, KwaZulu-Natal in 1995, during which they had killed an accomplice. Rogge suffered from diabetes and slept in the prison infirmary where he met Sithole, who wanted Rogge to steal some pills so that he could commit suicide. But first Rogge, Halligan and Schoeman persuaded him to tell his story on camera, on video equipment that the ex-cops got smuggled in. They even drew a contract giving each one a share in the profits – Sithole's would to go to his daughter when he was dead.

The use of such evidence was contentious. It was illegal to make unauthorized recordings or videos in prison. It was also illegal to publish a prisoner's story without the written permission of the Commissioner of the Department of Correctional Services, so it was unlikely that they could have made any financial gain. Indeed Charles Schoeman and his cohorts faced possible criminal charges. Then there was the vexed question of how the ex-cops got hold of the video equipment in the first place. When the video had first come to light, the Department of Correctional Services wanted to conduct an internal investigation, but the deputy attorney-general asked them to hold off so that she could keep the existence of the video secret until the trial.

This brought up all sorts of legal issues and the trial had to be suspended once again. When the proceedings resumed on 29 January 1997, Winnie Madikizela-Mandela, former-wife of President Mandela, was present. Sithole smiled at her; she did not smile back.

The video showed Sithole sitting back, smoking or casually eating an apple. He began with the first murder. In July 1995, he said, a woman he killed had shouted at him when he asked for directions. But he had turned on his not inconsiderable charm and arranged to meet her for a date. Then he had strangled her.

"I cannot remember her name," he said. "I killed her and left her there. I went straight home and had a shower."

He then relayed in detail how he had killed 29 women.

"I don't know where the other nine come from," he said. "If there was blood or injuries, they weren't my women."

He did not like blood and he did not want to see the faces of his victims as he took their lives. Consequently, he strangled his victims from behind, he said. However, he was obviously not so fastidious when he led his fresh victims into a field of rotting corpses.

He said that all his victims had reminded him of Buyiswa Swakamisa, the woman he claimed had "falsely" accused him of rape in 1989. He also said that he had not raped any of his victims, but that some had offered to have sex with him to save their lives. He had the opportunity to attack other women but did not do so because they were "sincere and without pretensions".

On the video, Schoeman asked Sithole if there was one victim that stuck out in his mind. Sithole said he particularly remembered Amelia Rapodile, one of the ten women found at the Van Dyk Mine. Training in karate, she put up fierce resistance.

"She started to fight," he said. "I gave her a chance to fight and I tell her, if you lose, you die . . . She was using her feet and kicked me. Then she tried to grab my clothes, but she could not grab me. I just tell her bye-bye."

Charles Schoeman said he did not want to testify, claiming that his life had been threatened. But after being promised indemnity for the making of the video and any charges surrounding it, he took the stand. He said that they had originally made audio recordings of Sithole's story, but he was so disturbed by what he had heard he had contacted the police. Then Captain Leon Nel of the East Rand Murder and Robbery Unit provided video equipment which was smuggled into prison by Schoeman's wife. But as there had been police involvement and Sithole had not been cautioned or told that the tapes might be used at his trial, his attorney objected to their use.

DNA evidence took days as it was new to South African courts and the techniques used had to be explained in detail. However, as many of the corpses were in an advanced state of decay when they were found, DNA evidence only linked Sithole to some of the victims.

There was another trial-within-a-trial over the confession Sithole made in the Military Hospital after his arrest. Sithole claimed he had been coached, coerced and denied legal representation. He also claimed that the crime scenes had been shown to him by the police, rather than the other way round. On 29 July, the judge admitted confessions made in the Military Hospital and the video tape into evidence. Finally, on 15 August, the prosecution rested.

Sithole took the stand in his own defence. He claimed that he was totally innocent of all charges. Everything he had said in his confession had been fed to him by the police. He admitted knowing one of the rape victims, Lindiwe Nkosi, as she was the sister of his girlfriend, but he denied raping her. He also protested his innocence of the rape he had been sent to prison for in 1989. But Sithole did not stand up well under cross-examination and *The Star* said his testimony was "rambling, often incoherent".

Finally, on 4 December 1997, Moses Sithole was found guilty on all 38 counts of murder, 40 counts of rape and six counts of robbery. One of the two assessors felt that Sithole should not be held accountable, but he was overruled by the judge and the other assessor. It took three hours to read the judgment. The following day, Judge David Curlewis sentenced Sithole to 2,410 years in prison. He was given 50 years for each of the murders, 12 years for each rape and five years for each count of robbery. These sentences would run consecutively, so that there would be no possibility of parole for at least 930 years. The judge said that he would have no qualms about imposing a sentence of death if it had been available and he refused to give life sentences as that would have meant Sithole could have been eligible for parole in 25 years and he had no faith in the parole boards or prison authorities to keep him in jail after that.

"Nothing can be said in favour of Sithole," said Justice Curlewis. "In this case I do not take leniency into account. What Sithole did was horrible . . . I want to make it clear I mean that Moses Sithole should stay in jail for the rest of his life."

Sithole listened to the sentence without emotion. He was taken to C-Max, the maximum security section of Pretoria Central Prison and the highest security cellblock in South Africa which each prisoner is allowed one hour a day outside his cell and three visits a month. One of the other 93 prisoners there is Eugene de Kock of the apartheid government's Counterinsurgency Unit, who was sentenced to 212 years for crimes against humanity.

Sithole has AIDS but, in prison, he has access to excellent medical care and his life expectancy is now longer than if he had remained outside.

The problem here is that there were more murders than Moses Sithole and David Selepe can account for. Sithole, in his video account, which there is no reason to doubt, denied nine of the murders he was charged with, and Selepe, presumably, was innocent of the four murders that Sithole was jailed for. And the police have never been able to link Sithole to Selepe, even though there is a strange overlap between the two cases.

There is the odd coincidence around Amanda Thethe. If the police are to be believed, David Selepe had taken them to her murder site and was revealing fresh details about the crime when he was shot. But it is undoubtedly true that Sithole knew Amanda. One or other of them used her cash card and Sithole was linked to her by DNA evidence.

A man phoned murder victim Dorah Mokoena's employer three days after she went missing, giving his name as "Martin". Although Sithole regularly used the alias Martin, he was not charged with Dorah Mokoena's murder.

Five days after Joyce Mashabela disappeared on 9 August 1994, a man phoned her employer, giving his name as "Moses Sima" and saying that he had found her identity papers. DNA linked Sithole to her body and he was charged with her murder. But Peggy Bodile's body was found in the same patch of veldt two months later. Sithole was not charged with her murder. It was attributed to Selepe. Then there is the name "Mandla", fingered by Selepe an accomplice but also used by Sithole the third time he called Monica Vilakazi's grandmother.

The police have never revealed whether any of the four murders initially attributed to Selepe which Sithole was charged with were among the six "positively" linked to David Selepe. FBI profiler Robert Ressler and Micki Pistorius concluded that the evidence indicated that Selepe had been involved in the Cleveland murders in some way; that it was likely that the Atteridgeville killer was working with an accomplice; and that it was possible that Selepe and the Atteridgeville killer may have known each other and may even have worked together. But if Selepe was telling the truth about "Mandla", why would he have lied about "Tito"? He may well be responsible for the murders not attributed to either Selepe and Sithole. And he is still at large.

While the trial of Moses Sithole was still underway, another serial killer was on the loose three hundred miles to the south in Transkei. Local people blame a *Mamlambo* – a legendary creature that is "half horse, half fish" from Xhosa tribal myth that inhabits the Mzintlava River near Mount Ayliff in the Eastern Cape. The creature is said to be 67 feet long, with short stumpy legs, a crocodilian body and the head and neck of a snake with a hypnotic gaze that shines at night with a green light. It drags human and animal victims in the water, drowning them, and sucking their blood and brains out. According to Xhosa tribal legend, *Mamlambo* brings great wealth to anyone brave enough to capture it.

Official sources say that seven human victims, along with several goats, were attributed to the creature in 1997 alone. But freelance journalist Andite Nomabhunga, says that nine human deaths have been blamed on the *Mamlambo*, including a schoolgirl. Mount Ayliff police claim that most of the alleged victims which have been found had simply drowned. Sometimes, crabs have eaten away at the soft tissues of the face and throat. Despite police explanations for the deaths, villagers claim that they are not just superstitious tribe people. There is a genuine fear that a real killer is at work under the guise of the *Mamlambo*.